W9-AXL-203

Frommer's®

Miami & the Keys

Here's what the critics say about Frommer's:

"Amazingly easy to use. Very portable, very complete."
—Booklist

♦

"The only mainstream guide to list specific prices. The Walter
Cronkite of guidebooks—with all that implies"
—Travel & Leisure

♦

"Complete, concise, and filled with useful information."
—New York Daily News

♦

"Hotel information is close to encyclopedic."
—Des Moines Sunday Register

Other Great Guides for Your Trip:

Frommer's® 99

Miami
& the Keys

by Victoria Pesce Elliott

MACMILLAN • USA

ABOUT THE AUTHOR

Victoria Pesce Elliott is a freelance journalist who contributes to many local and national newspapers and magazines, including the *New York Times*. A native of Miami, she returned there after nearly a decade in New York City, where she graduated from the Columbia University School of Journalism.

MACMILLAN TRAVEL

A Simon & Schuster Macmillan Company
1633 Broadway
New York, NY 10019

Find us online at **www.frommers.com**

ISBN 0-02-862258-8
ISSN 1047-790X

Editor: Jeff Soloway
Production Editor: Mark Enochs
Photo Editor: Richard Fox
Design by Michele Laseau
Digital Cartography by Raffaele DeGennaro and Ortelius Design
Page Creation by Jerry Cole, Trudy Coler, John Bitter and David Pruett

SPECIAL SALES

Bulk purchases (10+ copies) of Frommer's and selected Macmillan travel guides are available to corporations, organizations, mail-order catalogs, institutions, and charities at special discounts, and can be customized to suit individual needs. For more information write to Special Sales, Macmillan General Reference, 1633 Broadway, New York, NY 10019.

Manufactured in the United States of America.

Contents

List of Maps

AN INVITATION TO THE READER

In researching this book, we discovered many wonderful places—hotels, restaurants, shops, and more. We're sure you'll find others. Please tell us about them, so we can share the information with your fellow travelers in upcoming editions. If you were disappointed with a recommendation, we'd love to know that, too. Please write to:

Frommer's Miami & the Keys 1999
Macmillan Travel
1633 Broadway
New York, NY 10019

AN ADDITIONAL NOTE

Please be advised that travel information is subject to change at any time—and this is especially true of prices. We suggest, therefore, that you write or call ahead for confirmation when making your travel plans. The authors, editors, and publisher cannot be held responsible for the experiences of readers while traveling. Your safety is important to us, however, so we encourage you to stay alert and be aware of your surroundings. Keep a close eye on cameras, purses, and wallets, all favorite targets of thieves and pickpockets.

WHAT THE SYMBOLS MEAN

✪ Frommer's Favorites

Our favorite places and experiences—outstanding for quality, value, or both.

The following abbreviations are used for credit cards:

AE	American Express	EURO	Eurocard
CB	Carte Blanche	JCB	Japan Credit Bank
DC	Diners Club	MC	MasterCard
DISC	Discover	V	Visa

FIND FROMMER'S ONLINE

Arthur Frommer's Outspoken Encyclopedia of Travel (www.frommers.com) offers more than 6,000 pages of up-to-the-minute travel information—including the latest bargains and candid personal articles updated daily by Arthur Frommer himself. No other Web site offers such comprehensive and timely coverage of the world of travel.

Introducing Miami   1

I't's hard to know in which language to introduce yourself to this polyglot mini-nation. When you land at Miami International Airport, the nation's second-largest hub for international travelers, you'll hear Spanish, Portuguese, Creole, French, and Italian as a matter of course. Once in Miami, you'll find a curious mix of Caribbean immigrants, orthodox Jews, retirees seeking easier winters, models, actors, artists, wealthy real-estate moguls, and movie executives, as well as an already diverse crowd of long-time Floridians, black descendants of Bahamian railroad workers, Native Americans, and Hispanics. The city is a virtual mosaic of colors, sounds, and scents.

Although some residents say disdainfully, "It's just not like it used to be," the truth is Miami has always been a magnet for the masses. In fact, since 1980, Dade County's population, with Miami as its largest municipality, has grown nearly 33%.

Since the Spanish first colonized the area in the 16th century, Miami has been a home to runaways, castaways, and dreamers. Through its many incarnations, two Miami characteristics have remained constant—its predictable year-round warmth and its location on a peninsula pointing emphatically toward so many other nations. These traits have attracted newcomers year after year. Now Miami, known as "The Capital of the Americas," serves as Latin American and international headquarters for hundreds of multinational corporations. It's also the second-largest banking center in the United States.

Encompassing both the mainland and the barrier islands of Miami Beach, Greater Miami boasts about 2 million residents and hosts more than 9 million visitors annually. They come for different reasons. Some are drawn by the unadulterated sea and surf; some for the outrageous nightlife; others for the business opportunities; still others can't get enough of the natural wilderness right in the city's backyard.

Fortunately, the evolution of America's southernmost metropolitan region—from a simple playground to a vibrant cosmopolitan city—has not been achieved at the expense of the area's celebrated surf and sand. Despite Miami's quick transformation, the almost complete absence of heavy industry has left the air and water as clear, clean, and inviting as ever. Miami is not just a beach vacation, however—you'll also find high-quality hotels, distinctive restaurants, unusual attractions, and top shopping. Relaxing days on the water are now complemented by nights that include choice theater and opera, restaurants serving exotic and delicious food, a hopping club scene, and a lively cafe culture.

1 Frommer's Favorite Miami Experiences

- **Boating off the Coast of Miami Beach.** Jump on a party boat, take a sightseeing cruise, or rent a skiff. A boat ride off the coast of Miami Beach is the best way to see the elegant waterfront mansions, dramatic skyline, and gorgeous coastline that make Miami so alluring.
- **Shopping in Downtown and South Beach.** One of Miami's biggest draws is its incredible selection of stores. Many visitors from the Caribbean and Latin America come for the sole purpose of buying. From electronics to shoes and hardware to exotic grocery items, this is the place to shop. Bring the credit cards.
- **Cruising with the Top Down.** Driving with the roof down over the causeways to any of Miami's wonderful islands, especially Key Biscayne, is one of my favorite things to do. Tune the radio to a Latin station, catch a nice tan on your bare shoulders, and watch the water glimmer around you.
- **Lunching in Little Havana.** Miami's Cuban center is the city's most distinctive ethnic enclave. Located just west of Downtown, Little Havana is centered around "Calle Ocho," SW 8th Street. Car-repair shops, tailors, electronics stores, and restaurants all hang signs in Spanish; salsa rhythms thump from the radios of passersby; and old men in *guayaberas* chain-smoke cigars over their daily games of dominoes. Stop for a big filling lunch, and top it off with a Cuban coffee to really get the day going.
- **Biking, Blading, or Walking Through the Art Deco District on Ocean Drive.** The beauty of South Beach's celebrated Art Deco District culminates on the 15-block beachfront strip known as Ocean Drive. Most of the buildings on this stretch are hotels built in the late 1930s and early 1940s. You'll appreciate the architecture and the colorful characters as you go down this street—by bike, by in-line skates, or on foot.
- **Relaxing on Miami's Beaches.** You can choose your spot on dozens of miles of white-sand beaches, edged with coconut palms on one side and a clear turquoise ocean on the other. Each of Miami's many beach areas boasts its own distinctive character. While Europeans and naturalists enjoy a popular nude beach in North Dade, families barbecue on remote sandy stretches in Key Biscayne.
- **Dancing Until Dawn.** Choose your dance floor, from salsa at the Latin clubs to techno and house at European-style places to jamming at outdoor reggae bars.
- **Enjoying New World Cuisine.** World-class chefs have discovered the richness of locally harvested ingredients, including tropical fruits and seafood. This culling of techniques and ingredients from the Cuban, Haitian, and Asian communities has created the now-famous "New World Cuisine."
- **Doing Whatever On, In, or Above the Water.** One of the best ways to appreciate Miami is from the water—on it, in it, or above it. Options include parasailing, jet skiing, kayaking, sailing, scuba diving, snorkeling, and windsurfing. Of course, you can always swim or ride the waves, as well.
- **Snorkeling in Biscayne National Park.** The thriving reef system at Biscayne National Park, a unique ecological preserve that's mostly underwater, attracts thousands of scuba divers and snorkelers every year.
- **Canoeing Through the Everglades.** Paddling through the unique ecosystem that is the Everglades gives you a chance to slow down and appreciate the natural

beauty of South Florida. You're sure to see an alligator or two, and maybe even a manatee.

2 The City Today

Miami today is one of the most diverse metropolitan areas in the country. There are about 2.1 million residents in Greater Miami, of which 25% are non-Hispanic white, 20% black, and 55% Hispanic, according to estimates from the Dade County Planning Department. The city's heterogeneous mix includes more than 600,000 Cubans, 330,000 Jamaicans and Bahamians, 72,000 Puerto Ricans, 23,000 Dominicans, and perhaps as many as 110,000 Haitians. Add to this a 1997 total of almost 10 million visitors from around the world, and it's easy to understand why this is truly an international city.

In recent years, Miami has had a spate of publicity—some bad and some good. In the early 1990s, a rash of freeway shootings persuaded several European governments to issue advisories against travel to Florida, resulting in a sharp drop in the number of international visitors coming to the city and the state overall. In 1992, America's most destructive hurricane, Andrew, demolished billions of dollars worth of local real estate. Perhaps the most negative image of Miami came during the shooting of Italian fashion designer Gianni Versace by a spree killer in 1997. In 1998, the weather system El Niño wreaked havoc across the state and gave Miami an unusually cold and rainy winter.

Over the years, Miami has made the news for more positive reasons as well. After passing through the city during film shoots, many celebrities, such as Sylvester Stallone, Madonna, Cher, Sophia Loren, and Whitney Houston, have bought homes along the water. The Summit of the Americas, held in 1994, brought together more than 30 heads of state from throughout the Western Hemisphere. Extravagant celebrations in 1996, including an 850-pound cake, helped mark the city's centennial. On the sports front, celebrity coach Pat Riley joined the Miami basketball team, the Heat, while the former Cowboy's maverick, Jimmy Johnson, took over Don Shula's team, the Dolphins. In 1997, Everglades National Park celebrated its 50th anniversary, and Dade County officially changed its name to Miami-Dade County.

Thanks to the increased vigilance of Miami police, both the rates of violence against tourists and overall crime have dropped to an all-time low. The city, like many other large metropolises, still suffers from random muggings and the like, but in the more-touristy areas, visitors are relatively safe.

If we could isolate a single principle that has kept Miami afloat over its short but tumultuous lifetime, it would be resiliency. Problems are nothing new to Miami, but the city always seems to rebound. Over the years, hurricanes, riots, and waves of immigration have altered the city's physical and cultural landscape. With each cataclysm, however, a new stability has emerged, creating a city both more complex and more dynamic than the one that preceded it.

Impressions

In so many ways, Miami represents the promise of hemispheric integration. I have been deeply moved over the last few years when I've had the opportunity to go to Miami and see the heroic efforts that people have made to build a genuine, multicultural, multiracial society that would be at the crossroads of the Americas, and therefore at the forefront of the future.

　　　　　—U.S. President William Clinton, at the Summit of the Americas, 1994

Florida

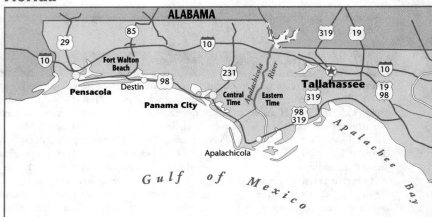

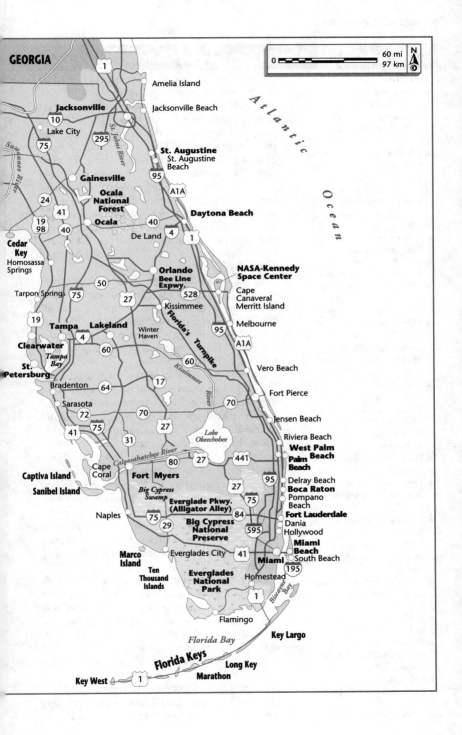

GEORGIA

60 mi
0   97 km

N

Jacksonville
10
Lake City
75
295

Amelia Island

Jacksonville Beach

St. Augustine
St. Augustine
Beach
95
A1A

Gainesville

**Ocala
National
Forest**
24
41
19
98
40
Ocala
40
De Land
4
1

Daytona Beach

**Cedar
Key**
Homosassa
Springs

Orlando
Bee Line
Expwy.

**NASA-Kennedy
Space Center**

50
Tarpon Springs
75
27
528
Kissimmee
Florida's Turnpike

Cape
Canaveral
Merritt Island

19
Tampa
Lakeland
4
Winter
Haven
60
95
Melbourne
A1A

Clearwater
**St.
Petersburg**
*Tampa
Bay*
60
60

Kissimmee River

Vero Beach

Bradenton
64
Sarasota
72
75
41
17
70
70
Fort Pierce

Jensen Beach

31
27
*Lake
Okeechobee*
441

Riviera Beach
**West Palm
Beach**
**Palm
Beach**

Captiva Island
Sanibel Island
Cape
Coral
Caloosahatchee River
80
27
Fort Myers
*Big Cypress
Swamp*
27
95
Delray Beach
Boca Raton
Pompano
Beach

Naples
75
**Everglade Pkwy.
(Alligator Alley)**
29
**Big Cypress
National
Preserve**
75
84
595
Fort Lauderdale
Dania
Hollywood

**Marco
Island**
Everglades City
41
**Miami
Beach**
South Beach
Miami
195

**Ten
Thousand
Islands**
**Everglades
National
Park**
Homestead

Biscayne Bay

Flamingo

Florida Bay

Key Largo

Florida Keys
Long Key
Marathon
Key West
1

Atlantic Ocean

St. Johns River

Suwannee River

3 A Look at the Past: A Century of Change

Dateline

- **1513** Juan Ponce de León is first European to land in Florida.
- **1600** Spanish colonization continues.
- **1763** England trades Havana for Florida. British plantations established.
- **1776** Florida fights on England's side during American Revolution.
- **1783** England returns Florida to Spain in exchange for the Bahamas and Gibraltar.
- **1785** Border disputes between Spain and America.
- **1821** U.S. acquires Florida. Andrew Jackson appointed first governor.
- **1835–1842** Seminole War; some 300 remaining natives deported to reservations.
- **1845** Florida becomes the 27th U.S. state.
- **1881** Philadelphia industrialist, Hamilton Disston, buys one million acres of Everglades, paving the way for South Florida's development.
- **1896** Henry M. Flagler extends railroad to Miami.
- **1898** Spanish-American War; army camps based in Miami.
- **1900** Florida's population is 530,000.
- **1915** Carl Fisher dredges Biscayne Bay to build Miami Beach.
- **1921** President-elect Warren Harding spends winter in Miami.
- **1925** Freedom Tower built in downtown Miami.
- **1926** Hurricane swamps Miami; the Biltmore Hotel completed in Coral Gables.
- **1930s** Hundreds of art deco hotels built in South Beach.

continues

Miami, a city that only recently celebrated its 100th birthday, is now defining itself as a cultural, historical, and financial capital of the Americas. Not so long ago, it was an uninhabitable wilderness, plagued by mosquitoes and warring natives. Until the final years of the 19th century, much of the Florida peninsula remained unsurveyed. To most Americans, southern Florida was arduously remote, a place only for enterprising explorers and hunters. Some adventurers attempted the journey south on horseback, following ancient Native American trails; others went by sea on one of the open sloops that carried the coastal trade. Either way, the voyage down Florida's east coast was both long and dangerous.

In 1825, the U.S. Army built the first permanent structure in South Florida, a lighthouse at the tip of Key Biscayne. It was destroyed during the Seminole wars, which lasted from 1835 to 1842. In the next years, a few dozen settlers and slaves came to the area and began clearing the brush and marshes to build homes and, eventually, towns.

In 1891, everything began to change. Even though an unescorted woman traveling alone at the time was considered nothing short of scandalous, Julia Tuttle, the widow of a wealthy Cleveland industrialist, journeyed to a small southeast Florida town. She brought determination and a dream. At that time, the town consisted of little more than a few plantations, a small trading post, and the ruins of a U.S. Army camp once known as Fort Dallas. Sensing the economic and social potential of America's most tropical land, Tuttle set out to transform the area into a full-blown city. Realization of her dream depended on easier access to the area, but the northern railroad magnates were less than enthusiastic.

Fate intervened, however, in the winter of 1895, when a gripping freeze practically destroyed the state's northern citrus crop. With a shipment of fresh orange blossoms as evidence of southern Florida's ability to rebound quickly from severe cold and its agricultural prospects, Tuttle again courted America's rail barons. The following year, Henry Flagler's first train steamed into town; Tuttle had given him half of her 600-acre prime riverfront property as a gift. Thus, Tuttle became the only woman in American history to start a major city.

It wasn't long before Miami's irresistible combination of surf, sun, and sand prompted wealthy Americans to build elaborate winter retreats overlooking Biscayne Bay. (One of these mansions, Villa Vizcaya, remains and is open to the public—see chapter 7, "What to See and Do.") Miami became a chic place to be, and, following World War I, widespread middle-class interest in the region prompted spectacular growth. The newcomers discovered that hefty windfalls could be made in real-estate speculation, and tales of million-dollar profits drove the population of Miami up from 30,000 to 100,000 in just 5 years. More than 300,000 vacationers visited Miami in the winter of 1924–1925 alone.

The building boom of the Roaring Twenties was directly responsible for the city's distinctive neighborhoods of today. Coral Gables, the single largest real-estate venture of the time, became one of the most beautiful, exclusive residential areas in Miami. The towns of Hialeah, Miami Springs, and Opa-Locka were planned and built by entrepreneur Glenn H. Curtiss as winter home sites for upper-middle-class northerners. Opa-Locka, his most celebrated development, was designed around an Arabian Nights theme, complete with domes, parapets, and minarets. Another fanciful developer, Carl Fisher, dredged Biscayne Bay and built up the islands of Miami Beach for his opulent hotels, tennis courts, golf courses, and polo fields.

The Great Depression slowed Miami's boom and changed the nature of the city's buildings, exemplified primarily by the art deco style of the hotels and other structures that went up on South Beach. These pastel structures are at the same time austere and whimsical, reflecting both a stark reality and the promise of better times. Regarded as architectural masterpieces today, the art deco hotels offer visitors an attractive, and less expensive, alternative to the luxurious accommodations up the beach.

Miami's belt-tightening days were short-lived. The end of World War II brought a second boom and another development frenzy. Again, entire communities were built and sold wholesale. Miami Beach's communities were redesigned and rebuilt as resorts. Some television shows, such as Arthur Godfrey's in the 1950s and Jackie Gleason's in the 1960s, began to be telecast coast-to-coast from Miami.

- **1947** Everglades National Park dedicated by President Harry S Truman.
- **1950** Frozen citrus concentrate becomes a major industry.
- **1954** Fontainebleau Hotel opens on Miami Beach.
- **1958** First jet passenger service between Miami and New York.
- **1959** Fidel Castro assumes power in Cuba; a mass exodus to South Florida follows.
- **1968** Richard Nixon nominated for president at the Republican National Convention in Miami Beach.
- **1973** Miami Dolphins win Super Bowl VII, completing the only undefeated season in NFL history.
- **1977** Orange juice spokesperson Anita Bryant leads fight against equal rights ordinance for gays; Dade County rejects rights bill.
- **1980** Four ex-Miami policemen acquitted of killing black insurance executive, Arthur McDuffie; riots leave 6 dead, 370 wounded. Some 140,000 Cubans enter South Florida when Castro opens port of Mariel.
- **1984** Miami's $1 billion Metrorail opens.
- **1991** Greater Miami's population reaches 1.9 million.
- **1992** Hurricane Andrew sweeps through Dade and Monroe counties, causing an estimated $30 billion in damage.
- **1994** Miami hosts the Summit of the Americas, in which heads of 34 countries from South, Central, and North America and the Caribbean meet in the first such hemispheric conference in 28 years.

continues

■ **1996** Miami celebrates its centennial with festivals and events throughout the year.
■ **1997** The Everglades National Park marks its 50th year.
■ **1997** Italian designer Gianni Versace is murdered in front of his oceanfront mansion. His killer, Andrew Cunanan, is found dead in a nearby houseboat days later.

Tourism waned again in the 1960s, but, at the same time, Miami began welcoming a new wave of dreamers. With a desire for a better life and a stead-fast belief in the American Dream, Cuban refugees and other sunbelt settlers started Miami's transformation from a resort community to a city of international stature. Most of the original 265,000 Cuban freedom-seekers came with little more than their entrepreneurial skills and a desire to build new lives. Their overwhelming accomplishments in constructing a strong educational, economic, and cultural base is one of America's greatest success stories.

In the early 1980s, Miami underwent its biggest building boom yet. Fantastically beautiful and unique skyscrapers sprang up downtown and along the boulevards flanking Biscayne Bay. The city's harbor became the biggest cruise-ship port in the world. Hundreds of multinational corporations, banks, and insurance firms opened offices. At the same time, Miami International Airport grew to be America's second-busiest international gateway, and a billion-dollar, futuristic Metrorail system whisked its way into the city. The 1988 reopening of the Miami Beach Convention Center, with its high-tech "new deco" facade, marked the rebirth of South Florida conventioneering.

Suddenly Miami wasn't just blooming; it was stylish. The hit television series, "Miami Vice," spotlighted the quirky and colorful city. Filmmakers found it hard to resist the rich texture and year-round accessibility of Miami as a backdrop. The show also put the city on the fashion map, with the world's top models and photographers seduced by the region's climate and colors. As Miami became more sophisticated, it began catering to the needs of commercial and artistic film crews with full-capacity studios, rental houses, film labs, and production equipment. In 1985, the Miami Office of Film, Television, and Print issued a total of about 350 permits; 10 years later, it issued nearly 5,000 permits. Moviegoers across the country got a memorable glimpse of South Beach in the 1996 film *The Birdcage*.

4 Famous Miamians

Muhammad Ali (b. 1942)   Like many other boxers who hit the big time, Muhammad Ali (born Cassius Clay) lived in Miami and trained in South Beach's Fifth Street Gym, demolished in the 1990s to make room for the spectacular growth in South Beach.

Al Capone (1899–1947)   In the late 1920s, Chicago's most infamous gangster moved his operations to Miami and settled into a white-stucco mansion on Palm Island.

Roy Cohn (1927–1986)   Disbarred just before he died, Roy Cohn is best known as the chief counsel for the "Red-baiting witch hunts" organized by Senator Joseph McCarthy in the 1950s. Cohn was raised in Miami Beach, where he was a childhood friend of television journalist Barbara Walters.

Amelia Earhart (1897–1937)   The world's most famous aviatrix began her ill-fated flight around the world from Miami. A city park is named in her honor.

Gloria Estefan (b. 1957)   She's come a long way from the Miami Sound Machine. Estefan sang for the Pope and composed the theme song for the 1996 Olympic Games in Atlanta. She is frequently spotted at one of her restaurants in town. She

Impressions

They say Miami Beach will make a comeback, and who knows, maybe it will . . . for me, Miami Beach is still one of the most beautiful places in the world.
        —Isaac Bashevis Singer, *My Love Affair with Miami Beach* (1986)

and her husband, record producer Emilio Estefan, keep a palatial mansion on Miami Beach's Star Island.

Perry Farrel (b. 1960 as Perry Bernstein)   The lead singer of alternative L.A. rock bands Jane's Addiction and Porno for Pyros grew up in North Miami Beach, where he spent most of his time surfing and performing until he hit the West Coast big.

Don Johnson (b. 1950)   New episodes of "Miami Vice" are no longer being produced, but Don Johnson, one of the show's stars, still likes to kick around the city that made him famous. Johnson bought a home on Star Island, a fancy parcel in the middle of Biscayne Bay.

Madonna (b. 1958)   Since purchasing her $4.9 million mansion in Coconut Grove, the platinum record singer has become a fixture on the Miami nightclub scene. She has also done many photo shoots here for her albums and books, including *Bedtime Stories* and *Sex.*

Bob Marley (1945–1981)   Perhaps one of the most influential figures in Jamaican history, Bob Marley was more than just a reggae musician. He was a spokesman for his people, a cultural leader of millions. Marley spent a lot of time in Miami and eventually died in a Miami hospital.

Richard M. Nixon (1913–1994)   Richard Nixon made Key Biscayne his "Winter White House" during his years as President of the United States. Subsequent owners have remodeled the property extensively, making it unrecognizable as the ex-president's ex-residence.

Mickey Rourke (b. 1956)   The actor/biker has started several restaurants and clubs in South Beach, his hometown, and often shows up at smoky bars throughout the city.

Sylvester Stallone (b. 1946)   A movie star, director, and producer, Stallone attended the University of Miami in the late 1960s, and then returned to Miami to purchase an $8 million bayfront estate that's next door to Madonna and near the famed Vizcaya. He is now very active in the community's cultural affairs.

Barbara Walters (b. 1931)   The renowned television interviewer grew up in Miami Beach and went to Beach High. Other notable Beach High alums are actor Andy Garcia and Roy Firestone, a sports commentator for ESPN.

5 Architecture 101

Miami's flamboyant, surprising, and fanciful architecture is one of the its greatest treasures. Three distinct forms, indigenous to specific periods, are in evidence.

The best of the "old" buildings were constructed between 1914 and 1925 by Miami's first developers. Designed primarily in an Italian Renaissance style are such structures as Villa Vizcaya, the Biltmore Hotel, and the Venetian Pool. The many Mediterranean Revival homes built in the late 1920s and 1930s feature antique Spanish tiles, arched doorways, and open courtyards. Other monuments in and around Coral Gables and Coconut Grove, including George Merrick's wonderful

Impressions

The first time I saw Miami, I experienced a series of emotions and was able to relive certain atmospheres, and breathe in the same imagination and creativity that was alive in the streets of Capri and St. Tropez' golden years. That is how I began my love affair with this city—with its people, its colors and its surprisingly contagious vitality.
—Fashion designer, Gianni Versace (1946–1997)

plazas and fountains, are timeless examples of tasteful wealth and beauty. See "Driving Tour 2" in chapter 8, "Driving & Strolling Around Miami," for more in-depth descriptions.

Miami's second distinct building style is its most famous. The celebrated Art Deco District in South Beach is a remarkable dreamlike foray into fashion and art on a grand scale. For the casual observer, the best buildings are the recently rehabilitated ones fronting the Atlantic on Ocean Drive. Until recently, South Beach had fallen into massive decay, but thanks to strong community involvement and support, the district is now protected by a 1979 listing in the National Register of Historic Places. Continuously undergoing intensive revitalization, South Beach's hotels are now some of the hippest in Miami. See "A Walking Tour" in chapter 8 for more in-depth information.

The sleek 21st-century skyline of downtown Miami represents the city's newest building wave. Almost every structure in the small bayfront cluster is a gem. Designed with independence, creativity, and a flamboyant flair, the skyscrapers in and around Brickell Avenue stand sharp and proud, like exotic entrants in a futuristic design competition. Viewed from across the bay, the cluster of shining buildings creates one of the most awesome cityscapes in the world. See "Driving Tour 2" in chapter 8.

Other innovative architecture includes internationally acclaimed designs by Arquitectonica in downtown Miami and Miami Beach. The critics have come up with a profusion of monikers for the brash designs that forever altered the Miami skyline: surrealistic, exuberant, Romantic Modernism, and Beach Blanket Bauhaus.

6 Miami's Bill of Fare

Miami is an exciting place to eat. What's on the menu? Everything from exotic fruits and vegetables to stone crab and fresh fish, from foreign cooking to delicious home-grown inventions. You can taste it all not only in the city's many restaurants, but also in the kiosks and grocery stores where locals buy their food.

Miami's regional cooking, dubbed "New World Cuisine," stems from the city's unique location, climate, and ethnic composition. Miami cuisine is based on the California model of creatively prepared dishes using fresh local ingredients. Many of the presentations are health-oriented fish and vegetable dishes, highlighted by delicate dashes of color. Fruity sauces topping succulent seafood are common, as are jazzed-up versions of traditional meat and poultry dishes. Local citrus fruits are widely used as garnishes in sauces, and as the primary ingredient in such recipes as Key lime pie.

Miami's ethnic edibles are as rich and diverse as the city's brilliant blend of cultures. In addition to the many straightforward rice-and-beans dishes served in traditional South and Central American restaurants (see "Little Havana" in chapter 6, "Dining," for details), you'll find Latin and Caribbean influences on even the most conservative menus. Cuban fried yucca, Bahamian conch fritters, tropical Caribbean preserves, Creole-style blackened fish, Spanish arroz con pollo, and all kinds of tapas are available all over town.

Here's a short list of readily available local specialties:

A variety of ✪ **smoked fish,** especially marlin, amberjack, and dolphin, appear on bar and restaurant menus and are sold at smokehouses throughout the city. The tender meat has a rough, smoky taste and is often served as a dip mixed with mayonnaise and spices.

Alligator, usually farm-raised, provides a smooth meat that is extremely lean, so it's likely to become tough if not cooked carefully. Usually it's battered and fried and very tasty. In some spots you may find alligator stew, an Old Florida specialty.

Conch, pronounced "conk," is a chewy shellfish that comes in those huge shells you can blow like horns or put next to your ear to "hear the ocean." This Bahamian specialty is usually served as an appetizer, either in a marinated ceviche or salad, in chowder, or battered and fried as "fritters."

Dolphin (also called mahi-mahi) is a popular fish that has nothing to do with "Flipper" or his marine mammal relatives. This Florida specialty is a plump, white-meat saltwater fish that is great blackened or skewered or just plain grilled.

Key lime pie is the region's most famous dessert. The citrus fruit that flavors the filling is small and yellow and indigenous to South Florida and the Florida Keys. The most authentic pie is sweetened with condensed milk and has a yellow pudding-like filling and a graham-cracker crust.

Florida **lobster,** also known as crawfish (though not the same as New Orleans crawfish), is smaller and somewhat sweeter than the Maine shellfish of the same name. But the spiny Florida variety has no claws, so look for a big meaty tail or a variety of pasta dishes that use the meat for filling or sauces.

Florida **mangos** grow for only a few short months, from roughly May to August, although they are used in sauces and chutneys throughout the year. The word *mango* derives from the Sanskrit word *ama* (meaning "of the people"), and mangos are truly a unifying force in this city. During the season, hundreds of varieties grow in yards and roadsides and are so plentiful that neighbors give each other bags of the luscious fruits and help their friends cut, peel, and process them.

Floridians wait for **stone crab** season the way the French wait for the new Beaujolais. The crab's claws are the only part of the animal you eat. Crabbers clip one or two claws, then toss the crustacean back in the water so it can grow new ones.

Citrus fruits are the area's largest legal cash crop, accounting for the lion's share of Florida's $12-billion agricultural industry. The state produces more than 80% of the nation's limes, 50% of the world's grapefruits, and 25% of the world's oranges. Needless to say, citrus juice is the drink of choice in these parts. Try starting your day with a cool glass of fresh orange or grapefruit juice. It's surprisingly hard to find fresh juices at most restaurants, although better places do offer it. At night, get a sense of the city's close Caribbean connections by mixing juice with rum from one of the nearby islands.

2 Planning a Trip to Miami

Although it's possible to land in Miami without an itinerary or reservations, your trip will be much more rewarding with a little bit of advance planning.

Of the many special events scheduled throughout the year, the bulk are staged from October through May. This reflects the close relationship between tourism and festivals, but in no way means that Miami's special events are canned tourist traps. In fact, these events are just the opposite; Miamians have a talent for creating popular outdoor festivals. Although the success of city festivals often relies on tourist dollars, the inspiration and creativity that goes into them is 100% home-grown.

1 Visitor Information & Money

VISITOR INFORMATION

The best source for any kind of specialized information about the city is the **Greater Miami Convention and Visitors Bureau,** 701 Brickell Ave., Miami, FL 33131 (☎ **800/283-2707** or 305/ 539-3063; **www.Miamiandbeaches.com** or gmcvb@aol.com). Even if you don't have a specific question, call ahead to request its free magazine, *Destination Miami,* which includes several good, easy-to-use maps. The office is open weekdays from 9am to 5pm.

For information on traveling in Florida, contact **Visit Florida,** P.O. Box 1100, 66 E. Jefferson St., Tallahassee, FL 32302 (☎ **904/ 488-5607**). The office is open weekdays from 8am to 5pm. Europeans should note that this agency maintains an office in Great Britain at 18/24 Westbourne Grove, 4th floor, London W2 5RH (☎ **071/727-1661**).

In addition to information on some of South Beach's funkier hotels, the **Miami Design Preservation League,** 1001 Ocean Dr. (PO Bin L), Miami Beach, FL 33139 (☎ **305/672-2014**), offers an informative free guide to the Art Deco District and several books on the subject. It's open Monday through Saturday from 10am to 7pm.

Greater Miami's various chambers of commerce also send maps and information about their particular neighborhoods, including the following:

- **Coconut Grove Chamber of Commerce,** 2820 McFarlane Rd., Miami, FL 33133 (☎ **305/444-7270**).
- **Coral Gables Chamber of Commerce,** 50 Aragon Ave., Coral Gables, FL 33134 (☎ **305/446-1657**).

What Things Cost in Miami	U.S. $
Taxi from Miami Airport to a downtown hotel	18.00–26.00
Local telephone call	.35
Double room at the Grand Bay Hotel (expensive)	285.00
Double room at the Indian Creek Hotel (moderate)	130.00
Double room at the Suez Motel (inexpensive)	70.00
Lunch for one at the News Cafe (moderate)	9.00
Lunch for one at Mrs. Mendoza's (inexpensive)	6.00
Dinner for one, without wine, at Chef Allen's (very expensive)	49.00
Dinner for one, without wine, at Versailles (inexpensive)	13.00
Pint of beer	2.75
Coca-Cola in a restaurant	1.50
Cup of coffee	1.25
Roll of ASA 100 film, 36 exposures	6.50
Admission to Miami Metrozoo, Adult	8.00
Movie ticket	6.50

- **Florida Gold Coast Chamber of Commerce,** 1100 Kane Concourse (Bay Harbor Islands), Miami, FL 33154 (☎ **305/866-6020**)—this office represents Bal Harbour, Sunny Isles, Surfside, and other North Dade waterfront communities.
- **Greater Homestead/Florida City Chamber of Commerce,** 160 US Hwy. (☎ **305/245-9180**); open daily 8am to 6pm.
- **Greater Miami Chamber of Commerce,** Omni International, 1601 Biscayne Blvd., Miami, FL 33132 (☎ **800/283-2707** or 305/539-3063).
- **Miami Beach Chamber of Commerce,** 1920 Meridian Ave., Miami Beach, FL 33139 (☎ **305/672-1270**).

The following organizations represent dues-paying hotels, restaurants, and attractions in their specific areas. These associations can arrange accommodations and tours as well as provide discount coupons to area sights: **Miami Beach Resort Hotel Association,** 407 Lincoln Rd., Miami Beach, FL 33139 (☎ **800/531-3553**, or 305/531-3553), and **Sunny Isles Beach Resort Association,** 17100 Collins Suite 208, Sunny Isles, FL 33160 (☎ **305/947-5826**).

MONEY

You never have to carry a lot of cash in Miami. Automated teller machines (ATMs) are located at virtually every bank in the city, and credit cards are accepted by the vast majority of Miami's hotels, restaurants, attractions, shops, and nightspots. U.S.-dollar traveler's checks are also widely accepted for goods and services and can be exchanged for cash at banks and check-issuing offices.

1st Nationwide Bank, 517 Arthur Godfrey Rd., accepts cards on Cirrus, Honor, and Metroteller networks. For the location of the nearest ATM, call **800/424-7787** for the Cirrus network or **800/843-7587** for the Plus system. Banks making cash advances against MasterCard and Visa cards include Citibank (☎ **800/ 627-3939**) and NationsBank (☎ **800/299-2265**). American Express cardholders can write a personal check, guaranteed against the card, for up to $1,000 in cash at any American Express office (see "Fast Facts: Miami" in Chapter 4 for locations).

2 When to Go

Miami's tourist season, from December through April, is more reflective of the weather up north than it is of climatic changes in South Florida. It's always warm in Miami. No matter what time of year you visit, you'll find that indoor spaces are always air-conditioned, cafes always have tables out on the sidewalk, and the beaches are always full.

Terrific weather has always been Miami's main appeal and is a particular delight during the winter, when the rest of the country is shivering. When it's winter in Wisconsin, it's still summer in the Sunshine State. The period from November to mid-May is considered the high season; many hotels tend to raise prices by the first week of November and lower them by the end of May.

Don't overlook traveling to Miami during the "off" seasons, when vacationing can be every bit as rewarding. The weather is still great, and hotel prices are significantly lower than at other times of the year. In addition, restaurants, stores, and highways are less crowded.

South Florida's unique climate is extremely tropical. Hot, sometimes muggy summers are counterbalanced by wonderfully warm winters. It's not uncommon for a sudden shower to be followed by several hours of intense sunshine. For natives, "winter" is too cold for swimming; however, for many visitors, 70° January afternoons are perfect beach days. It can't always be perfect, though—there are occasional cold snaps, and even one short tropical rain shower can ruin a day at the beach.

Finally, a word about Florida's tropical storms and hurricanes. Most occur between August and November. For local property owners, the tumultuous winds that sweep in from the Atlantic Ocean can be devastating. In August 1992, for example, Hurricane Andrew—one of the fiercest storms ever recorded in Florida— caused about $30 billion in damage to residential and business districts in Dade and Monroe Counties. More than 250,000 people were left homeless.

For visitors, the high winds and incessant rains usually mean little more than a delayed vacation. Even Hurricane Andrew caused relatively little damage to most of Miami's hotels and major tourist attractions, all of which have since reopened.

Meteorologists know far in advance when a storm is brewing off the Atlantic Coast and can determine pretty accurately what force it will have; the information is then broadcast nationwide. With respect to Andrew, the National Hurricane Center, located in Coral Gables, gave due warning of the storm and tracked it closely as it approached Florida, although it couldn't predict the exact spot where the storm would make landfall, causing many of the inland residents in Homestead and beyond to be unprepared for the hit. However, if there are reports of an impending storm before you leave for Florida, you may want to postpone your trip.

Miami's Average Temperatures & Rainfall

	Jan	Feb	Mar	Apr	May	June	July	Aug	Sept	Oct	Nov	Dec
Avg. High (°F)	75	76	79	82	85	87	89	90	88	84	80	76
Avg. Low (°F)	59	60	64	68	72	75	76	77	76	72	66	61
Avg. Rain (in.)	2.0	2.0	2.3	3.6	6.3	8.6	6.7	7.2	8.6	6.9	2.9	1.9

MIAMI CALENDAR OF EVENTS

January

- **Orange Bowl,** Miami. Two of the year's college football teams do battle at Pro Player Stadium, preceded by the King Orange Jamboree Parade (see December listing, below). Tickets are available starting March 1 of the previous year through the Orange Bowl Committee. Call ☎ **305/371-4600** for details. Usually January 1 (but note that dates of this and the other college bowl games mentioned below may vary to accommodate TV schedules).

- **Art Miami,** Miami. This annual fine art fair attracts more than a hundred galleries from all over the world. International, modern, and contemporary works are featured here, bringing thousands of visitors and buyers to the Coconut Grove Convention Center. For information and ticket prices, call ☎ **561/220-2690.** Early January.

- **Three Kings Parade,** Miami. Since Cuban President Fidel Castro outlawed this religious celebration more than 25 years ago, Cuban-Americans in Little Havana have put on a bacchanalian parade winding through Calle Ocho from 4th Avenue to 27th Avenue, with horse-drawn carriages, native costumes, and marching bands. Call ☎ **305/447-1140** for the exact date during the first week of January.

- ✪ **Art Deco Weekend,** South Beach, Miami. Held along the beach between 5th and 15th streets, this festival—with bands, food stands, antiques vendors, artists, tours, and other festivities—celebrates the whimsical architecture that has made South Beach one of America's most unique neighborhoods. Call ☎ **305/672-2014** for details. Usually held on Martin Luther King weekend.

- **Martin Luther King Day Parade,** Miami. This parade along NW 62nd Avenue, north of Downtown, honors Dr. King. For information, call ☎ **305/636-1924.**

- ✪ **Royal Caribbean Classic,** Key Biscayne. World-renowned golfers compete for more than $1 million in prize money at Crandon Park Golf Course, formerly known as The Links. Lee Trevino is a two-time winner of this championship tournament. Call ☎ **305/374-6180** for more information. Late January.

- **Winter Antique Show,** Miami Beach. Antique glasswork, coins, jewelry, furniture, and more fill 800 booths and two halls at the mammoth Miami Beach Convention Center. Call ☎ **305/754-4931** for details. Late January to early Febuary.

- **Taste of the Grove Food and Music Festival,** Coconut Grove. This fundraiser in the Grove's Peacock Park is an excellent chance for visitors to sample menu items from some of the city's top restaurants and sounds from international and local performers. Call ☎ **305/444-7270** for details. Mid-January.

- **The Key Biscayne Art Festival,** Key Biscayne. Really one of the finest in the country, this art festival, held in Cape Florida State Park, brings hundreds of artists, some crafts makers, and lots of great international food together for a high-quality, juried fine art show—and it's all for charity. Call ☎ **305/361-5207** for details. Last weekend in January.

February

- **Everglades Seafood Festival,** Florida City. As many as 75,000 people show up each year for this two day eating festival in the quaint old town of Florida City. Florida delicacies like stone crab and gator tails are dished up from shacks and food booths on the outskirts of town. Friday night is family night where a carnival and craft fair attract the youngsters. No admission charge. Call ☎ 941/695-4100 for more details. First full weekend in February.

- ✪ **Miami Film Festival,** Miami. This 10-day festival has made an impact as an important screening opportunity for Latin American cinema and American independents. It's relatively small, well-priced, and easily accessible to the general public. Contact the Film Society of Miami at ☎ 305/377-FILM. Early February.

- ✪ **Coconut Grove Art Festival,** Coconut Grove. This is the state's largest art festival and the favorite annual event of many locals. More than 300 artists are selected from thousands of entries to show their works at this prestigious outdoor festival. Almost every medium is represented, including the culinary arts. Call ☎ 305/447-0401 for details. Presidents' Day weekend.

- ✪ **Miami International Boat Show,** Miami. This show draws almost a quarter of a million boat enthusiasts to the Miami Beach Convention Center and surrounding locations to see the mega-yachts, sailboats, dinghies, and accessories. It's the biggest anywhere. Call ☎ 305/531-8410 for more information and ticket prices. Mid-February.

- **Doral Ryder Golf Open,** West Miami. One of the country's most prestigious annual tournaments. Call ☎ 305/477-GOLF for more information. Late February to early March.

March

- **Winter Party,** Miami. The Dade Human Rights Foundation hosts this gay and lesbian weekend-long party, which features several activities at clubs around town and culminates in a huge all-day dance fest on the beach on Sunday. Travel reservations can be made through Different Roads Travel—the official travel company of the event—at ☎ 888/ROADS-55, ext. 510. For more information on specific events and ticket prices, call ☎ 305/538-5908 or check out their Web site at **www.winterparty.com.** Early March.

- **The Italian Renaissance Festival,** Miami. Stage plays, music, and period costumes complement Villa Vizcaya's neo-Italianate architectural style. Call ☎ 305/250-9133 for more information. Mid-March.

- **Miami Gay & Lesbian Film Festival,** Miami. A 10-day festival of short and feature-length films and videos by gay filmmakers is presented at South Beach's Colony Theater on Lincoln Road and other smaller venues. For details, call Robert Rosenberg ☎ 305/532-7256. Mid-March.

- **Grand Prix of Miami,** Homestead. This high-purse, high-profile auto race rivals the big ones in Daytona. It attracts the top Indy car drivers and large crowds. For information and tickets, contact Homestead Motorsports Complex at ☎ 305/230-5200. First week of March.

- ✪ **Calle Ocho Festival,** Miami. This salsa-filled blowout marks the end of a 10-day extravaganza called Carnival Miami. It's one of the world's biggest block parties, held along 23 blocks of Little Havana's Southwest 8th Street between 4th and 27th avenues. Call ☎ 305/644-8888 for more information. Early to mid-March.

- **Lipton Championship,** Miami. One of the world's largest tennis events is hosted at the lush Tennis Center at Crandon Park on Key Biscayne. Call ☎ 305/446-2200 for details. Mid- to late March.

April

- **Blues Festival,** Coral Gables. Mozart Stub restaurateur Harald Neuweg hosts this all-day street fest featuring down-home blues tunes as well as great food and lots of beer. Call ☎ **305/446-1600** for more details or see "Oktoberfest" listing below. Third weekend in March.

May

- **Arabian Nights Festival,** Opa-Locka. This yearly event commemorates the distinctive Moorish architecture in the heart of Opa-Locka. Historical tours, street festivals, live music, and food booths are part of the fun. For details, call ☎ **305/688-4611.** Early May.
- **Texaco/Hemingway Key West Classic,** Key West. Hailed as the top fishing tournament in Florida, this catch-and-release competition offers $50,000 in prizes to be divided between the top anglers in three divisions: sailfish, marlin, and light tackle. Call ☎ **305/294-4440** for more information. Mid-May.
- **Coconuts Dolphin Tournament,** Key Largo. This is the largest fishing tournament in the Keys, offering $5,000 and a Dodge Ram pickup truck to the person who breaks the record for the largest fish caught. The competition is fierce! Call ☎ **305/451-4107** for details. Mid-May.
- **The Great Sunrise Balloon Race & Festival,** Homestead. Every Memorial Day weekend, dozens of multicolored balloons rise up over Homestead Air Reserve Base as sky divers fall from the sky. The race is celebrated on the ground with a variety of food, music, arts, and crafts. For information, call ☎ **305/275-3317.**

June

- **Super Boat Racing Series,** Key West. A day of food, fun, and powerboat racing in downtown Key West. Call ☎ **305/296-8963** for details. Early June.
- ✪ **Coconut Grove Goombay Festival,** Miami. This bash, one of the country's largest black-heritage festivals, features Bahamian bacchanalia with dancing in the streets of Coconut Grove and music from the Royal Bahamian Police marching band. The food and music draw thousands to an all-day celebration of Miami's Caribbean connection. It's lots of fun—if the weather isn't scorching. Call ☎ **305/372-9966** for festival details. Early June.

July

- **Independence Day,** Miami. Celebrate July 4th on the beach, where parties, barbecues, and fireworks flare all day and night. For a weekend's worth of events on Key Biscayne, call ☎ **305/361-5207.** You can also find one of the wildest parties around—complete with fireworks and top-notch festivities—at Bayfront Park, 301 N. Biscayne Blvd. For more on this free event, call ☎ **305/358-7550.** It's a good idea, though, to check local papers for a more detailed list of events.
- **Miccosukee Everglades Music and Crafts Festival,** Miami. Native American rock, Razz (reservation jazz), and folk bands perform while visitors gorge themselves on exotic treats like pumpkin bread and fritters. Watch the hulking old gators wrestle with Native Americans. Call ☎ **305/223-8380** for prices and details. Late July.
- ✪ **Lower Keys Underwater Music Fest,** Looe Key. At this outrageous celebration, boaters go out to the underwater reef of Looe Key Marine Sanctuary off Big Pine Key, drop speakers into the water, and pipe in music. It's entertainment for the fish and swimmers alike! A snorkeling Elvis can usually be spotted. Call ☎ **800/872-3722** for details. Second Saturday of July.

August

- **Miami Reggae Festival,** Miami. Jamaica's best dance-hall and reggae artists turn out for this 2-day festival. Burning Spear, Steel Pulse, Spragga Benz, and Jigsy King have participated recently. Call Jamaica Awareness at ☎ **305/891-2944** for more details. Early August.

September

- **Festival Miami,** Miami. A 4-week program of performing arts featuring local and invited musical guests. Based in the University of Miami School of Music and Maurice Gusman Concert Hall. For a schedule of events, call ☎ **305/284-4940.** Mid-September to mid-October.
- ✪ **Columbus Day Regatta,** Miami. Find anything that can float—from an inner tube to a 100-foot yacht—and you'll fit right in. Yes, there actually is a race, but how can you keep track when you're partying with a bunch of semi-naked psychos in the middle of Biscayne Bay? It's free and it's wild. Rent a boat, jet ski, or sailboard to get up close. Be sure to secure a vessel early, though—everyone wants to be there. Check local newspapers for exact date and time. Columbus Day weekend.

October

- **Oktoberfest,** Miami. They close the streets for this German beer and food festival thrown by the Mozart Stub Restaurant in Coral Gables. You'll find loads of great music and dancing at this wild party. Call Harald Neuweg (☎ **305/446-1600**) to find out where and when.
- ✪ **Fantasy Fest,** Key West. It might feel as though the rest of the world is joining you if you're in Key West for this world-famous Halloween festival, Florida's version of Mardi Gras. Crazy costumes, wild parades, and even wilder revelers gather for an opportunity to do things Mom said not to. Definitely leave the kids at home! Call ☎ **305/296-1817.** Last week of October.
- ✪ **Goombay Festival,** Key West. Sample Caribbean dishes and purchase art and ethnic clothing in this celebration with a Jamaican flair that coincides with Fantasy Fest (see above).

November

- **The Jiffy Lube Miami 300 Weekend of NASCAR,** Homestead. Here's more world-class racing at a recently constructed 344-acre motorsports complex. For information and tickets, contact Homestead Motorsports Complex, One Speedway Blvd., Homestead (☎ **305/230-5200**). Mid-November.
- **Chili Cook-Off,** Miami. Sample some of the nation's best chili as the area's "hottest" restaurants compete for the glory of being the best. For details, call ☎ **305/441-6677.** Mid-November.
- ✪ **Miami Book Fair International,** Miami. An event that draws hundreds of thousands of visitors, including foreign and domestic publishers and authors from around the world, with great lectures and readings by world-renowned authors. Call ☎ **305/237-3258.** Mid-November.
- **The Ramble,** Miami. Old-time Floridians love this yearly event at the Fairchild Tropical Gardens. Here you can buy antiques, exotic orchids, or vintage clothes. If you're not shopping, it's still worth strolling around the lush park where you can learn about various botanical miracles. For more information, call ☎ **305/667-1651.** Mid-November.
- ✪ **Mercury Outboards Cheeca/Redbone Celebrity Tournament,** Islamorada, in the Upper Keys. Curt Gowdy from American Sportsman hosts this tournament, the proceeds of which go to finding a cure for cystic fibrosis. The likes of Wade

Boggs, actor James B. Sikking, and Gen. Norman Schwartzkopf compete almost yearly. Call ☎ **305/664-2002** for details. This event is followed by the **George Bush Cheeca Lodge Bonefish Tournament**. Call ☎ **305/743-7000** for more information. Second and third weekends of November.

- ❂ **White Party Week,** Miami. This week-long AIDS fundraiser begins with a series of events in Miami Beach nightclubs and leads up to the Sunday night gala, where Miami's gay community comes out to celebrate at Vizcaya, the Renaissance mansion. Since this gala always sells out, make sure to buy your tickets as soon as they go on sale October 1. Call ☎ **305/759-6181** for details. Thanksgiving weekend.

December

- • **King Mango Strut,** Coconut Grove, Miami. This fun-filled march encourages everyone to wear wacky costumes and join the floats in a spoof of the King Orange Jamboree Parade, held the following night. Runs from Commodore Plaza to Peacock Park in Coconut Grove. Comedians and musical entertainment follow in the park. Call ☎ **305/444-7270** for details. December 30.

- ❂ **King Orange Jamboree Parade,** Miami. The world's largest nighttime parade is followed by a long night of festivities leading up to the Orange Bowl football game (see January listing, above). Runs along Biscayne Boulevard. For information and tickets (which cost $7.50 to $13), contact the Greater Miami Convention and Visitors Bureau at ☎ **305/539-3063**. Usually December 31.

3 Insurance & Safety Concerns

INSURANCE

Many travelers are covered by their hometown health-insurance policies in the event of an accident or sudden illness while away on vacation. Make sure your Health Maintenance Organization (HMO) or insurance carrier can provide services for you while you're in Florida. If there's any doubt, a health-insurance policy that specifically covers your trip is advisable.

You can also protect yourself with insurance against lost or damaged baggage and trip-cancellation or interruption costs. These coverages are often combined into a single comprehensive plan, sold through travel agents, credit- and charge-card companies, and automobile and other clubs.

Most travel agents can sell low-cost health, loss, and trip-cancellation insurance to their vacationing clients. Compare these rates and services with those offered by local banks as well as by your personal insurance carrier.

PERSONAL SAFETY

Reacting to several highly publicized crimes against tourists, both local and state governments have taken steps to help protect visitors. These measures include special, highly visible police units patrolling the airport and surrounding neighborhoods, and better signs on the state's most tourist-traveled routes. Also, look for bright orange sunbursts on highway exit signs that point the way to tourist-friendly zones.

When driving around Miami, always have a good map, and know where you are going. Never stop on a highway—if you get a flat tire, drive to the nearest well-lighted, populated place. Keep car doors locked and stay alert. If you are arriving in Miami at night and plan to rent a car, I suggest taking a taxi from the airport to your hotel and arranging to have a rental car delivered to your hotel. Opt for any additional safety features in the car, such as cellular telephones or electronic maps. For short stays or trips that will be centered in one area of the city, such as

South Beach, you could dispense with a rental car altogether, and just rely on taxis, which are generally safe and relatively inexpensive.

Don't walk alone at night, and be extra wary when walking or driving though Little Haiti and Downtown.

During the hurricane season, listen to radio and television broadcasts, which will describe evacuation routes. Better hotels will arrange transportation for their guests to safe areas.

4 Tips for Travelers with Special Needs

FOR TRAVELERS WITH DISABILITIES   Many hotels offer special accommodations and services for wheelchair-bound visitors and travelers with disabilities, including large bathrooms, ramps, and telecommunication devices for the deaf. The Greater Miami Convention and Visitors Bureau (see "Visitor Information," above) has the most up-to-date information.

The **City of Miami Department of Parks and Recreation,** 2600 S. Bayshore Dr. (Coconut Grove), Miami, FL 33133 (☎ 305/860-3800; TTY 305/579-3436), maintains many programs for people with disabilities at parks and beaches throughout the city. Call or write for a listing of special services. The office is open weekdays from 8am to 5pm. **The Metro-Dade County Parks & Recreation Department** also runs hundreds of programs from swimming to sailing for visitors with disabilities. For a complete listing, call the department (☎ 305/755-7848) weekdays from 9am to 5pm. Primarily a referral service, the **Deaf Services Bureau,** 4800 W. Flagler St., Suite 213, Miami, FL 33134 (☎ 305/668-4407; TTY 305/668-3323) may be contacted for any special concerns you have about traveling in and around Miami. Hours are weekdays from 9am to 5pm. The **Division of Blind Services,** 401 NW 2nd Ave., Suite 700, Miami, FL 33128 (☎ 305/377-5339), offers services similar to those of the Deaf Services Bureau, above, but to those with visual impairments. The office is open weekdays from 8am to 5pm.

Many of the major car rental companies now offer hand-controlled cars for disabled drivers. Avis can supply such a vehicle at any of its locations in the United States with 48-hour advance notice; Hertz requires between 24 and 72 hours of advance reservation at most of its locations. **Wheelchair Getaways** (☎ 800/873-4973 for information, or try the Web site, **www.blvd.com/wg.htm**) rents specialized vans with wheelchair lifts and other features for the disabled throughout the United States, including in Florida.

FOR GAY & LESBIAN TRAVELERS   Miami, particularly South Beach, has a significant gay community, supported by a wide range of services. There are many gay-oriented publications with information, up-to-date calendars, and listings of gay-friendly businesses and services. *TWN* is the only local gay newspaper in town; you'll find it in lavender boxes throughout the city and at bookstores and gay bars. Other local publications include *WIRE, Miamigo, Out Pages,* and *Scoop.*

The **Gay and Lesbian Community Hotline** (☎ 305/759-3661), an interactive recording that can be reached with a push-button phone, lists categories of information of interest to the gay community. These items include political issues, gay bars, special events, support groups, businesses serving the gay community, doctors and lawyers, help wanted, and others.

The **Lambda Passages/Gay Community Bookstore,** 7545 Biscayne Blvd. (☎ 305/754-6900), features quality literature, newspapers, videos, music, cards, and more. It's open Monday to Saturday from 11am to 9pm and Sunday from noon to 6pm.

For a map and directory of gay businesses or a copy of the gay and lesbian community calendar (sponsored by the Dade Human Rights Foundation), contact the **South Florida Business Guild** at ☎ **305/534-3336** or 305/893-5595. For a copy of the calendar and other information, you can also log on to the foundation's Web site at **www.dhrf.com**.

FOR SENIORS   Miami is well versed in catering to seniors. Ask for discounts everywhere, at hotels, movie theaters, museums, restaurants, and attractions—you'll be surprised how often you're offered reduced rates. Many restaurants offer early-bird specials and honor AARP memberships.

FOR STUDENTS   A valid high school or college ID often entitles you to discounts at attractions (particularly at museums) and sometimes to reduced rates at bars during "college nights." You're most likely to find these discounts at places near the local colleges, in downtown Miami and Coral Gables.

You'll find lots of students at the large main campus of the **University of Miami,** located in south Coral Gables. This campus encompasses dozens of classrooms, a huge athletic field, a large lake, a museum, a hospital, and more. For general information, call the university (☎ **305/284-2211**). The school's main student building is the Whitten University Center, 1306 Stanford Dr. (☎ **305/284-2318**). Social events are often scheduled here, and important information on area activities is always posted. The building houses a recreation area, a pool, a snack shop, and a Ticketmaster outlet.

The **Jerry Herman Ring Theatre,** on the University of Miami campus, 1380 Miller Dr. (☎ **305/284-3355**), is the main stage for the Department of Theater Arts' advanced-student productions. Faculty and guest actors are regularly featured, as are contemporary works by local playwrights.

The **Gusman Concert Hall,** 1314 Miller Dr. (☎ **305/284-2438** voice; 305/284-6477 recording), features performances by faculty and students of the university's School of Music, as well as concerts by special guests. Call for schedules and tickets.

For tickets to Miami Hurricanes basketball, football, and baseball home games, call the **U of M Athletic Department** (☎ **305/284-3822,** or 800/GO-CANES in Florida). See "Spectator Sports" in chapter 7, "What to See and Do," for more information.

The University's **Bill Cosford Cinema** (☎ **305/284-4861**) is named after the deceased Miami Herald's film critic and features new and classic films. Call for ticket prices and screening schedules. The theater closes during school holidays, including a month over Christmas.

5 Getting There

One hundred years ago, Miami, basically a swampy jungle, was a hard place to reach—but no more. Today, transportation companies, most notably airlines, fight perpetual price wars to woo tourists to the Sunshine State. In fact, airfares are so competitive that, unless you are visiting from an adjacent state, flying to Miami will almost always be your most economical option. However, take a look at your alternatives, too. An overland journey to Florida's Gold Coast is both a more scenic and a more flexible way to travel. Greyhound/Trailways offers several types of bus passes, and Amtrak offers a host of rail services to the South.

BY PLANE

More than 80 scheduled airlines service Miami International Airport, including almost every major domestic and foreign carrier. The city is so well connected that the problem isn't getting there, but rather deciding what service and fare to select.

CyberDeals for Net Surfers

It's possible to get some great deals on airfare, hotels, and car rentals via the Internet. So go grab your mouse and start surfing before you hit the real waves in Miami—you could save a bundle on your trip. The Web sites highlighted below are worth checking out, especially since all services are free.

Microsoft Expedia (www.expedia.com)   The best part of this multipurpose travel site is the "Fare Tracker": You fill out a form on the screen indicating that you're interested in cheap flights to Miami (for example) from your hometown, and, once a week, they'll e-mail you the best airfare deals. The site's "Travel Agent" will steer you to bargains on hotels and car rentals, and you can book everything, including flights, right online. This site is even useful once you're booked: Before you go, log on to Expedia for oodles of up-to-date travel information, including weather reports and foreign exchange rates.

Preview Travel (www.reservations.com and www.vacations.com)   Another useful travel site, Reservations.com has a "Best Fare Finder," which will search the Apollo computer reservations system for the three lowest fares for any route on any days of the year. Say you want to go from Chicago to Miami and back between December 6th and 13th: Just fill out the form on the screen with times, dates, and destinations, and within minutes, Preview will show you the best deals. If you find an airfare you like, you can book your ticket right online—you can even reserve hotels and car rentals on this site. If you're in the preplanning stage, head to Preview's Vacations.com site, where you can check out the latest package deals for destinations around the world by clicking on "Hot Deals."

Travelocity (www.travelocity.com)   This is one of the best travel sites out there. In addition to its "Personal Fare Watcher," which notifies you via e-mail of the lowest airfares for up to five different destinations, Travelocity will track the three lowest fares for any routes on any dates in minutes. You can book a flight right

Major American carriers offering regular flights to Miami include **American Airlines,** 150 Alhambra Plaza, Coral Gables (☎ **800/433-7300** or 305/358-6800); **Continental,** 38 Biscayne Blvd., Downtown (☎ **800/525-0280** or 305/871-1400); **Delta Airlines,** 201 Alhambra Circle, Suite 516, Coral Gables (☎ **800/221-1212** or 305/448-7000); **Northwest Airlines,** 150 Alhambra Plaza, Coral Gables (☎ **800/447-4747**); and **United Airlines,** Miami International Airport (☎ **800/521-4041**).

Florida destinations are often at the heart of the "fare wars" that airlines wage; flights to Miami are usually pretty reasonable, if not downright cheap. The lowest round-trip airfares from New York usually dip below $200, and are around $300 from Chicago and $400 from Los Angeles. Sometimes you can do better, especially by calling the airlines directly.

You might be able to get a great deal on airfare by calling a consolidator, such as **Travac,** 989 Ave. of the Americas, New York, NY 10018 (☎ **800/TRAV-800** or 212/563-3303); and **Unitravel,** 1117 N. Warson Rd. (P.O. Box 12485), St. Louis, MO 63132 (☎ **800/325-2222** or 314/569-0900).

MIAMI INTERNATIONAL AIRPORT

Originally carved out of scrubland in 1928 by Pan American Airlines, Miami International Airport (MIA) has emerged as one of the busiest airports in the world.

then and there, and if you need a rental car or hotel, Travelocity will find you the best deal via the SABRE computer reservations system (a huge database used by travel agents worldwide). Click on "Last Minute Deals" for the latest travel bargains, including a link to "H.O.T. Coupons" (**www.hotcoupons.com**), where you can print out electronic coupons for travel in the United States and Canada.

Trip.Com (www.thetrip.com)   This site is really geared toward the business traveler, but vacationers-to-be can also use Trip.com's valuable fare-finding engine, which will e-mail you every week with the best city-to-city airfare deals on your selected route or routes.

Discount Tickets (www.discount-tickets.com)   Operated by the ETN (European Travel Network), this site offers discounts on airfares, accommo-dations, car rentals, and tours. It deals in flights between the United States and other countries, not domestic U.S. flights, so it's most useful for travelers coming to Miami from abroad.

Airline Web Sites   Here's a list of airlines and their Web sites, where you can not only get on the e-mailing lists, but also book flights directly:

- **American Airlines:** www.americanair.com
- **Continental Airlines:** www.flycontinental.com
- **TWA:** www.twa.com
- **Northwest Airlines:** www.nwa.com
- **US Airways:** www.usairways.com

Epicurious Travel (travel.epicurious.com)   Another good travel site; it allows you to sign up for all these airline e-mail lists at once.

—Jeanette Foster

Unfortunately, as it undergoes major reconstruction to expand its capacity, the airport can feel like a maze with inadequate signage and surly employees.

The route down to the baggage-claim area is clearly marked. You can change money or use your Honor or Plus System ATM card at Barnett Bank of South Florida, located near the exit.

Like most good international airports, MIA has its fair share of boutiques, shops, and eateries. Unless you are starving or forgot to get a gift for the person picking you up, bypass these overpriced establishments. The airport is literally surrounded by restaurants and shops; if you can wait to get to them, you will save a lot of money. If you are exiting Miami on an international flight, don't miss the excellent duty-free selection in the departure lounge.

Visitor information is available at the Miami International Airport Main Visitor Counter, Concourse E, 2nd level (☎ **305/876-7000**). Open 24 hours a day.

RELAXING AT THE AIRPORT HOTEL   If you find yourself waiting in the airport with time to kill, consider going up to the Miami International Airport Hotel to catch a few rays. For a $5 fee, the Top of the Port Health Club allows anyone to use their facilities, which include a sundeck, weights, sauna, showers, and a pool.

Although the hotel is literally in the airport, finding it is a little tricky. From the second level of the airport at Concourse E, take the elevator to the seventh floor, and then turn right and find another elevator that will take you to the eighth floor. When you exit, you'll see the health club right in front of you.

GETTING INTO TOWN   The airport is located about 6 miles west of Downtown and about 12 miles from the beaches, so it's likely you can get from the plane to your hotel room in less than an hour. Of course, if you're arriving from an international destination, it will take more time to go through Customs and Immigration.

By Car   All the major car-rental firms operate off-site branches reached via shuttle from the terminals. See "Getting Around" in chapter 4 for a list of major rental companies. Signs at the airport's exit clearly point the way to various parts of the city. However, if you're arriving at night, I suggest taking a taxi to your hotel and having the car-rental firm deliver a car to your hotel the next day.

By Taxi   Taxis line up in front of a dispatcher's desk outside the airport's arrivals terminals. Most cabs are metered, though some have flat rates to popular destinations. The fare should be about $12 to Coral Gables, $18 to Downtown, and $24 to South Beach, plus tip, which should be at least 10% and more for each bag the driver handles. Depending on traffic, the ride to Coral Gables or Downtown takes about 15 to 20 minutes, and to South Beach, 20 to 25 minutes.

By Limo or Van   Group limousines (multipassenger vans) circle the arrivals area looking for fares. Destinations are posted on the front of each van, and a flat rate is charged for door-to-door service to the area marked.

   SuperShuttle (☎ **305/871-2000**) is one of the largest airport operators, charging between $10 and $20 per person for a ride within Dade County. Its vans operate 24 hours a day and accept American Express, MasterCard, and Visa.

   Private limousine arrangements can be made in advance through your local travel agent. A one-way meet-and-greet service should cost about $50.

By Public Transportation   I do not recommend taking public transportation to get from the airport to your hotel. Buses heading Downtown leave the airport only once per hour (from the arrivals level), and connections are spotty at best. It could take about an hour and a half to get to South Beach. Journeys to Downtown and Coral Gables are more direct. The fare is $1.25, plus an additional 25 cents for a South Beach transfer.

BY CAR

No matter where you start your journey, chances are you'll reach Miami by way of I-95. This north-south interstate is the city's lifeline and an integral part of the region. The highway connects all of Miami's different neighborhoods, the airport, and the beach, and it connects all of South Florida to the rest of America. Unfortunately, many of Miami's road signs are completely confusing and notably absent when you need them. Take time out to study I-95's placement on the map. You will use it as a reference point time and again.

   Other major highways to Florida include I-10, which originates in Los Angeles and terminates in Jacksonville, and I-75, which begins in North Michigan and runs through the center of Florida.

   Before you set out on a long car trip, you might want to join the **American Automobile Association** (AAA) (☎ **800/222-4357**), which has hundreds of offices nationwide. Members receive excellent maps (they'll even help you plan an exact itinerary) and emergency road service. Other auto clubs include the **Allstate Motor Club,** 1500 Shure Dr., Arlington Heights, IL 60004 (☎ **847/253-4800**), and the **Amoco Motor Club,** P.O. Box 9046, Des Moines, IA 50369 (☎ **800/334-3300**).

BY TRAIN

Amtrak (☎ **800/USA-RAIL**) may be a good option. Two trains leave daily from New York—the Silver Meteor at 7:05pm and the Silver Star at 11:50am. They both take from 26¹/₂ to 29 hours to complete the journey to Miami. At press time, the lowest-priced round-trip ticket from New York to Miami cost $146 for a coach seat, climbing to a whopping $417 for a sleeper (based on double occupancy).

If you are planning to stay in South Florida for some time, you might consider taking your car on Amtrak's **East Coast Auto Train**. The 16¹/₂-hour ride, connecting Lorton, Virginia (near Washington, D.C.), with Sanford, Florida (near Orlando), has a glass-domed viewing car and includes breakfast and dinner in the ticket price. Round-trip fares are only a few dollars higher than one-way—about $170 for adults, $85 for children under 12, and $300 for your car. One-way fares are discounted as much as 50% when most traffic is going in the opposite direction.

You'll pull into Amtrak's Miami terminal at 8303 NW 37th Ave. (☎ **305/ 835-1205**). Unfortunately, none of the major car-rental companies has an office at the train station; you'll have to go to the airport, just over 5 miles away, to rent a car.

Taxis meet each Amtrak arrival. The fare to Downtown will cost about $22; the ride takes less than 20 minutes.

BY BUS

Bus travel is an inexpensive and flexible option. **Greyhound/Trailways** (☎ **800/ 231-2222**) can get you to Miami from anywhere, and it offers several money-saving multiday bus passes. Round-trip fares vary depending on your point of origin.

Greyhound/Trailways buses pull into a number of stations around the city, including 700 Biscayne Blvd. (Downtown); 16560 NE 6th Ave., North Miami Beach; and 4111 NW 27th St., Miami.

3 For Foreign Visitors

This chapter gives you specific suggestions about getting to the United States as economically and effortlessly as possible, plus some helpful information about how things are done in Miami—from receiving mail to making a local or long-distance telephone call.

1 Preparing for Your Trip

ENTRY REQUIREMENTS

Immigration laws are a hot political issue in the United States these days, and the following requirements may have changed somewhat by the time you plan your trip. Check at any U.S. embassy or consulate for current information and requirements.

DOCUMENT REGULATIONS   Citizens of Canada and Bermuda may enter the United States without visas, but they will need to show proof of nationality, the most common and hassle-free form of which is a passport.

The U.S. State Department has a Visa Waiver Pilot Program that allows citizens of certain countries to enter the United States without a visa for stays of fewer than 90 days of holiday travel. At press time, they included Andorra, Argentina, Australia, Austria, Belgium, Brunei, Denmark, Finland, France, Germany, Iceland, Ireland, Italy, Japan, Liechtenstein, Luxembourg, Monaco, the Netherlands, New Zealand, Norway, San Marino, Spain, Sweden, Switzerland, and the United Kingdom. (The program as applied to the United Kingdom refers to British citizens who have the "unrestricted right of permanent abode in the United Kingdom," that is, citizens from England, Scotland, Wales, Northern Ireland, the Channel Islands, and the Isle of Man, and not, for example, citizens of the British Commonwealth of Pakistan.)

Citizens from these countries need only a valid passport and a round-trip air or cruise ticket in their possession upon arrival. If they first enter the United States, they may then visit Mexico, Canada, Bermuda, and/or the Caribbean islands and return to the United States without needing a visa. Further information is available from any U.S. embassy or consulate.

Citizens of countries other than those specified above, or those traveling to the U.S. for reasons or a length of time outside the restrictions of the Visa Waiver program, or those who require waivers of inadmissibility must have these two documents:

- A valid passport, with an expiration date at least 6 months later than the scheduled end of the visit to the United States. (Some countries are exceptions to the 6-month validity rule. Contact any U.S. embassy or consulate for complete information.)
- A tourist visa, available from the nearest U.S. consulate. To get a visa, the traveler must submit a completed application form (either in person or by mail) with a 1¹/₂-inch square photo and the required application fee. There may also be an issuance fee, depending on the type of visa and other factors.

Usually you can get a visa right away or within 24 hours, but it may take longer during the summer rush period (June to August). If you cannot go in person, contact the nearest U.S. embassy or consulate for directions on applying by mail. Your travel agent or airline office may also be able to give you visa applications and instructions. The U.S. consulate or embassy that issues your visa will determine whether you receive a multiple- or single-entry visa. The Immigration and Naturalization Service officers at the port-of-entry in the United States will make an admission decision and determine your length of stay.

MEDICAL REQUIREMENTS   No inoculations are needed to enter the United States unless you are coming from, or have stopped over in, areas known to be suffering from epidemics, particularly cholera or yellow fever.

If you have a condition requiring treatment with medications containing narcotics or drugs requiring a syringe, carry a valid signed prescription from your physician to allay any suspicions that you are smuggling drugs.

CUSTOMS REQUIREMENTS   Every adult visitor may bring in free of duty 1 liter of hard liquor, 200 cigarettes or 100 cigars (but no cigars from Cuba) or 3 pounds of smoking tobacco, and $100 worth of gifts. These exemptions are offered to travelers who spend at least 72 hours in the United States and who have not claimed them within the preceding 6 months. It is altogether forbidden to bring food-stuffs (particularly cheese, fruit, and cooked meats) and plants (vegetables, seeds, tropical plants, and so on) into the country. Foreign tourists may bring in or take out up to $10,000.00 in U.S. or foreign currency with no formalities; larger sums must be declared to Customs on entering or leaving.

INSURANCE

There is no national health system in the United States. Because the cost of medical care is extremely high, I strongly advise all travelers to secure health coverage before setting out.

You may want to take out a comprehensive travel policy that covers (for a relatively low premium) sickness or injury costs (medical, surgical, and hospital); loss or theft of your baggage; trip-cancellation costs; guarantee of bail in case you are arrested; and costs of accident, repatriation, or death. Automobile clubs sell packages (for example, "Europe Assistance" in Europe) at attractive rates; packages are also offered by insurance companies and travel agencies.

MONEY

CURRENCY   The U.S. monetary system has a decimal base: one American dollar ($1) = 100 cents (100¢). Dollar bills commonly come in $1 ("a buck"), $5, $10, $20, $50, and $100 denominations (the last two are not welcome when paying for small purchases and are not always accepted in taxis).

There are six coin denominations: 1¢ (one cent or "penny"), 5¢ (five cents or "nickel"), 10¢ (10 cents or "dime"), 25¢ (25 cents or "quarter"), 50¢ (50 cents or "half dollar"), and the $1 pieces (both the older, large silver dollar and the newer, small Susan B. Anthony coin).

TRAVELER'S CHECKS   It's actually cheaper and faster to get cash at an automatic teller machine (ATM) than to fuss with traveler's checks. If you do bring them, traveler's checks denominated in U.S. dollars are readily accepted at most hotels, restaurants, and large stores.

CREDIT CARDS   The most widely used method of payment is the credit card: Visa, MasterCard (EuroCard in Europe, Access in Britain, Diamond in Japan), American Express, Discover, Diners Club, enRoute, JCB, and Carte Blanche, in descending order of acceptance.

You can save yourself trouble by using "plastic" rather than cash or traveler's checks in 95% of all hotels, motels, restaurants, and retail stores. A credit card can also serve as a deposit for renting a car, as proof of identity, or as a "cash card," enabling you to draw money from automated teller machines (ATMs) that accept them.

You can telegraph money or have it wired to you very quickly by using the Western Union system (☎ **800/325-6000**).

SAFETY

While tourist areas are generally safe, crime is a persistent problem everywhere, and U.S. urban areas tend to be less safe than those in Europe or Japan. Visitors should always stay alert. This is particularly true of large U.S. cities such as Miami. It is wise to ask the city's or area's tourist office if you're in doubt about which neighborhoods are safe. Avoid deserted areas, especially at night. Don't go into any city park at night unless there is an event that attracts crowds.

Remember also that hotels are open to the public, and in a large hotel, security may not be able to screen everyone entering. Always lock your room door—don't assume that once inside your hotel, you are automatically safe and no longer need to be aware of your surroundings.

DRIVING   Safety while driving is particularly important. Question your rental agency about personal safety or ask for a brochure of traveler safety tips. Get written directions, or a map with the route marked in red, from the agency showing how to get to your destination. Opt for any additional safety features in the car, such as cellular telephones or electronic maps. And, if possible, arrive and depart during daylight hours. If you are arriving at night, consider taking a taxi from the airport to your hotel and then having your rental car delivered.

Recently, more and more crime has involved cars and drivers. If you drive off a highway into a doubtful neighborhood, leave the area as quickly as possible. If you have an accident, even on the highway, stay in your car with the doors locked until you assess the situation or until the police arrive. If you are bumped from behind on the street or are involved in a minor accident with no injuries and the situation appears to be suspicious, motion to the other driver to follow you. Never get out of your car in such situations. Go directly to the nearest police precinct, well-lighted service station, or all-night store.

If you see someone on the road who indicates a need for help, do not stop. Take note of the location, drive into a well-lighted area, and telephone the police by dialing 911.

Park in well-lighted, well-traveled areas if possible. Always keep your car doors locked, whether attended or unattended. Look around you before you get out of your car, and never leave any packages or valuables in sight. If someone attempts to rob you or steal your car, do not try to resist the thief/carjacker—report the incident to the police department immediately.

Impressions

As we rode over the causeway, I could hardly believe my eyes. It was almost unimaginable that in Miami Beach it was 80 degrees while in New York it was 20. Everything—the buildings, the water, the pavement—had an indescribable glow to it. The palm trees especially made a great impression on me.

—Isaac Bashevis Singer, describing his first visit to Miami in 1948

Reacting to several highly publicized crimes against tourists in Florida, both the local and state governments have taken steps to help protect visitors. These measures include special, highly visible police units patrolling the airport and surrounding neighborhoods and better signs on the state's most tourist-traveled routes. Still, especially in Miami, the signs can be extremely confusing. Make sure to chart your course before leaving an area. If you are staying on South Beach, you might want to consider skipping a car rental altogether, or at least for the time you are on the island. Taxis are plentiful and relatively inexpensive (see chapter 4, "Getting Around").

2 Getting to the United States

Travelers from overseas can take advantage of the APEX (Advance Purchase Excursion) fares offered by all the major U.S. and European carriers. **British Airways** (☎ 081/897-4000 from within the U.K.) offers direct flights from London to Miami and Orlando, as does **Virgin Atlantic** (☎ 02/937-47747 from within the U.K.). Canadian readers might book flights with **Air Canada** (☎ 800/776-3000), which offers service from Toronto and Montreal to Miami and Tampa.

Miami International Airport is a hub for flights to and from Latin America. Carriers include **Aerolineas Argentinas** (☎ 800/333-0276), **Aeromexico** (☎ 800/245-8585), **American Airlines** (☎ 800/433-7300), **Avianca** (☎ 800-284-2622), **Lan Chile Airlines** (☎ 800/735-5526), and **Varig Brazilian Airlines** (☎ 800/468-2744).

The visitor arriving by air, no matter what the port of entry, should cultivate patience and resignation before setting foot on U.S. soil. Getting through Immigration control could take as long as 2 hours on some days, especially summer weekends, so have your guidebook or something else to read handy. Add the time it takes to clear Customs, and you will see you should make a very generous allowance for delay in planning connections between international and domestic flights—figure on 2 to 3 hours at least.

In contrast, for the traveler arriving by car or by rail from Canada, the border-crossing formalities have been streamlined to the vanishing point. For the traveler by air from Canada, Bermuda, and some places in the Caribbean, you can sometimes go through Customs and Immigration at the point of departure, which is much quicker and less painful.

For further information about getting to Miami, see "Getting There," in chapter 2.

3 Getting Around the United States

See "Getting There" in chapter 2 for more information about travel to Miami.

BY AIR   On their transatlantic or transpacific flights, some large U.S. airlines offer special discount tickets for any of their U.S. destinations (American Airline's **Visit USA** program and Delta's **Discover America** program, for example). The tickets or coupons are not on sale in the United States and must be purchased before you leave your point of departure. This system is the best, easiest, and fastest way to see the United States at low cost. You should get information well in advance from your travel agent or the office of the airline concerned, since the conditions attached to these discount tickets can be changed without advance notice.

BY RAIL International visitors can also buy a **USA Railpass** good for 15 or 30 days of unlimited travel on **Amtrak** (☎ **800/USA-RAIL**). The pass is available through many foreign travel agents. Prices in 1998 for a 15-day pass were $260 off-peak, $375 peak; a 30-day pass was $350 off-peak, $480 peak (peak is June 17 to August 21). With a foreign passport, you can also buy passes at some Amtrak offices in the United States, including locations in San Francisco, Los Angeles, Chicago, New York, Miami, Boston, and Washington, D.C. Reservations are generally required and should be made for each part of your trip as early as possible.

Visitors should be aware of the limitations of long-distance rail travel in the United States. With a few notable exceptions (for instance, the Northeast Corridor line between Boston and Washington, D.C.), service is rarely up to European standards: Delays are common, routes are limited and often infrequently served, and fares are rarely significantly lower than discount airfares. Therefore, cross-country train travel should be approached with caution.

BY BUS Although ticket prices for short bus trips between cities are often the most economical form of public transit, at this writing, bus passes are priced slightly higher than similar train passes. **Greyhound** (☎ **800/231-2222**), the nationwide bus line, offers an **Ameripass** for unlimited travel for 7 days (for $199), 15 days (for $299), 30 days (for $399), and 60 days (for $599). Bus travel in the United States can be both slow and uncomfortable, so this option is not for everyone. In addition, bus stations are often located in undesirable neighborhoods.

FAST FACTS: For the Foreign Traveler

Automobile Organizations Auto clubs will supply maps, suggested routes, guidebooks, accident and bail-bond insurance, and emergency road service. The major auto club in the United States, with 983 offices nationwide, is the **American Automobile Association** (AAA). Members of some foreign auto clubs have reciprocal arrangements with the AAA and enjoy its services at no charge, so inquire about AAA reciprocity before you leave. The AAA can give you an International Driving Permit validating your foreign license, although drivers with valid licenses from most home countries don't really need this permit. You may be able to join the AAA even if you are not a member of a reciprocal club. To inquire, call ☎ **800/926-4222**. In addition, some car-rental agencies now provide these services, so ask when you rent your car.

Automobile Rentals To rent a car, you need a major credit or charge card and a valid driver's license. Sometimes a passport or international driver's license is also required if your driver's license is in a language other than English. Also, you usually need to be at least 25, although some companies do rent to younger people at a higher rate.

Business Hours Banks are open weekdays from 9am to 3pm or later and sometimes Saturday morning. There's daily 24-hour access to the automatic tellers (ATMs) at most banks and other outlets. Business offices are usually open weekdays from 9am to 5pm. Shops, especially department stores and those in shopping complexes, tend to stay open late—until about 9pm weekdays and until 6pm weekends.

Climate   See "When to Go" in chapter 2.

Currency   See "Money" in "Preparing for Your Trip" earlier in this chapter.

Currency Exchange   The "foreign-exchange bureaus" so common in Europe are rare in the United States. You'll find one in Concourse E of the Miami International Airport—**BankAmerica International** (☎ **305/377-6000**; open 24 hours). **Thomas Cook Currency Services** offers a wide variety of services: more than 100 currencies, commission-free traveler's checks, drafts and wire transfers, and check collections. Rates are competitive and service is excellent. The Miami office is downtown at 155 SE Third Ave. (☎ **305/381-9252**); it's open weekdays from 9am to 5pm. Another downtown money-changing office is **Abbot Foreign Exchange**, 255 E. Flagler St. (☎ **305/374-2336**); it's open weekdays from 8am to 5pm and Saturday from 8am to 2pm.

Drinking Laws   The legal age to drink alcohol is 21.

Electricity   The United States uses 110–120 volts, 60 cycles, compared to 220–240 volts, 50 cycles, as in most of Europe. Besides a 100-volt converter, small appliances of non-American manufacture, such as hair dryers or shavers, will require a plug adapter, with two flat, parallel pins. The easiest solution is to purchase dual-voltage appliances that operate on both 110 and 220 volts; then all that's required is a U.S. adapter plug.

Embassies/Consulates   All embassies are located in the national capital, Washington, D.C.; some consulates are located in Miami. Travelers from other countries can get telephone numbers for their embassies and consulates by calling "Information" in Washington, D.C. (☎ **202/555-1212**).

Brazil's Consulate General is in Coconut Grove at 2601 S. Bayshore Dr., Suite 800, Miami, FL 33133 (☎ **305/285-6200**); the British Consulate is also located in Coconut Grove at the Brickell Bay Tower, Suite 2110, 1001 S. Bayshore Dr., Miami, FL 33131 (☎ **305/374-1522**); a Canadian Consulate is at 200 S. Biscayne Blvd., Suite 1600, Miami, FL 33132 (☎ **305/579-1600**); Germany's Consulate General is at 100 N. Biscayne Blvd., Miami, FL 33132 (☎ **305/358-0290**); and the Portuguese Consulate is in Coral Gables at 1901 Ponce de Leon Blvd., Miami, FL (☎ **305/444-6311**).

Emergencies   Call 911 for fire, police, and ambulance. If you encounter such traveler's problems as sickness, accidents, or lost or stolen baggage, call **Advocates for Victims** (☎ **305/758-2546**), an organization that specializes in helping distressed travelers.

U.S. hospitals have emergency rooms, with a special entrance where you will be admitted for quick attention. **Health South Doctors' Hospital,** 5000 University Dr., Coral Gables (☎ **305/666-2111**), is a 285-bed acute-care hospital with a 24-hour physician-staffed emergency department.

Gasoline (Petrol)   One U.S. gallon equals 3.75 liters, while 1.2 U.S. gallons equals one Imperial gallon. A gallon of unleaded "gas" (short for "gasoline"), which most rental cars require, costs about $1.30 if you fill your own tanks (it's called "self-serve"), and 10¢ more if the station attendant does it (called "full-service"). Most Miami gas stations are self-serve, with credit card processors right on the pump.

Holidays   On the following legal national holidays, banks, government offices, post offices, and many stores, restaurants, and museums are closed: January 1 (New Year's Day); third Monday in January (Martin Luther King Day); third Monday in February (Presidents' Day, Washington's Birthday); last Monday in May

(Memorial Day); July 4 (Independence Day); first Monday in September (Labor Day); second Monday in October (Columbus Day); November 11 (Veterans Day/Armistice Day); fourth Thursday in November (Thanksgiving); and December 25 (Christmas). The Tuesday following the first Monday in November is Election Day.

Languages   Most hotels in Greater Miami have bilingual employees (Spanish and English). Unless your language is very obscure, they can usually supply a translator on request. Because more than half of Miami residents speak Spanish fluently, most signs and brochures are printed in both English and Spanish. In addition, since a large number of French, Canadian, Italian, and German tourists visit Miami, most visitor information is available in their languages.

Legal Aid   If you are stopped for a minor infraction (for example, of the highway code, such as speeding), never attempt to pay the fine directly to a police officer; you may be arrested on the much more serious charge of attempted bribery. Pay fines by mail, or directly into the hands of the clerk of the court. If accused of a more serious offense, it is best to say and do nothing before consulting a lawyer. Under U.S. law, an arrested person is allowed one telephone call to a party of his or her choice. Call your embassy or consulate.

Mail   You'll find the **Main Post Office,** 2200 Milam Dairy Rd., Miami, FL 33152 (☎ **305/639-4280**) just west of Miami International Airport. Letters addressed to you and marked "c/o General Delivery" can be picked up at 500 NW 2nd Ave., Miami, FL 33101. The addressee must pick it up in person and produce proof of identity (driver's license, credit card, passport, or the like). Mailboxes are blue with a red-and-white logo, and carry the inscription "U.S. Mail."

Within the United States, it costs 20¢ to mail a standard-size postcard and 32¢ to send an oversize postcard (larger than $4^1/_4 \times 6$ inches, or 10.8×15.4 centimeters). Letters that weigh up to 1 ounce (that's about five pages, $8^1/_2 \times 11$ inches, or 20.5×28.2 centimeters) cost 32¢, plus 23¢ for each additional ounce. A postcard to Mexico costs 35¢, a $^1/_2$-ounce letter 40¢; a postcard to Canada costs 40¢, a $^1/_2$-ounce letter 46¢. A postcard to Europe, Australia, New Zealand, the Far East, South America, and elsewhere costs 50¢, while a $^1/_2$-ounce letter is 60¢, and a 1-ounce letter is $1.

Medical Emergencies   See "Emergencies," above.

Newspapers/Magazines   *The Miami Herald* and the magazines *Newsweek* and *Time* cover world news and are available at newsstands. Most magazine racks at drugstores, airports, and hotels include a good selection of foreign periodicals, such as *Stern, The Economist,* and *Le Monde. El Herald* and *Diarios Las Americas* are Spanish-language newspapers. Spanish-language magazines are particularly abundant.

Post   See "Mail," above.

Safety   See "Safety" in "Preparing for Your Trip," above.

Taxes   In the United States, there is no VAT (value-added tax), or other indirect tax at a national level. There is a $10 Customs tax, payable on entry to the United States, and a $6 departure tax.

A 6% state sales tax (plus .5% local tax, for a total of 6.5% in Miami) is added on at the register for all goods and services purchased in Florida. These taxes are not refundable. In addition, most municipalities levy special taxes on restaurants and hotels. In Surfside, hotel taxes total 10.5%; in Bal Harbour, 9.5%; in Miami Beach (including South Beach), 11.5%; and in the rest of Dade County, a whopping 12.5%. In Miami Beach, Surfside, and Bal Harbour, the resort (hotel) tax also applies to hotel restaurants and restaurants with liquor licenses.

Telephone and Fax Look for **pay phones** on street corners, as well as in bars, restaurants, public buildings, stores, and at service stations. In most areas, local calls cost 35¢.

For **long-distance or international calls** from a pay phone, it's most economical to charge the call to a telephone charge card or a credit card, or you can use a lot of change. The pay phone operator will instruct you how much to deposit and when to deposit it into the slot on the telephone box.

For local **directory assistance** ("information"), dial 411; for long-distance information, dial 1, then the appropriate area code, and then 555-1212.

For **long-distance calls** in the United States, dial 1 followed by the area code and number you want. For direct **overseas calls,** first dial 011, followed by the country code (Australia, 61; Republic of Ireland, 353; New Zealand, 64; United Kingdom, 44), and then by the city code (for example, 71 or 81 for London, 21 for Birmingham, 1 for Dublin) and the number of the person you wish to call.

For **reversed-charge or collect calls** and for **person-to-person calls,** dial 0 (zero, not the letter *O*) followed by the area code and number you want; an operator will then come on the line, and you should specify that you are calling collect, or person-to-person, or both. If your operator-assisted call is international, immediately ask to speak with an overseas operator.

Before **calling from a hotel room,** always ask the hotel phone operator if there are any telephone surcharges. There almost always are, often as much as 75¢ or $1, even for a local call. Avoid these charges by using a public phone, calling collect, or using a telephone charge card.

In the past few years, many American companies have installed **voice-mail systems.** Listen carefully to the instructions (you'll probably be asked to dial 1, 2, or 3 or wait for an operator to pick up); if you can't understand, sometimes dialing zero will put you in touch with a company operator. It's frustrating even for locals!

Many rental car companies also rent **cellular phones,** a wise and convenient option when traveling in unfamiliar territory.

Most hotels have **fax machines** available for their customers and usually charge to send or receive a facsimile. You will also see signs for public faxes in the windows of small shops.

Telephone Directory The local phone company provides two kinds of telephone directories. The general directory, called the "white pages," lists businesses and personal residences separately, in alphabetical order. The first few pages are devoted to community-service numbers, including a guide to long-distance and international calling, complete with country codes and area codes.

The second directory, the "yellow pages," lists all local services, businesses, and industries by type, with an index at the back. The listings cover not only such obvious items as automobile repairs by make of car, or drugstores (pharmacies), often by geographical location, but also restaurants by type of cuisine and geographical location, bookstores by special subject and/or language, places of worship by religious denomination, and other information that a visitor might otherwise not readily find. The yellow pages also include city plans or detailed area maps, often showing postal ZIP codes and public transportation.

Time The United States is divided into six time zones. Miami, like New York, is in the eastern standard time zone. America's eastern seaboard is 5 hours behind Greenwich mean time. Between April and October, eastern daylight savings time

is adopted, and clocks are set 1 hour ahead. To find out what time it is, call
☎ **305/324-8811**.

Tipping   Waiters and bartenders expect a 15% tip, as do taxi drivers and hair-dressers. Porters should be tipped 50¢ to $1 per bag, and parking valets should be given $1. It's nice to leave a few dollars on your pillow for the hotel maid, and lavatory attendants will appreciate whatever change you have.

Toilets   Visitors can usually find a rest room in a bar, restaurant, hotel, museum, department store, or service station—and it will probably be clean (although the last-mentioned sometimes leaves much to be desired). The cleanliness of toilets at railroad stations and bus depots may be more questionable. You'll also find toilets at many public beaches and large parks. Some public places are equipped with pay toilets, which require you to insert one or more coins into a slot on the door before it will open. Rest rooms in cafes and restaurants usually are for patrons only, but in an emergency you can just order a cup of coffee or try simply asking to use the pay phone, usually conveniently positioned beside the rest rooms.

Miami is not a complicated city to negotiate, but, like all unfamiliar territories, this metropolis will take a little time to master.

1 Orientation

VISITOR INFORMATION

The best up-to-date, specialized information is provided by the **Greater Miami Convention and Visitors Bureau,** 701 Brickell Ave., Miami, FL 33131 (☎ **800/283-2707** or 305/539-3063; e-mail: **gmcvb@aol.com**; Web site: **www.miamiandbeaches.com**). Chambers of commerce in Greater Miami also send out information on their particular neighborhoods; for additional sources of information, please refer to the "Visitor Information" section in chapter 2, "Planning a Trip to Miami."

When you arrive at the Miami International Airport, you can pick up visitor information at the airport's main visitor counter on the second floor of Concourse E. It's open 24 hours a day.

You can also get more maps and brochures from your hotel concierge or from the following visitor information offices:

- **Coconut Grove Chamber of Commerce,** 2820 McFarlane Rd. in Peacock Park between Main Highway and South Bayshore Drive (☎ **305/444-7270**). Open Monday through Friday from 9am to 5pm; some weekend hours are planned in the future.
- **The Coral Gables Chamber of Commerce,** 50 Aragon Ave., 1 block north of Miracle Mile. (☎ **305/446-1657**). Open Monday through Thursday from 8:30am to 5pm and Friday until 4pm.
- **The Miami Beach Chamber of Commerce,** 1920 Meridian Ave. (☎ 305/672-1270). Open Monday through Friday from 9am to 6pm, Saturday and Sunday 10am to 4pm.
- **The Greater Homestead/Florida City Chamber of Commerce,** 160 US Hwy. 1 (☎ **305/245-9180**). Open daily 8am to 6pm.
- **The Sunny Isles Beach Resort Association Visitor Information Center**, 17100 Collins Ave., Suite 208 (☎ **305/947-5826**). Open Monday through Friday from 9am to 2pm.

Always check local newspapers for special things to do during your visit. The city's only daily, the *Miami Herald,* is an especially good source for current-events listings, particularly the "Weekend" section in Friday's edition.

CITY LAYOUT

Miami may seem confusing at first, but it quickly becomes easy to negotiate. The small cluster of buildings that make up the Downtown area is at the geographical heart of the city. You can see these sharp stalagmites from most anywhere, making them a good reference point. In relation to Downtown, the airport is northwest, the beaches are east, Coconut Grove is south, Coral Gables is west, and the rest of the country is north.

FINDING AN ADDRESS   Miami is divided into dozens of areas with official and unofficial boundaries. Street numbering in the city of Miami is fairly straightforward, but you must first be familiar with the numbering system. The mainland is divided into four sections—NE, NW, SE, and SW—by the intersection of Flagler Street and Miami Avenue. Street numbers (First St., Second St., and so forth) start from here and increase as you go further out, as do numbers of Avenues, Places, Courts, Terraces, and Lanes. Streets in Hialeah are the exceptions to this pattern; they are listed separately in map indexes.

Establishment addresses are often descriptive; 12301 Biscayne Boulevard is located at 123rd Street. It's also helpful to remember that avenues generally run north–south, while streets go east–west.

Getting around the barrier islands that make up Miami Beach is somewhat easier than moving around the mainland. Street numbering starts with First Street, near Miami Beach's southern tip, and increases to 192nd Street, in the northern part of Sunny Isles. Collins Avenue makes the entire journey from head to toe. As in the city of Miami, some streets in Miami Beach have numbers as well as names. When they are part of listings in this book, both names and numbers are given.

You should know that the numbered streets in Miami Beach are not the geographical equivalents of those on the mainland, but they are close. For example, the 79th Street Causeway runs into 71st Street on Miami Beach.

STREET MAPS   It's easy to get lost in sprawling Miami, so a reliable map is essential. If you are not planning on moving around too much, the tourist board's maps, located inside its free publication "Destination Miami," may be adequate. If you really want to get to know the city, it pays to invest in one of the large accordion-fold maps, available at most gas stations and bookstores. The Trakker Map of Miami ($2.50) is a four-color accordion map that encompasses all of Dade County.

Some maps of Miami list streets according to area, so you'll have to know which part of the city you are looking for before the street can be found. All the listings in this book include area information for just this reason.

NEIGHBORHOODS IN BRIEF

Much of Miami is sprawling suburbia. But every city has its charm, and aside from a fantastic tropical climate and the vast stretch of beach that lies just across its glistening Biscayne Bay, Miami's unique identity comes from extremely interesting cultural pockets within its residential communities. Here's a brief rundown of the characteristics of its diverse neighborhoods.

Miami Beach—The Mid and Central Areas, Including Surfside, Bal Harbour, and Sunny Isles   To tourists in the 1950s, Miami Beach was Miami. Its huge

Miami at a Glance

self-contained resort hotels were vacations unto themselves, providing a full day's worth of meals, activities, and entertainment. Then, in the 1960s and 1970s, people who fell in love with Miami began to buy apartments rather than rent hotel rooms. Tourism declined, and many area hotels fell into disrepair.

However, since the late 1980s, Miami Beach has experienced a tide of revitalization. Huge beach hotels are finding their niche with new, international tourist markets and are attracting large convention crowds. The **Miami Beach Convention Center,** 1901 Convention Center Dr., Miami Beach, FL 33139 (☎ **305/673-7311**), has more than 1 million square feet of exhibition space. New generations of Americans have discovered the special qualities that originally made Miami Beach so popular, and they are finding out that the beach now comes with a thriving, international, exciting city.

The north part of "The Beach"—Surfside, Bal Harbour, and Sunny Isles, plus other small neighborhoods—is, for the most part, an extension of the beach community below it. Collins Avenue crosses town lines with hardly a sign, while hotels, motels, restaurants, and beaches continue to line the strip. For visitors, it seems that—with some outstanding exceptions—the farther north one goes, the cheaper lodging becomes. All told, excellent prices, location, and facilities make Surfside and Sunny Isles, although a little rough around the edges, attractive places to stay. To keep up with demand for beachfront property, many of the area's moderately priced hotels have been converted to condominiums, leaving fewer and fewer kitschy and afford-able places to stay.

In exclusive **Bal Harbour,** a huge alfresco mall attracts decked-out shoppers. A few elegant hotels remain amid the many beachfront condominium towers. Fancy homes, tucked away on the bay, hide behind walls, gates, and security cameras.

Note that **North Miami Beach,** a residential area near the Dade–Broward county line, is a misnomer. It is actually northwest of Miami Beach on the mainland and has no beaches. North Miami Beach is part of North Dade County and has some of Miami's better restaurants and shops.

Key Biscayne   Miami's forested and fancy Key Biscayne is technically one of the first islands in the Florida Key chain. However, this luxurious island is nothing like its southern neighbors. Located south of Miami Beach, off the shores of Coconut Grove, Key Biscayne is protected from the troubles of the mainland by the long Rickenbacker Causeway and a $1 toll. Key Biscayne is largely an exclusive residen-tial community with million-dollar homes and sweeping water views, although it also offers visitors great beaches, some top resort hotels, and several good restaurants. Hobie Beach, adjacent to the causeway, is the city's premier spot for sail-boarding and jet skiing (see "Water Sports" in chapter 7, "What to See and Do"). On the island's southern tip, Bill Baggs State Park has great beaches, bike paths, and dense forests for picnicking and partying.

South Beach—The Art Deco District   In the last several years, South Beach has been the hottest area of Miami. While technically it's just 15 blocks at the southern tip of Miami Beach, South Beach has a style all its own. The thriving Art Deco District within South Beach contains the largest concentration of art deco architec-ture in the world. In chapter 8, "Driving & Strolling Around Miami," there's an in-depth walking tour of Miami's most fascinating area.

Young investors, artists, handsome model-types, and the usual Miami smattering of Cubans, African-Americans, and Caribbeans populate this vibrant community. Hip clubs and cafes are filled with vacationing Europeans, working models, photog-raphers, musicians, and writers who enjoy the exciting and sophisticated atmosphere.

Downtown   Miami's downtown boasts one of the world's most beautiful cityscapes. If you do nothing else in Miami, make sure you take your time studying the area's inspired architectural designs. During the day, a vibrant community of students, businesspeople, and merchants make their way through the bustling streets. Vendors sell fresh-cut pineapples and mangos while young Latin American consumers on shopping sprees lug bags and boxes. The Downtown area has its mall (Bayside Marketplace, where many cruise passengers come to browse), its culture (Metro-Dade Cultural Center), and a number of good restaurants (listed in chapter 6, "Dining").

Little Haiti   During a brief period in the late 1970s and early 1980s, almost 35,000 Haitians arrived in Miami. Most of the new refugees settled in a decaying 200-square-block area north of Downtown. Extending from 41st to 83rd streets and bordered by I-95 and Biscayne Boulevard, Little Haiti is a relatively depressed neighborhood with at least 60,000 residents, more than half of whom were born in Haiti.

On Northeast Second Avenue, Little Haiti's main thoroughfare, is the now-closed, once-colorful Caribbean Marketplace, located at the corner of 60th Street. Previously filled with bustling shops, it stands as a sad reminder of the neighborhood's economic distress.

Little Havana   Miami's Cuban center is the city's most important ethnic enclave. Referred to locally as "Calle Ocho" (pronounced *Ka*-yey *O*-choh), SW Eighth Street, just west of Downtown, is the region's main thoroughfare. Car-repair shops, tailors, electronics stores, and inexpensive restaurants all hang signs in Spanish. Salsa rhythms thump from the radios of passersby, while old men in guayaberas chain-smoke cigars over their daily game of dominoes.

Coral Gables   Just over 70 years old, Coral Gables is the closest thing to "historical" that Miami has. It's also one of the prettiest parcels in the city. Created by George Merrick in the early 1920s, the Gables was one of Miami's first planned developments. The houses here were built in a "Mediterranean style" along lush tree-lined streets that open onto beautifully carved plazas, many with centerpiece fountains. The best architectural examples of the era have Spanish-style tiled roofs and are built from Miami *oolite,* a native limestone commonly called "coral rock." Coral Gables is a stunning example of "boom" architecture on a grand scale—plus it's a great area to explore. Some of the city's best restaurants are located here, as are top hotels and good shopping. See the appropriate chapters for listings and "Driving Tour 2," in chapter 8, for details.

Coconut Grove   There was a time when Coconut Grove was inhabited by artists, intellectuals, hippies, and radicals, but times have changed. Gentrification has pushed most alternative types out, leaving in their place a multitude of cafes, boutiques, and nightspots. The intersection of Grand Avenue, Main Highway, and McFarlane Road pierces the area's heart, which sizzles with dozens of interesting shops and eateries. Sidewalks here are often crowded with businesspeople, high school students, and loads of foreign visitors—especially at night, when it becomes a great place to people-watch.

Coconut Grove's link to the Bahamas dates from before the turn of the century, when islanders came to the area to work in a newly opened hotel called the Peacock Inn. Bahamian-style wooden homes, built by these early settlers, still stand on Charles Street. Goombay, the lively annual Bahamian festival, celebrates the Grove's Caribbean link and has become one of the largest black-heritage street festivals in America (see "Miami Calendar of Events" in chapter 2, "Planning a Trip to Miami").

Greater Miami South   To locals, South Miami is both a specific area, southwest of Coral Gables, and a general region that encompasses all of southern Dade County and includes Kendall, Perrine, Cutler Ridge, and Homestead. For the purposes of clarity, this book has grouped all these southern suburbs under the rubric "Greater Miami South." Similar attributes unite the communities: They are heavily residential, and all are packed with condominiums and shopping malls as well as acres upon acres of farmland. Tourists don't stay in these parts, as there are no beaches and few cultural offerings, but Greater Miami South does contain many of the city's top attractions (see chapter 7), making it likely you'll spend some time during the day here.

2 Getting Around

Officially, Dade County has opted for a "unified, multimodal transportation network," which basically means you can get around the city by train, bus, and taxi. However, in practice, the network doesn't work too well. In most cases, unless you are going from downtown Miami to a not-too-distant spot, you are better off in a rented car or a taxi.

With the exception of downtown Coconut Grove and South Beach, Miami is not a walker's city. Because it is so spread out, most attractions are too far apart to make walking between them feasible. In fact, most Miamians are so used to driving that they drive even when going just a few blocks.

BY PUBLIC TRANSPORTATION

BY RAIL   Two rail lines, operated by the **Metro-Dade Transit Agency** (☎ 305/ 638-6700 for information), run in concert with each other.

Metrorail, the city's modern high-speed commuter train, is a 21-mile elevated line that travels north-south, between downtown Miami and the southern suburbs. If you are staying in Coral Gables or Coconut Grove, you can park your car at a nearby station and ride the rails Downtown. Unfortunately for visitors, the line's usefulness is limited. There are plans to extend the system to service Miami International Airport, but until those tracks are built, these trains don't go most places tourists go. Metrorail operates daily from about 6am to midnight. The fare is $1.25.

Metromover, a 4.4-mile elevated line, connects with Metrorail at the Government Center stop and circles Downtown. Riding on rubber tires, the single-train car winds past many of the area's most important attractions and shopping and business districts. Metromover offers a fun, futuristic ride that you might want to take to complement your Downtown tour. You get a beautiful perspective from the towering height of the suspended rails. System hours are daily from about 6am to midnight. The fare is 25¢.

BY BUS   Miami's suburban layout is not conducive to getting around by bus. Lines operate, and maps can be had, but instead of getting to know the city, you'll find that relying on bus transportation will acquaint you only with how it feels to wait at bus stops. You can get a bus map by mail, either from the Greater Miami Convention and Visitors Bureau (see "Visitor Information" in chapter 2) or by writing the Metro-Dade Transit System, 3300 NW 32nd Ave., Miami, FL 33142. In Miami, call ☎ 305/638-6700 for public-transit information. The fare is $1.25.

BY CAR

Tales circulate about vacationers who have visited Miami without a car, but they are very few indeed. If you are counting on exploring the city, even to a modest degree, a car is essential. Miami's restaurants, attractions, and sights are far from one another, so any other form of transportation is impractical. You won't need a car, however, if you are spending your entire vacation at a resort, are traveling directly to the Port of Miami for a cruise, or are here for a short stay centered in one area of the city, such as South Beach.

When driving across a causeway or through Downtown, allow extra time to reach your destination because of frequent drawbridge openings. Some bridges open about every half hour for large sailing vessels that make their way through the wide bays and canals that crisscross the city, stalling traffic for several minutes. Don't get frustrated by the wait. It's all part of the easy pace of South Florida life.

RENTALS   It seems as though every car-rental company, big and small, has at least one office in Miami. Consequently, the city is one of the cheapest places in the world to rent a car. Many firms regularly advertise prices in the neighborhood of $100 per week for their bottom-of-the-line tin can—not an unreasonable sum for 7 days of transportation in the land of sun and fun.

A minimum age, generally 25, is usually required of renters. Some rental agencies have also set maximum ages. A national car-rental broker, **A Car Rental Referral Service** (☎ 800/404-4482), can often find companies willing to rent to drivers over the age of 21 and can also get discounts from major companies as well as some regional ones.

National car-rental companies with toll-free numbers include **Alamo** (☎ 800/327-9633), **Avis** (☎ 800/331-1212), **Budget** (☎ 800/527-0700), **Dollar** (☎ 800/800-4000 or 800/327-7607), **Hertz** (☎ 800/654-3131), **National** (☎ 800/328-4567), and **Thrifty** (☎ 800/367-2277). Literally dozens of other regional companies—some offering lower rates—can be found in the Miami yellow pages under "Automobile Renting & Leasing." One excellent company that has offices in every conceivable part of town and offers extremely competitive rates is **Enterprise** (☎ 800/325-8007).

Many companies offer cellular phones or electronic map rental. It might be wise to opt for these additional safety features, although the cost can be exorbitant; the phone especially can come in handy if you get disoriented. There is nothing worse than being lost in a foreign city in a questionable area with no one to turn to.

Finally, think about splurging on a convertible. Few things in life can match the feeling of cruising along warm Florida highways with the sun smiling on your shoulders and the wind whipping through your hair. At most companies, the price is only about 20% more.

PARKING   Always keep plenty of quarters on hand to feed hungry meters. Parking is usually plentiful (except on South Beach and Coconut Grove), but when it's not, be careful: Fines for illegal parking can be stiff, up to $18.

In addition to parking garages, valet services are commonplace and often used. Expect to pay from $3 to $10 for parking in Coconut Grove and on South Beach's Ocean Drive on busy weekend nights.

LOCAL DRIVING RULES   Florida law allows drivers to make a right turn on a red light after a complete stop, unless otherwise indicated. In addition, all passengers are required to wear seat belts, and children under 3 must be securely fastened in government-approved car seats.

BY TAXI

If you're not planning on traveling much within the city, an occasional taxi is a good alternative to renting a car. If you plan on spending your holiday within the confines of South Beach's Art Deco District, you might also want to avoid the parking hassles that come with renting your own car. Taxi meters start at $1.50 for the first 1/4 mile and 25¢ for each 1/8 mile. There are standard flat-rate charges for frequently traveled routes—for example, Miami Beach's Convention Center to Coconut Grove would cost about $16.

Major cab companies include **Metro** (☎ 305/888-8888), **Yellow** (☎ 305/444-4444), and, on Miami Beach, **Central** (☎ 305/532-5555).

BY BICYCLE

Miami has several interesting areas to bike, including most of Miami Beach, where the hard-packed sand and boardwalks make it an easy and scenic route. However, unless you are a former New York City bicycle messenger, you won't want to use a bicycle as your main means of transportation.

For more information on bicycles, including where to rent the best ones, see chapter 7.

FAST FACTS: Miami

Airport   See "Getting There," in chapter 2.

American Express   You'll find American Express offices in downtown Miami at 330 Biscayne Blvd. (☎ **305/358-7350**); 9700 Collins Ave., Bal Harbour (☎ **305/ 865-5959**); and 32 Miracle Mile, Coral Gables (☎ **305/446-3381**). Offices are open weekdays from 9am to 5pm and Saturday from 10am to 4pm. The Bal Harbour office is also open on Sunday from noon to 6pm. To report lost or stolen traveler's checks, call ☎ **800/221-7282**.

Area Code   The original area code for Miami and all of Dade County was 305. That is still the code for older phone numbers, but all phone numbers assigned since July of 1998 have the area code 786 (SUN). Even though the Keys still share the Dade County area code of 305, calls to there from Miami are considered long distance and must be preceded by 1-305. Within the Keys, simply dial the seven-digit number.

Baby-Sitters   Hotels can often recommend a baby-sitter or child-care service.

Business Hours   Banking hours vary, but most banks are open weekdays from 9am to 3pm. Several stay open until 5pm or so at least one day during the week, and many banks feature automated-teller machines (ATMs) for 24-hour banking. Most stores are open daily from 10am to 6pm; however, there are many exceptions. Shops in the Bayside Marketplace are usually open until 9 or 10pm, as are the boutiques in Coconut Grove. Stores in Bal Harbour and other malls are usually open an extra hour one night during the week (usually Thursday). As far as business offices are concerned, Miami is generally a 9am–5pm town.

Car Rentals   See "Getting Around," above.

Climate   See "When to Go" in chapter 2.

Curfew   Although not strictly enforced, there is a curfew in effect for minors after 11pm on weeknights and midnight on weekends in all of Miami-Dade County. After those hours, children under 17 cannot be out on the streets or driving unless accompanied by a parent or on their way to work.

Dentists   The East Coast District Dental Society staffs an **Emergency Dental Referral Service** (☎ **305/285-5470**). **A&E Dental,** 11400 N. Kendall Dr., Mega Bank Building (☎ **305/271-7777**), also offers round-the-clock care and accepts MasterCard and Visa.

Doctors   In an emergency, call an ambulance by dialing 911 from any phone. The Dade County Medical Association sponsors a **Physician Referral Service** (☎ **305/324-8717**) weekdays from 9am to 5pm. **Health South Doctors' Hospital,** 5000 University Dr., Coral Gables (☎ **305/666-2111**), is a 285-bed acute-care hospital with a 24-hour physician-staffed emergency department.

Driving Rules   See "Getting Around," above.

Drugstores   See "Pharmacies," below.

Embassies/Consulates   See chapter 3, "For Foreign Visitors."

Emergencies   To reach the police, ambulance, or fire department, dial 911 from any phone. No coins are needed. Emergency hotlines include **Crisis Intervention** (☎ **305/358-HELP** or 305/358-4357) and **Poison Information Center** (☎ **800/ 282-3171**).

Eyeglasses   Pearle Vision Center, 7901 Biscayne Blvd. (☎ **305/754-5144**), in Miami, can usually fill prescriptions in about an hour.

Hospitals   See "Doctors," above.

Information   See "Visitor Information," above.

Laundry/Dry Cleaning   For dry cleaning, self-service machines, and a wash-and-fold service by the pound call **All Laundry Service,** 5701 NW 7th St. (west of Downtown, ☎ **305/261-8175**); it's open daily from 7am to 10pm. **Clean Machine Laundry,** 226 12th St., South Beach (☎ **305/534-9429**), is convenient to South Beach's art deco hotels; it's open 24 hours. **Coral Gables Laundry & Dry Cleaning,** 250 Minorca Ave., Coral Gables (☎ **305/446-6458**), has been dry cleaning, altering, and laundering since 1930. It offers a lifesaving same-day service and is open weekdays from 7am to 7pm and Saturday from 8am to 3pm.

Liquor Laws   Only adults 21 or older may legally purchase or consume alcohol in the state of Florida. Minors are usually permitted in bars that serve food. Liquor laws are strictly enforced; if you look young, carry identification. Beer and wine are sold in most supermarkets and convenience stores. The city of Miami's liquor stores are closed on Sunday. Liquor stores in the city of Miami Beach are open all week.

Lost Property   If you lost it at the airport, call the **Airport Lost and Found office** (☎ **305/876-7377**). If you lost it on the bus, Metrorail, or Metromover, call **Metro-Dade Transit Agency** (☎ **305/638-6700**). If you lost it somewhere else, phone the **Dade County Police Lost and Found** (☎ **305/375-3366**). You might also want to fill out a police report for insurance purposes.

Luggage Storage/Lockers   In addition to the baggage check at Miami International Airport, most hotels offer luggage-storage facilities. If you are taking a cruise from the Port of Miami (see "Cruises and Other Caribbean Getaways" in chapter 11, "Side Trips from Miami"), bags can be stored in your ship's departure terminal.

Maps   See "City Layout" earlier in this chapter.

Newspapers/Magazines   The well-respected *Miami Herald* is the city's only English-language daily. It is especially known for its Latin American coverage and its excellent Friday "Weekend" entertainment guide. There are literally dozens of specialized Miami magazines geared toward visitors and natives alike. Many are free and can be picked up at hotels, at restaurants, and in vending machines all around town. The most respected alternative weekly is the tabloid *New Times.* You can pick up *Ocean Drive,* a gorgeous oversized glossy magazine, at most South Beach establishments.

For a large selection of **foreign-language newspapers and magazines,** check out News Cafe at 800 Ocean Drive, South Beach (☎ **305/538-6397**) or in Coconut Grove at 2901 Florida Ave. (☎ **305/7746397**); Bus Terminal News, 2320 Salzedo St., Coral Gables (☎ **305/443-7979**); Eddie's Normandy, 1096 Normandy Dr., Miami Beach (☎ **305/866-2026**); Plaza News, 7900 Biscayne Blvd., Miami (☎ **305/751-NEWS**); and Worldwide News, 1629 NE 163rd St., North Miami Beach (☎ **305/940-4090**).

Pharmacies   The most ubiquitous drugstore is **Walgreens Pharmacy,** located all over town, including 8550 Coral Way (☎ **305/221-9271**), in Coral Gables; 1845 Alton Rd. (☎ **305/531-8868**), in South Beach; and 6700 Collins Ave. (☎ **305/861-6742**), in Miami Beach. The branch at 5731 Bird Rd. at SW 40th Street (☎ 305/666-0757) is open 24 hours, as is **Eckerd Drugs,** 1825 Miami Gardens Dr. NE, at 185th Street, North Miami Beach (☎ **305/932-5740**).

Photographic Needs   One of the more expensive places to have your film developed is **One Hour Photo** in the Bayside Marketplace (☎ 305/377-FOTO). They charge $17 to develop and print a roll of 36 pictures, and they're open Monday to Saturday from 10am to 10pm and Sunday from noon to 8pm. **Coconut Grove Camera,** 3317 Virginia St. (☎ 305/445-0521), features 30-minute color processing and maintains a huge selection of cameras and equipment. It rents, too. Walgreens or Eckerd's will develop film for the next day for about $6 or $7.

Police   For emergencies, dial 911 from any phone. No coins are needed. For other matters, call ☎ **305/595-6263**.

Post Office   The Main Post Office, 2200 Milam Dairy Rd., Miami, FL 33152 (☎ **305/639-4280**), is located west of Miami International Airport. Letters addressed to you and marked "c/o General Delivery" can be picked up at 500 NW 2nd Ave. Conveniently located post offices include 1300 Washington Ave. (☎ **305/531-7306**), in South Beach, and 3191 Grand Ave. (☎ **305/443-0030**), in Coconut Grove.

Radio   About five dozen radio stations can be heard in the Greater Miami area. On the AM dial, 610 (WIOD), 790 (WNWS), 1230 (WJNO), and 1340 (WPBR) are all talk. There is no all-news station in town, although 940 (WINZ) does give traffic updates and headline news in between its talk shows. WDBF (1420) is a good Big Band station and WPBG (1290) features golden oldies. The best rock stations on the FM dial are WZTA (94.9) and the progressive-rock station WVUM (90.5). WKIS (99.9) is the top country station. Public radio can be heard either on WXEL (90.7) or WLRN (91.3). WGTR (97.3) plays easy listening. WDNA (88.9) has the best Latin jazz and multi-ethnic sounds.

Religious Services   Miami houses of worship are as varied as the city's population and include **St. Patrick Catholic Church,** 3716 Garden Ave., Miami Beach (☎ 305/531-1124); **Temple Judea,** 5500 Granada Blvd., Coral Gables (☎ 305/667-5657); **Coconut Grove United Methodist,** 2850 SW 27th Ave. (☎ 305/443-0880); **Christ Episcopal Church,** 3481 Hibiscus St. (☎ 305/442-8542); and **Plymouth Congregational Church,** 3400 Devon Rd., at Main Highway (☎ 305/444-6521).

Restrooms   Stores rarely let customers use the restrooms, and many restaurants offer their facilities for customers only. Most malls have bathrooms, as do many of the ubiquitous fast-food restaurants. Many public beaches and large parks provide toilets, though in some places you have to pay or tip an attendant. Most large hotels have clean restrooms in their lobbies.

Safety   Don't walk alone at night, and be extra wary when walking or driving though Downtown Miami and surrounding areas. It's always a good idea to stay aware of your surroundings when you're in any unfamiliar city, even in the most heavily touristed areas. Always consult a good map and know where you are going before getting in your car. Never stop on a highway—if you get a flat tire, drive to the nearest well-lighted, populated place. Keep car doors locked and stay alert.

Taxes   A 6% state sales tax (plus .5% local tax, for a total of 6.5% in Miami) is added on at the register for all goods and services purchased in Florida. In addition, most municipalities levy special taxes on restaurants and hotels. In Surfside, hotel taxes total 10.5%; in Bal Harbour, 9.5%; in Miami Beach (including South Beach), 11.5%; and in the rest of Dade County, a whopping 12.5%. In Miami

Beach, Surfside, and Bal Harbour, the resort (hotel) tax also applies to hotel restaurants and restaurants with liquor licenses.

Taxis   See "Getting Around" earlier in this chapter.

Television   The local stations are Channel 6, WTVJ (NBC); Channel 4, WCIX (CBS); Channel 7, WSVN (Fox); Channel 10, WPLG (ABC); Channel 17, WLRN (PBS); Channel 23, WLTV (independent); and Channel 33, WBFS (independent).

Time Zone   Miami, like New York, is in the eastern standard time zone. Between April and October, eastern daylight saving time is adopted, and clocks are set 1 hour ahead. America's eastern seaboard is 5 hours behind of Greenwich mean time. To find out what time it is, call ☎ **305/324-8811**.

Transit Information   For Metrorail or Metromover schedule information, phone ☎ **305/638-6700.**

Weather   Hurricane season runs from August through November. For an up-to-date recording of current weather conditions and forecast reports, call ☎ **305/ 229-4522.**

5 Accommodations

There's hardly a block on Miami Beach without a hotel or condominium under construction. Since the renaissance that began in the early 1980s, the beach has turned into an upscale boomtown. In 1998, Loews completed an 850-room hotel on Collins Avenue (the first large-scale new hotel to be built on South Beach in more than 30 years), Marriott and Crowne Plaza both broke ground on large hotels, and Merv Griffin opened a small hotel called Blue Moon on Collins Avenue.

And it's not just the beach that's growing. In Coconut Grove, the Ritz-Carlton started construction on a 250-room luxury hotel due to open in late 1999. On Key Biscayne, Carnival Resorts & Casinos is planning a 250-room Grand Bay Resort for the year 2000.

All this upscale building means that there are more good choices than ever for travelers. Unfortunately, it has also made prices skyrocket. Visitors can no longer find a decent room overlooking the ocean for 100 bucks a night. Don't despair, however—there are plenty of great options at bargain prices in and around the hot tourist areas. Always remember to ask about packages, since it's often possible to get a better deal than the "official" rates.

Many of the old hotels from the 1930s, 1940s, and 1950s (when most Miami resorts were constructed) have been totally overhauled, but others have survived with occasional coats of paint and new carpeting, which some owners like to call "renovation." When checking them out, be sure to ask about exactly what work has been done; especially on the ocean, sea air and years of tourist wear can result in musty, paint-peeled rooms. Also, be sure to find out if the hotel you're booking is undergoing reconstruction while you're there. There's nothing worse than the sounds of jackhammers over breakfast. I've omitted the more worn hotels and tried to list only those that have been fully upgraded recently. Exceptions are noted.

If you can't get a room after inquiring at the hotels listed in this guide (an extremely unlikely prospect), look along South Beach's Collins Avenue. There are dozens of hotels and motels on this strip—in all price categories—so there's bound to be a vacancy.

SEASONS & RATES   South Florida's tourist season is well defined, beginning in mid-November and lasting until Easter. Hotel prices escalate until about March, after which they begin to decline. During the off-season, hotel rates are typically 30% to 50% lower than their winter highs.

But timing isn't everything. In many cases, rates also depend on your hotel's proximity to the beach and how much ocean you can see from your window. Small motels a block or two from the water can be up to 40% cheaper than similar properties right on the sand. When a hotel *is* right on the beach, its oceanfront rooms are significantly more expensive than similar accommodations in the rear.

Rates below have been broken down into two broad categories: winter (generally, Thanksgiving through Easter) and off-season (about mid-May through August). The months in between, the shoulder season, should fall somewhere in between the highs and lows. Rates always go up on holidays. Remember that state and city taxes can add as much as 12.5% to your bill in some parts of Miami. Some hotels, especially those in South Beach, also tack on an additional service charge.

LONG-TERM STAYS   If you plan to visit Miami for a month, a season, or more, think about renting a room in a long-term hotel or condominium apartment. Long-term accommodations exist in every price category, from budget to deluxe, and in general are extremely reasonable, especially during the off-season. Check with the reservation services below, or write a short note to the chamber of commerce in the area where you plan to stay. In addition, many local real estate agents also handle short-term rentals (meaning less than a year).

RESERVATION SERVICES   **Central Reservations** (☎ 800/950-0232 or 305/274-6832; Web site: www.reservation-services.com; e-mail: rooms@america.com) works with many of Miami's hotels and can often secure discounts of up to 40%. It also gives advice on specific locales, especially in Miami Beach and Downtown.

The **South Florida Hotel Network** (☎ 800/538-3616 or 305/538-3616) lists more than 300 hotels throughout the area, from Palm Beach to Miami and down to the Keys.

1 Best Bets

- **Best Historical Hotel:** The Biltmore Hotel Coral Gables (☎ 800/228-3000 or 305/445-1926) just celebrated its 70th birthday. The founder of Coral Gables, George Merrick, built this grand old hotel in a Mediterranean style, with a huge bell tower based on the Giralda tower in Seville. It's now restored to its original 1926 splendor, and rooms are large and luxurious.
- **Best for Business Travelers:** The **Hotel Inter-Continental Miami** (☎ 800/332-4246 or 305/577-1000) wins for its amenities and convenient location, near the Metrorail and only a 10-minute drive from Miami International Airport. It features an extensive variety of well-appointed meeting rooms and every imaginable executive service on sight. The dining options are also superb.
- **Best for a Romantic Getaway:** The ivy-covered **Hotel Place St. Michel** (☎ 800/848-HOTEL or 305/444-1666) in Coral Gables is a small Old-World–style hotel. Warm architectural details like arched doorways and teak floors covered by Oriental rugs make visitors feel as if they're staying in an Italian mansion.
- **Best Trendy Hotel:** With its Alice-in-Wonderlandesque interior designed by Philip Starck, the recently reinvented **Delano Hotel** (☎ 800/555-5001 or 305/672-2000), on South Beach, wins the vote for Miami's trendiest spot.
- **Best Hotel Lobby for Pretending You're Rich:** If you lounge around one of the tapestried divans in the **Fisher Island Club** (☎ 305/535-6026) long enough, you'll find yourself calling for Jeeves in a heavily affected accent. You can't help it in this magnificent marbled palace.
- **Best for Families:** The **Sonesta Beach Resort Hotel Key Biscayne** (☎ 800/SONESTA or 305/361-2021) has family-friendly everything: restaurants, game

rooms, gym, tennis courts, and a pool. Add to that the entertaining and educational programs, and you'll find your children will be coming back with their children. It's the perfect place for the entire family.

- **Best Moderately Priced Hotel:** South Beach's **Hotel Leon** (☎ **305/673-3767**) is hip, gorgeous, and well-appointed, and for the location you can't beat the price. Slightly north in Bay Harbor is the **Bay Harbor Inn** (☎ **405/868-4141**), an antique-laden hotel in the exclusive Bal Harbour area. Its impeccable service and style make it so popular with discriminating budget-conscious travelers that it's booked a year in advance in season.

- **Best Hotel Pool:** The **Fontainebleau Hilton's** (☎ **800/HILTONS** or 305/538-2000) dramatic grotto and waterfall make its pool one of the most interesting and fun in the area. On the other hand, the pool at the **Biltmore** (☎ **800/228-3000** or 305/445-1926) is the nation's largest, graced with Italian statues and columns beneath a huge Gothic tower.

- **Best Spa:** When you want to relax or be pampered, there's no better place to go than the world-famous **The Spa at the Doral,** at the **Doral Golf Resort and Spa** (☎ **800/22-DORAL,** 800/71-DORAL, or 305/592-2000). And the exclusive facilities at **Fisher Island Club** (☎ **305/535-6026**) are the most luxurious I've ever seen.

2 South Beach

South Beach's art deco hotels were mostly built in the late 1930s, just after the Depression, in an area originally planned as an affordable destination for middle-class northeasterners. None of them were really luxurious—they just happened to be situated on one of the most beautiful strips of beach in the country. Large resorts like the Fontainebleau and Eden Roc were built later, 20-some-odd blocks north of South Beach, to cater to celebrities and jet-setters. These were the spots where Sinatra and his gang hung out.

But after many years of transition, South Beach gained national recognition for its unique art deco architecture. The area is now South Florida's number-one tourist destination and home to many of the city's best restaurants and nightclubs.

The most expensive rooms are on Ocean Drive or Collins Avenue, just across the street from the beach. Thankfully, for at least most of South Beach, new buildings cannot be built directly on the sand and cannot exceed three stories. Remember that the art deco hotels are generally small and have tiny bathrooms and few services and facilities.

Unless I noted otherwise, most offer no-smoking rooms. Inquire before booking.

Some very well-located chain hotel options include the **Howard Johnson Tudor Hotel** (☎ **800/446-4656** or 305/534-2934) at 1111 Collins Ave., one block from the beach but right in the happening South Beach nightlife area. Rates are moderate, starting at $115 a night in season. Cheaper options are the **Days Inn** (☎ **800/325-2525** or 305/538-6631) at 100 21st St. (off Collins Avenue), or the **Holiday Inn** (☎ **800/HOLIDAY** or 305/534-1511) at 2201 Collins Ave. They're right on the ocean at the north edge of the historic district, within walking distance of the nightlife scene. They both play up the tropical look and offer standard chain-hotel–style rooms for under $90 even in season. The Holiday Inn has lushly landscaped grounds, hidden behind an Eckerd's drugstore, and lots of amenities, including a private beach, water-sports equipment rentals, and car-rental desk. The Days Inn is on a public beach and has a car rental deck, but no water-sports equipment.

South Beach Accommodations

To Central Miami Beach

The Bass Museum of Art

Collins Park

Miami Beach Convention Center

Jackie Gleason Theater of Performing Arts

Lincoln Road Mall — Lincoln Rd.

Venetian Causeway

Belle Island

Biscayne Bay

Flamingo Park

Española Way

Miami Beach Post Office

Beach Patrol Station

Art Deco Welcome Center

Lummus Park

Atlantic Ocean

South Pointe Park

Government Cut

The Albion Hotel **6**
Avalon Hotel **20**
Banana Bungalow **1**
Brigham Gardens **5**
Casa Grande Suite Hotel **18**
Cavalier **12**
Clay Hotel & Int'l Hostel **10**
The Delano **5**
Essex House **16**
Fisher Island Club **21**
The Governor Hotel **2**
Hotel Astor **17**
Hotel Continental Riande **3**
Hotel Leon **19**
The Kent **14**
Loew's Miami Beach Hotel **9**
Marseilles Hotel **4**
The National Hotel **7**
Park Washington Hotel **15**
The Tides **13**
Villa Paradiso **11**

0   .2 mi
0   .124 km

N

NA-0162

VERY EXPENSIVE

✪ **Casa Grande Suite Hotel.** 834 Ocean Dr., South Beach, FL 33139. ☎ **800/OUTPOST** or 305/672-7003. Fax 305/673-3669. 33 units. A/C MINIBAR TV TEL. Winter $245–$400 double; $495 two-bedroom suite; $1,125 three-bedroom suite. Off-season $160–$265 double; $345 two-bedroom suite; $750 three-bedroom suite. Additional person $15 extra. Children 11 and under stay free in parents' room. AE, CB, DC, DISC, MC, V. Valet parking $14.

Europeans and vacationing celebs looking for privacy enjoy the casual elegance and thoughtful service of this hotel right on "Deco Drive." Here you'll feel as though you're staying in a very stylish apartment, not in a cookie-cutter hotel room. Every room is outfitted in a slightly different style with fully equipped kitchenettes, beautifully tiled baths, reed rugs, mahogany beds, handmade batik prints, and antiques from all over the world, particularly Indonesia. There's no pool on the property, but considering that you can see the ocean, stock your own fridge, and veg out with a good stereo and VCR, this is one of the most desirable hotels on South Beach. Some rooms facing the ocean can be loud, especially on a weekend night.

Amenities: Room service, overnight dry cleaning and laundry, complimentary newspaper and evening turndown with chocolates, twice-daily maid service, express checkout, baby-sitting arrangements. VCRs and videos are available to rent. Full kitchens, CD/cassette stereo, conference rooms, car rental, activities desk, access to a nearby health club.

The Delano. 1685 Collins Ave., South Beach, FL 33139. ☎ **800/555-5001** or 305/672-2000. Fax 305/532-0099. 209 units, 1 penthouse. A/C MINIBAR TV TEL. Winter $310–$415 double; $475 loft; $700 suite; $800 bungalow; $1,850 two-bedroom; $2,200 penthouse. Off-season $180–$265 double (weekend rates for double same as winter rates); all other room rates same as winter rates. Additional person $35 extra. Children 17 and under stay free in parents' room. AE, DC, DISC, MC, V. Valet parking $16.

When the Delano—pronounced like FDR's middle name—opened in 1995, it made the front page of nearly every architecture and style magazine in the country for its whimsical and elegant design. Look for a huge hedge with a simple blue arched door in its center, or look up for a rocketlike fin (an original 1947 detail) sprouting from the top of the all-white building. New York's Ian Shrager, of Studio 54 fame, brought in designer Philippe Starck, who went wild with the decor, including 40-foot sheer white curtains hanging outside, mirrors everywhere, white billowing curtains, Adirondack chairs, and fur-covered beds. The guest rooms are all white; a perfectly crisp green Granny Smith apple in each one is the only dose of color. It may sound antiseptic, but it actually comes across as sexy and sophisticated. The poolside cabanas are the most desirable rooms because of their huge size, but they can be noisy, since they're on an active poolside walkway.

Unfortunately, the model-gorgeous staff is often aloof or simply unavailable. But the location is ideal; it's just north of the Art Deco District strip of bars and restaurants, away from the noisy street traffic but close enough to walk to hopping Lincoln Road Mall. And of course, it's right on the ocean.

Dining/Diversions: An elegant bar attracts curious beautiful people nightly. The Blue Door (owned in part by Madonna) is known more as a place to be seen than for great cuisine. Food and service are inconsistent. The thatched Beach Bar restaurant serves fantastic sandwiches and salads. A cozy kitchen table is loaded alternately with homemade pastries, stone crabs, or champagne and caviar.

Amenities: Concierge, room service, same-day dry cleaning and laundry, newspaper delivery, evening turndown, in-room massage, executive business services, express checkout. VCRs, video rentals, children's movie theater and child activity programs, large outdoor pool, wide guarded beach, business center, conference rooms, rooftop solarium, extensive water-sports recreation, funky gift shop, 24-hour state-of-the-art David Barton gym with sauna. Aqua Spa is $10 for hotel guests; open for women 9am–7pm, men 7:30pm–11pm, and closed Tuesday night. Offers facials and a plethora of massages and water treatments.

Fisher Island Club. One Fisher Island Dr., Fisher Island, FL 33190. ☎ **305/535-6026**. Fax 305/535-6037. 60 units. A/C TV TEL. Winter $385–$900 double; $955–$1,350 suite; $725–$1,450 cottage and villa. Off-season $330–$670 double; $725–$1,155 suite; $550–$1,200 cottage and villa. Golf, tennis, and spa packages available seasonally. 20% gratuity added to all food and beverages. AE, DC, MC, V.

This secluded island, just off Miami Beach in the middle of the bay, is the height of luxury. Luciano Pavarotti, Oprah Winfrey, and other celebrities keep condos here. There are no bridges or roadways to the mainland, just a ferry that operates every 15 minutes around the clock. Attendants rinse each Mercedes and Rolls with fresh water as it glides off the docks. Don't worry if you are car-less, however—on this exclusive island, golf carts get you anywhere you need to go.

As for location, you're only minutes from the airport, South Beach, Coral Gables, or The Grove (not counting ferry time). Still, considering the pampering you'll receive in this former Vanderbilt mansion turned resort extraordinaire, you probably won't want to leave the island. A world-class spa and club offer anything you could possibly imagine. Ask and you shall receive. Most of the other buildings are million-dollar condos owned by seasonal visitors.

Dining/Diversions: The elegant Vanderbilt Club offers continental cuisine. The Beach Club and Golfer's Grill serve basic but expensive sandwiches and salads, including a great club sandwich. An Italian Cafe prepares exceptional pastas and seafood. A dinner theater features live music.

Amenities: Concierge, room service (7am–10pm), dry cleaning, laundry, national newspaper delivery, nightly turndown, twice-daily maid service, baby-sitting, secretarial service, valet parking, courtesy airport transportation. The huge Spa Internazionale, P.B. Dye Golf Course, 18 tennis courts, two deep-water marinas, boutiques, huge corporate board room, helipad, seaplane ramp, auto-ferry system.

The National Hotel. 1677 Collins Ave., South Beach. ☎ **800/327-8370** or 305/532-2311. Fax 305/534-1426. E-mail: sales@nationalhotel.com. 200 units. A/C MINIBAR TV TEL. Winter $225–$345 one-bedroom suite; $570 tower suite. Off-season $180–$280 one-bedroom suite; $245 one-bedroom with balcony; $440–$490 tower suite. Rates include continental breakfast. AE, DC, DISC, MC, V. Valet parking $16.

This elegant newcomer has joined the ranks of South Beach's particular brand of luxury resorts. Since there is so much to offer in the neighborhood, these "resorts" tend to offer limited on-site facilities and concentrate more on style and service. The National does a super job. With its towering ceilings, sultry furnishings, and massive gilded mirrors, the elegant 1940s lobby ought to be the backdrop for a gangster flick. At 11 stories, the main building stands taller than most of its neighbors and offers grand views of the beach and ocean below. Rooms in the garden wing are slightly larger and have balconies. All are decorated in tropical bamboo and pastel tones. The hotel is located right on the ocean and just a block from each of the best shopping and dining streets in town.

Dining/Diversions: The Oval Room is an elegant and formal dining room with an eclectic American menu and extensive wine list. Two outside dining spots overlook the pool and serve drinks, light meals, snacks, and sandwiches. There are three bars, including The Deco Lounge, which features live jazz most nights in season and free appetizers on Thursday evenings.

Amenities: Concierge, room service (24 hours), dry-cleaning and laundry service, newspaper delivery, evening turndown, twice-daily maid service, baby-sitting, express checkout. Stereos in suites, two TVs in suites, VCRs, video rental, two outdoor pools, large beach, small fitness room, small business center, water-sports concession (including scuba and sailing).

✪ **The Tides.** 1220 Ocean Dr., South Beach, FL 33139. ☎ **800/OUTPOST** or 305/604-5000. Fax 305/672-6288. www.islandlife.com. E-mail: outpost800@aol.com. 45 units. A/C MINIBAR TV TEL. Winter $275 superior; $350–$425 suites; $900–$2,000 penthouse suite. Off-season $150 superior; $200–$275 suite; $600–$1,100 penthouse suite. Additional person $20 extra. Rates include continental breakfast. AE, CB, DC, DISC, MC, V. Valet parking $15.

Opened in late 1997 to rave reviews, this 12-story art deco masterpiece is one of the tallest buildings on the strip of Ocean Drive. It is the latest addition to the Island Outpost group, which includes the Cavalier, The Kent, Casa Grande (reviewed in this section), and others. Rooms are starkly white but luxurious. The warm staff and central location, across the street from a popular beach, are definite strong points. Also, all rooms are large and have ocean views. Guests can also enjoy the terraces and a freshwater pool on the rear mezzanine.

Dining/Diversions: Twelve Twenty is the hotel's fine restaurant. It serves dinner nightly 6pm–midnight. The Terrace, a gorgeous marble-floored outdoor cafe overlooking the ocean, does a fine job of breakfast and lunch. There's also a lobby lounge with live entertainment.

Amenities: Concierge, room service (24 hour), dry cleaning, laundry service, newspaper delivery, in-room massage, twice-daily maid service, baby-sitting, secretarial services, express check-out. Stereos with cassette and CD player and a selection of CDs in each room, VCRs, video rentals, heated outdoor pool, small health club and discount at nearby Club Bodytech, one conference room.

EXPENSIVE

Albion Hotel. 1650 James Ave. (at Lincoln Rd.). ☎ **888/665-0008** or 305/913-1000. Fax 305/674-0507. 100 units. A/C MINIBAR TV TEL. Winter $205–$215 double; $375–$700 suite. Off-season $125–$145 double; $195–$550 suite. AE, DC, DISC, MC, V. Valet parking $15.

An architectural masterpiece originally designed in 1939 by internationally acclaimed architect Igor Polivitzky, this large Streamline Moderne building looks like a cruise ship with portholes, smokestack, and sleek curved lines. It was totally renovated in 1997, under the guidance of the hip New York family, the Rubells. Although you have to walk a few blocks to find beach access, you may not want to. A huge pool and artificial beach are original features at this unusual and recommendable resort. Rooms are furnished with wonderful modern furnishings custom-designed for the space. The hotel is popular with those in the music and modeling industry and often serves as the backdrop for parties and shoots.

Dining: Plans are in the works to open two restaurants, one by the pool.

Amenities: Concierge, room service, dry cleaning and laundry, evening turndown, in-room massage, newspaper delivery, twice-daily maid service, baby-sitting, executive business services, valet parking, airport limo service. VCRs available on request, large outdoor heated pool with adjacent artificial sand beach, access to nearby health club, business services on request, small conference and production rooms, stereos with CD and cassette player (but no CDs), state-of-the-art phones with data port and voice mail.

✪ **Hotel Astor.** 956 Washington Ave., South Beach, FL 33139. ☎ **800/270-4981** or 305/531-8081. Fax 305/531-3193. 40 units. A/C MINIBAR TV TEL. Winter $145–$200 rms;

$275–$320 suites. Off-season $115–$190 rms; $245–$290 suites. Astor suite $420–$600. Additional person $30. AE, MC, V. Valet parking $14.

For the price (about half that of the Delano), this is a great option for those who like intimate but terribly hip accommodations. A small but elegant and modern hotel, the Astor attracts many loyal, return guests. Originally built in 1936, the renovation in 1995 greatly improved on the original design of this simple three-story gem. There is a small lap pool and a beautiful waterfall outside the sleek lobby bar area. All the details are pure luxury, like swivel stands for the large-screen TVs, Belgian linens and towels, and funky custom lighting with dimmer switches. The hotel staff is known for bending over backwards. This is definitely a place for those in the know. Unfortunately, the few moderately priced standard rooms are usually booked months in advance.

Dining: Astor Place is one of Miami's best restaurants. The Florida-style menu is diverse and delicious (see listing under "South Beach" in chapter 6, "Dining"). Sunday brunch is one of the best in town.

Amenities: 24-hour concierge service, room service, dry cleaning, laundry, newspaper delivery, in-room massage, twice-daily maid service, baby-sitting, secretarial service, express checkout. VCRs available on request, video rental, outdoor pool with jet-streams, access to nearby health club, two phones in suites.

Loews Miami Beach Hotel. 1601 Collins Ave., South Beach, FL 33139. ☎ **800/23LOEWS** or 305/604-1601. 857 units. A/C MINIBAR TV TEL. Winter, from $300 double. Off-season, from $250 double. AE, DC, DISC, MC, V.

Not yet completed at press time, this 800-room hotel is the first new hotel to be built in South Beach for the past 30 years. It's also the largest, which is a good thing—the Beach was sorely in need of a large hotel to accommodate business travelers who come to the nearby convention center. Accordingly, it will feature plenty of meeting rooms, ballrooms, a large health club, and seven restaurants and lounges. Like the Fontainebleau and Eden Roc 30 blocks north, the Loews will be a full-service, beachfront resort. However, it will have the advantage of being brand-new and situated right in the heart of the bustling Art Deco district.

MODERATE

Avalon Hotel. 700 Ocean Dr. (at 7th St.), South Beach, FL 33139. ☎ **800/933-3306** or 305/538-0133. Fax 305/534-0258. 106 units. A/C TV TEL. Winter $120–$180 double. Off-season $65–$145 double. Rates include continental breakfast, full breakfast off-season. Additional person $10 extra. Children 11 and under stay free in parents' room. 10% discount for stays of 7 days or more. AE, CB, DC, DISC, MC, V. Valet parking $14.

This striking hotel on a pretty parcel of land offers classic art deco digs right on the beach. The rooms are well decorated in traditional 1930s style. The modest lobby holds a casual restaurant, best for lunch either inside or on the breezy outdoor patio. The experienced management, known for its excellent inns in Newport, Rhode Island, runs this hotel with an even hand.

Room service, free coffee, refreshments, and breakfast are also available. If the Avalon is full, don't hesitate to accept a room in its companion property, the Majestic, located across the street.

Cavalier. 1320 Ocean Dr., South Beach, FL 33139. ☎ **800/OUTPOST** or 305/604-5000. Fax 305/531-5543. 45 units. A/C MINIBAR TV TEL. Winter $125–$195 double; $275–$350 suite. Off-season $95–$155 double; $230–$250 suite. Additional person $15 extra. Children 11 and under stay free in parents' room. AE, DC, DISC, MC, V. Valet parking $14; self-parking $6.

The Cavalier, a hip, well-priced hotel, is kept in shape by yearly refurbishments. You can't beat its oceanfront location, adjacent to shops and restaurants. Palm trees brush the ceilings of the modest lobby, where young trendy guests make their way to their rooms. Funky prints cover the walls, which are the colors of a tequila sunrise. A young, competent staff waits on guests and offers lots of good advice about local clubs, restaurants, and shopping. Rooms come equipped with CD players and discs. You can also use a VCR and rent videos. Despite the Ocean Drive location, most rooms are relatively quiet.

Essex House. 1001 Collins Ave., South Beach, FL 33139. ☎ **800/55-ESSEX** or 305/534-2700. Fax 305/532-3827. 79 units. A/C TV TEL. Winter $155–$195; 255–$300 suite. Off-season $99–139 double; $199–245 suite. Rates include deluxe continental breakfast. Minimum stay 2 nights on weekends in season, 3 nights on holidays. AE, CB, DC, DISC, MC, V. Valet parking $14. Nearby parking available for $4 weekdays, $6 weekends and holidays.

This art deco landmark, just a block from the ocean, is one of South Beach's architectural gems, especially since the $3-million renovation completed in 1998. The pretty Essex House is a textbook example of Streamline Moderne style, complete with large porthole windows, original etched glasswork, ziggurat arches, and detailed crown moldings. The solid-oak bedroom furnishings are also original and, like many other details in this special hotel, were carefully restored. Suites feature minibars, coffeemakers, and VCRs. Ask for a room with a refrigerator, since more than a dozen standard rooms do have them. The Essex also features 24-hour reception, a baby grand, self-playing piano in the lobby/lounge, and a state-of-the-art security system. This hotel is spic-and-span, almost too much like a chain, but the staff is extremely pleasant and helpful.

A very small pool is just one of the many new additions here. A new martini bar and piano lounge are on the way.

The Governor Hotel. 35 21st St., Miami Beach, FL 33139. ☎ **800/542-0444** or 305/532-2100. Fax 305/532-9139. 125 units. A/C TV TEL. Winter $89–$125 double. Off-season $69–$89 double. Children under 18 stay free. AE, DC, DISC, MC, V. Free parking.

This reasonably priced hotel on the northernmost border of South Beach is frequented by conventioneers who until recently had no real hotel to stay in. The Governor is nothing special, but the rooms are decent enough and the rates are pretty cheap. However, as an example of art deco architecture, this hotel is one of the most stylish in the area. It has streamlined details, from the checkerboard floor tiles to the steel marquee and looming flagstaffs, but don't expect too much inside. A recent revamping improved the slightly tacky decor and introduced some better staff. You'll want to drive to the beach since it's a few long blocks through a not-so-scenic neighborhood of mostly unrenovated and seedy hotels. The Governor has a medium-size pool and a small cafe and bar.

Hotel Continental Riande. 1825 Collins Ave., South Beach, FL 33139. ☎ **800/RIANDE-1** or 305/531-3503. Fax 305/531-2803. 251 units. A/C MINIBAR TV TEL. Winter $135–$160 double. Off-season $105–$135 double. Additional person $10 extra. Children 11 and under stay free in parents' room. Frommer's readers get a 20% discount. AE, DC, DISC, MC, V. Valet parking $8.

The Riande is just the ticket if you want value and convenience right on South Beach. Catering to a largely Latin and European clientele, this hotel overlooking the ocean has become quite well known. It's just 2 blocks from The Delano and the best of South Beach. The rooms and lobby areas are clean and well maintained, but not too fussy. A large outdoor pool and sundeck are just out back. There's also a restaurant/coffeeshop with both buffet and menu service. Room service is available daily for breakfast and dinner.

✪ Hotel Leon. 841 Collins Ave., South Beach, FL 33139. ☎ **305/673-3767**. Fax 305/673-5866. E-mail: hotel-leon@travelbase.com. 18 units. A/C TV TEL. Winter $125 rm; $165–$215 suite; $375 penthouse. Off-season $100 rm; $135–$185 suite; $315 penthouse. $10 for an extra bed. AE, DC, MC, V. Valet parking $14.

A true value, this stylish sliver of a property has won the loyalty of fashion industrialists and romantics alike. The very central location, 1 block from the sea and in the heart of shopping and dining, means a car isn't necessary. The spacious well-renovated rooms are sparkling clean and warmly appointed. Gleaming wood floors and simple pale furnishings are appreciated in a neighborhood where many others overdo the art deco motif. Each room has two phones, sunken oval tubs, robes, CD players, and CDs. Unfortunately, there's no pool. A meeting room and business center make it a fine choice for business trips. In the standard rooms, there are no minibars or fridges, but you can order room service anytime. In the morning, enjoy a moderately priced breakfast ($8.50) of croissants, fresh rolls, ham, cheese, and eggs cooked to order. The owners, a young German couple, have made a commitment to providing excellent service with a distinctly personal touch, and they have succeeded.

The Kent. 1131 Collins Ave., South Beach, FL 33139. ☎ **800/OUTPOST** or 305/604-5000. Fax 305/531-0720. www.islandlife.com. E-mail: outpost800@aol.com. 54 units. A/C MINIBAR TV TEL. Winter $125–$195 double; $275 suite. Off-season $95–$155 double; $230 suite. Additional person $15 extra. Children 11 and under stay free in parents' room. AE, DC, DISC, MC, V. Valet parking $14; self-parking $6.

This is an excellent value right in South Beach's active center. Even if the other Island Outpost hotels are full, you're likely to find a spot here. The prices are the same as the group's beachside hotels, the Cavalier and the Leslie, but the rooms tend to be less noisy. The staff includes an eager-to-please group of Caribbeans, and the clientele comes largely from the fashion industry. Frequent shoots are coordinated in the lobby and conference room, where full office services are available. Thanks to a vacant lot in the backyard (for now), some rooms in the rear offer nice views of the ocean. The decor is modest but tasteful. CD players are standard, as are bright and whimsical furnishings. VCRs and video rentals are available. There's no pool or sundeck, but you're only 1 block from the beach.

Marseilles Hotel. 1741 Collins Ave., South Beach, Fl 33139. ☎ **800/327-4739** or 305/538-5711. Fax 305/673-1006. www.marseilleshotel.com. E-mail: peter@marseilleshotel.com. 116 units. A/C TV TEL. Winter $115–$135 double; $180 suite. Off-season $79–$99 double; $145 suites. Frommer's readers get 10% discount in winter and 20% in the off-season. AE, DC, DISC, MC, V. Valet parking $10.

The Marseilles is one of the very best deals in this super-trendy area. It's a full-service, inexpensive, classic art deco hotel, located right on the beach and near the best of everything. The staff is pleasant, the restaurant and bar very recommendable, and the decor is thoroughly tasteful. Still, it's a little worn around the edges, although Lloyd and Clara Mandell are continuing to make improvements.

With only about 100 rooms, the Marseilles is more intimate than the larger Riande, a few doors away. The suites (three of which have Jacuzzis at no extra charge) are an exceptionally good deal if you want to spend a lot of time in your room. You'll find a telescope for spying on naked sunbathers below. The rooms are on the small side but clean and comfortable. All have small refrigerators and bottled water upon check-in. The bar and restaurant are popular with budget-seeking locals. When the Marseilles is full, the staff may suggest putting you at the nearby Dorchester. It's cheaper and decent but not nearly as recommendable.

○ **The Mermaid Guesthouse.** 909 Collins Ave., Miami Beach, FL 33140. ☎ **305/538-5324**. 8 units, all with bathroom. A/C TEL. Winter $105–$115 single or double; $200 suite. Off-season $75–$95 single or double; $175 suite. Additional person $10 extra; small children stay free in parents' room. Discounts available for longer stays. AE, MC, V.

There's something magical about this little hideaway tucked behind tropical gardens in the very heart of South Beach. You won't find the amenities of the larger hotels here, but the charm and hospitality at this one-story guesthouse keeps people coming back. Plus, it's smack in the middle of the hottest part of South Beach and less than 2 blocks from the ocean.

In 1996 the new owners, Ana and Gonzalo Torres, did a thorough clean-up, adding new brightly colored fretwork around the doors and windows and installing phones in each room. Also, the wood floors have been stripped or covered in straw matting, one of the many Caribbean touches that make this place so cheery. There are no TVs, so guests tend to congregate in the lush garden in the evenings. The owners sometimes host free impromptu dinners for their guests and friends. New in 1998 is live Latin music on the patio two or three nights a week.

INEXPENSIVE

Banana Bungalow. 2360 Collins Ave., Miami Beach, FL 33139. ☎ **800/7-HOSTEL** or 305/538-1951. Fax 305/531-3217. E-mail: MIAMIres@bananabungalow.com. 90 units. A/C TV TEL. Winter $13–$16 per person in shared rms; $54–$60 single; $64–$70 double. Off-season $12–$14 per person in shared rms; $40–$46 single; $50–$56 double. MC, V. Free parking.

Opened in late 1996, this youth hostel-ish hotel is the most recent and recommendable addition to the South Beach budget scene. Across the street is a popular beach; the best shops, clubs, and restaurants are only 6 or 7 blocks away. This redone 1950s two-story newcomer surrounds a pool and deck complete with shuffleboard, a small alfresco restaurant, and a tiki bar where young European travelers hang out.

The best rooms face a narrow canal where motorboats and kayaks are available for a small charge. In general, rooms are clean and well kept, despite a few rusty faucets and chipped Formica furnishings. Guests in shared rooms need to bring their own towels. This is one of the only hotels in this price range with a private pool. Guests can also enjoy free nightly movies, sightseeing tours, discounts at local clubs, and a great community spirit.

○ **Brigham Gardens.** 1411 Collins Ave., South Beach, FL 33139. ☎ **305/531-1331**. Fax 305/538-9898. 19 units. A/C TV TEL. Winter $85–$130 double. Off-season $60–$110 double. Additional person $5 extra. 10% discount on all stays of 1 week or longer. Pets stay for $6 a night, and young children stay in parents' room free. AE, MC, V.

There's no pool or other niceties, but you'll find this funky place a homey and affordable oasis in the midst of high prices and commercialization. Also, the location is prime. Because most rooms have full kitchens, you'll find many people staying for longer than a weekend. You may, too. All rooms have microwaves and coffeepots, at least. You can do your laundry on the premises.

When you enter the tropically landscaped garden, you'll hear macaws and parrots chirping and see cats and lizards running through the bougainvillea. The tiny but lush grounds are framed by quaint Mediterranean buildings—they're pleasant, although in need of some sprucing up. This happy spot is run by a mother and daughter who go out of their way to see that guests and their pets are well cared for. A warning: Like most other small properties on South Beach, parking can be a pain.

Clay Hotel & International Hostel. 1438 Washington Ave. (at Española Way), South Beach, FL 33139. ☎ **305/534-2988**. Fax 305/673-0346. 350 beds in singles, doubles, and dorm rms. $40–$50 single; $45–65 double; $14–$16 dorm beds. Sheets $2 extra. Pay for 6 nights in advance and get 7th night free. JCB, MC, V.

A member of the International Youth Hostel Federation (IYHF), the Clay occupies a beautiful 1920s-style Spanish Mediterranean building at the corner of historic Española Way. Like other IYHF members, this hostel is open to all ages and is a great place to meet people. The usual smattering of Australians, Europeans, and other budget travelers makes it Miami's best clearinghouse of "insider" travel information. Even if you don't stay here, you might want to check out the ride board or mingle with fellow travelers over a beer at the sidewalk cafe.

Although a thorough renovation in 1996 made this hostel an incredible value and a step above any others in town, don't expect nightly turndown service or chocolates. You will find a self-serve laundromat, occasional movie nights, and a tour desk with car rental available. Reservations are essential for private rooms year-round and recommended in season. In summer, be sure to ask for a room with air-conditioning. Don't bother with a car in this congested area.

Park Washington Hotel. 1020 Washington Ave., South Beach, FL 33139. ☎ **305/ 532-1930.** Fax 305/672-6706. 36 units. A/C TV TEL. Winter $79–$99 double; $129 suite. Off-season $59–$69 double; $99 suite. Rates include self-serve coffee and Danish. Additional person $20 extra. Children stay free in parents' room. AE, MC, V.

The Park Washington is a large, refurbished hotel just 2 blocks from the ocean that offers some of the best values in South Beach—good rooms at incredible prices. Designed in the 1930s by Henry Hohauser, one of the beach's most famous architects, the Park Washington reopened in 1989. Most of the rooms have original furnishings and well-kept interiors, and some have kitchenettes. Guests also enjoy a decent-sized outdoor heated pool with a sundeck, bikes for rent, and access to a nearby health club.

The same owners run the adjacent Taft House and Kenmore hotels. All three attract a large gay clientele, and all offer privacy, lush landscaping, a great pool and sundeck, consistent quality, and a value-oriented philosophy. You can't park on the premises, but there's a public garage at 7th Street, less than 3 blocks away.

Villa Paradiso. 1415 Collins Ave., Miami Beach, FL 33139. ☎ **305/532-0616.** Fax 305/ 673-5874. E-mail: villap@gates.net. 17 units. A/C TV TEL. Winter $100–$145 apt. Off-season $69–$105 apt. Weekly rates are 10% less. Additional person $5–10 extra. AE, DC, MC, V.

This guesthouse, like Brigham Gardens, is more like a cozy apartment house than a hotel. There's no elegant lobby or restaurant, but the amicable hosts, Lisa and Pascal Nicolle, are happy to give you a room key and advice on what to do. The apartments are simple, but the style is fine for the beach, since you'll be spending most of your time outside anyway. Plus, the spacious apartments are quiet considering their location, a few blocks from Lincoln Road and all of Miami Beach's best clubs. Most have full kitchens, and Murphy beds or foldout couches for extra friends. There are also laundry facilities on the premises and free local phone service.

3 Miami Beach: Surfside, Bal Harbour & Sunny Isles

The area just north of South Beach encompasses Surfside, Bal Harbour, and Sunny Isles. Unrestricted by zoning codes throughout the 1950s, 1960s, and especially the 1970s, area developers went nuts, building ever-bigger and more brazen structures, especially north of 41st Street, which is now known as "Condo Canyon." Consequently, there's now a glut of medium-quality condos, with a few scattered holdouts of older hotels and motels casting shadows over the beach by afternoon.

Miami Beach, as described here, runs from 24th Street to 192nd Street, a long strip that varies slightly from end to end. Staying in the southern section, from 24th to 42nd streets, can be a good deal—it's still close to the South Beach scene but the rates are more affordable. Bal Harbour and Bay Harbor are at the center of Miami Beach and retain their exclusivity and character. The neighborhoods north and south of here, like Surfside and Sunny Isles, have nice beaches and some shops, but are a little worn around the edges.

Just north of South Beach is the **Days Inn** (☎ **800/325-2525** or 305/673-1513) at 42nd Street and Collins Avenue. It's very well kept and right on the ocean. The **Howard Johnson** (☎ **800/446-4656** or 305/532-4411) at 4000 Alton Rd., just off the Julia Tuttle Causeway (I-95), is a generic eight-story building on a strip of land near a busy road, but it's convenient to the beach, by car or bike. Rooms, renovated in 1995, are clean and spacious, and some have pretty views of the city and the intracoastal waterway. Farther north in Miami Beach, in an uncrowded section of beach, there is an oceanfront **Ramada Inn** (☎ **800/272-6232** or 305/865-8511) at 6701 Collins Ave. and a **Howard Johnson** (☎ **800/446-4656** or 305/868-1200) at 6261 Collins Ave.

VERY EXPENSIVE

✪ **Alexander All-Suite Luxury Hotel.** 5225 Collins Ave., Miami Beach, FL 33140. ☎ **800/327-6121** or 305/865-6500. Fax 305/341-6553. Telex 808172. 150 units. A/C TV TEL. Winter $325 one-bedroom suite; $470 two-bedroom suite. Off-season $250 one-bedroom suite; $370 two-bedroom suite. Additional person $35 extra. Children 17 and under stay free in parents' room. Packages available. AE, CB, DC, DISC, MC, V. Valet parking $12.50.

This stunning hotel is a good luxury choice if you want to be off the beaten path. It's expensive, but worth it for the service and attention. The Alexander features spacious one- and two-bedroom mini-apartments. Each contains a living room, a fully equipped kitchen, two bathrooms, and a balcony. The rooms are elegant without being pretentious and have every convenience you could want, including hair dryers, coffeemakers, VCRs upon request, and cable TVs. The hotel itself is well decorated, with sculptures, paintings, antiques, and tapestries, most of which were garnered from the Cornelius Vanderbilt mansion. The two oceanfront pools are surrounded by lush vegetation; one of these "lagoons" is fed by a cascading waterfall.

Dining/Diversions: A pricey steak house was opened here in 1998 by former Dolphins football coach, Don Shula. A more casual garden restaurant, a piano lounge, and a pool bar are also available.

Amenities: Concierge, room service (24 hours), dry cleaning and laundry service, newspaper delivery, evening turndown on request, in-room massage on request, twice-daily maid service, secretarial services, express checkout. Two large outdoor pools, beach, small state-of-the-art health club, four Jacuzzis, sauna, business center and conference rooms, car rental through concierge, sundeck, water-sports equipment, beauty salon.

Fontainebleau Hilton. 4441 Collins Ave., Miami Beach, FL 33140. ☎ **800/HILTONS** or 305/538-2000. Fax 305/674-4607. Telex 519362. 1,266 units. A/C TV TEL. Winter $310–$340 double; $525–$725 suite. Off-season $205–$310 double; $475–$675 suite. Additional person $30 extra. Children under 18 stay free in parents' room. Weekend and other packages available. AE, CB, DC, DISC, MC, V. Overnight valet parking $10.

The most famous hotel in Miami, the Fontainebleau (pronounced "fountain-blue") has built its reputation on garishness and excess. Its sheer size, with its full complement of restaurants, stores, and recreational facilities, plus over 1,100 employees, makes it a perfect place for conventioneers. Unfortunately, the same recommendation cannot be extended to individual travelers. It's easy to get lost here, both physically and personally. The lobby is terminally crowded, the staff is overworked, and lines are always long. Renovations to the rooms in 1995 and 1996 did manage to freshen up the decor with new furnishings and pastel accents.

Miami Beach Accommodations

ACCOMMODATIONS:
Alexander All-Suite Luxury Hotel **7**
Bay Harbor Inn **2**
Baymar Ocean Resort **4**
Compostela Motel **5**
Dezerland Surfside Beach Hotel **6**
Doral Ocean Beach Resort **8**
Eden Roc Resort & Spa **9**
Fontainebleau Hilton **10**
Indian Creek Hotel **12**
Miami Beach Ocean Resort **11**
Sheraton Bal Harbour
    Beach Resort **3**
Suez Oceanfront Resort **1**

NA-0163

Still, this is the one and only Fontainebleau, in many ways the quintessential Miami hotel. See it as a tourist attraction; you really shouldn't miss the incredible lagoon-style pool and waterfall. Since its opening in 1954, the hotel has hosted presidents, pageants, and movie productions—including the James Bond thriller *Goldfinger*. No matter if it suits your taste; this is one place you'll never forget.

Dining/Diversions: The Steak House serves dinner until 11pm. A continental restaurant offers a huge Sunday buffet brunch. There are five other cafes and coffeeshops (including two by the pool), as well as a number of cocktail lounges, such as the Poodle Lounge, which offers live entertainment and dancing nightly. Another lounge features a Las Vegas–style floor show with dozens of performers and two orchestras.

Amenities: Concierge, room service, dry cleaning and laundry, newspaper delivery, nightly turndown on request, in-room massage, baby-sitting, secretarial services, valet parking. VCRs, two large outdoor pools, beach, large state-of-the-art health club, three whirlpool baths, sauna, game rooms, special year-round activities for children and adults, elaborate business center, conference rooms, car-rental and tour desks, sundeck, seven lighted tennis courts, water-sports equipment rental, beauty salon, boutique, large shopping arcade.

✪ **Sheraton Bal Harbour Beach Resort.** 9701 Collins Ave., Bal Harbour, FL 33154. ☎ **800/ 999-9898** or 305/865-7511. Fax 305/864-2601. Telex 519355. 642 units. A/C MINIBAR TV TEL. Winter $319–$409 double; $600 suite or villa. $225–$315 double; $600 suite. Off-season $279– $379 double; $600 suite or villa. Additional person $25 extra. Children 17 and under stay free in parents' room. Weekend and other packages and senior discounts available. Lowest rates reflect bookings made at least 14 days in advance for rooms without ocean views. AE, CB, DC, DISC, JCB, MC, V. Valet parking $12.

This hotel has the best location in Bal Harbour, on the ocean and just across from the swanky Bal Harbour Shops. Bill and Hillary Clinton have stayed here, and Bill even jogged along the beach with local fitness enthusiasts. It's one of the nicest Sheratons I've seen, with a glass-enclosed two-story atrium lobby and large, well-decorated rooms that include convenient extras like coffeemakers and hair dryers. A spectacular staircase wraps itself around a cascading fountain full of wished-on pennies. One side of the hotel caters to corporations and comes complete with ballrooms and meeting facilities, but the main sections are relatively uncongested and removed from the convention crowd.

Dining/Diversions: Guests have their choice of four restaurants and lounges. An Argentinean steak house serves good, heavy meals with live Latin music nightly. The other less formal spots serve Mediterranean-influenced beach food, pizzas, and gourmet coffees. A lounge serves good tropical drinks.

Amenities: Concierge, room service (24 hours), laundry and dry cleaning, valet, newspaper delivery, nightly turndown, in-room massage, twice-daily maid service on request, baby-sitting, secretarial services, express checkout, valet parking, free coffee and refreshments in the lobby. VCRs in some rooms, a full complement of aquatic playthings for rent on the beach (including sailboats and jet skis), outdoor heated pool, sundeck, large state-of-the-art fitness center and spa (with aerobics, Jacuzzi, sauna, and sundeck), two outdoor tennis courts, jogging track, games room, children's programs, large business center, conference rooms, tour desk, gift shop and shopping arcade, nearby golf course.

EXPENSIVE

✪ **Eden Roc Resort and Spa.** 4525 Collins Ave., Miami Beach, FL 33140. ☎ **800/327-8337** or 305/531-0000. Fax 305/674-5568. 350 units. A/C TV TEL. Winter $195–$350 double; $275– $1,500 suite. Off-season $120–$250 double; $175–$1,000 suite. Additional person $15 extra.

Children 16 and under stay free in parents' room. Weekend, spa, and honeymoon packages available. AE, CB, DC, DISC, MC, V. Valet parking $12.

Just next door to the mammoth Fontainebleau, this flamboyant and large hotel, opened in 1956, seems almost intimate by comparison. The accommodations here are a bit gaudy, but this is Miami Beach, after all. The amenities by far make up for the ostentation. The huge, modern spa has excellent facilities and exercise classes, including yoga. The popular pool deck overlooking the ocean is a great place to spend the afternoon.

The big, open, and airy lobby is dressed in solid tropical colors, diamond-pattern carpeting, and fleur-de-lis wallpaper. It's often full of name-tagged conventioneers. The rooms, uniformly outfitted with purple and aquatic-colored interiors and retouched 1930s furnishings, are unusually spacious. Because of the hotel's size, you should be able to negotiate a good rate unless there's a big event going on.

Dining/Diversions: A steakhouse serves exceptionally good Angus beef and seafood. From Jimmy Johnson's, the poolside sports bar, patrons can watch swimmers through an underwater "porthole" window. A lobby lounge and bar has occasional jazz.

Amenities: Concierge, room service, dry cleaning and laundry, newspaper delivery, in-room massage, nightly turndown, baby-sitting, secretarial services, express checkout, valet parking. Kitchenettes in suites and penthouses, VCRs for rent, two outdoor pools, beach, full-service spa and health club with sauna, business center and conference rooms, car-rental desk, sundeck, squash, racquetball and basketball courts as well as a rock-climbing arena, water-sports equipment, tour desk, beauty salon, sundries shop.

Miami Beach Ocean Resort. 3025 Collins Ave., Miami Beach, FL 33140. ☎ **800/550-0505** or 305/534-0505. Fax 305/534-0515. 243 units. A/C TV TEL. Winter $170–$200, one to four people; $220–$600 suite. Off-season $140–$170, one to four people; $200–$550 suite. AE, DC, MC, V.

Popular with tour groups and Europeans, this oceanfront resort is a great choice for those who want a quiet place on the ocean in close proximity to South Beach and the mainland. It's priced like many other chains on the oceanfront, but it's one of the best. The elegant vast lobby is done up in Mexican tile, wood fretwork, and attractive furnishings. Rooms are basic but very tastefully decorated with new wicker and rattan furnishings. A huge outdoor area is landscaped with palms and hibiscus and has a large heated pool as its centerpiece. It faces a popular boardwalk for runners and strollers as well as a large beach where water-sports equipment is available.

Dining/Diversions: The recommendable restaurant serves a breakfast and dinner buffet of simple but good Caribbean and international cuisine to many who choose the meal programs. À la carte offerings and lunch are also available. A patio garden offers cake and coffee, a pool bar serves snacks and drinks, and a colorful indoor/outdoor lounge features cocktails and live music most nights.

Amenities: Concierge, room service, valet parking, laundry and dry-cleaning services, baby-sitting. Outdoor heated pool, beach, sundeck, bicycle rental, game room, self-service laundromat, currency exchange, tour desk, conference rooms, car-rental desk, beauty salon, boutique.

MODERATE

✪ Bay Harbor Inn. 9601 E. Bay Harbor Dr., Bay Harbor Island, FL 33154. ☎ **305/868-4141.** Fax 305/867-9094. 24 units. A/C TV TEL. Winter $139 double; $149 suite; $169 penthouse suite. Off-season $60 double; $70 suite; $90 penthouse suite. Additional person $25 extra. Children

12 and under stay free in parents' room. Rates include continental breakfast. AE, MC, V. Free parking.

This quaint little inn looks as if it ought to be in Vermont, but it's just moments from the beach, fine restaurants, and some of the city's best shopping. The inn comes in two parts. The more modern section sits squarely on a little river, called "the creek," and overlooks a heated outdoor pool and a boat named *Celeste* where guests eat breakfast. On the other side of the street is the cozier, antique-filled portion, where glass-covered bookshelves hold good beach reading. The rooms have a hodgepodge of wood furnishings, like oak-framed mirrors, canopied beds, Victorian chairs, and modern vanities. Some of the rooms are slightly larger (like nos. 301, 305, 308, and 311) and boast an extra half bath at no extra cost. You can at times smell the aroma of cooking from the restaurant below, but you might find that this only adds to the charm of this homey inn.

Adjacent to the hotel is The Palm, a clubby steak-and-lobster house. Students from a nearby culinary institute run a superb restaurant and bar in the creekside building across the street. A deluxe continental breakfast is served on a nearby yacht.

Baymar Ocean Resort. 9401 Collins Ave., Miami Beach, FL 33154. ☎ **800/8-BAYMAR** or 305/866-5446. Fax 305/866-8053. 96 units. A/C TV TEL. Winter $115–$125 double; $125–$135 efficiency; $150–$235 suite. Off-season $85–$95 double; $95–$105 efficiency; $125–$185 suite. Additional person $10 extra. Children 11 and under stay free in parents' room. AE, DISC, MC, V. Parking $5.

Depending on what you're looking for, this hotel could be one of the beach's best buys. It's just south of Bal Harbour, right on the ocean, with a low-key beach that attracts few other tourists. It offers all the modern conveniences, including some kitchenettes and large closets. You won't flip over the decor, but it's pleasant enough and all brand-new. A recent renovation has done wonders. There isn't much within walking distance from this spot (much of the rest of the area is run-down or has been converted into condos), but you're close to everything by car. It may not be worth it to pay more for the oceanfront rooms since they tend to be smaller than the others. Rooms overlooking the large pool and sundeck area can get loud on busy days. The first-floor ocean-view rooms have a nice shared balcony space. This hotel is popular with budget travelers and conservative religious groups.

A small restaurant serving basic American fare and a tiki bar are popular with guests.

Dezerland Surfside Beach Hotel. 8701 Collins Ave., Miami Beach, FL 33154. ☎ **800/331-9346** in the U.S., 800/331-9347 in Canada, or 305/865-6661. Fax 305/866-2630. 225 units. A/C TV TEL. Winter $80–$125 double. Off-season $60–$85 double. Additional person $10 extra. Children 18 and under stay free in parents' room. Special packages and group rates available. AE, CB, DC, DISC, MC, V. Self-parking.

Designed by car enthusiast Michael Dezer, the Dezerland is a one-of-a-kind—part hotel and part 1950s automobile wonderland. Visitors, many of them German tourists, are welcomed by a 1959 Cadillac stationed by the front door, one of a dozen mint-condition classics around the grounds and lobby. Though not pristine, this beachfront hotel is clean and pleasant. Constant renovations improve it every year. Some rooms contain fully equipped kitchenettes. Look for the mosaic of a pink Cadillac at the bottom of its surfside pool.

Other amenities include a Jacuzzi, adjacent tennis courts and jogging track, Windsurfer and jet-ski rental, game room, laundry, car-rental and tour services desk, and an antique shop featuring 1950s memorabilia. There's also a restaurant and a lobby lounge with all-you-can-eat buffets and nightly entertainment.

Indian Creek Hotel. 2727 Indian Creek Dr., Miami Beach, FL 33140. ☎ **800/491-2772** or 305/531-2727. Fax 305/531-5651. 61 units. A/C TV TEL. Winter, from $130 double; from $220 suite. Off-season $90 double; $150 suite. Additional person $10 extra. Group packages available. 18% gratuity added to room service. AE, CB, DC, DISC, MC, V. Limited parking available on street.

Although there isn't much in the way of views or amenities, this small hotel just north of South Beach is pleasant and not too far from the action. Every detail of the 1936 building has been meticulously restored, from one of the beach's first operating elevators to the period steamer trunk in the lobby. The modest rooms are outfitted in art deco furnishings, with pretty tropical prints and all the modern amenities. Just one short block from a good stretch of sand, the hotel is also within walking distance to shops and inexpensive restaurants. A landscaped pool area is a great place to lounge in the sun. There's a small fitness center and conference facilities. A tiny restaurant serves continental breakfast; beer and wine can be purchased in the lobby.

INEXPENSIVE

Compostela Motel. 9040 Collins Ave., Miami Beach, FL 33154. ☎ **305/861-3083**. Fax 305/861-2996. 20 units. A/C TV TEL. Winter, from $75 suite; from $65 one-bedroom apt.; $55 efficiency. Off-season, from $65 suite; $55 one-bedroom apt.; $45 efficiency. Additional person $10 extra. Children 17 and under stay free in parents' room. AE, MC, V. Free parking.

At this hotel, you get a lot of space and a great location for a low price. The owners of the Compostela have recently set to renovating their three buildings, all within walking distance of the exclusive Bal Harbour Shops and many good shopping and dining areas. Although the buildings were full of run-down efficiencies for many years, the new interiors are really quite nice. All are carpeted and most have full kitchenettes. You'll find no fancy lobby, no doorman to greet you as you enter, and no amenities to speak of save an outdoor pool and laundry facilities. But you're across the street from a great beach, the area is safe, and the staff is courteous, though at some hours only Spanish speakers are available.

Suez Oceanfront Resort. 18215 Collins Ave., Sunny Isles, FL 33160. ☎ **800/327-5278** or 305/932-0661. Fax 305/937-0058. 150 units. A/C TV TEL. Winter $67–$100 double; $82–$117 suite. Off-season $39–$85 double; $54–$100 suite. Kitchenettes $10–$15 extra. 15% gratuity added to food. AE, DC, MC, V. Free parking.

Guarded by an undersize replica of Egypt's famed Sphinx, the campy Suez offers decent rooms on the beach, where most of the other old hotels have turned condo. Its Sunny Isles location is actually closer to Hallandale in Broward County than to South Beach.

The strict orange-and-yellow motif makes the Suez look more like a fast-food restaurant than anything in ancient Egypt. The thatch umbrellas over the beach lounges and the Spanish-style fountains in the courtyard add to the confused decor. There are several convenient pluses, however, like a low-priced restaurant, fully equipped kitchenettes in some rooms, a large heated outdoor pool, a kiddie pool, an exercise room with saunas, lighted tennis courts, and a free laundromat. A kitschy but pleasant and inexpensive lounge reminds you that you are indeed in a tropical paradise. For the price, it's not a bad place, and you can say you saw the pyramids.

4 Key Biscayne

There are only a couple of hotels here, not counting the super-luxurious Grand Bay Resort, due to be completed in 2000. All are on the beach, and room rates are uniformly high. If you can afford it, Key Biscayne is a great place to stay. The island is far enough from the mainland to make it feel like a secluded tropical paradise, yet close enough to Downtown to take advantage of everything Miami has to offer.

Silver Sands Oceanfront Motel. 301 Ocean Dr., Key Biscayne, FL 33149. ☎ **305/361-5441.** Fax 305/361-5477. 56 units. A/C TV TEL. Winter $149–$179 minisuite; $300 cottage; $385 oceanfront suite. Off-season $109–$129 minisuite; $200 cottage; $385 oceanfront suite. Additional person $30 extra. Children 14 and under stay free in parents' room. Weekly rates available. AE, DC, MC, V. Free parking.

If Key Biscayne is where you want to be and you don't want to pay the prices of the next-door Sonesta, consider this quaint, one-story motel. Everything is crisp and clean, and the pleasant staff will help with anything you may need, including baby-sitting. But it's certainly no resort. Except for the beach and pool, you'll have to leave the premises for almost everything, including food. The well-appointed rooms are very beachy, sporting a tropical motif and simple furnishings; extras include micro-waves, refrigerators, and coffeemakers. Oceanfront suites have the added convenience of full kitchens with stoves and pantries. You'll sit poolside with an unpretentious set of Latin American families and Europeans who have come for a long and simple vacation—and get it.

Amenities: Secretarial services, twice-daily maid service. VCRs in some rooms, medium-sized outdoor pool, beach, kitchenettes, coin laundry.

✪ **Sonesta Beach Resort Key Biscayne.** 350 Ocean Dr., Key Biscayne, FL 33149. ☎ **800/SONESTA** or 305/361-2021. Fax 305/361-3096. 303 units. A/C MINIBAR TV TEL. Winter $255–$395 double; $600–$1,650 suite or villa. Off-season $195–$315 and $160–$275 double; $525–$1,325 suite or villa. Up to two children 17 and under stay free in parents' room. 15% gratuity added to food and beverage bills. Special packages available. AE, CB, DC, DISC, EURO, JCB, MC, V. Valet parking $12.

One of South Florida's most private and luxurious resorts, the Sonesta is an ideal retreat. From the moment the valets, clad in tropical prints, take your car, you'll know you've entered a world of no concern. Each of the nearly 300 rooms has a private balcony or terrace. Sports, from tennis to jet skiing, are available all around you. Although you may not want to leave the lush grounds, Bill Baggs State Recreation Area and the area's best beaches are right at hand, and if you choose to venture out, you're only about 15 minutes from Miami Beach and even closer to the mainland and Coconut Grove. The vacation homes have fully equipped kitchenettes.

Dining/Diversions: The hotel has four restaurants, including Purple Dolphin, for "New World" cuisine, and Two Dragons, for Chinese. There's also an excellent sea-food restaurant with a terrace, and several lounges and bars. The restaurants regularly draw locals, who have few dining options on "The Key."

Amenities: Concierge, room service (24 hours), dry cleaning and laundry, news-paper delivery, nightly turndown, baby-sitting, secretarial services, express checkout, complimentary transportation to and from Miami's shopping districts. Children are well cared for, with day and night field trips and activities. Olympic-size pool, beach, large state-of-the-art fitness center, Jacuzzi, sauna, nearby jogging track, bicycle rental, access to nearby championship golf course, game rooms, children's programs, elabo-rate business center, conference rooms, car-rental and tour desks, sundeck, nine tennis courts (three lighted), water-sports equipment rental, beauty salon, boutiques.

5 Downtown

Most Downtown hotels cater primarily to business travelers, but tourists can get well-located, good-quality accommodations, too. Although business hotels are expensive, quality and service are of a high standard. Look for discounts and packages for the weekend, when offices are closed and rooms often go empty. Downtown is closest to some of Miami's best shopping. Be warned that after dark there's virtually nothing to do outside of the hotels; the streets are often deserted and crime can be a problem.

In downtown Miami, the **Wyndham** (☎ **800/WYNDHAM** or 305/374-0000) at 1601 Biscayne Blvd., above the Omni Mall, is a good option for the thrifty business traveler. It has a full business center as well as a heated rooftop pool. It's just a few minutes away from Bayside and Miami Beach. Rates are from $95 to $170.

VERY EXPENSIVE

✪ **Hotel Inter-Continental Miami.** 100 Chopin Plaza, Miami, FL 33131. ☎ **800/327-3005** or 305/577-1000. Fax 305/577-0384. Telex 153127. 644 units. A/C MINIBAR TV TEL. Winter $209–$289 double; $325–$450 suite. Off-season $159–$259 double; $325–$450 suite. Additional person $20 extra. Weekend and other packages available. AE, CB, DC, DISC, MC, V. Valet parking $12.

Especially since the $5-million renovation of all their guest rooms and some common areas, the Inter-Continental is downtown's swankiest hotel. It boasts more marble than a mausoleum (both inside and out), but it's warmed by colorful, homey touches. The five-story lobby features a marble centerpiece sculpture by Henry Moore and is topped by a pleasing skylight. Plenty of plants, palm trees, and brightly colored wicker chairs also add charm and enliven the otherwise stark space. Brilliant downtown and bay views add luster to already posh rooms, outfitted with every convenience known to hotel-dom, including VCRs. Some suites have fully equipped kitchenettes.

Dining/Diversions: Three restaurants cover all price ranges and are complemented by two full-service lounges.

Amenities: Concierge, room service, dry cleaning and laundry, newspaper delivery, twice-daily maid service, express checkout, free refreshments in lobby, babysitting. Olympic-size heated outdoor pool, health spa, sundeck, jogging track, large business center, 15 conference rooms, self-service laundromat, car-rental desk, travel-agency/tour desk, beauty salon and barbershop, shopping arcade, access to nearby golf course.

MODERATE

Everglades Hotel. 244 Biscayne Blvd., Miami, FL 33136. ☎ **800/327-5700** or 305/379-5461. Fax 305/577-8445. 371 units. A/C TV TEL. Year-round $92 double; $125 suite. AE, CB, DC, DISC, MC, V. Parking $7.

This hotel has been around about forever on Downtown's active Biscayne Boulevard. And it shows: The lobby and rooms border on dive quality. Many traveling business types and Latin American families stay here, however, because of its convenient, safe location, low rates, and many services, which include a bank in the building. It's also one of the only Downtown properties with a pool. The hotel is near the highways and Metrorail, and there's great shopping across the street at Bayside Marketplace.

Miami River Inn. 118 SW South River Dr., Miami, FL 33130. ☎ **305/325-0045**. Fax 305/325-9227. E-mail: miami100@ix.netcom.com. A/C TV TEL. 40 units. Winter $89–$120. Off-season $69–$89 double. Rates include continental breakfast. Additional person $15 extra; children 11 and under stay free in parents' room. AE, CB, DC, DISC, MC, V. Free parking.

The Miami River is a great deal for those who want to be in a central location—close to the highway, public transportation, downtown eateries, and museums. Extras include a small outdoor pool, Jacuzzi, and complimentary coffee and wine in the lobby. Although many predict that the riverfront will soon undergo a renaissance, for now the area is still a bit seedy. Don't venture too far out of the enclave, unless you want to see the ugly underside of Miami.

Rooms are nicely furnished with a mix of antiques from all eras and gentle wallpaper prints. In the common area is a collection of books about old Miami, with histories of this land's former owners: Julia Tuttle, William Brickell, and Henry Flagler. The low year-round rates make this hotel an attractive option for those who appreciate old things. There's a small outdoor pool on the premises and a Jacuzzi.

Riande Continental Bayside. 146 Biscayne Blvd., Miami, FL 33132. ☎ **800/RIANDE-1** or 305/358-4555. Fax 305/371-5253. 250 units. A/C MINIBAR TV TEL. Winter $115–$175 double. Off-season $85–$155 double. Frommer's readers get a 20% discount. Children stay free in parents' room. AE, DC, MC, V. Parking $7.50.

Like its sister hotel in South Beach, this Riande caters to a Latin American crowd that descends on Downtown in droves to shop for clothes and electronics. The location is ideal, only steps away from a Bayside shopping center, many great ethnic restaurants, and a Metrorail stop. The reasonable prices and helpful staff are reason enough to consider staying here, if you want to be right in downtown Miami.

Sheraton Brickell Point Miami. 495 Brickell Ave., Miami, FL 33131. ☎ **800/325-3535** or 305/373-6000. Fax 305/374-2279. Telex 6811701. 598 units. A/C TV TEL. Winter $129–$169 double; $305–$375 suite. Off-season $129–$159 double; $275–$375 suite. Additional person $10. Children under 18 stay free in parents' room. Senior discounts and weekend and other packages available. AE, CB, DC, DISC, MC, V. Parking $11.

This Downtown hotel's waterfront location is its greatest asset. Nestled between Brickell Park and Biscayne Bay, the Sheraton is set back from the main road and surrounded by a pleasant bayfront walkway. Just as clean and reliable as other hotels in the Sheraton chain, Brickell Point also has good water views from most of the rooms. Its identical rooms are well furnished and comfortable. There isn't much to do in the area, but you're within a short drive to anything Miami has to offer.

Dining/Diversions: Ashley's, overlooking Biscayne Bay, serves continental and American cuisine. The Coco Loco Club serves you indoors and out.

Amenities: Concierge services, room service (7am–11:30pm), laundry and dry-cleaning services, newspaper delivery, nightly turndown, in-room massage, twice-daily maid service upon request, baby-sitting, express checkout, valet parking, free refreshments in the lobby. Large heated outdoor pool, state-of-the-art health club, access to nearby health club, sundeck, nearby golf course, game room, adequate business center, conference rooms, car-rental and tour desk, small gift shop.

6 West Miami/Airport Area

As Miami continues to grow at its rapid pace, expansion has begun westward, where land is plentiful. Several resorts have taken advantage of the space to build world-class tennis and golf courses. While there's no sea to swim in, a plethora of facilities makes up for the lack of an ocean view.

There are dozens of chain hotels by the airport, including a **Sheraton Gateway** at 3900 NW 21st St. (☎ **800/933-1100**) and a **Holiday Inn Select** at 950 NW LeJeune (☎ **800/428-9582**).

Don Shula's Hotel and Golf Club. Main St., Miami Lakes, FL 33014. ☎ **800/24-SHULA** or 305/821-1150. Fax 305/820-8190. 330 units. A/C TV TEL. Winter, from $230 double; $279 suite. Off-season $139–$159 double; $189–$209 suite. Additional person $10 extra. Children stay free in parents' room. Business packages available. AE, CB, DC, MC, V.

Guests come to Shula's mostly for the golf, but there's plenty here to keep non-golfers busy, too. Opened in 1992 to much fanfare from the sports and business community, Shula's resort is an all-encompassing oasis in the middle of a highly planned residential neighborhood, complete with a Main Street and nearby shopping facilities—a good thing, since the site is more than a 20-minute drive on the highways from anything. The guest rooms, located in the main building or surrounding the golf course, are plain but pretty, and come with VCRs (on request).

Dining: The award-winning Shula's Steak House and the more casual Steak House Two rank in the top 10 nationwide. They serve huge Angus beef steaks and seafood. Another restaurant on the premises serves health food.

Amenities: Concierge, room service, newspaper delivery, express checkout, valet parking, free morning coffee in the lobby. Large outdoor swimming pool, Don Shula's state-of-the-art athletic club (with aerobics, Cybex equipment, and trainers who assist all exercisers), Jacuzzi, sauna, sundeck, 16 outdoor tennis courts, racquetball courts, two golf courses (one championship course), 22 conference and banquet rooms, beauty salon, and shopping arcade.

✪ Doral Golf Resort and Spa. 4400 NW 87th Ave., Miami, FL 33178. ☎ **800/22-DORAL**, 800/71-DORAL, or 305/592-2000. Fax 305/594-4682. 623 units (plus an additional 58 suites at the spa). A/C MINIBAR TV TEL. Winter $225–$315 double; $315–$945 suite; $350–$1,280 spa suite. Off-season $95–$275 double; $175–$380 golf suite; $350–$825 spa suite. Additional person $35 extra. One or two children 15 and under stay free in parents' room. 18% service charge added. Golf and spa packages available. AE, CB, DC, DISC, MC, V. Valet parking $8.50.

The Doral epitomizes the luxury resort in Florida. While the pamperings in the spa attract worldwide attention, the next-door golf resort hosts world-class tournaments and is home to the Blue Monster Course—rated one of the top 25 in the country. The season is booked well in advance by those who have been here before or have just read about the fantastic offerings on this 650-acre, fully self-contained resort. It's just moments from the Miami airport.

The spacious lobbies and dining areas shimmer with polished marble, mirrors, and gold. The rooms, too, are luxuriously large and tastefully decorated; big windows allow views of the tropical gardens or golf courses below. The resort is surrounded by warehouses and office buildings.

Dining/Diversions: The Spa restaurant serves delicious low-fat cuisine, including reduced-calorie desserts. Other options include a cafe with super Italian sandwiches, salads, and pasta. A sports bar at the golf club offers excellent club fare.

Amenities: Concierge, room service, laundry and dry cleaning, newspaper delivery, evening turndown, in-room massage in spa suites by appointment, baby-sitting, secretarial services, express checkout, courtesy car or limo, shuttle to the Doral Ocean Resort. Olympic-size outdoor heated pool, access to the spa ($25), small exercise room, steam room and sauna, jogging track, bicycle rentals, extensive golf facilities, game rooms, children's programs during the holidays, business center, conference wing, car-rental desk, sundeck, 15 outdoor tennis courts, tour and activities desks, beauty salon, boutiques.

Miami International Airport Hotel. P.O. Box 997510. NW 20th St. and LeJeune Rd., Airport Terminal Concourse E., Miami, FL 33299-7510. ☎ **800/327-1276** or 305/871-4100. Fax 305/871-0800. 260 units. A/C TV TEL. Winter $135–$185 double; $250–$650 suite. Off-season $150–$170 double; $250–$265 suite. Additional person $10. Up to two children under 12 stay free. AE, CB, DC, EURO, JCB, MC, V. Parking $9.

If you need to be at the airport and want excellent service, this is your best bet. I don't know of a nicer airport hotel, and you can't beat the convenience—it's actually in the airport at Concourse E. You'll find every amenity of a first-class tourist hotel here, including a large rooftop pool, health club, Jacuzzi, sauna, sundeck, racquetball courts, jogging track, small business center, conference room, beauty salon, tour desk, boutiques, and several cocktail lounges and restaurants. The rooms are modern, clean, and spacious, with industrial-grade carpeting. The furnishings are nondescript but tasteful. You might think you'd be deafened by the roar of the planes, but all of the rooms have been sound-proofed and actually allow very little noise. In addition, the hotel has modern security systems and is extremely safe.

7 North Dade

✪ **Turnberry Isle Resort and Club.** 19999 W. Country Club Dr., Aventura, FL 33180. ☎ **800/327-7028** or 305/932-6200. Fax 305/933-6550. 340 units. A/C MINIBAR TV TEL. Winter $375–$495 resort room or suite; $295–$335 yacht club room or suite. Off-season $195–$300 resort room or suite; $150–$175 yacht club room or suite. AE, DC, DISC, MC, V. Valet parking $8; free self-parking.

A top-rated resort, this gorgeous 300-acre compound has every possible facility for active guests, particularly golfers. You'll pay a lot to stay at here—but it's worth it. The main attractions are two newly renovated Trent Jones courses, available only to members and guests of the hotel. Impeccable service from check-in to checkout brings loyal fans back for more. The North Miami Beach location is about halfway between Fort Lauderdale and Miami, but you'll find excellent shopping and some of the best dining in Miami right in the neighborhood.

Unless you're into boating, the higher-priced resort rooms are where you'll want to stay. Here you're steps from perfect spa facilities and the renowned Veranda restaurant. The well-proportioned rooms are gorgeously tiled to match the Mediterranean-style architecture. The bathrooms even have a color TV mounted within reach of the whirlpool bathtubs. Video rental is available.

Dining/Diversions: There are six restaurants, including the Veranda, which serves healthful and tropical New World cuisine in an elegant dining room. The several bars and lounges, including a popular disco, also have enough entertainment and local flavor to keep anyone busy for weeks.

Amenities: Concierge, room service (24 hours), same-day laundry service, newspaper delivery, in-room massage, nightly turndown, twice-daily maid service, baby-sitting services, express checkout. Four large swimming pools, complete state-of-the-art health spa, beach, Jacuzzi, sauna, two 36-hole golf courses, nature trails, sundeck, 24 outdoor tennis courts (including 16 lighted for night play), squash/racquetball courts, water-sports equipment, 3-mile jogging course, bicycle rental, game room, children's center and programs, large business center, four large meeting and conference centers, tour desk, boutiques, limousine and car-rental desks, helipad, beauty salon.

8 Coral Gables

Coconut Grove eases into Coral Gables, which extends north toward Miami International Airport. "The Gables," as it's affectionately known, was one of Miami's original planned communities and is still among the city's prettiest neighborhoods. It's close to the shops along the Miracle Mile and the University of Miami. Two popular and well-priced chain hotels are a **Holiday Inn** (☎ **800/327-5476** or 667-5611) at 1350 S. Dixie Hwy. and a **Howard Johnson** (☎ **800/446-4656** or 305/665-7501) at 1430 S. Dixie Hwy., both located across the street from the University of Miami.

VERY EXPENSIVE

✪ Biltmore Hotel Coral Gables. 1200 Anastasia Ave., Coral Gables, FL 33134. ☎ **800/ 727-1926**, 305/445-1926, or Westin at 800/228-3000. Fax 305/442-9496. 275 units. A/C TV TEL. Winter $259 double; $379–$479 suite. Off-season $189 double; $309–409 suite. Additional person $20 extra. Children 17 and under stay free in parents' room. Special packages available. AE, CB, DC, DISC, MC, V. Valet parking $9.

Just 5 minutes from the airport and excellent dining and shopping selections, and about 20 minutes from Miami Beach, this hotel is a wonderful option for those seeking a luxurious getaway. The Biltmore is the oldest Coral Gables hotel and a city landmark. In 1996, it was granted national recognition as an official National Historical Landmark—one of only two operating hotels in Florida to receive the designation. Always a popular destination for golfers, including President Clinton, the Biltmore is situated on a lush rolling 18-hole course that is as challenging as it is beautiful.

Now under the management of the Westin Hotel group, the hotel boasts large rooms decorated with tasteful period reproductions, as well as high-tech amenities like VCRs (on request). The enormous lobby, with its 45-foot ceilings, serves as an entry point for hundreds of weddings and business meetings each year. Rising above the Spanish-style estate is a majestic 300-foot copper-clad tower, modeled after the Giralda bell tower in Seville and visible throughout the city. Over the years, the Biltmore has passed through many incarnations (for example, it was used as a VA hospital after World War II), but is now back to its original 1926 splendor.

Dining/Diversions: An elegant European restaurant serves excellent French/Italian cuisine nightly and champagne brunch on Sunday. An impressive wine cellar and cigar room are popular with local connoisseurs. The more casual Courtyard Café and Poolside Grille both serve three meals daily. There's also a lounge and piano bar where drinks are accompanied by live music nightly.

Amenities: Concierge, room service (24 hours), laundry and dry cleaning, newspaper delivery, nightly turndown on request, twice-daily maid service, baby-sitting, secretarial services, express checkout. Kitchenettes in tower suite, VCR and video rentals, 21,000-square-foot swimming pool surrounded by arched walkways and classical sculptures, state-of-the-art health club, full-service spa, sauna, 18-hole golf course, elaborate business center, conference rooms, car rental through concierge, sundeck, 10 lighted tennis courts, beauty salon, boutiques.

Hyatt Regency Coral Gables. 50 Alhambra Plaza, Coral Gables, FL 33134. ☎ **800/ 233-1234** or 305/441-1234. Fax 305/442-0520. Telex 529706. 242 units. A/C MINIBAR TV TEL. Winter $260 double; $299–$1,800 suite. Off-season $150 double; $175–$1,800 suite. Additional person $25. Packages and senior discounts available. AE, CB, DC, DISC, MC, V. Valet parking $10; self-parking $9.

High on style, comfort, and price, this Hyatt is part of Coral Gables' Alhambra, an office-hotel complex with a Mediterranean motif. The building itself is gorgeous, designed with pink stone, arched entrances, grand courtyards, and tile roofs. Inside you'll find overstuffed chairs on marble floors, surrounded by opulent antiques and chandeliers. The hotel opened in 1987, but, like many historical buildings in the neighborhood, the Alhambra attempts to mimic something much older and much farther away.

The good-size rooms are outfitted with everything you'd expect from a top hotel— terry robes and all. Most furnishings are antique.

Dining/Diversions: A good New World cuisine restaurant serves a varied menu with many local specialties. Alcazaba is a fun Latin-style dance spot (see "Latin Clubs" in chapter 10, "Miami After Dark").

Amenities: Full concierge services, room service (6am–midnight), same-day laundry and dry-cleaning services, newspaper delivery, nightly turndown on request, in-room massage, baby-sitting arrangements available, secretarial services, express checkout, valet parking. Large outdoor heated pool, health club with Nautilus equipment, Jacuzzi, two saunas, nearby golf course, basic business center, conference rooms, small gift shop.

EXPENSIVE

Hotel Place St. Michel. 162 Alcazar Ave., Coral Gables, FL 33134. ☎ **800/848-HOTEL** or 305/444-1666. Fax 305/529-0074. 27 units. A/C TV TEL. Winter (including continental breakfast) $165 double; $200 suite. Off-season $125 double; $160 suite. Additional person $10 extra. Children 11 and under stay free in parents' room. AE, DC, MC, V. Parking $7.

This unusual little hotel in the heart of Coral Gables is one of the city's most romantic options. The accommodations and hospitality are straight out of old-world Europe, complete with dark wood-paneled walls, cozy beds, beautiful antiques, and a quiet elegance that seems startlingly out of place in trendy Miami. Everything here is charming—from the parquet floors to the paddle fans. One-of-a-kind furnishings make each guest room special. Guests are treated to fresh fruit baskets upon arrival and enjoy every imaginable service throughout their stay.

Dining/Diversions: The Restaurant St. Michel is a very romantic and elegant dining choice. A lounge and deli complete the hotel options.

Amenities: Concierge, room service, laundry and dry cleaning, newspaper delivery, evening turndown, in-room massage, twice-daily maid service, complimentary continental breakfast.

The Omni Colonnade Hotel. 180 Aragon Ave. (at Ponce de Leon and Miracle Mile), Coral Gables, FL 33134. ☎ **800/THE OMNI** or 305/441-2600. Fax 305/445-3929. 157 units. A/C MINIBAR TV TEL. Winter $195–$265 double; $405 suite. Off-season $125–$225 double; $365 suite. Packages available. AE, CB, DC, DISC, MC, V. Valet parking $10.

The Colonnade occupies part of a large historic building, originally built by Coral Gables's founder George Merrick in 1926. Faithful to its original style, the hotel is a successful amalgam of new and old, with an emphasis on modern conveniences. The structure stands 14 elegant stories high, although guest rooms occupy only four floors. It's popular with business travelers.

The oversized rooms are worthy of the hotel's rates. They feature sitting areas, historic photographs, marble counters, gold-finished faucets, and solid wood furnishings. Thoughtful extras include complimentary shoe-shines and champagne upon arrival.

Dining/Diversions: Doc Dammers Saloon is a good happy hour for the 30-something crowd. There's live entertainment on weekends.

Amenities: 24-hour concierge and room service, same-day laundry and dry-cleaning service, newspaper delivery, evening turndown on request, in-room massage, twice-daily maid service on request, baby-sitting, express checkout, valet parking, free morning coffee and tea in the lobby. Heated outdoor pool on rooftop, small modern rooftop fitness center, Jacuzzi, sundeck, large conference centers and meeting rooms, laundromat, car-rental and tour desks, gift shop and shopping arcade.

INEXPENSIVE

Riviera Inn. 5100 Riviera Dr. (on U.S. 1), Coral Gables, FL 33146. ☎ **800/368-8602** or 305/665-3528. 30 units. A/C TV TEL. Winter $68 rms; $78 efficiencies. Off-season $55 rms; $78 efficiencies. 10% discount for seniors and AAA members. AE, CB, DC, DISC, MC, V.

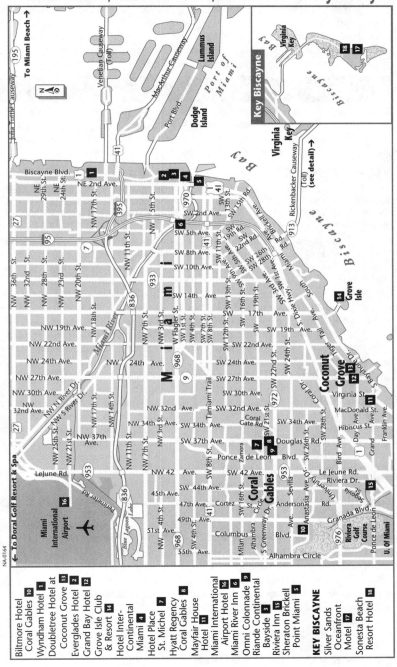

Biltmore Hotel Coral Gables **10**
Wyndham Hotel **1**
Doubletree Hotel at Coconut Grove **13**
Everglades Hotel **2**
Grand Bay Hotel **12**
Grove Isle Club & Resort **14**
Hotel Inter-Continental Miami **4**
Hotel Place St. Michel **7**
Hyatt Regency Coral Gables **8**
Mayfair House Hotel **11**
Miami International Airport Hotel **16**
Miami River Inn **6**
Omni Colonnade **9**
Riande Continental Bayside **3**
Riviera Inn **15**
Sheraton Brickell Point Miami **5**

KEY BISCAYNE

Silver Sands Oceanfront Motel **17**
Sonesta Beach Resort Hotel **18**

Besides the newly renovated Holiday Inn down the road, this family-owned motel is the best discount option in the area. The comfortable and clean two-story property, dating from 1954, has a small pool and is set back from the road, so that the rooms are all relatively quiet. Vending machines are the only choice for refreshments, but guests are near many great dining spots. You can also choose to stay in one of the efficiencies, which all have fully stocked kitchens.

9   Coconut Grove

This intimate enclave hugs the shores of Biscayne Bay, just south of U.S. 1 and about 10 minutes from the beaches. The Grove is a great place to stay, offering ample nightlife, excellent restaurants, and beautiful surroundings. Unfortunately, all hotel rates are very high. There are no chains here.

VERY EXPENSIVE

Grand Bay Hotel. 2669 S. Bayshore Dr., Coconut Grove, FL 33133. ☎ **800/327-2788** or 305/858-9600. Fax 305/859-2026. E-mail: grandbay@von.net. 178 units. A/C MINIBAR TV TEL. Winter, from $295 double. Off-season $255 double. Year-round $350–$1,400 suite. Additional person $20 extra. Packages available. AE, CB, DC, MC, V. Valet parking $15.

The Grand Bay opened in 1983 and immediately won praise as one of the most elegant hotels in the world. This stunning pyramid-shaped hotel is a masterpiece both inside and out. The rooms are luxurious, each featuring high-quality linens, comfortable overstuffed love seats and chairs, a large writing desk, and all the amenities you'd expect in deluxe accommodations, including VCRs and video rentals. It has recently added ironing boards, irons, and voice mail to all rooms as well. Original art and armfuls of fresh flowers are generously displayed throughout.

The Grand Bay consistently attracts wealthy, high-profile people, and it basks in its image as a rendezvous for royalty, socialites, and superstars. Guests come here to be pampered and to see and be seen.

Dining/Diversions: The hotel's Grand Café is excellent. Drinks are served in the Ciga Bar, and the Lobby Lounge offers a traditional afternoon tea.

Amenities: Concierge, room service (24 hours), same-day laundry and dry cleaning, newspaper delivery, evening turndown, masseuse on call, twice-daily maid service, baby-sitting, secretarial services, express checkout, courtesy limousine service to Cocowalk, free refreshments in the lobby. Heated indoor pool, small health club, access to nearby health club, Jacuzzi, sauna, VCR and video rentals, sundeck, watersports equipment rental, bicycle rental, good-sized business center, conference rooms, car-rental and activities desks, beauty salon, gift shop, nearby golf course.

Grove Isle Club and Resort. Four Grove Isle Dr., Coconut Grove, FL 33133. ☎ **800/88-GROVE** or 305/858-8300. Fax 305/854-6702. 49 units. A/C TV TEL. Winter $245–$325 double; $475 suite. Off-season $195–$295 double; $475 suite. Rates include breakfast. Children under 14 stay free. Additional person $20. AE, DC, MC, V. Free valet parking.

A 1994 renovation has turned Grove Isle into one of the nicest spots to stay in Coconut Grove. Its location is stunning. From the lobby and many rooms, guests look out onto glimmering Biscayne Bay, where sailboats drift lazily about and dolphins sometimes leap circles in the clear blue water. You'd almost think the property is on an island; actually, it's only a few minutes from Coconut Grove's business district.

Grove Isle feels like a country club. Everyone dresses in white and pastels, and if they're not on their way to a set of tennis, they're not in a rush to get anywhere. Rooms are nicely furnished, as is the elegant but uncluttered lobby.

Dining/Diversions: Mark's Place offers a relaxed menu of New World cuisine.

Amenities: Concierge service, room service (6:30am–10pm), laundry and dry-cleaning services, newspaper delivery, nightly turndown, in-room massage, twice-daily maid service, baby-sitting, secretarial services, express checkout, valet parking, free coffee in the lobby. VCRs, movie channels, video rental delivered to room ($5), large heated outdoor pool, deluxe fitness facilities, 12 outdoor tennis courts, water-sports equipment rental available, jogging track, nature trails, conference rooms, beauty salon.

Mayfair House Hotel. 3000 Florida Ave., Coconut Grove, FL 33133. ☎ **800/433-4555** or 305/441-0000. Fax 305/441-1647. 182 units. A/C MINIBAR TV TEL. Winter $235–$450 suite; $450 penthouse. Off-season $205–$440 suite; $450 penthouse. Packages available. AE, DC, DISC, MC, V. Valet parking $15; self-parking $6.

If you want to be in the Grove, this hotel is a good choice. Situated inside the posh Mayfair Shops complex, the all-suite Mayfair House is about as centrally located as you can get. Each guest unit has been individually designed. All are extremely comfortable, with extras like VCRs. Some suites are downright opulent and include a private, outdoor, Japanese-style hot tub. The top-floor terraces offer good views, and all are hidden from the street by leaves and latticework. Since the lobby is in a shopping mall, recreation is confined to the roof, where a small pool, sauna, and snack bar are located.

Dining/Diversions: The Mayfair Grill serves a varied menu with particularly good steaks and seafood. There's also a rooftop snack bar for poolside snacks and a private nightclub open late.

Amenities: Concierge and room service (24 hours), dry cleaning, newspaper delivery, nightly turndown, twice-daily maid service, secretarial services, express checkout. VCRs and video rentals, outdoor pool, access to nearby health club, Jacuzzi, elaborate business center, conference rooms.

6 Dining

Florida's chefs have taken their place at the international culinary table. Norman van Aken of Norman's received the prestigious James Beard award as Best American Chef in the Southeast in 1997, following in the footsteps of Allen Susser of Chef Allen's who took the award in 1994. *Esquire* magazine cited Johnny Vinczencz of Astor Place as a "Chef To Keep Your Eye On," and a few years ago named Jonathan Eismann's Pacific Time the best new restaurant. These chefs, like so many visitors, are attracted to the tropical environment of Miami, where produce grows in backyards and fish are so fresh they're still flapping on the prep line.

No longer do chefs get their start here with hopes of moving on to New York or Los Angeles. Quite the contrary. There are literally hundreds of successful restaurants that have opened first in the Northeast and then have opted to join the other successful outlets in sunny South Florida. They bring with them recipes and distinctive ideas about food that add even more variety to this hodgepodge of regional cuisine known as "New World."

This regional style of cooking is hard to define. It encompasses the varied tastes of the Caribbean, especially Cuba, as well as an old-Floridian and California nouvelle influence. The idea is to use locally available tropical ingredients, such as mango, papaya, avocado, jicama, coconut, snapper, lobster, and stone crab. Though at times it can be more than a bit overwhelming, in general, the results are deliciously exciting. Think of mango-infused oils over jerk tuna with jicama slaw served in a cracked coconut with yuca fries. You may need a translator. Welcome to the new world.

In addition to the exciting inventions of native chefs, you can always find the exotic foods of almost every ethnicity—from Cuban to Haitian to Jamaican to Vietnamese.

Many restaurants keep extended hours in season (roughly December to April), and may close for lunch and/or on Mondays, when the traffic is slower. Call for updated schedules. If you want to picnic on the beach or pick up some dessert, check out the gourmet food shops, green markets, and bakeries listed in chapter 9, "Shopping."

1 Best Bets

- **Best Spot for a Romantic Dinner:** The newly revitalized **Forge Restaurant,** 432 Arthur Godfrey Rd. (at 41st Street), Miami

Beach (☎ 305/538-8533), is where everyone's parents went in the 1950s for a really elegant meal. It's still the most romantic spot in town for black-tie service, stupendous food, and private conversation. For a truly intimate experience, reserve a booth in "The Library," perfect for popping the question.

- **Best Wine List**: The extensive and well-chosen wine list at **Smith & Wollensky,** at South Pointe Park, South Beach (☎ 305/673-2800), beats other Miami restaurants hands-down. The wine list at **The Forge,** 432 Arthur Godfrey Rd, Miami Beach (☎ 305/538-8533), a tome really, encompasses more than 3,000 vintages and 250,000 bottles from all over the world.

- **Best for Kids:** There may not be fun video games in the entryway, but **The Beverly Hills Cafe,** 17850 West Dixie Hwy., North Miami Beach (☎ 305/935-3660), offers simple and delicious kids' meals for less than you'd pay at McDonald's. Who could complain about fresh pasta marinara, turkey and chicken sandwiches, grilled cheese, and burgers all served with fries and a choice of beverage for less than $4? Also good on the beach is **Van Dyke's** at 846 Lincoln Rd., South Beach (☎ 305/534-3600).

- **Best Chinese Cuisine**: **Chrysanthemum,** 1248 Washington Ave., South Beach (☎ 305/531-5656), has the city's very finest Chinese food—by far. The signature dish, chicken with crispy spinach, melts in your mouth while sparking a small flame. The Szechuan menu features lots of spicy favorites made of the very best-quality ingredients.

- **Best Continental Cuisine:** The offerings at **Crystal Café,** 726 41st St., Miami Beach (☎ 305/673-8266), have been dubbed "New Continental" by local food reviewers who rightfully consider it a shame to saddle the menu of this fantastic little spot with the pedestrian-sounding label of plain old "continental."

- **Best Cuban Cuisine:** Cuban restaurants here range from take-out windows to diners to elegant establishments. The food comes in so many different styles that it's hard to choose a "best." If you're looking for a classic and filling Cuban meal, **Versailles,** 3555 SW 8th St., in Little Havana (☎ 305/444-0240), is it. If you want a lighter, more expensive, nouvelle experience, **Yuca** is *el más sabroso* (the most delicious). You can find it in South Beach at 501 Lincoln Rd. (☎ 305/532-9822).

- **Best French Cuisine:** There are plenty of places to enjoy French fare in Miami, but the best is **The Bistro,** 2611 Ponce de Leon Blvd., Coral Gables (☎ 305/754-1707), where typical fare is livened up with uncommon spices and accouterments.

- **Best Italian Cuisine:** With so many good pasta places, it's great to see Miami also knows how to enjoy elegant Italian like they have at **Osteria del Teatro,** 1443 Washington Ave., South Beach (☎ 305/538-7850).

- **Best Seafood:** For all-around good seafood, including tasty stews, ceviche, and shellfish, the **Fishbone Grille,** 650 S. Miami Ave., Downtown (☎ 305/530-1915), is the place to go. The bonus is the price—downright cheap.

- **Best Steakhouse:** There are suddenly dozens of steakhouses in Miami (see box below) but none is as popular as **Shula's,** at 7601 NW 154th St., Miami Lakes (☎ 305/820-8102) and in Miami Beach, at the Alexander Hotel, 5225 Collins Ave. (☎ 305/341-6565). Other steakhouses offer big portions. Shula's are bigger. For a really delicious prime cut at a prime price, try **The Forge,** 432 Arthur Godfrey Rd, Miami Beach (☎ 305/538-8533).

- **Best Late-Night Dining:** You'll find dozens of good 24-hour spots, especially on South Beach, but I say, go to Little Havana, where Casa Juancho, 2436 SW 8th St. (☎ 305/642-2452), serves hearty good meals 'til all hours.

- **Best People-Watching:** Nowhere will you find better people to watch than at the **Blue Door,** at the Delano Hotel, 1685 Collins Ave., South Beach (☎ **305/ 674-6400**). From any seat in the house, you'll have a full parade of hipsters in view.
- **Best Place to Shock Your Relatives:** The food may not be great at **Lucky Cheng's,** 600 Lincoln Rd. (☎ **305/672-1505**), but the entertainment is. There are some seriously talented drag queens here, guaranteed to fool your most astute friends and terrify your uptight relatives. Bring lots of dollar bills for stuffing into plunging necklines.
- **Best Pre-Theater Dinner:** The menu at **Kaleidoscope,** 3112 Commodore Plaza (☎ **305/446-5010**), is so reasonable all the time that they need no special fixed-price pre-theater meal. It's a popular spot for those on their way to the Coconut Grove theater. For an even more elegant experience, try the $28 special at **Norman's,** 21 Almera Ave., in the Gables (☎ **305/446-6767**), offered between 5 and 7pm. Even if you don't have tickets to a show, it's a great way to eat cheap at this otherwise exorbitantly priced hotspot.
- **Best Fast Food: Mrs. Mendoza's,** 1040 Alton Rd., South Beach (☎ **305/ 535-0808**), is the best fast food and the best Mexican in Miami. Time after time, this place turns out the tastiest burritos, tacos, and enchiladas with a super-zingy salsa for the brave. There's another location at Doral Plaza, 9739 NW 41 St. (☎ **305/477-5119**). **Pollo Tropical** ranks a close second with its superior rice and beans and roast chicken. Plus, it has drive-through windows at most locations for unbeatable speed and convenience. Locations include 1454 Alton Rd., Miami Beach (☎ **305/672-8888**); 11806 Biscayne Blvd. North Miami (☎ **305/ 895-0274**); and 18710 S. Dixie Hwy. (at 186th Street), South Miami (☎ **305/ 254 0666**). Check the phone book for others.
- **Best Brunch:** The combination of sensational food and lively jazz makes **Astor Place** in the Astor Hotel, 956 Washington Ave, South Beach (☎ **305/672-7217**), a great spot for Sunday brunch.
- **Best Happy Hour:** The food at **John Martin's,** 253 Miracle Mile, in Coral Gables (☎ **305/445-3777**), tastes even better when you've had one of their single-malt scotches or a pint of ale. Professionals and Irish nationals complete the scene at this weekday gala from 5 to 7pm. Drinkers can feast on hot pizza, chicken wings, cheeses, and fruits. Well drinks are usually 50 to 75¢ each. Another good deal can be had at **Monty's,** downstairs at 400 Alton Road on South Beach (☎ **305/ 672-1148**). Not only are drinks half price between 4 and 8pm weekdays, but you can also get great deals on shellfish and raw bar items. Stone crab claws are three for $5, and shrimps, oysters, or clams are two for $1.
- **Best Ice Cream:** Nothing's better than a cool cone in the middle of a hot day at the beach. Surprisingly, there aren't a lot of fresh ice cream places worth getting excited about. One notable exception is the **Frieze** at 947 Lincoln Rd., South Beach (☎ **305/538-2028**). It does mango, banana, guanabana, mamey, coconut, and anything else in season, plus all the usual chocolatey specialties.

2 Restaurants by Cuisine

AMERICAN

Beverly Hills Cafe (North Dade, *I*)
Biscayne Miracle Mile Cafeteria
  (Coral Gables, *I*)

Blue Door (South Beach, *VE*)
Christy's (Coral Gables, *VE*)
Curry's (Miami Beach, *I*)

Key to Abbreviations: *E* = Expensive; *I* = Inexpensive; *M* = Moderate; *VE* = Very Expensive

The Forge Restaurant
(Miami Beach, *VE*)
Gables Diner (Coral Gables, *M*)
Here Comes the Sun
(North Dade, *I*)
Kaleidoscope (Coconut Grove, *M*)
News Café (South Beach, *I*)
News Cafe in the Grove
(Coconut Grove, *I*)
Sergio's (Coral Gables, *I*)
Sheldon's Drugs (Miami Beach, *I*)
The Strand (South Beach, *E*)
Sundays on the Bay
(Key Biscayne, *E*)
Tony Roma's Famous For Ribs
(West Dade, *M*)
Van Dyke Cafe (South Beach, *I*)

ASIAN

Lucky Cheng's (South Beach, *E*)
Pacific Time (South Beach, *VE*)

BARBECUE

Shorty's (South Miami, *I*)
Tony Roma's (West Dade, *I*)

BISTRO

Jeffrey's (South Beach, *M*)

CANTONESE

The Red Lantern
(Coconut Grove, *M*)

CONTINENTAL

Cafe Hammock
(South Miami, *M*)
Crystal Café (Miami Beach, *E*)
Green Street Cafe
(Coconut Grove, *M*)
Jeffrey's (South Beach, *M*)
The Lagoon (North Dade, *M*)
The Palm (Miami Beach, *E*)
Rusty Pelican (Key Biscayne, *E*)

CREPES

The Crepe Maker (Downtown, *I*)
The Crepe Maker Cafe
(South Miami, *I*)

CUBAN/SPANISH

Casa Juancho (Little Havana, *M*)
La Carreta (Little Havana, *I*)

La Cibeles Cafe (Downtown, *I*)
Larios on the Beach
(South Beach, *M*)
The Oasis (Key Biscayne, *I*)
Puerto Sagua (South Beach, *I*)
Pollo Tropical (South Miami, *I*)
Sergio's (Coral Gables, *I*)
Versailles (Little Havana, *I*)
Victor's Cafe (Little Havana, *VE*)
Yuca (South Beach, *VE*)

DELI

Bagel Factory (South Beach, *I*)
Stephan's Gourmet Market & Cafe
(South Beach, *I*)
Wolfie Cohen's Rascal House
(Miami Beach, *M*)

DINER FARE

S & S Restaurant (Downtown, *I*)

ENGLISH TEA

The Tea Room (South Miami, *I*)

EUROPEAN/AMERICAN

The Estate Wines & Gourmet Foods
(Coral Gables, *I*)

FAST FOOD

Mrs. Mendoza's Tacos al Carbon
(South Beach, *I*)
Pollo Tropical (South Miami, *I*)
Raja's (Downtown, *I*)

FONDUE

The Melting Pot
(North Dade, *M*)

FRENCH

The Bistro (Coral Gables, *E*)
Brasserie Les Halles
(Coral Gables, *M*)
The Crepe Maker Cafe
(South Miami, *I*)
La Boulangerie (Key Biscayne, *I*)
La Sandwicherie (South Beach, *I*)
Le Festival (Coral Gables, *E*)
L'Entrecote de Paris
(South Beach, *M*)
The Gourmet Diner
(North Dade, *M*)
Lemon Twist (Miami Beach, *M*)

GREEK

The Greek Place (Miami Beach, *I*)

HAITIAN

Tap Tap (South Beach, *M*)

HEALTH FOOD

Amos' Juice Bar (North Dade, *I*)
Here Comes the Sun
(North Dade, *I*)

INDIAN

House of India (Coral Gables, *I*)
Nirvana (South Beach, *M*)
Raja's (Downtown, *I*)

INTERNATIONAL

Balans (South Beach, *M*)
Cafe Tu Tu Tango
(Coconut Grove, *I*)
The Globe (Coral Gables, *M*)
Norma's (South Beach, *E*)

IRISH PUB

John Martin's (Coral Gables, *M*)

ITALIAN

Anacapri (South Miami, *M*)
Bocca di Rosa
(Coconut Grove, *E*)
Cafe Prima Pasta
(Miami Beach, *M*)
Cafe Ragazzi (Miami Beach, *M*)
Caffe Abbracci (Coral Gables, *E*)
Laurenzo's Cafe (North Dade, *I*)
Miami Beach Place
(Miami Beach, *I*)
Oggi Caffe (Miami Beach, *M*)
Osteria del Teatro
(South Beach, *VE*)
Sport Cafe (South Beach, *I*)
Stefano's (Key Biscayne, *E*)
Stephan's Gourmet Market & Cafe
(South Beach, *I*)
Tula (Coconut Grove, *M*)

JAMAICAN

Caribbean Delite (Downtown, *I*)
Norma's (South Beach, *E*)

JAPANESE

Toni's (South Beach, *M*)

MEXICAN

Mrs. Mendoza's Tacos al Carbon
(South Beach, *I*)
Señor Frogs (Coconut Grove, *M*)

NEW WORLD CUISINE

Astor Place in the Astor Hotel
(South Beach, *VE*)
Blue Door (South Beach, *VE*)
Chef Allen's (North Dade, *VE*)
China Grill (South Beach, *VE*)
Crystal Café (Miami Beach, *E*)
Nemo's (South Beach, *E*)
Norman's (Coral Gables, *VE*)
Pacific Time (South Beach, *VE*)
Le Pavillon (Downtown, *VE*)

PIZZA

Miami Beach Place
(Miami Beach, *I*)

SEAFOOD

Bayside Seafood Restaurant and
Hidden Cove Bar
(Key Biscayne, *I*)
East Coast Fisheries
(Downtown, *M*)
Fishbone Grille (Downtown, *M*)
The Fish Market (Downtown, *E*)
Grillfish (South Beach, *M*)
Joe's Stone Crab Restaurant
(South Beach, *VE*)
The Lagoon (North Dade, *M*)
Monty's Bayshore Restaurant
(Coconut Grove, *M*)
Monty's Stone Crab/Seafood House
(South Beach, *E*)

SPANISH

Cafe Tu Tu Tango
(Coconut Grove, *I*)
Casa Juancho (Little Havana, *M*)
Las Tapas (Downtown, *M*)
Macarena (South Beach, *M*)
Puerto Sagua (South Beach, *I*)

STEAKHOUSE

Shula's Steak House (West Dade
and Miami Beach, *VE*)
Smith & Wollensky
(South Beach, *VE*)

SUSHI
Toni's (South Beach, *M*)
World Resources (South Beach, *I*)

SZECHUAN/PEKINESE
Chrysanthemum
  (South Beach, *M*)

THAI
Thai House South Beach
  (South Beach, *M*)
World Resources (South Beach, *I*)

VIETNAMESE
Hy-Vong (Little Havana, *I*)

3 South Beach

The renaissance of South Beach has spawned dozens of first-rate restaurants. In fact, big names from across the country have decided to capitalize on South Beach's international appeal and have begun to open branches here with great success. A few old standbys remain from the *Miami Vice* days, but the flock of newcomers dominates the scene, with places going in and out of style as quickly as the tides. The listings below represent the restaurants that have quickly gained national attention or should.

The **Lincoln Road area** is packed with places offering good food and great atmosphere. Since it's impossible to list them all, I recommend strolling and browsing. Most restaurants post a copy of their menu outside, and staff are happy to chat with curious passersby.

With very few exceptions, the places on **Ocean Drive** are crowded with tourists and priced accordingly. You'll do better to venture a little farther into the pedestrian-friendly streets just west of Ocean Drive.

VERY EXPENSIVE

❂ **Astor Place in the Astor Hotel.** 956 Washington Ave. South Beach. ☎ **305/672-7217.** Reservations recommended. Main courses $15–$30. AE, DC, MC, V. Daily 7am–2:30pm; Sun–Thurs 7–11pm; Fri–Sat 6pm–midnight . NEW FLORIDA BARBECUE.

The Astor Hotel not only has a great bar, but perhaps the very best restaurant on the beach. Known as the Caribbean Cowboy, chef Johnny Vinczencz has created an elegant but never stuffy menu that features local ingredients and a lot of imagination. From his signature corn-crusted yellowtail snapper with lemon boniato mash and roasted corn sauce to his sushi salad (a concoction of curry, fresh tuna, ginger shrimp, caviar, wasabi, and smoked salmon dressed in an orange sesame vinaigrette), all his dishes are dramatic and delicious. A stack of portobello mushrooms is served pancake style with balsamic syrup and sundried tomato butter. Nightly specials consistently sell out and are always worth a try. Another hot seller is the decadent lobster pot pie with shrimp and vegetables. If it's available, order it.

The sleek dining room, with low-level lighting, a glass-enclosed atrium, and marble floors, is romantic in an ultra-modern way. Well-dressed hipsters flock to the restaurant, especially on weekend nights. A sophisticated family crowd shows up for the Sunday jazz brunch, which features all kinds of eggs and luscious sandwiches on crisp homemade bread. There are also Italian rice dishes, salads, and soups.

Blue Door. At the Delano Hotel, 1685 Collins Ave., South Beach. ☎ **305/674-6400.** Reservations recommended for dinner. Main courses $19–$34; soups and salads $6–$12. AE, DC, MC, V. Daily 7am–1am. AMERICAN NOUVELLE.

The Blue Door's setting—with plump circular booths, billowy white curtains, and polished oak accents—could be a backdrop for a 1930s movie. Celebrity sightings are almost guaranteed; with Madonna as a part owner, you would expect no less.

The problem is that everyone, including your waiter, thinks he's the next big star. In the dining room, a steady stream of beautiful people parade through a center corridor on their way to the Alice-in-Wonderlandesque pool deck, where more people are posing on the luxurious furnishings. You'll want to sit on the patio if the weather is nice.

If your waiter deigns to take your order, try the delicate crabcakes, two to an order, served on a peppery fennel and tomato salad. On a recent visit, the stone crab claws were badly cracked, making the experience frustrating. The fish options, on the other hand, were fresh and prepared in a simple but elegant style. The choices include sea bass with a mashed combination of acorn squash and fennel, grilled lobster, salmon, and sautéed mahi-mahi in a sweet vinegar sauce.

China Grill. 404 Washington Ave. (at the corner of Fifth St.), South Beach. ☎ **305/534-2211.** Reservations recommended. Main courses $19–$30. AE, DC, MC, V. Mon–Fri 11:45am–5pm; Sun–Thur 6pm–midnight; Fri–Sat 6pm–1am. NEW WORLD CUISINE/MULTICULTURAL.

Imported from New York, like so many other Miami institutions, China Grill took Miami Beach by storm when it opened in late 1995. Unfortunately, the attitude and prices are so up there that it tends to attract mostly the aging beautiful people and a few hangers-on. It's worth going to the bar for a drink to soak up some atmosphere and to people-watch. But be warned—the food sounds better than it is in this night-club pretending to be a restaurant.

The menu and management explain that the prices are so high because the dishes are meant to be shared; however, when we tried that approach, we were left hungry. Others have complained that the service is slow and the food inconsistent. I know that I could get addicted to the Confucius Chicken Salad, which has crispy fried noodles and a perfect blend of sesame and soy in the vinaigrette. But both the duck salad and the crispy spinach can be greasy with a sour, dusty taste.

Joe's Stone Crab Restaurant. 227 Biscayne St. (at the corner of Washington Ave. south of 1st St.), South Beach. ☎ **305/673-0365.** Reservations not accepted. No shorts allowed. Market price varies but averages $42 for a serving of jumbo crab claws, $30 for large claws. AE, CB, DC, DISC, MC, V. Tues–Sat 11:30am–2pm; Sun–Thurs 5–10pm; Fri–Sat 5–11pm. Closed mid-May to mid-Oct. SEAFOOD.

Open since 1913 and steeped in tradition, this restaurant is famous in Florida and beyond, as evidenced by the ubiquitous long lines waiting to get in. A full menu is available, but to order anything but stone crabs is unthinkable, and the waiters will let you know it. Service tends to be brusque and pushy.

Even after a $5 million renovation, which more than doubled the size of the place, the lines are still ridiculously long. Too many locals claim they "know someone" at the door, which usually means they were introduced through their mutual friend, Ben Franklin. Even after heavy tipping, the wait can exceed 2 hours. If you have to say you were there, brave it and enjoy drinks in the newly renovated oak bar. Otherwise, try the take-out bar next door for the same price and less hassle. The claws here are the best, but also pricier than at other local restaurants. Remember, you are paying for history.

✪ Osteria del Teatro. 1443 Washington Ave. (at Española Way), South Beach. ☎ **305/ 538-7850.** Reservations recommended. Main courses $21–$32. AE, CB, DC, JCB, MC, V. Wed–Mon 6pm–midnight; Fri–Sat 6pm–1am. NORTHERN ITALIAN.

The curved entryway of this well-established enclave of reliable, if slightly overpriced, Italian cuisine is a-buzz nightly. Reams of locals and tourists wait for a seat at one of the small tables. Move the fresh orchid aside to make room for a big

South Beach Dining

To Mid Beach↗
& North Beach

Dade Boulevard

The Bass
Museum of Art

Collins
Park

Miami Beach
Convention Center

20th St.

19th St.

James Ave.

Jackie Gleason Theater
of Performing Arts

18th St.

Dade Boulevard

17th St.

Venetian
Causeway

West Ave.

Lenox Ave.

Alton Rd.

West Ave.

Bay Rd.
Purdy Ave.

Lincoln Road Mall

Lincoln Rd.

Collins Ave.

Biscayne
Bay

16th St.

15th St.

Española Way

14th Pl.

14th St.

Miami Beach
Post Office

13th St.

Michigan Ave.

Meridian Ave.

Flamingo
Park

12th St.

11th St.

10th St.

9th St.

Pennsylvania Ave.

Washington Ave.

Ocean Dr.

Beach
Patrol
Station

Art Deco
Welcome
Center

Lummus
Park

Atlantic
Ocean

Astor Place **19**
Bagel Factory **34**
Balans **1**
Blue Door **9**
China Grill **27**
Chrysanthemum **15**
Grillfish **11**
Jeffrey's **4**
Joe's Stone Crab
  Restaurant **31**
L'Entrecote de Paris **28**
La Sandwicherie **13**
Larios on the Beach **20**
Les Deux Fontaines **18**
Lucky Cheng's **7**
Macarena **14**
Monty's Stone Crab/
  Seafood House **29**
Mrs. Mendoza's
  Tacos al Carbon **33**
Nemo's **30**
News Cafe **21**
Nirvana **24**
Norma's **6**
Osteria del Teatro **10**
Pacific Time **2**
Puerto Sagua **22**
Smith & Wollensky **32**
Sport Cafe **25**
Stephan's Gourmet
  Market & Cafe **12**
The Strand **23**
Tap Tap **26**
Thai House
  South Beach **17**
Toni's **16**
Van Dyke Cafe **3**
World Resources **5**
Yuca **8**

Alton Rd.

Lenox Ave.

Michigan Ave.

Jefferson Ave.

8th St.

7th St.

6th St.

5th St.

4th St.

3rd St.

2nd St.

1st St.

Commerce St.

Biscayne St.

Washington Ave.

Collins Ave.

Ocean Dr.

South Pointe
Park

Government Cut

0   .2 mi
     .124 km

N

NA-0165

basket of lightly toasted chunks of real Italian bread and then wait for your very knowledgeable waiter to recommend a daily special.

A good start is any of the grilled vegetables, particularly the portobello mushrooms with fontina or the garlic-infused peppers. All the pastas are handmade and done to perfection. The risotto al'aragosta is a creamy rice dish with a decadent lobster and shrimp sauce full of tasty morsels of seafood. Of the five or so entrees offered nightly, usually at least three are seafood. The tuna loin is served with a rich mushroom sauce with just a hint of rosemary. The duck breast, doused in a sweet balsamic honey sauce and fanned over a bed of wilted radicchio leaves, is rightfully very popular. Each slice of duck is perfectly seared on the outside and tender throughout without a hint of gamey flavor.

Pacific Time. 915 Lincoln Rd. (between Jefferson and Michigan avenues), South Beach. ☎ 305/534-5979. Reservations recommended. Main courses $19.50–$29. AE, CB, DC, MC, V. Sun–Thurs 6–11pm; Fri–Sat 6pm–midnight. PAN ASIAN.

This exciting Lincoln Road restaurant has received accolades from *The Miami Herald, Esquire* magazine, and *Bon Appetit.* Chef and co-owner Jonathan Eismann puts out some of the funkiest dishes ever spotted this side of the equator. One of the best for meat-eaters is the Mongolian lamb salad, which has a lightly sweet, earthy taste with a crunchy kick of onion. For a main course, the ever-changing menu offers many locally caught fish specialties, including grouper served on a bed of shredded shallots and ginger with a sweet sake-infused sauce and tempura-dunked sweet potato slivers on the side. Under the midnight-blue sky ceiling and against the pale yellow distressed walls, you'll probably see stars. I'm told Arnold Schwarzenegger recently ordered the famous chocolate bomb for Maria Shriver. It is every bit as decadent as they've said, with hot bittersweet chocolate bursting from the cupcake-like center. Some folks are put off by the exotic dishes, but more adventurous eaters return over and over again to wait in line at this stunning Pacific-inspired meteor.

Smith & Wollensky. 1 Washington Ave. (in South Pointe Park), South Beach. ☎ 888/517-8325 or 305/673-2800. Reservations suggested. Main courses $20–$30. DC, DISC, MC, V. Daily noon–midnight. The Grill open 3pm–1am. STEAK/AMERICAN

This pricey New York steakhouse opened its doors in late 1997 and was packed from the start. The handsome clubby atmosphere is enhanced by views of the intercoastal waterway that leads to the Port of Miami. The menu is basic, almost austere, with a few chicken and fish choices and beef served about a dozen ways. The classic is the sirloin seared lightly and served naked. Also good is the filet mignon, a thick and buttery cut also served unadorned. Delicious side dishes such as asparagus, baked potato, onion rings, creamed spinach, and hash browns are sold a la carte. Ask for advice from the wine steward, since the vast and impressive menu can be overwhelming. Service here, unlike so many other South Beach restaurants, is actually professional and polite. Desserts are superb, too. Just hope someone else is paying.

To avoid the clanking bustle of the main dining rooms, ask for a seat upstairs or, better yet, in The Grill, where you can order from a more casual and less expensive menu. You'll find meat entrees at about 30 percent less than in the regular restaurant. Portions in here are thankfully a bit smaller, too, eliminating the need for doggie bags.

☼ Yuca. 501 Lincoln Rd. (corner of Drexel), South Beach. ☎ 305/532-9822. Reservations required. Main courses $19–$32. AE, DC, DISC, MC, V. Tues–Sun noon–4pm and 6pm–midnight; Mon 6–11pm. NOUVELLE CUBAN.

This is the place to take out-of-towners you want to impress with a dose of upscale Latin culture. The menu is large and exotic. Unfortunately, it's also badly translated, so don't be shy about asking for a waiter who is proficient in English (most are) if you don't *habla español.* By the way, don't give yourself away as a gringo by pronouncing it "Yucka." It's "Yoo-ka," and is a play on words, being the name of a staple root vegetable and an acronym for Young Upscale Cuban-Americans (like a yuppie).

To enjoy your meal, insist on being seated in the front of the restaurant, facing Lincoln Road; otherwise you'll be in the hectic path of the kitchen and too close to the very talented but loud salsa band that plays on weekends. Start with the lobster medallions with sautéed spinach and a portobello mushroom stuffed with vegetarian paella. The pieces of lobster tail are expertly grilled, with a touch of oil over just-wilted greens. The mushrooms are good, but the paella can be a bit pasty. For a main course, the pork tenderloin is a favorite. It must have been marinated for days because you could cut it with a butter knife. The hearty *congri,* a mash of red beans and rice, and a green apple and mango salsa make a perfect balance. The veal loin, the menu's most expensive entree, has a rich meaty flavor but can be a bit dry. Try the succulent side dish of lobster and purple potatoes. A full selection of traditional and exotic dessert choices is available, as well as some of the best coffee in town.

Go on the weekend for a late dinner and then head upstairs for live music. If Cuban diva Albita is playing, you're in for a real experience. It's pricey but well worth it.

EXPENSIVE

Lucky Cheng's. 600 Lincoln Rd., South Beach. ☎ **305/672-1505.** Reservations suggested on weekends. Main courses $13–$20. AE, DC, DISC, MC, V. Daily 6:30–midnight; brunch 11am–4pm. PAN-ASIAN.

The food is nothing to speak of, but oh, those "waitresses." It's worth the inflated prices to watch these truly lovely transvestites vamp, pose, and generally do their thing. On weekdays, shows are at 8 and 10pm; weekends, they're at 8pm, 10pm, and midnight. As for the food, stick with safe choices like chicken satay or spring rolls. The moist and tender wok-seared pork loin with crispy leeks and yuca pancakes is an anomaly. A good feature of the menu is that many of the entrees and salads come in small and large sizes. Be sure to bring lots of small bills to tip the entertainers.

✪ **Monty's Stone Crab/Seafood House.** 300 Alton Rd., South Beach. ☎ **305/673-3444.** Reservations recommended. Main courses $20–$37. AE, DC, MC, V. Sun–Thurs 5:30–11pm; Fri–Sat 5:30pm–midnight. SEAFOOD.

Seafood fans have long been enamored of Monty's various menus in the Grove and in Boca. Now Monty's has moved in to South Beach, burnished the rustic oak floor, set up a raw bar outside around a large swimming pool, and opened the doors for business. The best deal in town is still the all-you-can-eat stone crabs—about $40 for the large ones and $35 for the mediums. That's about the same price that Joe's, located 2 blocks away, charges for just three or four claws. (But don't order stone crabs in summer.) Enjoy the incredible views and off-season fish specialties, including the Maryland she-crab soup, rich and creamy without too much thickener. Year-round, you can enjoy the saffron and tomato-base bouillabaisse; Monty's is always worth a trip. The Key lime pie is authentic.

✪ **Nemo's.** 100 Collins Ave., South Beach. ☎ **305/532-4550.** Reservations recommended. Main courses $17–$20; sandwiches and platters $4–$12; Sun brunch $19. AE, MC, V. Mon–Sat noon–3pm and 7pm–midnight; Sun noon–3pm and 6–11pm. NEW WORLD CUISINE/MULTICULTURAL.

This dark and super-stylish hotspot is an oasis in a newly hip area of South Beach below 5th Street. Here models and celebrities rub elbows—literally, since the tables are so close together. Ask to be seated in the more private back room, which has a pleasant garden and is the only place where you can hear your dining companions or your waiter. In the main dining room, the din is unbearable. The staff here is professional, personable, and efficient, the best on the beach.

The menu offers many fish dishes. One of the most popular is the charred salmon. The flash-cooking in a wok gives it a unique flavor, slightly blackened outside and tender and sweet inside. If you're in the mood for something light, try the grilled portobello mushroom appetizer, served with a rich, creamy garlic polenta. The spicy Vietnamese beef salad is indeed very spicy, but it's too small a portion. Daily specials are always superb. Try the pork loin if they've got it, and the side dish of roasted beets with a super-chunky Maytag blue dressing. An exotic and delicious choice for dessert is the California figs soaked in port syrup and surrounded with balls of tamarind (said to be an aphrodisiac) ice cream.

⚫ **Norma's.** 646 Lincoln Rd., South Beach. ☎ **305/532-2809.** Reservations recommended. Main courses $12–$24. AE, DC, MC, V. Tues–Thur noon–11pm; Fri–Sat noon–midnight; Sun noon–10pm. NEW CARIBBEAN.

This tiny jewel on Lincoln Road sparkles with its eclectic mix of classical and Caribbean cooking. The multilingual staff is polite if sometimes slightly flustered. The daily specials are always good, but you may want to call in advance to reserve whatever sounds best, because they sell out quickly.

For starters, try the smoked marlin platter with cucumbers, capers, and onion, plus a spicy pepper salsa and a creamy dipping sauce. Cindy, the cook, has the tender filets flown in weekly from Montego Bay. At lunch, a surprisingly tasty jerk tofu salad is served on *callaloo* (a slightly sweeter version of spinach) with tomatoes and onions. The seared jerk tuna has a kick (like all the jerk-seasoned dishes) and is one of the Beach's best. If you prefer something milder, the rasta chicken is a good bet. A different homemade soup is offered daily; carrot is one of the best. If you like it hot, ask for a splash of pepper sherry. To cool off, try the refreshing mango or guava mousse served with fresh tropical berries, melons, or tropical fruits. And don't drive after you've had the Appleton Rum cake and rum whipped cream.

The Strand. 671 Washington Ave., South Beach. ☎ **305/532-2340.** Reservations recommended on weekends. Main courses $13–$24; pasta and vegetarian dishes $12–$16. AE, DC, MC, V. Daily 8:30pm–midnight. Club open daily midnight–5am. AMERICAN.

Nothing on the menu will disappoint you, which explains why, after more than 10 years (an eternity for South Beach), The Strand is still going strong. It's kept up with the times and still offers an exceptional value with enough glitz to keep it popular. Still the place to be and be seen, this old standby has candlelit tables and a large, open-room layout, a setting conducive both to intimate dining and table hopping. Lots of model types hang out at the bar where hundreds of people crunch into an expansive and elegant deco-style marble and glass area. After hours, the restaurant becomes a packed nightclub called the Living Room.

If it's in season, definitely consider the seafood and tropical salad, which combines stone crab, lobster, shrimp, and fish in a passion fruit vinaigrette. The crab cakes are very gently browned on the outside and super moist inside. Other Italian-inspired dishes, like the fusili con fungi or the penne all'arrabiata, are true to form with a slightly al dente noodle and a subtle hand with the sauce. The reasonably tasty lamb medaillons are served with a fragrant herb sauce, sautéed vegetables, and plump spinach-and-mushroom-stuffed ravioli.

MODERATE

Balans. 1022 Lincoln Rd. (between Lenox and Michigan), South Beach. ☎ **305/534-9191.** Reservations not accepted on weekends. Main courses $9–$17; pastas and noodles $8–$10. AE, DISC, MC, V. Daily 8am–1 am. INTERNATIONAL.

This well-run sidewalk cafe, a London import, is a good value, especially when the weather is right. It's a favorite hang-out for the gay community, and is right at home on fabulous Lincoln Road. Dinners here are a bargain, with winning entrees like a hearty lobster club sandwich served with bacon, lettuce, and tomato on toasted onion bread, and a hoisin Port filet nestled over baby bok choy and crisp leek spring rolls. The tempting starters are relatively small, so you can try a few. Try Thai soup, as well as the concoction of goat, cheese, and lightly breaded fried mushrooms. A large herb salad with a mix of more than five types of baby greens is a refreshing and crisp way to start any meal. The tahini chicken salad, however, is sadly lacking in spice. Noodle dishes are especially good. A favorite is the linguini with eggplant and pork.

✪ Chrysanthemum. 1256 Washington Ave., South Beach. ☎ **305/531-5656.** Main courses $11–$20. AE, CB, DC, MC, V. Tues–Thurs and Sun 6pm–10:30pm; Fri–Sat 6pm–midnight. SZECHUAN/PEKINESE.

At first, the unpretentious atmosphere may be a surprise in glitzy South Beach, but after you have tried the simple and tasty dishes in what many consider to be the best Chinese restaurant in Miami, you'll want to come back. Count on the service to be prompt but not solicitous. The many vegetarian specialties include spicy eggplant strips in a rich balsamic vinegar sauce and black mushrooms sautéed with tiny Shanghai lettuce hearts. Start with the Chinese salad, which comes heaped with a fresh mix of greens, vermicelli, bean sprouts, and coriander. The steamed whole fish is best with the ginger and scallions. It comes with bones, but ask the waiter to remove them; he will gladly and expertly oblige.

Grillfish. 1444 Collins Ave. (corner of Española Way), South Beach. ☎ **305/538-2203.** Reservations recommended on weekends. Main courses $8–$13. AE, DC, MC, V. In season daily 6pm–midnight; off-season daily 6–11pm. SEAFOOD.

From the beautiful Byzantine-style mural and the gleaming oak bar, you'd think you were eating in a much more expensive restaurant. No doubt Grillfish manages to pay the exorbitant South Beach rent because the restaurant has a loyal following of locals, who come for the fresh and simple seafood in a relaxed but upscale atmosphere. As the name implies, fish, fish, and fish is what you'll get.

The waiters are friendly and know the limited menu well. The barroom seafood chowder is full of chunks of shellfish, as well as some fresh white fish filets in a tomato broth. The small ear of corn, included with each entree, is about as close as you'll get to any type of vegetable offering besides the pedestrian salad. Still, at these prices, it's worth a visit to try some local fare including mako shark, swordfish, tuna, marlin, and wahoo. They'll grill it or sauté it. Also, choose the spicy red sauce on the pasta as a great complement to this rustic, Italian-inspired seafood fare.

Jeffrey's. 1629 Michigan Ave. (half-block south of Lincoln Rd.), South Beach. ☎ **305/ 673-0690.** Main courses $11–$17. AE, CB, DC, MC, V. Tues–Sat 6–11pm; Sun 5–10pm. CONTINENTAL/BISTRO.

Jeffrey's is a real find on South Beach. Here you get a genuinely concerned and doting owner, Jeffrey, who treats everyone as a regular and calls grandmothers and children alike "kids." Some say this is the most romantic restaurant on the beach—South Beach's gay crowd certainly seem to think so. Old-fashioned lace curtains and candle-light are a welcome repast from the glitz and chrome of the rest of the island.

You can choose a basic burger or try a hearty chicken breast marinated in a balsamic sauce served with freshly mashed sweet potatoes over spinach. Some of the better seafood options include the conch fritters, which are not too oily, or the crab cakes. Jeffrey's is known for its perfectly dressed Caesar salad, which could use some more anchovies for my taste, but is nonetheless delicious. Most desserts are tasty, but the homemade tarte-tartin, a caramelly deep-dish apple tart, is superb. Go early before it sells out.

Larios on the Beach. 820 Ocean Dr., South Beach. ☎ **305/532-9577.** Reservations recommended. Main courses $8–$15. AE, MC, V. Sun–Thurs 11:30am–midnight; Fri–Sat 11:30am–2am. CUBAN.

Gloria and Emilio Estefan brought their favorite chef to create this ultra-stylish restaurant in the heart of the South Beach hustle. Enjoy a few appetizers at the handsome chrome and wood bar while you wait for a seat amid the sea of Spanish-speaking regulars.

Portions are large and prices are reasonable. The menu runs the gamut, from diner-style *medianoches* (Cuban sandwiches with pork and cheese) to a tangy and tender *serrucho en escabeche* (pickled kingfish) with just enough citrus to mellow the fishiness but not enough to cause a pucker. You could get away with ordering three or four *aperitivos* and *ensaladas* (appetizers and salads) for two people. If you are still hungry, try the *camarones al ajillo* (shrimp in garlic sauce), *fabada asturiana* (hearty soup of black beans and sausage), or *palomilla* (thinly sliced beef served with onions and parsley). Save room for the rich custard desserts, which include a few stunning variations on the standard flan. A spoonful of pumpkin or coffee-accented custard with a cup of *cortadito* (espresso-style coffee with milk and sugar) will get you prepped for a full night of dancing.

L'Entrecote de Paris. 413 Washington Ave., South Beach. ☎ **305/673-1002.** Reservations suggested on weekends. Prix-fixe $14–18 (includes potatoes and salad). DC, MC, V. Daily 6pm–1am. FRENCH BRASSERIE.

Everything in this classy little bistro is simple. For dinner, you choose between salmon or steak. Yes, that's it, beyond a few salads. But both are great, although the salmon looks like spa cuisine. It's served with a pile of bald steamed potatoes and a salad with pedestrian greens and an unmatchable vinaigrette. The steak, on the other hand, is the stuff cravings are made of, even if you're not a die-hard carnivore. Its salty sharp sauce is rich but not thick and full of the beef's natural flavor. The slices are served on top of your own little habachi, which also keeps the accompanying fries warm.

Most diners are very Euro and pack a *petit* attitude. Tables and booths are squeezed tight together. On the other hand, the waiters are super-quick and professional, almost friendly, in a French kind of way. A short and very French wine list includes several well-priced bottles for under $20. Even if you are on a diet or have forsaken chocolate, try the *profiteroles au chocolat,* a perfect puff pastry filled with vanilla ice-cream and topped with a dark bittersweet chocolate sauce.

✪ **Macarena.** 1334 Washington Ave. South Beach. ☎ **305/531-3440.** Reservations suggested on weekdays. AE, DC, MC, V. Daily 7pm–midnight (later on Fri and Sat) SPANISH/TAPAS.

Despite its unfortunate name, this South Beach newcomer is a great place to eat and enjoy. It's looked after by a young crew of Spanish imports whose families own several popular restaurants in Madrid. If you're a gringo, you'll probably show up before 9pm, when you're sure to get a table. However, after then, especially on weekends, it's standing room only.

The gorgeous Euro crowd shows up for foot-stomping flamenco (every Wednesday, Friday, and Saturday) and an outrageous selection of tapas, including this town's very best paella. Order a large portion and share it among at least four people. The garlic shrimp is tasty and aromatic. A yellow squash stuffed with seafood and cheese is especially delicious. All the seafood, such as mussels in marinara sauce and clams in green sauce, is worth sampling. With such reasonable prices, you can taste lots of dishes and leave satisfied. Try some of the terrific sangria made with slices of fresh fruit and a subtle tinge of sweet soda.

Nirvana. 630 6th St. (off Washington Ave.), South Beach. ☎ **305/534-3700.** Reservations accepted. Main courses $8–$16. AE, DC, DISC, MC, V. Sun–Thur 6–11pm; Fri–Sat 6–midnight. NORTHERN INDIAN.

With heavy emphasis on vegetarian dishes and many extraordinary meat, chicken, seafood, and lamb dishes, this reasonably priced, trendy hot spot qualifies as the best Indian restaurant in Miami. Expert chef-owner Raghu Raturi has created a simple and elegant menu with all the favorites, such as saag paneer and chicken vindaloo, plus a variety of curries and a few unusual specialties. Baigan Bharta, a creamy concoction of mashed eggplant, is a rich, hearty main dish served, like all other entrees, with a large helping of fragrant pulao rice. A rich chicken curry, although not listed on the menu, is one of the restaurant's finest offerings. The gentle mustard-colored sauce is savory but not overly thick, spicy but not sharp.

Despite the budget prices, the atmosphere is romantic and elegant enough for a Saturday-night date. So far, it is mostly popular with the young locals and a few East Indians in the know. It seems most Miamians have a real problem with Indian food. Good. There's more for those of us who know better.

Tap Tap. 819 Fifth St. (between Jefferson and Meridian Aves., next to the Shell station), South Beach. ☎ **305/672-2898.** Reservations recommended in season and for special events. Main courses $8–$15. AE, DC, MC, V. Sun–Thur 6pm–midnight; Fri–Sat 6pm–2am. HAITIAN.

The whole place looks like an overgrown *tap tap*, a brightly painted jitney common in Haiti. Every space of wall and floor and furniture is painted a neon blue or pink or purple and every color in between. The atmosphere is always fun. It's where the Haiti-philes and Haitians hang out, from journalists to politicians. Even Manno Charlemagne, the mayor of Port-au-Prince, shows up when he can to play his old brand of protest music and drink lots of Rhum Barbancourt.

You don't really come here for the food, although meals aren't bad, when you can get served. On crowded nights, the service is impossible. I recommend going for appetizers and drinks. The *Lanbi nan citron,* a tart, marinated conch salad, is perfect with a tall tropical drink and maybe some lightly grilled goat tidbits, which are served in a savory brown sauce and are less stringy than a typical goat dish. Another super-satisfying choice is the pumpkin soup, a rich brick-colored purée of subtly seasoned pumpkin with a dash of pepper. An excellent salad of avocado, mango, and watercress is a great finish. Even if you don't stay for a full meal, try the pumpkin flan with coconut caramel sauce, an ultra-Caribbean sweet-treat.

Thai House South Beach. 1137 Washington Ave., South Beach. ☎ **305/531-4841.** Reservations recommended on weekends. Main courses $7–$13 ($15–$18 for fish). AE, MC, V. Mon–Fri noon–3pm; daily 5pm–midnight. THAI.

The third in a series of successful Thai Houses in Miami, this most recent addition has perhaps the most complete and inspired menu. A whole page of tofu options for vegetarians includes massaman tofu with sweet potato, snow peas, and pineapple in a curry-based sauce. The pad Thai is nearly perfect, with a hint of fish and just a tinge of sweetness. The shrimp are few and small, but the peanut flavor and the scallions provide the required bulk. As a side, try the Thai fries, strips of *boniato* (a sweet potato-like root) dunked in coconut meat and deep fried.

The service in this quaint little storefront is spotty at best, but pleasant none-theless. For a taste of South Beach with your meal, sit in the sidewalk area, which overlooks hectic Washington Avenue, where club-hoppers and teeny-boppers perform nightly. You'll find other Thai Houses at 715 East 9th St., Hialeah, and 2250 NE 163rd St., North Miami Beach. Try Thai Toni's across the street for a more upscale experience.

○ Toni's. 1208 Washington Ave., South Beach. ☎ **305/673-9368.** Reservations recommended. Main courses $11–$22; rolls $3.50–$8.50. AE, MC, V. Daily 6pm–midnight; Fri–Sat 6pm–1am. SUSHI/JAPANESE.

One of Washington Avenue's first tenants, Toni's has withstood the test of time on fickle South Beach. By serving local fish caught daily and some imports from the Pacific and beyond, Toni has created a vast menu with options from teriyaki to hand rolls. The atmosphere is comfortable and even allows for quiet conversation—a rarity on the beach. The hundreds of appetizers and rolls you can order makes it a fun place to go with a group.

Consider the seaweed salad, a crunchy and salty green plant dressed with a light sesame sauce. The miso soup is hearty and a bit sweet. A good appetizer from the sushi bar is Miami Heat, which contains slabs of tuna with bits of scallion in a peppery sesame oil. I suggest skipping the entrees unless you are somehow still hungry after all the warm-ups. However, many main dishes are good, like the lobster teriyaki in a dark sweet sauce over white rice.

INEXPENSIVE

Bagel Factory. 1427 Alton Rd., South Beach. ☎ **305/674-1577.** Sandwiches $1–$7. No credit cards. Mon–Sat 5:30am–5pm; Sun 5:30am–3:30pm. BAGELS/DELI.

There are bagel joints all over South Beach, but this narrow storefront on Alton Road is one of the best. The Rishty family makes the city's finest hand-rolled bagels in every imaginable flavor, from sunflower to banana raisin to sundried tomato. The bagels are deliciously chewy, but not too doughy. Add to that the phenomenal salads, including a range of decent fat-free options, and you'll understand why every weekend hungry customers wait in a line that snakes out the door. Grab a spot at one of the three small inside tables or take the order to go, as most loyal patrons do.

○ La Sandwicherie. 229 14th St. (behind the Amoco station), South Beach. ☎ **305/ 531-9883.** Sandwiches and salads $4.50–$7. No credit cards. Daily 9:30am–5am. FRENCH SNACK BAR.

If you want the most incredible gourmet sandwich you've ever tasted, stop by the green-and-white awning that hides this fabulously French lunch and snack counter. Choose pâté, saucisson, salami, prosciutto, turkey, tuna, ham, roast beef, or any of the perfect cheeses (Swiss, mozzarella, cheddar, or provolone). Vegetarians can make a meal out of the optional sandwich toppings, which include black olives, cornichons, cucumbers, lettuce, onions, green or hot peppers, or tomatoes. You can choose to have your sandwich made on delicious fresh French bread or on a relatively uninspired croissant.

If the six or so wooden stools are all taken, don't despair; you can stand and watch the tattoo artist do his work through the glass wall next door. Or douse your creation with the light tangy vinaigrette and bring lunch to the beach—that is, if you can make it 2 blocks without eating the whole thing. In addition to the cans and bottles of teas, sodas, juices, and waters, you can get a killer cappuccino here.

Mrs. Mendoza's Tacos al Carbon. 1040 Alton Rd., South Beach. ☎ **305/535-0808.** Main courses $3–$5; side dishes 79¢–$3. No credit cards. Mon–Thur 11am–10pm; Fri–Sat 11am–11pm; Sun noon–9pm. FAST FOOD/MEXICAN.

This hard-to-spot storefront is a godsend. It's the only fresh California-style Mexican place around. The steak and chicken are grilled as you wait and then stuffed into homemade flour or corn wrappings. You order at the tile counter and pick up your dish on a plastic tray in minutes. This is a popular spot for locals and those who work in the area.

The vegetarian offerings are huge and hearty. One of my favorites is the veggie burrito, which includes rice, black beans, cheese, lettuce, and guacamole doused in tomato salsa. They offer three types of salsa, from mild to super hot. You can see the fresh-cut cilantro and taste the super-hot chilies. The chips are hand cut and flavorful, but a bit too coarse. Skip them and enjoy an order of the rich chunky guacamole with a fork.

There's another location at Doral Plaza, 9739 NW 41st St.

News Café. 800 Ocean Dr., South Beach. ☎ **305/538-6397.** Salads $4–$8; sandwiches $5–$7. AE, MC, V. Daily 24 hours. AMERICAN.

Of all the chic spots around trendy South Beach, News Café has been around the longest. Inexpensive breakfasts and cafe fare are served at about 20 perpetually congested tables. Most of the seating is outdoors, and terrace tables are most coveted. Ocean Drive's multitude of fashion photography crews and their models meet here regularly to get the international newspapers and magazines.

The food isn't remarkable, but the people-watching is. Delicious and often health-oriented dishes include yogurt with fruit salad, various green salads, imported cheese and meat sandwiches, and a choice of quiches.

Puerto Sagua. 700 Collins Ave., South Beach. ☎ **305/673-1115.** Main courses $7–$17; sandwiches and salads $3–$9. AE, DC, MC, V. Daily 7:30am–2am. SPANISH/CUBAN.

This dingy brown-walled diner is one of the only old hold-outs on South Beach. Its steady stream of regulars range from *abuelitos,* little old grandfathers, to hipsters who stop in after clubbing. It has endured because the food is good, if a little greasy. Some of the less heavy dishes are a super-chunky fish soup with pieces of whole flaky grouper, the chicken and seafood paella, or the marinated kingfish. Also good are most of the shrimp dishes, especially the shrimp in garlic sauce served with white rice and salad.

This is one of the most reasonably priced places left on the beach for simple hearty fare. Don't be intimidated by the hunched older waiters in their white button shirts and black pants. Even if you don't speak Spanish, they're usually willing to do charades. Anyway, the extensive menu, which ranges from BLTs to grilled lobsters to yummy fried plantains, is translated into English. Hurry, before another boutique goes up in its place.

Sport Cafe. 538 Washington Ave., South Beach. ☎ **305/674-9700.** Reservations accepted for four or more. Main courses $7.95–$10.95; sandwiches and pizzas $4.50–$8. AE, MC, V. Daily noon–1am; sometimes earlier for coffee. ITALIAN.

Don't expect to see the latest football or baseball games at this Sports Cafe; instead you're more likely to find a soccer match or bicycle race on the television. The Sport Cafe's owners, brothers Tonino and Paolo Doino, hail from Rome. They've put together an authentic Italian menu, listing only three entrees and a few pizzas. It can be a challenge placing your order with one of the waiters, but do try to ask for a plate of fresh crushed garlic when they bring your bread and oil. Ask for the day's specials and order one of them. Always good is the perfectly al dente penne with salmon served with a pink sauce. The eggplant parmigiano, almost always available though not on the menu, is the best in the county. For dessert, try the great tiramisu, which, unlike the more common cake or pudding style, is served *semi-freddo,* or partially frozen, like an ice cream.

The atmosphere is rustic and young and the prices so cheap that on some nights you may have to wait for a seat, especially for the sidewalk tables. Thanks to their great success on Washington Avenue, the brothers have opened a second, similar restaurant called Al Vicolo Caffe on Lincoln Road.

Stephan's Gourmet Market & Cafe. 1430 Washington Ave. (at Española Way), South Beach. ☎ **305/674-1760.** Main courses $6–$12; dinner special for two with salad and a bottle of wine $24.95. AE, MC, V. Sun–Thur 8am–midnight; Fri–Sat 8am–2am; dinner special served daily 5:30–11pm. DELI/ITALIAN.

This deli, which could be in New York's Little Italy, sells a huge assortment of fresh pastas, breads, and salads as well as cold cuts, cheeses, and grocery items. Upstairs, however, in a tiny loft used to store wine bottles is a cozy dining room with space for about 10 couples. Dinner is also served out on the sidewalk or delivered to your hotel.

A chalkboard displays the chef's special, usually a pasta dish with some kind of chicken or fish. One of my favorites is the linguini Alfredo with tender pieces of chicken breast mixed into the light cheesy sauce. While you wait, you'll want to eat baskets and baskets of the very garlicky garlic bread and get started on the bottle of wine that comes with the daily special. The red is an excellent full-bodied Italian Merlot. (The pinot grigio, however, is undrinkable.) If the special doesn't strike you, consider any of the other moderately priced dishes, such as rotisserie chicken with potatoes and vegetables, ziti, sausage and peppers, or eggplant parmigiano. Choose whatever looks good to you from the glass case downstairs or see what else the chef is dishing out. Other locations: 2 NE 40th St. (☎ **305/571-4070**) and 19495 Biscayne Blvd. (One Turnberry Pl.; ☎ **305/932-8885**).

Van Dyke Cafe. 846 Lincoln Rd., South Beach. ☎ **305/534-3600.** Reservations recommended for evenings. Main courses $6–$11. AE, DC, MC, V. Daily 8am–1am; Fri–Sat 8am–3am. AMERICAN.

Owned by the same group who owns the successful News Café, the Van Dyke has used the same formula to guarantee its longevity on Lincoln Road. The smart, upscale decor inside and the European sidewalk cafe outside are always crowded because of the diner-like prices and fast, friendly service.

There is nothing too ambitious on the menu, which offers basic sandwiches and salads and, best of all, breakfast all day long. The pastas are decent, although not too exciting. House specialties include an excellent smoked salmon on thick black bread and a smooth lemony hummus with pita chips. Also, since you are in Miami Beach, you may want to consider a nice hot bowl of cure-all chicken soup with matzoh balls. In the evenings, the sounds of a talented jazz band waft down from the dark elegant club upstairs.

✪ World Resources. 719 Lincoln Rd., South Beach. ☎ **305/535-8987.** Main courses $6–$8; sushi hand rolls $3–$4. AE, DC, MC, V. Daily noon–midnight. SUSHI/THAI.

World Resources is an excellent little cafe and sushi bar masquerading as an Indonesian furniture and bric-a-brac store. Local hippie types and hipsters frequent this downright cheap hangout instead of cooking at home. Offerings include some of the freshest, most innovative sushi in Miami, plus many Thai specialties. The portions are generous and the cooking simple. The basil chicken, for example, is a

Steak Is No Longer So Rare

Miami's always had more than its share of pricey fish houses, and don't forget the huddle of trendy restaurants serving "New World" cuisine, pasta joints, Cuban cafeterias, and fast-food drive-throughs. In this multicultural metropolis you can find cuisine from Delhi, Honduras, or Peking. But a good old-fashioned steak? It wasn't always so easy.

The old standbys like **Christy's** in Coral Gables (☎ **305/446-1400**), **Ruth's Chris** in North Miami Beach (☎ **305/949-0199**), and **The Palm** in Bay Harbor Islands (☎ **305/868-7256**) were the lonely mainstays for years. When Don Shula's took over the old Legends steakhouse in Miami Lakes in 1989 and renamed it **Shula's Steak House** (☎ **305/820-8102**), it became so popular—even in its remote location—that over the years five more branches have opened around the country. One of the latest Shula's (☎ **305/341-6565**) opened in the luxurious Alexander Hotel on Miami Beach.

And who could forget **The Forge** in Miami Beach (☎ **305/604-9798**), one of the premier dining spots in town? Its steak was voted number one in America by *Wine Spectator* in 1996. However, that was before the stampede of new restaurants came to town to capitalize on a renewed desire for flesh.

The National Cattlemen's Association reported a 41.6% increase of restaurant traffic at both casual and upscale steakhouses between 1993 and 1996. Following that trend, Miami has seen a glut of new steakhouses opening up over the years. From the Argentine **La Fusta** in Sunny Isles (☎ **305/949-0888**) to downtown's Brazilian **Porcao** (☎ **373-2777**) and the more upscale **Capital Grille** (☎ **305/374-4500**), it seems that every month a new one jumps in the fire.

In late 1997, New York's **Smith & Wollensky** expanded with its first restaurant outside Manhattan. This clubby elegant haven for beef lovers now occupies a scenic spot in South Pointe Park on South Beach (☎ **305/673-2800**). The venerable **Morton's** of Chicago turned up the heat in December 1997 with a luxurious spot in Downtown Miami (☎ **305/400-9990**). Another superb newcomer is the French **Brasserie Les Halles** in Coral Gables (☎ **305/461-1099**).

So far, it seems each of the establishments has found its niche and is serving up its own kind of beef in all price ranges. Less expensive spots around town include **Houston's** in North Miami (☎ **305/947-2000**) and three **Outback Steak Houses** in Kendall, Miami Beach, and Sunny Isles. Don Shula's also has a more casual spot in Miami Lakes called **Shula's Steak 2** (☎ **305/820-8047**).

tasty combination of white meat sautéed in a coconut sauce with subtle hints of basil and garlic. The Thai salad is heaped with fresh vegetables.

Although you can get better Thai at a number of spots on the beach, you can't beat the atmosphere here, which includes dozens of outside tables surrounding a tiny pond and a stage where World Beat musicians perform nightly. From African drumming to Indian sitar playing, there is always some action at this standout on the Road. It also offers a vast selection of coffees, teas, wines, beers, and cigarettes from around the world.

4 Miami Beach: Surfside, Bal Harbour & Sunny Isles

The area north of the Art Deco District—from about 21st Street to 163rd Street— had its heyday in the 1950s when its huge hotels and gambling halls blocked the view of the ocean. Now many of the old hotels have been converted into condos or budget lodgings and the bayfront mansions renovated by and for wealthy entrepreneurs, families, and speculators. The area now has many more residents, albeit seasonal, than visitors. On the culinary front, the result is a handful of super-expensive, traditional restaurants and a number of value-oriented spots.

VERY EXPENSIVE

○ **The Forge Restaurant.** 432 Arthur Godfrey Rd. (41st St.), Miami Beach. ☎ **305/ 538-8533.** Reservations required. Main courses $19–$30. AE, DC, MC, V. Sun–Thurs 6pm–midnight; Fri–Sat 6pm–1am. AMERICAN.

English oak paneling and Tiffany glass suggest high prices and haute cuisine, and that's exactly what you get from The Forge. Each elegant dining room possesses its own character and features high ceilings, ornate chandeliers, and high-quality European artwork. The most intimate room is the library in the back. The Forge attracts a mix of young, well-dressed Euros, Saudi royalty, and moneyed Miamians. The atmosphere is elegant but not too stuffy, especially on Wednesday nights, when the singles scene shows up for mingling at the bar and dancing next door at Jimmy's.

Like the rest of the menu, appetizers are mostly classics, from Beluga caviar to baked onion soup to shrimp cocktail and escargot. When they're in season, order the stone crabs. For the main course, any of the seafood, chicken, or veal dishes are recommendable, but The Forge is especially known for its steaks. In fact, in 1996, *Wine Spectator* magazine voted the Super Steak the Best in America. Finally, The Forge still has one of Miami's best wine lists and an extensive cellar. Ask for a tour.

EXPENSIVE

○ **Crystal Café.** 726 41st St., Miami Beach. ☎ **305/673-8266.** Reservations recommended on weekends. Main courses $11–$25. AE, DC, DISC, MC, V. Tues–Thur 5–10pm; Fri–Sat 5–11pm. CONTINENTAL/NEW WORLD.

The setting is sparse, with Lucite salt and pepper grinders and a bottle of wine as the only centerpiece on each of the 15 or so tables. I promise you won't need the seasoning. Chef Klime has done it all with the help of his affable wife and a superb waitstaff. Enjoy his unique sparkle at this little-known hideaway, which attracts stars like Julio Iglesias and other discriminating guests.

With something like 30 entrees, including a few nightly specials, I can't figure out how each appears perfectly prepared and beautifully presented. The shrimp-cake appetizer, for example, is the size of a bread plate and rests on top of a small mound of lightly sautéed watercress and mushrooms. Surrounding the delicately breaded disc are concentric circles of beautiful sauces. The veal marsala is served in a luscious brown sauce thickened not with heavy cream or flour but with delicate vegetable broth and a hearty mix of mushrooms. Most main courses come with a choice of three side dishes, such as zucchini, carrots, mashed potatoes, or pasta. The osso buco is a masterpiece.

The Palm. 9650 E. Bay Harbor Dr., Bay Harbor Island. ☎ **305/868-7256.** Reservations highly recommended. Main courses $17–$29. AE, CB, DC, MC, V. Daily 5–11pm. From Collins Ave., turn west onto 96th St.; at Bal Harbour Shops, go over a small bridge, and turn right onto East Bay Harbor Drive. The restaurant is half a block down on the left. CONTINENTAL.

You feel like you're in New York in this dark clubby steakhouse, known for enormous sirloins and jumbo Maine lobsters. The same celebrity caricatures and photos adorn the walls as in the other Palms in Los Angeles and New York. There are currently more than a dozen branches throughout the country, all known for pleasing a demanding corporate and tourist clientele.

Miami Beach Dining

BAL HARBOUR

SURFSIDE

Biscayne Park

NE 125th St.
Miami Blvd.
NE 103rd St.
NE 79th St.

1

Biscayne Blvd.

Broad Causeway

96th St.

Harding Ave.

Collins Ave.

77th St.
North Shore Dr.
South Shore Dr.
Normandy Dr.
71st St.

Harbor Island
John F. Kennedy Causeway
North Bay Island
Treasure Island
Normandy Isle
La Gorce Island
Allison Island

934

N. Bay Rd.
W. 63rd St.

907

Creek

MIAMI BEACH

Biscayne Bay

W. 51st St.

W. 47th St.

Alton Rd.
W. 47th St.

Godfrey Rd.
Arthur
Sheridan Ave.
Pine Tree Dr.
Indian Creek Dr.
44th St.

195

Julia Tuttle Causeway

907

30th St.
24th St.

Sunset Isles

Rivo Alto Island
Belle Isle
Bay Rd.

W. 20th St.
Dade Blvd.
23rd St.

City Park

Collins Park

Lincoln
Rd. Mall

Flamingo Park
14th St.
11th St.

Bay Rd.
Alton Rd.
9th St.
7th St.
Collins Ave.
Ocean Dr.

Lummus Park

Star Island

A1A

41

1st St.
Biscayne St.

South Pointe Park

Atlantic Ocean

Fisher Island

DINING:

Cafe Prima Pasta **8**
Cafe Ragazzi **3**
Chef Allen's **14**
Crystal Cafe **12**
Curry's **6**
The Forge Restaurant **11**
The Gourmet Diner **14**
The Greek Place **4**
Here Comes the Sun **13**
Lemon Twist **9**
Miami Beach Place **7**
Oggi Caffe **10**
The Palm **2**
Sheldon's Drugs **5**
Wolfie Cohen's Rascal House **1**

0   0.6 mi / 1 km

N

NA-0166

You can't go wrong with the limited, simple menu filled with old standbys, such as Caesar salad, shrimp cocktail, clams oreganata, salmon, broiled chicken, and veal. A selection of steak ranges from chopped to filet mignon. The prices are as big as the portions. You'll find more martini drinkers than health-conscious types here.

MODERATE

Cafe Prima Pasta. 414 71st St. (half a block east of the Byron movie theater), Miami Beach. ☎ **305/867-0106.** Main courses $12–$14; pastas $7–$9. No credit cards. Sun–Thurs 5pm–midnight; Fri 5pm–1am; Sat 1pm–1am. ITALIAN.

Here's another tiny pasta joint that serves phenomenal homemade noodles with good old Italian sauces, such as carbonara, dioliva, putanesca, and pomodoro. There are only 30 seats, so you might feel a bit cramped, but the crowd is generally a pleasant, young, laid-back set. The stuffed agnolotti with either tomato or pesto, spinach, and ricotta are so delicate and flavorful that you'll think you're eating dessert. Speaking of which, you'll want to try the apple tart with a pale golden caramel sauce. Ask for it à la mode and plan to come back again for more.

Its location, closer to Collins Avenue, makes this place more popular than the superior Oggi just a few miles west. Be prepared to stand in line.

Cafe Ragazzi. 9500 Harding Ave. (on corner of 95th St.), Surfside. ☎ **305/866-4495.** Reservations not accepted. Main courses $11–$15; MC, V. Mon–Fri 11:30am–3pm and 5:30–11pm; Sat 5:30pm–11pm; Sun 5–10:30pm. ITALIAN.

A relative newcomer in an area of old-time delis and diners, this little Italian cafe, with its rustic decor and a handsome waitstaff, enjoys great success for its tasty simple pastas. The spicy putanesca sauce with a subtle hint of fish is perfectly prepared, with just enough bits of tomato to give it some weight. Also recommended is the salmon with radicchio. You can choose from many decent salads and carpacci, too. Lunch specials are a real steal at $7, including soup, salad, and daily pasta. The mostly Italian/Argentinian staff is efficient, although sometimes limited in their ability to communicate. Expect a wait on weekend nights.

Lemon Twist. 908 71st St. (on 79th St. Causeway) , Miami Beach/Normandy Isle. ☎ **305/868-2075.** Reservations suggested on weekends. Main courses $8–$16; pastas $7–$9.50. AE, MC, V. Daily 6pm–midnight. FRENCH MEDITERRANEAN.

This hip little French bar and restaurant in a burgeoning neighborhood is certainly worth a visit. The specialties are salads and seafood. Both are excellent. A good dish is the tender lamb shank and the very tasty chicken with lemon and cream sauce. A favorite salad features a mound of herbed goat cheese in a puff pastry shell over a bed of fresh baby greens dressed in a delicate but spicy vinaigrette. The pastas, on the other hand, are not even worth a try. Most are overcooked and others underseasoned. You're sure to like the complimentary lemon vodka shots that are offered after each meal. The waitstaff is super-attentive, and the atmosphere is clubby and comfortable.

✪ Oggi Caffe. 1740 79th St. Causeway (in the White Star shopping center next to the Bagel Cafe), North Bay Village. ☎ **305/866-1238.** Reservations accepted. Main courses $12–$20; pastas $8–$10. AE, CB, DC, MC, V. Mon–Fri 11:30am–2:30pm; daily 6–11:00pm. ITALIAN.

Tucked away in a tiny strip mall on the 79th Street Causeway, this neighborhood favorite makes fresh pastas daily. Every one, from the agnolotti stuffed with fresh spinach and ricotta to the wire-thin spaghettini, is tender and tasty. Also notable are the daily soups. A hearty *pasta e fagiola* is filled with beans and vegetables and could almost be a meal. The creamy spinach soup, when on the menu, is also delicious and not laden with starch or other thickeners. Though you could fill up on the starters, the entrees, especially the grilled dishes, are superb. The salmon is served on a bed of spinach with a light lemon-butter sauce. The place is small and a bit rushed, but it's well worth the slight discomfort for this authentic, moderately priced food.

Wolfie Cohen's Rascal House. 17190 Collins Ave., Sunny Isles. ☎ **305/947-4581.** Omelets and sandwiches $4–$13; other dishes $5–$14. AE, MC, V. Open 24 hours. JEWISH/ DELICATESSEN/BAKERY.

Opened in 1954 and still going strong, this historic, nostalgic culinary extravaganza is one of Miami Beach's greatest traditions. Simple tables and booths as well as plenty of patrons fill the airy 425-seat dining room. The menu is as huge as the portions; try the corned beef, schmaltz herring, brisket, kreplach, chicken soup, or other authentic Jewish staples. Take-out service is available.

INEXPENSIVE

Curry's. 7433 Collins Ave., Miami Beach. ☎ **305/866-1571.** Reservations accepted. $8–$17, including appetizer, main course, dessert, and coffee. MC, V. Daily 4–10pm. AMERICAN.

Established in 1937, this large dining room on the ocean side of Collins Avenue is one of Miami Beach's oldest restaurants. Neither the restaurant's name nor the Polynesian wall decorations are indicative of its offerings, which are straightforwardly American and reminiscent of the area's heyday. Broiled and fried fish dishes are available, but the best selections, including steak, chicken, and ribs, come off the open charcoal grill perched by the front window. Prices are incredibly reasonable here, and all include an appetizer, soup, or salad, as well as a potato or vegetable, dessert, and coffee or tea.

✪ The Greek Place. 233 95th St. (between Collins and Harding Aves.), Surfside. ☎ **305/ 866-9628.** Main courses $5–$6. No credit cards. Mon–Fri 10am–6pm. GREEK.

The only drawback of this tiny hole in the wall is that it's open only on weekdays. It's a little diner with sparkling white walls and about 10 wooden stools that serves fantastic Greek and American diner-style food. Daily specials like pastitsio, chicken alcyone, and roast turkey with all the fixings are big lunchtime draws for locals working in the area. Typical Greek dishes like shish kebab, souvlakis, and gyros are cooked to perfection as you wait. Even the hamburger, prime ground beef delicately spiced and fresh grilled, is exemplary.

Miami Beach Place. 6954 Collins Ave., Miami Beach. ☎ **305/866-8661.** Main courses (served with spaghetti, vegetables, or rice and garlic rolls) $10–$13; pizzas and pastas $7–$16. MC, V. Sun–Fri 5pm–midnight; Sat 1pm–midnight. ITALIAN/PIZZA.

This Brazilian-owned pizza parlor is full most weekends, not only because of its good inexpensive pastas and pizzas, but also because of the fun Brazilian bands that play most weekend nights after 9pm. By midnight, the place is packed with Portuguese-speaking dancers who enjoy a late-night buffet and lots of wine and beer. I think the light garlicky garlic rolls wrapped in golden twists are addictive. While the pizza tends to be too cheesy for my taste, it's topped with fresh toppings instead of the canned variety offered at other places. If you've never tasted the ubiquitous Brazilian soda, *Guaraná,* I suggest trying a sip; it's like a rich ginger ale with not as much zing.

Sheldon's Drugs. 9501 Harding Ave., Surfside. ☎ **305/866-6251.** Main courses $4.50–$5; soups and sandwiches $2–$5. AE, DISC, MC, V. Mon–Sat 7am–9pm; Sun 7am–4pm. AMERICAN/DRUGSTORE.

This typical old-fashioned drugstore counter was a favorite breakfast spot of Isaac Bashevis Singer. Consider stopping into this historic site for a good piece of pie and a side of history. According to legend, he was sitting at Sheldon's, eating a bagel and eggs, when his wife got the call in 1978 that he had won the Nobel Prize for

Literature. The menu hasn't changed much since then. You can get eggs and oatmeal and a good tuna melt. A blue-plate special might be generic spaghetti and meatballs or grilled frankfurters. The food is pretty basic, but you can't beat the prices.

5 Key Biscayne

Key Biscayne has some of the world's nicest beaches, hotels, and parks, yet it's not known for great food. Most visitors eat at the island's largest hotel, where the food is reliable if not outstanding. Locals, or "Key rats" as they're known, tend to go off-island for meals or take-out, but here are some of the best on-the-island choices.

EXPENSIVE

Rusty Pelican. 3201 Rickenbacker Causeway, Key Biscayne. ☎ **305/361-3818.** Reservations recommended. Main courses $16–$20. AE, CB, DC, MC, V. Daily 11:30am–4pm; Sun–Thurs 5–11pm; Fri–Sat 5pm–midnight. CONTINENTAL.

The Pelican's private tropical walkway leads over a lush waterfall into one of the most romantic dining rooms in the city, located right on beautiful blue-green Biscayne Bay. The restaurant's windows look out over the water onto the sparkling stalagmites of Miami's magnificent downtown. Inside, quiet wicker paddle fans whirl overhead and saltwater fish swim in pretty tableside aquariums.

The restaurant's surf-and-turf menu features conservatively prepared prime steaks, veal, shrimp, and lobster. The food is good, but the atmosphere is even better, especially at sunset, when the view over the city is magical.

Stefano's. 24 Crandon Blvd., Key Biscayne. ☎ **305/361-7007.** Reservations recommended on weekends. Main courses $15–$23; pastas $11–$15. AE, DC, MC, V. Mon–Fri 11:30am–2:30pm; Sun–Thurs 6pm–11pm; Fri–Sat 6pm–12:30am. Disco open later. NORTHERN ITALIAN.

For retro-elegance, Stefano's has no match. Its restaurant and disco share the same strobe-lit atmosphere. Food is traditional and reliable, if a little pricey. You'll find an older country club crowd here in the evenings enjoying steaks and pastas and seafood. One of the best entrees is the *Delfino Livornese*, a dolphin (not Flipper—a type of saltwater fish) sautéed with a spicy sauce of tomato, olives, capers, and onions. Stefano's also serves some rare game, such as guinea hen in wine sauce and quails wrapped in pancetta. I recommend sticking with the pastas and fish.

After 7:30pm, the band starts playing pop American and Latin favorites. Some nights you feel as if you accidentally happened upon your long-lost cousin's wedding, as you watch the parade of taffeta dresses and tipsy uncles. Stefano's has continued to do well over time because of its dependable service and kitchen.

Sundays on the Bay. 5420 Crandon Blvd., Key Biscayne. ☎ **305/361-6777.** Reservations accepted; recommended for Sunday brunch. Main courses $15–$24; Sunday brunch $18.95. AE, CB, DC, MC, V. Daily 11am–11:45pm; Sun brunch 11am–4pm. AMERICAN.

Although its food is fine, Sundays is really a fun tropical bar that features an unbeatable view of Downtown, Coconut Grove, and the Sunday's marina. The menu features local favorites—grouper, tuna, snapper, and good shellfish in season. Competent renditions of such classic dishes as oysters Rockefeller, shrimp scampi, and lobster fra diablo are recommendable. Particularly popular is the Sunday brunch, when a buffet the size of Bimini attracts the city's late-rising in-crowd.

The lively bar stays open all week until midnight and weekends until 2am, with a DJ spinning most nights from 9pm.

INEXPENSIVE

✪ **Bayside Seafood Restaurant and Hidden Cove Bar.** 3501 Rickenbacker Causeway, Key Biscayne. ☎ **305/361-0808.** Reservations accepted only for groups of more than 15.

Appetizers, salads, and sandwiches $4.50–$6; platters $7–$13. AE, MC, V. Sun–Thurs 11:30am–10:30pm; Fri–Sat 11:30am–1am; disco on weekends ($5 cover) 11pm–4am. SEAFOOD/PASTA.

Known by locals as "the Hut," this ramshackle restaurant and bar is a laid-back outdoor tiki hut and terrace that serves pretty good sandwiches and fish platters on paper plates. A blackboard lists the latest catches, which can be prepared blackened, fried, broiled, or in a garlic sauce. I prefer the blackened, which is super-crusty, spicy, and dark. The fish dip is wonderfully smoky and moist, if a little heavy on mayonnaise. Lately the Hut has been offering happy hours on weekday evenings with open bar and snacks for $25 per person. It's a good deal if you drink a lot.

But if you come here, do bring bug spray or ask the waiters for some (they usually keep packets behind the bar). For some reason, this place is plagued by mosquitoes even when the rest of town is not. Local fishermen and yacht owners share this rustic outpost with equal enthusiasm and loyalty.

☼ **La Boulangerie.** 328 Crandon Blvd. (in Eckerd's shopping mall), Key Biscayne. ☎ **305/361-0281.** Sandwiches and salads $5–$7. MC, V. Mon–Sat 7:30am–8pm; Sun 7:30am–6pm. FRENCH BAKERY.

Beware. You'll stop into this inconspicuous French bakery for a loaf of bread and find yourself walking out with an armload of the freshest sandwiches, salads, groceries, and pastries anywhere. You can also sit and enjoy a great breakfast, lunch, or early dinner with the jet-set in their designer sweatsuits. There are about 15 tables inside where diners enjoy vegetarian omelets, gourmet sandwiches, and dangerous desserts. The prosciutto and goat cheese sandwich on crusty French bread is unbeatable. There must be something in the mustard.

The friendly proprietors behind the counter will no doubt talk you into a heavenly fruit tart, like the pointy-tipped apricot tart with plump fruit halves painted with a thin layer of sweet glaze. Try any of the cakes or rustic breads, too.

The Oasis. 19 Harbor Dr. (on corner of Crandon), Key Biscayne. ☎ **305/361-5709.** Main courses $4–$12; sandwiches $3–$4. No credit cards. Daily 6am–9pm. CUBAN.

Even Hurricane Andrew couldn't blow down this rugged little shack where everyone, from the city's mayor to the local handymen, meet for delicious paella or a good Cuban sandwich. In fact, after the storm, the place expanded and now provides seating for those who used to gather around the little window for super-powerful *cafesitos* and rich *croquetas*. It's a little dingy, but the food is good and cheap.

6 Downtown

Downtown Miami is a large sprawling area divided by the Brickell bridge into two distinct areas: Brickell Avenue and the bayfront area near Biscayne Boulevard. You shouldn't walk from one to the other because it's too far a distance and unsafe at night. Convenient Metromover stops do adjoin the areas, so for a quarter, it's better to hop on the scenic sky-tram (closed after midnight).

If your hotel is not Downtown and you aren't going to a show at the Gusman, the Knight Center, or Bayside, put your visit off until the afternoon when you'll join Latin American shoppers, college students, and lots of professionals in suits. Although some shopkeepers in the area have tried to revitalize the nighttime scene, Downtown Miami mostly shuts down after dark. A few of the better restaurants, especially in the hotels, stay open late.

VERY EXPENSIVE

☼ **Le Pavillon.** 100 Chopin Plaza (in the Hotel Inter-Continental, adjacent to the Bayside Marketplace), Downtown. ☎ **305/577-1000.** Reservations recommended. Main courses

$18–$23. AE, CB, DC, DISC, MC, V. Mon–Fri noon–2:30pm; Tues–Sat 6:30–10:30pm. NEW WORLD CUISINE.

Once a private club, Le Pavillon maintains an air of exclusivity with leather sofas and an expensive salon setting. Dark-green marble columns divide the spacious dining room, while well-spaced booths and tables provide comfortable seating and a sense of privacy. The menu features both heavy club-room fare and lighter dishes prepared with a masterful Miami Regional hand.

Standout appetizers include the chilled trout, stuffed with seafood and basil, and an unusual grilled shrimp cocktail with pineapple relish and citrus-flavored lobster mayonnaise. Skillfully prepared main dishes include boneless quail Louisiana, stuffed with oysters and andouille sausage. Meat, fish, and chicken dishes are abundant, as are a host of creative pastas, including ravioli stuffed with artichokes, garlic, truffles, and cheese.

EXPENSIVE

The Fish Market. 1601 Biscayne Blvd. (at The Wyndham, corner of 16th St.), Downtown. ☎ 305/374-4399. Reservations recommended. Main courses $17–$22. AE, CB, DC, DISC, MC, V. Mon–Fri 11:30am–2:30pm; Mon–Sat 6–11pm. SEAFOOD.

One of Miami's most celebrated seafood restaurants is this understated, elegant dining room right in the heart of the city. It's spacious and comfortable, featuring high ceilings, marble floors, and a sumptuous dessert table centerpiece. Local fish, prepared and presented simply (either sautéed or grilled), is always the menu's main feature. Don't overlook the appetizers, which include meaty Mediterranean-style seafood soup and delicate yellowfin tuna carpaccio. Prices are very reasonable.

MODERATE

✪ **East Coast Fisheries.** 360 W. Flagler St., Downtown (south). ☎ 305/372-1300. Reservations recommended. Main courses $9–$25. AE, MC, V. Daily 11am–10pm. From I-95 South, exit at NW 8th Street. Drive straight to NW 3rd Street and turn right. The next block is River Drive. Turn left, and you'll see the restaurant 3 blocks down on the right-hand side. SEAFOOD.

East Coast Fisheries is a no-nonsense retail market and restaurant offering a terrific variety of the freshest fish available. The dozen or so plain wood tables are surrounded by refrigerated glass cases filled with snapper, salmon, mahi-mahi, trout, tuna, crabs, oysters, lobsters, and the like. The absolutely huge menu features every fish imaginable, cooked the way you want it—grilled, fried, stuffed, Cajun-style, Florentine, hollandaise, or blackened. However, the smell of frying grease detracts from the otherwise quaint old-Miami feel. Service is fast, but good prices and good food still mean long lines on weekends.

✪ **Fishbone Grille.** 650 S. Miami Ave. (SW 7th Ave., next to Tobacco Rd.), Downtown. ☎ 305/530-1915. Reservations recommended on weekends. Entrees $6–$16; pizzas and pastas $9–$20. AE, CB, DC, DISC, MC, V. Mon–Thurs 11:30am–10pm; Fri 11:30am–11pm; Sat 5:30–11pm. SEAFOOD.

This is by far Miami's best and most reasonably priced seafood restaurant. Located in a small strip mall it shares with Tobacco Road, this sensational fish shop prepares dozens of outstanding specials daily. The atmosphere is nothing to speak of, although at one cool table you can stare into a fish tank.

Try the excellent ceviche, which has just enough spice to give it a zing, yet doesn't overwhelm the fresh fish flavor. The stews, crab cakes, and all the starters are superb. If you like a nice Caribbean flavor, try the jerk Covina (the Biblical fish) or one of the excellent dolphin specialties.

Las Tapas. 401 Biscayne Blvd. (in the Bayside Marketplace), Downtown. ☎ 305/372-2737. Reservations accepted. Tapas $4–$7; main courses $12–$29. AE, CB, DC, DISC, MC, V. Sun–Thurs 11am–midnight; Fri–Sat 11am–1am. SPANISH.

Occupying a large corner of Downtown's Bayside Marketplace, glass-wrapped Las Tapas is a fun place to dine in a laid-back, easy atmosphere. *Tapas,* small dishes of Spanish delicacies, are the featured fare here. Good chicken, veal, and seafood main dishes are on the menu, but it's more fun to taste a variety of the restaurant's tapas. The best include shrimp in garlic, smoked pork shank with Spanish sausage, baby eel in garlic and oil, and chicken sautéed with garlic and mushrooms.

The open kitchen in front of the entrance greets diners with succulent smells. The long dining room is outlined in red Spanish stone and decorated with hundreds of hanging hams.

INEXPENSIVE

✪ **Caribbean Delite.** 236 NE First Ave. (across the street from Miami Dade Community College), Downtown. ☎ **305/381-9254.** Menu items $5.50–$9; full meals $4–$7. AE, MC, V. Mon–Sat 8:30am–7pm. JAMAICAN.

You'd never spot this tiny storefront diner on a one-way street, although you might smell it from the sidewalk. The aroma of succulent jerk chicken or pork beckons regulars back over and over again. Try Jamaican specialties, such as the oxtail stew or the curried goat, tender tasty pieces of meat on the bone in a spicy yellow sauce. The kitchen can be stingy with its spectacular sauces, leaving the dishes a bit dry, so ask for an extra helping on the side. They are happy to oblige. Also, if you come early in the day, you can get a taste of Jamaica's national dish, salt fish and ackee (usually served for breakfast). Ask chef-owner Carol Whyte to tell you the story of this interesting dish made with "brain fruit" or quiz one of the many Jamaicans who stop in while they are in port off the cruise ships a few blocks away.

The Crepe Maker. 70 Biscayne Blvd. (East Flagler St. in the Columbus Bazaar) ☎ **305/377-2218** (for catering). Crêpes $2.50–$6. No credit cards. Mon–Fri 11am-2:30pm. CREPES.

If you don't mind standing, The Crepe Maker carts prepare some of the freshest, most delicious fare available Downtown. Inspired by the wooden crêpe carts in Paris, Christopher Hoffman and his wife Maria decided Miamians would appreciate the cheap, healthful ease of fresh meats and vegetables quickly sautéed at sidewalk carts. They were right. Lawyers, students, and tourists wait in line to watch the little pancakes turn golden brown on the edges in time for a cheerful chef in a flouncy white hat to throw a dash of olive oil and a handful of spinach leaves in the center.

Specials change daily but include classics like Cordon Bleu with ham, chicken, and cheese and innovations like Havana chicken with sweet red peppers, black beans, and sweet pesto. You can also design whatever you like. For dessert, there are fruit-and-jam–filled specialties.

La Cibeles Cafe. 105 NE 3rd Ave. (1 block west of Biscayne Blvd.), Downtown. ☎ **305/577-3454.** Main courses $5–$9. No credit cards. Mon–Sat 7:30am–7:30pm. CUBAN/BRAZILIAN/SPANISH.

This very typical Latin diner serves some of the best food in town. Just by looking at the line that runs out the door every afternoon between noon and 2pm, you can see that you're not the first to discover it. For about $5, you can have a huge and filling meal. Pay attention to the daily lunch specials and go with them. A pounded, tender chicken breast (*pechuga*) is smothered in sautéed onions and served with rice and beans and a salad. Also good is the trout or the roast pork. When available, try the *ropa vieja,* a shredded beef dish delicately spiced and served with peas and rice.

Raja's. 243 E. Flagler St. (in the Galeria International mall), Downtown. ☎ **305/539-9551.** Menu items $3–$6; specials, including salad, rice, and vegetable side dishes $5. No credit cards. Thurs–Tues 9am–6:30pm; Sun 9am–4:30pm. SOUTH INDIAN/FAST FOOD.

Nearly impossible to find, this tiny counter in the hustling Downtown food court serves some of the feistiest chicken stews and vegetarian dishes in Miami. It's surrounded by mostly Brazilian fast-food places packed with tour groups on shopping sprees.

If you like it spicy, try the rich Masala Spicy Chili Chicken. For vegetarians, the heaping platters of dahl, cauliflower, eggplant, broccoli, and chickpeas are a valuable find. For those who know to request them, there are half a dozen tasty condiments, including lemon chutney with fresh orange rinds, bright green cilantro sauce, and glistening gold mango chutney that will complement the rough stews and tasty soups. The Masala Dosa (rice crêpes stuffed with vegetable mash) is a filling lunch or dinner made fresh when ordered. The side salad with fresh onions, cucumbers, and lettuce is free with the specials, but only if you ask for it. Try a mango lassi to finish off the meal and to cool your tongue.

S & S Restaurant. 1757 NE Second Ave., Downtown. ☎ **305/373-4291.** Main courses $5–$11. No credit cards. Mon–Fri 6am–7pm; Sat 6am–2:30pm (later on Heat game nights). DINER.

This tiny chrome-and-linoleum-counter restaurant in the middle of Downtown looks like a truck stop. But locals have been coming back since it opened in 1938. Expect a wait at lunch time while the mostly male clientele, from lawyers to linemen, wait patiently for old-fashioned fast food served in large quantities.

You'll get a slice of pie and a slice of Miami history at the same time at S & S. Although the neighborhood has become pretty undesirable, the food—basic diner fare with some excellent stews and soups—hasn't changed in years. It's one of the only places in town I know that serves creamed chicken on toast. Also good when it's on the specials board is the stuffed cabbage roll in a pale brown sauce. In addition to cheap breakfasts, the diner serves up some of the most comfortable comfort food in Miami.

7 Little Havana

The main artery of Little Havana is a busy commercial strip called Southwest 8th Street, or *Calle Ocho.* Auto body shops, cigar factories, and furniture stores line this street, and on every corner there seems to be a pass-through window serving super-strong Cuban coffee and snacks. In addition, many of the Cuban, Dominican, Nicaraguan, Peruvian, and Latin American immigrants have opened full-scale restaurants ranging from intimate candlelit establishments to bustling stand-up lunch counters.

VERY EXPENSIVE

Victor's Cafe. 2340 SW 32nd Ave. (1 block south of Coral Way), Little Havana. ☎ **305/445-1313.** Reservations recommended. Main courses $19–$32. AE, DC, MC, V. Sun–Thurs noon–midnight; Fri–Sat noon–1am. CUBAN.

At Victor's, you'll get good food in an upscale setting—it's a place for tourists and celebrations. Locals say it's overpriced. Strolling guitarists add an air of romance to this kitschy old Havana-style restaurant. Lively salsa music wafts through the regal dining room where attentive waiters look after most details. Stick around for the wild cabaret most nights after 11pm. Ask to sit on El Patio where oversized umbrellas shade you from the sun and create a private little cocoon overlooking the lush courtyard.

The cooking takes liberties with Cuban classics with generally good results. Some of the best dishes are the fish and shrimp plates, all served with rice and beans.

Cuban Coffee

Forget Starbucks and the other fancy coffeehouses that have sprouted up all over the country. Of course, a few of the national chains have made it this far south with their pricey cappuccinos and frothy blends, but for a real taste of Florida, you need to head where the locals go.

Cuban coffee is a long-standing tradition in Miami. You'll find it served from the take-out windows of hundreds of *cafeterías* or *luncherías* around town, especially in Little Havana, Downtown, Hialeah, and the beaches. Depending on where you are and what you want, you'll spend between 40 and 95¢ per cup.

The best *café cubano* has a rich layer of foam on top formed when the hot espresso shoots from the machine into the sugar below. The result is the caramelly, sweet, potent concoction that's a favorite of locals of all nationalities.

To partake, you've just got to learn how to ask for it *en español.*

The most commonly ordered take-out coffee is the *colada.* This large cup of sweet black coffee is served in a Styrofoam cup with five or six thimble-size plastic cups on top, meant to be shared with friends or co-workers.

If you're alone, you'll probably want a *café* or *cafecito,* a thimble-size cup of the same thick black espresso with lots of sugar. It's usually swallowed in one quick gulp. Unless you ask for it to go (*para llevar*), you'll probably get it in a miniature ceramic cup and saucer. Don't be fooled by the small size. Caffeine-wise, one shot of this stuff is equal to two or three mugs of the American version.

For the less brave, there is the *cortado* or *cortadito,* the same dose of strong coffee cut with a bit of steamed milk.

Even more mild is the is the *café con leche,* a large cup of steamed milk with a single shot of coffee. You can ask for it *oscuro* (dark) or *claro* (light), but count on it being sweet. This coffee is especially popular at breakfast, when it often accompanies *pan tostada,* a long hunk of grilled, flattened, and buttered bread that you dunk in the cup, donut style.

To avoid the sweetness, order your coffee *sin azúcar,* without sugar, or *con poco azúcar,* with a little sugar—but even then, you'll have to be vigilant. The person behind the counter has probably heaped thousands of spoons of sugar over the years. It's an automatic motion. Ask twice and watch closely. If you want artificial sweetener, ask for *azúcar de dieta.*

You can even find decaffeinated coffee, *café descafeínado,* in some shops. Café Bustelo, the most ubiquitous brand of Cuban coffee, began marketing a neutered version of its famous espresso several years ago. It's not bad, but it certainly doesn't have the same effect as the real stuff. Low-fat or skim milk is harder to find.

Finally, if you insist, you can usually get a cup of American coffee, *café americano,* in a Latin restaurant, although I wouldn't advise it. It was probably brewed hours ago. Locals sometimes call it *agua sucia,* dirty water, and that's most likely what your coffee will taste like. It's worse than airline coffee; I wouldn't recommend it. Stick with the real stuff, but watch out—it can be habit-forming. Remember, you're supposed to relax in Miami.

My favorite appetizer is the snapper ceviche marinated in Cachucha pepper and lime juice. The beef dishes are also good. The *bistec alo Victor con tamal en balsa* is a tender oak-grilled top sirloin served with Cuban-style polenta.

MODERATE

✪ **Casa Juancho.** 2436 SW 8th St., Little Havana. ☎ **305/642-2452.** Reservations recommended, but not accepted Fri–Sat after 8pm. Tapas $6–$8; main courses $13–$20. AE, CB, DC, MC, V. Sun–Thurs noon–midnight; Fri–Sat noon–1am. SPANISH.

One of Miami's finest Hispanic restaurants, Casa Juancho offers an ambitious menu of excellently prepared main dishes and tapas. The several dining rooms are decorated with traditional Spanish furnishings and enlivened nightly by strolling Spanish musicians. Try not to be frustrated with the older staff who don't speak English or respond quickly to your subtle glance. They are used to an aggressive clientele.

I suggest ordering lots of tapas, small dishes of Spanish "finger food." Some of the best include mixed seafood vinaigrette, fresh shrimp in hot garlic sauce, and fried calamari rings. A few entrees stand out, like roast suckling pig, baby eels in garlic and olive oil, and Iberian-style snapper.

INEXPENSIVE

✪ **Hy-Vong.** 3458 SW 8th St. (between 34th and 35th Aves.), Little Havana. ☎ **305/446-3674.** Reservations not accepted. Main courses $8–$15. No credit cards. Wed–Sun 6–11pm. Closed 2 weeks in Aug. VIETNAMESE.

Expect to wait hours for a table, and don't even think of mumbling a complaint. It's worth it, despite the poor service. Vietnamese cuisine combines the best of Asian and French cooking with spectacular results. Food at Hy-Vong is elegantly simple and super-spicy. Appetizers include small, tightly packed Vietnamese spring rolls, and *kimchee*, a spicy, fermented cabbage. Star entrees include pastry-enclosed chicken with watercress cream-cheese sauce and fish in tangy mango sauce.

Enjoy the wait with a traditional Vietnamese beer and lots of company. Outside this tiny storefront restaurant, you'll meet interesting students, musicians, and foodies who come for the large delicious portions, not for the plain wood-paneled room or painfully slow, inattentive service.

La Carreta. 3632 SW 8th St., Little Havana. ☎ **305/446-4915.** Main courses $3–$9. DC, MC, V. Daily 24 hours. CUBAN.

This cavernous family-style restaurant is filled with relics of an old farm and college kids eating *medianoches* (midnight sandwiches with ham, cheese, and pickles) after partying all night. Waitresses are brusque but efficient and will help anglos along who may not know all the lingo. The menu is vast and very authentic. Try the *sopa de pollo*, a rich golden stock loaded with chunks of chicken and fresh vegetables or the *ropa vieja*, a shredded beef stew in a thick brown sauce.

Because of its immense popularity and low prices, La Carreta has opened several branches throughout Miami. Check the white pages for locations.

✪ **Versailles.** 3555 SW 8th St., Little Havana. ☎ **305/444-0240.** Soup and salad $2–$10; main courses $5–$8. DC, DISC, MC, V. Mon–Thurs 8am–2am; Fri 8am–3:30am; Sat 8am–4:30am; Sun 9am–2am. CUBAN.

Versailles is the meeting place of Miami's Cuban power brokers, who meet daily over *café con leche* to discuss the future of the exiles' fate. A glorified diner, the place sparkles with glass, chandeliers, murals, and mirrors meant to evoke the French palace. There's nothing fancy here—nothing French, either—just straightforward food from the home country. The menu is a veritable survey of Cuban cooking and includes specialties such as Moors and Christians (flavorful black beans with white rice), ropa vieja, and fried whole fish.

From Ceviche to Picadillo: Latin Cuisine at a Glance

In Little Havana and wondering what to eat? Many restaurants list menu items in English for the benefit of *norteamericano* diners. In case you're wondering what to eat, though, here are translations and suggestions for filling and delicious meals:

Arroz con pollo　Roast chicken served with saffron-seasoned yellow rice and diced vegetables.

Café cubano　Very strong black coffee, served in thimble-size cups with lots of sugar. It's a real eye-opener.

Camarones　Shrimp.

Ceviche　Raw fish seasoned with spice and vegetables and marinated in vinegar and citrus to "cook" it.

Croquetas　Golden-fried croquettes of ham, chicken, or fish.

Paella　A Spanish dish of chicken, sausage, seafood, and pork mixed with saffron rice and peas.

Palomilla　Thinly sliced beef, similar to American minute steak, usually served with onions, parsley, and a mountain of French fries.

Pan cubano　Long, white crusty Cuban bread. Ask for it *tostada,* toasted and flattened on a grill with lots of butter.

Picadillo　A rich stew of ground meat, brown gravy, peas, pimientos, raisins, and olives.

Plátano　A deep-fried, soft, mildly sweet banana.

Pollo asado　Roasted chicken with onions and a crispy skin.

Ropa vieja　A delicious shredded beef stew, whose name literally means "old clothes."

Sopa de pollo　Chicken soup, usually with noodles or rice.

Tapas　A general name for Spanish-style hors d'oeuvres, served in grazing-size portions.

8 West Dade

As all of South Florida expands westward, good restaurants will follow as well. So far, however, only a few have distinguished themselves, and they are reviewed here.

VERY EXPENSIVE

Shula's Steak House. 7601 NW 154th St. (Miami Lakes Golf Resort off the Palmetto Expressway), Miami Lakes. ☎ **305/820-8102.** Reservations recommended. Main courses $18–$58. AE, CB, DC, MC, V. In season Mon–Fri 6:30am–2:30pm and 6–11pm; Sat–Sun 7–11am and 6–11pm; call for hours off-season (May–Nov). STEAKHOUSE.

This is the place to get huge slabs of red meat cooked however you like. A limited à la carte menu lists entrees by weight. You could start with the petite 12-ounce filet mignon, so tender and juicy you could almost cut it with your fork. Linebackers might consider the 48-ounce porterhouse. I haven't tried it myself, but am told it's one of the best. Potatoes and a few vegetables are available, but don't bring your vegetarian friends here. They'd go hungry.

Retired Miami Dolphin coach Don Shula is said to be spending more time around this shrine to his old Dolphins as he puts the final touches on his new location in the Alexander Hotel in Miami Beach.

MODERATE

Tony Roma's Famous For Ribs. 6728 Main St. (at Ludlum Rd.), Miami Lakes. ☎ **305/558-7427.** Main courses $9–$14; sandwiches $6. AE, CB, DC, DISC, MC, V. Mon–Thurs 11am–11pm; Fri–Sat 11am–1am. AMERICAN.

Rib lovers rave over this Miami-based chain that now has more than a dozen locations in South Florida. In Miami Lakes, the place is packed with regulars who order full slabs of thick meaty pork with the usual side dishes, such as cole slaw and a crispy onion loaf. You can't beat the prices and the dark woody atmosphere makes you feel like you're in a much more upscale place.

Other locations include 15700 Biscayne Blvd., North Miami (☎ **305/949-2214**); 18050 Collins Ave., Miami Beach (☎ **305/932-7907**); and 2665 SW 37th Ave., Coral Gables (☎ **305/443-6626**).

9 North Dade

Although there aren't many hotels in North Dade, the population in the winter months explodes because of the large number of seasonal residents from the Northeast. A number of exclusive condominiums and country clubs, including William's Island, Turnberry, and The Jockey Club, breed a demanding clientele, many of whom dine out nightly. That's good news for visitors who can find superior service and cuisine at value prices.

VERY EXPENSIVE

○ **Chef Allen's.** 19088 NE 29th Ave. (at Biscayne Blvd.), North Miami Beach. ☎ **305/935-2900.** Reservations suggested. Main courses $26–$31. AE, DC, MC, V. Sun–Thurs 6–10:30pm; Fri–Sat 6–11pm. NEW WORLD CUISINE.

For one of South Florida's finest dining experiences, Chef Allen's is a must. There simply isn't better food to be found in the county. Owner-chef Allen Susser, of New York's Le Cirque fame, has built a classy yet relaxed restaurant with art deco furnishings, a glass-enclosed kitchen, and a hot-pink swirl of neon surrounding the dining room's ceiling. It's more than a little kitschy, but this is Miami, after all. In a town of flash-in-the-pan restaurants, this 14-year-old spot has become an institution, helped by a young, energetic staff.

Appetizers are alluring and may include lobster-and-crab cakes served with strawberry-ginger chutneys, or baked brie with spinach, sun-dried tomatoes, and pine nuts. Favorite main dishes include crisp roast duck with cranberry sauce, and mesquite-grilled Norwegian salmon with champagne grapes, green onions, and basil spaetzle. Local fish dishes, in various delectable guises, and homemade pastas are always on the menu. The extensive wine list is well chosen and features several good buys. Handmade desserts are works of art and sinfully delicious.

MODERATE

The Gourmet Diner. 13951 Biscayne Blvd. (between NE 139th and 140th Sts.), North Miami Beach. ☎ **305/947-2255.** Reservations not accepted. Main courses $10–$17. MC, V. Mon–Fri 11am–11pm; Sat 8am–11:30pm; Sun 8am–10:30pm. BELGIAN/FRENCH.

This retro 1950s-style diner serves plain old French fare without pretensions. The atmosphere is a bit brash, and the lines are often out the door. You'll want to get there early anyway to taste some of the house specialties, such as beef Burgundy, the trout amandine, and frog legs Provençale—these dishes tend to sell out quickly.

Check the blackboard, which—depending on where you are seated—can be hard to see. The salads and soups are all prepared to order. Even a simple hearts of palm becomes a gourmet treat under the basic, tangy vinaigrette. A well-rounded wine list with reasonable prices makes this place a standout and a great deal. The homemade pastries are also delicious.

The Lagoon. 488 Sunny Isles Blvd. (163rd St.), North Miami Beach. ☎ **305/947-6661.** Reservations accepted. Main courses $12–$22; lobster special $22.95. AE, CB, MC, V. Daily 4:30–11pm; early-bird dinner 4:30–6pm. SEAFOOD/CONTINENTAL.

This old bayfront fish house has been around since 1936. Major road construction nearby should have guaranteed its doom years ago, but the excellent view and incredible specials make it a worthwhile stop. If you can disregard the somewhat dirty bathrooms and nonchalant service, you'll find the best-priced juicy Maine lobsters around.

Yes, it's true! Lobster lovers can get two 1 1/4 pounders for $22.95. Try them broiled with a light buttery seasoned coating. This dish is not only inexpensive but incredibly succulent, too. Side dishes include fresh vegetables, like broccoli or asparagus, as well as a huge baked potato, stuffed or plain. The salads are good but come with too much commercial-tasting dressing. To be safe, ask for oil and vinegar on the side, or, better yet, skip all the accouterments to save room for the lobster.

The Melting Pot. 3143 NE 163rd St. (between U.S. 1 and Collins Avenue, in Sunny Isles Plaza shopping center), North Miami Beach. ☎ **305/947-2228.** Reservations recommended on weekends. Main courses $9–$11 for cheese fondue; $11–$18 for meat and fish fondues. AE, DISC, MC, V. Sun–Thurs 5:30–10:30pm; Fri–Sat 5:30pm–midnight. FONDUE.

Traditional fondue is supplemented by combination meat-and-fish dinners, which are served with one of almost a dozen different sauces. The place, with its lace curtains and cozy booths, was voted most romantic restaurant in the local alternative paper several years ago.

As more diners become health conscious, the owners have introduced a more healthful version of fondue, in which you cook vegetables and meats in a low-fat broth. It tastes good, although this version is less fun than watching drippy cheese flow from the hot pot. Best of all, perhaps, is dessert: chunks of pineapple, bananas, apples, and cherries you dip into a creamy chocolate fondue. No liquor is served here, but the wine list is extensive, and beer is available.

A second Melting Pot is located at 9835 SW 72nd St. (Sunset Drive) in Kendall (☎ **305/279-8816**).

INEXPENSIVE

Amos' Juice Bar. 18315 W. Dixie Hwy. (1 block west of Biscayne Blvd.), North Miami Beach. ☎ **305/935-9544.** Sandwiches and salads $4–$6. No credit cards. Mon–Sat 8:30am–6:30pm. HEALTH FOOD.

This brightly painted stand in the middle of a busy road attracts a varied crowd, from young pony-tailed Europeans to bikers. If you don't mind a bit of car exhaust with your snapper sandwich, consider this landmark in North Dade.

The food is made on the premises and includes one of the most unusual tuna salads I've ever run across, served in a pita with tons of crisp vegetables, including alfalfa sprouts, tomato, and lettuce. The hummus is also superb, although garlic lovers might want a hint more spark. You can also get a fresh smoothie or vegetable juice made on the spot.

Beverly Hills Cafe. 17850 West Dixie Hwy., North Miami Beach. ☎ **305/935-3660.** Salads and sandwiches $5–$7; main courses $8–$13. AE, DISC, MC, V. Mon–Thurs 11:30am–9:30pm; Fri–Sat 11:30am–10pm. AMERICAN.

🐘 Family-Friendly Restaurants

Beverly Hills Cafe *(see p. 105)* This restaurant offers a varied selection for children under 10 years old. Choices include the regular offerings of hamburgers, hot dogs, and grilled cheese sandwiches, as well as healthier options such as pasta marinara and a turkey sandwich. Entrees cost around $4 and include French fries, soda, apple juice, or milk.

The Crepe Maker Cafe *(see p. 114)* This little French café lets you and the kids create your own crepe concoctions. You can even get ice cream crepes for dessert. Afterwards, the kids can entertain themselves in a small play area.

Señor Frogs *(see p. 113)* This Coconut Grove restaurant, with its lively atmosphere and universally appealing Mexican dishes, plus margaritas for the adults, is a good choice for the entire family. The service is generally efficient, and the food is reasonably priced. If you ask for half portions of some of the more popular dishes, such as the quesadilla, the kitchen will happily oblige. High chairs and booster chairs are available.

Van Dyke's *(see p. 90)* One of South Beach's only family-friendly sit-down restaurants, Van Dyke is a large indoor/outdoor cafe whose whole menu is for children. From PB and Js to grilled cheese to burgers, this is the spot for kids of all ages.

Versailles Restaurant *(see p. 102)* This quirky, bustling Cuban diner is great for kids. Although there's no specific children's menu, the place is used to catering to patrons of all ages. You'll find *abuelitos* and *niños,* little old grandparents and children, as well as high-powered politicians and teenage revelers. The prices are cheap, and there are plenty of choices for even the most finicky eater. Try *croquetas* of ham, chicken, or fish, or a Cuban sandwich.

It isn't pink, and it isn't in Los Angeles, but this pleasant little spot in a cobble-pathed mini-mall is a perfect choice for an affordable business lunch or family dinner. The varied menu includes Mexican dishes, like quesadillas and fajitas, and good old classics, like Caesar salads or Philly cheese steak sandwiches. Some more healthful options include a fragrant stir-fried chicken on saffron-flavored rice and a blackened dolphin sandwich. A spicy Southwestern chicken penne dish with grilled pepper and onions is a particularly good choice for those who enjoy a little heat.

While none of the dishes are overly ambitious, the presentation and large portions make this a popular place for the predominantly budget-conscious diners in the neighborhood. Be warned that you can fill up on the toasty warm bread before one of the well-meaning but overworked waitresses arrives to take your order. Save room for the renowned tollhouse pie, a hot-fudge-sundae slab of ice cream atop a chocolate chip cookie dough crust. A limited but affordable selection of wines and beers is available.

Another Beverly Hills Cafe is located at 1559 Sunset Dr., Coral Gables (☎ **305/ 666-6618**).

Here Comes the Sun. 2188 NE 123rd St. (west of the Broad Causeway), North Miami. ☎ **305/893-5711.** Reservations recommended in season. Main courses $10–$14; early-bird special $7.95; sandwiches and salads $5–$7.50. AE, DC, DISC, MC, V. Mon–Sat 11am–8:30pm. AMERICAN/HEALTH FOOD.

One of Miami's first health-food spots, this bustling grocery-store-turned-diner serves hundreds of plates a night, mostly to blue-haired locals. It's noisy and hectic but worth it. In season, all types pack the place for a $7.95 special, served between 4 and 6:30pm, which includes one of more than 20 choices of entrees, soup or salad, coffee or tea, and a small frozen yogurt. Fresh grilled fish and chicken entrees are reliable and served with a nice array of vegetables. The miso burgers with "sun sauce" are a vegetarian's dream.

Laurenzo's Cafe. 16385 West Dixie Hwy. (at the corner of 163rd St.), North Miami Beach. ☎ 305/945-6381. Main courses $4–$5; salads $2–$5. AE, MC, V. Mon–Sat 8am–7pm; Sun 8am–4pm. SOUTHERN ITALIAN CAFETERIA.

This little lunch counter in the middle of a chaotic grocery store has been serving delicious buffet lunches to the *paesanos* for years. A meeting place for the growing Italian population in Miami, the store has been open for more than 40 years. Daily specials usually include a lasagna or eggplant parmigiano and two or three salad options.

Choose a wine from the vast selection and take your meal to go or sit in the trellis-covered seating area amid busy shoppers buying their evening's groceries. You'll get to eavesdrop on some great conversations over your plastic tray of real southern-style Italian cooking.

10   Coral Gables & Environs

VERY EXPENSIVE

Christy's. 3101 Ponce de Leon Blvd., Coral Gables. ☎ **305/446-1400.** Reservations strongly recommended. Main courses $17–$30. AE, CB, DC, MC, V. Mon–Thur 11:30am–4pm; Fri 4–11:30pm; Sat 5pm–midnight; Sun 5–11pm. AMERICAN.

Arrive famished. One of the Gables' most expensive and elegant establishments, Christy's is known primarily for its generous cuts of thick, juicy steaks and ribs, despite its demure Victorian style. Some say it's one of the most romantic spots in Miami. I say it's just fine for serious carnivores.

The prime rib is so thick that even a small cut weighs about a pound. New York strip, filet mignon, and chateaubriand are all on the menu here, and all steaks are fully aged without chemicals or freezing. Each entree is served with a jumbo Caesar salad and a baked potato. Seafood, veal, and chicken dishes are also available; however, ordering anything but a steak at this pricey little candlelit spot would be a disappointment.

Norman's. 21 Almera Ave. (between Douglas and Ponce de Leon), Coral Gables. ☎ **305/446-6767.** Reservations highly recommended. Main courses $25–$32. Mon–Thurs noon–2pm and 6–10:30pm; Fri noon–2pm and 6–10:30pm; Sat 6–11pm. AE, DC, MC, V. NEW WORLD CUISINE.

Master chef Norman Van Aken, one of the originators of New World Cuisine, re-emerged after a 2-year break from restauranting to open what he has called his "culmination." The result is an open kitchen, surrounded by well-dressed diners, where a handful of silent industrious chefs prepare Asian- and Caribbean-inspired dishes.

The food is the main focus of attention. Some think the exotic-sounding menu is pretentious or overwrought. I think there's plenty to enjoy, like pizzas and pastas with a good glass of wine and a hunk of bread. The fish, too, is out of this world. The Rhum-and-pepper-painted grouper on mango-Habanero Mojo is an exotic-tasting dark-fleshed fish with an explosion of sauces to complement its heavy flavor.

The staff is adoring and professional and the atmosphere tasteful without being too formal. The portions are realistic, but still, be careful not to overdo it. You'll want to try some of the wacky desserts, such as mango ice cream served with Asian pears and crushed red pepper (the pepper really just adds color to the plate).

EXPENSIVE

The Bistro. 2611 Ponce de Leon Blvd., Coral Gables. ☎ **305/442-9671.** Reservations recommended. Main courses $16–$26. AE, CB, DC, DISC, MC, V. Mon–Fri 11:30am–2pm; Mon–Thurs 6–10:30pm; Fri–Sat 6–11pm. FRENCH.

The Bistro's intimate atmosphere is heightened by soft lighting, 19th-century European antiques and prints, and an abundance of flowers atop crisp white table-cloths. Co-owners Ulrich Sigrist and André Barnier keep a watchful eye over their experienced kitchen staff, which regularly dishes out artful French dishes with an international accent. Look for the house specialty *terrine maison*, a country-style veal-and-pork appetizer. Common French-bistro fare like *escargots au Pernod* and *coquilles St-Jacques* are prepared with uncommon spices and accouterments, livening a rather typical continental menu. Especially recommended are the roasted duck with honey-mustard sauce and the chicken breasts in mild curry sauce, each served with fried bananas and pineapple.

✪ **Caffe Abbracci.** 318 Aragon Ave. (between LeJeune Rd. and Miracle Mile), Coral Gables. ☎ **305/441-0700.** Reservations recommended for dinner. Main courses $16–$24; pasta $14–$20. AE, CB, DC, MC, V. Mon–Fri 11:30am–2:30pm; Sun–Thurs 6–11pm; Fri–Sat 6pm–midnight. NORTHERN ITALIAN.

You'll be greeted with a hug by the owner and maître d' Nino, who oversees this remarkable spot as only an Italian could. The food is remarkable, yet the restaurant is not known to many outside of the Gables. Still, it's packed on weekends by those in the know. You are guaranteed perfect service in a pretty wood and marble setting, with the only drawback being the unfortunately loud dining room.

It's hard to get beyond the appetizers here, which are all so good that you could order a few and be satisfied. My favorite is the shrimp with a bright pesto sauce that has just enough garlic to give it a kick, but not so much you won't get a kiss later. The excellent risottos are served in half portions so that you'll have room for the indescribable fish dishes. A snapper entree comes in a light olive oil and wine sauce dotted with fresh marjoram and tomatoes. The grilled tuna and the swordfish are also flawless.

Le Festival. 2120 Salzedo St. (5 blocks north of Miracle Mile), Coral Gables. ☎ **305/442-8545.** Reservations required for dinner. Main courses $16–$25. AE, CB, DC, DISC, MC, V. Mon–Fri 11:45am–2:30pm; Mon–Thurs 6–10:30pm; Fri–Sat 6–11pm. FRENCH.

Le Festival's contemporary pink awning hangs over one of Miami's most traditional Spanish-style buildings, hinting at the unusual combination of cuisine and decor that awaits inside. The modern dining rooms, enlivened with New French features and furnishings, belie the traditional highlights of a well-planned menu.

Shrimp and crab cocktails, fresh pâtés, and an unusual cheese soufflé are star starters. Both meat and fish are either simply seared with herbs and spices or doused in wine and cream sauces. Dessert can be a delight if you plan ahead: Grand Marnier and chocolate soufflés are individually prepared and must be ordered at the same time as the entrees. There's also a wide selection of other homemade sweets.

MODERATE

Brasserie Les Halles. 2415 Ponce de Leon Blvd. (at Miracle Mile), Coral Gables. ☎ **305/461-1099.** Reservations suggested on weekends. Main courses $14.50–$21.50. AE, DC, DISC, MC, V. Daily 11:30am–midnight. FRENCH BISTRO.

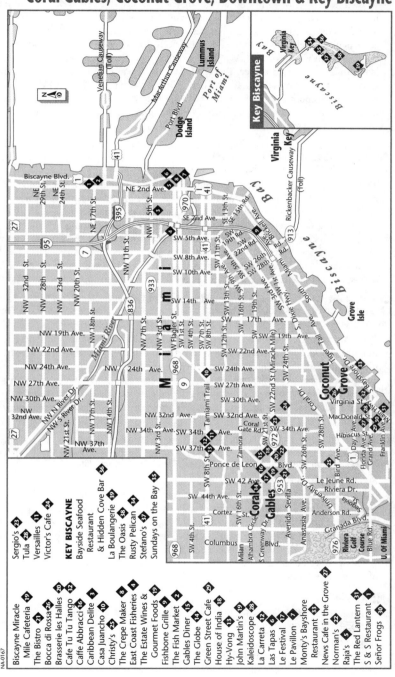

Biscayne Miracle
Mile Cafeteria
The Bistro **28**
Bocca di Rossa **26**
Brasserie les Halles **20**
Cafe Tu Tu Tango **32**
Caffe Abbracci **16**
Caribbean Delite **3**
Casa Juancho **10**
Christy's **25**
The Crepe Maker **8**
East Coast Fisheries **4**
The Estate Wines &
Gourmet Foods **19**
Fishbone Grille **9**
The Fish Market **2**
Gables Diner **15**
The Globe
Green Street Cafe **29**
House of India **18**
Hy-Vong **13**
John Martin's **19**
Kaleidoscope **28**
La Carreta **12**
Las Tapas **17**
Le Festival **7**
Le Pavillon **21**
Monty's Bayshore
Restaurant
News Cafe in the Grove **33**
Norman's **22**
Raja's **5**
The Red Lantern **31**
S & S Restaurant **1**
Señor Frogs **30**

Sergio's **23**
Tula **28**
Versailles **11**
Victor's Cafe **24**

KEY BISCAYNE

Bayside Seafood
Restaurant
& Hidden Cove Bar **36**
La Boulangerie **39**
The Oasis **38**
Rusty Pelican **34**
Stefano's **37**
Sundays on the Bay **35**

Known especially for its fine steaks and delicious salads, this very welcome addition to the Coral Gables dining scene became popular as soon as it opened in 1997 and has since continued to do a brisk business. The modest and moderately priced menu is particularly welcome in an area of overpriced, stuffy restaurants. For starters, try the mussels in white wine sauce and the escargot. For a main course, the duck confit is an unusual and rich choice. Pieces of duck meat wrapped in duck fat are slow-cooked and served on salad frissé and baby potatoes with garlic. Service by the young French staff is polite but a bit slow. The tables tend to be a little too close, although there is a lovely private balcony space overlooking the long thin dining room where large groups can gather.

Gables Diner. 2320 Galiano Dr. (between Ponce de Leon Blvd. and 37th Ave.), Coral Gables. ☎ **305/567-0330.** Main courses $9–$16; pasta $10–$12; burgers and sandwiches $7–$9; salads $8–$10. AE, DC, DISC, MC, V. Daily 8am–10pm. AMERICAN.

This upscale diner serves an eclectic mix of comfort food and nouvelle health food. From meatloaf to Chinese chicken salad, there are moderately priced options for everyone. My favorite is the chicken pot pie, a flaky homemade crust filled with big chunks of white meat, pearl onions, peas, and mushrooms. Also good are the large burgers with every imaginable condiment. Vegetarians can find a few good choices, including pastas, bean soups, pizzas, a vegetable stir-fry, and some hearty salads. All the ingredients are fresh and crisp. No need to dress up here, although the clean, almost romantic setting is as appropriate for first dates as it is for families.

✪ **The Globe.** 377 Alhambra Circle (just off Le Jeune Rd.), Coral Gables. ☎ **305/445-3555.** Reservations only for more than six. Salads $4–$10; pizzas and sandwiches $7–$11. AE, DISC, MC, V. Mon–Fri 11:30-midnight; Sat 6:30pm–2am. INTERNATIONAL/CASUAL.

This funky coffee shop/travel agency is an odd and welcome addition to a neighborhood dominated by fancy eateries and hotels. Take advantage of the hip surroundings and enjoy the quite decent food. Especially good are the salads and pizzas, particularly the chicken and blue cheese pizza, my favorite. In addition to an extensive list of wines and specialty beers, there are many interesting non-alcoholic choices. More important, sample some of the excellent live music every weekend.

John Martin's. 253 Miracle Mile, Coral Gables. ☎ **305/445-3777.** Reservations recommended on weekends. Main courses $12–$20; sandwiches and salads $4–$8. AE, DC, DISC, MC, V. Mon–Thurs 11:30am–midnight; Fri–Sat 11:30am–1am. IRISH PUB.

Food at this Irish pub is a step above average. The basic menu is loaded with fried bar snacks as well as some Irish specialties, such as bangers and mash and shepherd's pie. Some decent salads include a blackened chicken Caesar salad with nice pieces of white meat doused in a spicy seasoning.

Of course to wash it down, you'll want to try one of the ales on tap or one of the more than 20 single-malt scotches. The crowd is upscale and chatty, as is the young waitstaff. Check out happy hour on weeknights, plus the Sunday brunch with loads of hand-carved meats and seafood.

INEXPENSIVE

Biscayne Miracle Mile Cafeteria. 147 Miracle Mile, Coral Gables. ☎ **305/444-9005.** Main courses $3–$4. Cash only. Mon–Sat 11am–2:15pm and 4–8pm; Sun 11am–8pm. SOUTHERN.

Here you'll find no bar, no music, and no flowers on the tables—just great Southern-style cooking at unbelievably low prices. The menu changes, but roast beef, baked fish, and barbecue ribs are typical entrees, few of which exceed $5.

Food is picked up cafeteria-style and brought to one of the many unadorned Formica tables. The restaurant is always busy. The kitschy 1950s decor is an asset in this last of the old-fashioned cafeterias, where the gold-clad staff is proud and attentive. Enjoy it while it lasts.

The Estate Wines & Gourmet Foods. 92 Miracle Mile, Coral Gables. ☎ **305/442-9915.** Main courses $6–$8. AE, MC, V. Mon–Fri 10am–8pm; Sat 10am–4pm. EUROPEAN/AMERICAN.

This storefront, in the heart of Coral Gables' main shopping strip, is primarily a wine shop, but one of the friendliest storekeepers in Miami also serves gourmet meals to a handful of lucky diners. Deliciously thick soups are served with pâtés, salads, and sandwiches around an overturned barrel that can accommodate only about a dozen diners. It has no food license, but officials wink at the technicality. The only advertisement is word of mouth, and knowledgeable locals are dedicated regulars.

House of India. 22 Merrick Way, Coral Gables (near Douglas and Coral Way, a block north of Miracle Mile). ☎ **305/444-2348.** Reservations accepted. Main courses $7–$10. AE, DC, DISC, MC, V. Daily 11:30am–3pm; Sun–Thurs 5–10pm; Fri–Sat 5–11pm. INDIAN.

House of India's curries, kormas, and kebabs are very good, but the restaurant's well-priced all-you-can-eat lunch buffet is unsurpassed. All the favorites are on display, including tandoori chicken, naan bread, various meat and vegetarian curries, as well as rice and dahl (lentils). This place isn't fancy and could use a good scrub-down (in fact, I've heard it described as a "greasy spoon"), but it is nicely decorated with hanging batik prints.

Sergio's. 3252 Coral Way, Coral Gables. ☎ **305/529-0047.** Reservations not accepted. Main courses $5–$7. AE, DC, MC, V. Sun–Thurs 6am–midnight; Fri–Sat 24 hours. CUBAN/AMERICAN.

Located across from Coral Gables' Paseos Mall, Sergio's stands out like a Latin-inspired International House of Pancakes, with red-clothed tables, neon signs in the windows, and video games along the back wall.

The family-style restaurant serves everything from ham-and-eggs breakfasts to grilled steak sandwich lunches and dinners, but it specializes in native Cuban-style dishes, as well as grilled chicken, fajitas, and a variety of sandwiches. Low prices and late-night dining keep it popular with locals.

11 Coconut Grove

Coconut Grove was long known as the artists' haven of Miami, but the rush of developers trying to cash in on the laid-back charm of this old settlement has turned it into something of an overgrown mall. Nonetheless, a few old haunts that retain the flavor of the hippie days still remain, and a few good newcomers are also worth a visit. Saturday nights are a scene, with young wealthy Latin kids cruising down Main Highway in convertibles blasting loud music. The area's popular streets are shrinking as muggings and car break-ins cause more and more people to stay within the relatively safe confines of the CocoWalk and Mayfair areas.

EXPENSIVE

Bocca di Rosa. 2833 Bird Ave. (between SW 27th and Virginia Sts.), Coconut Grove. ☎ **305/444-4222.** Reservations suggested. Main courses $16–$24; pastas $11–$17. AE, DC, DISC, MC, V. Sun–Thurs 6pm–11pm; Fri–Sat 6pm–midnight. ITALIAN.

This elegant restaurant is nestled in a cozy corner of the Grove, but from the smells and tastes here you might as well be in Roma or Sicily. With dishes like *coniglio all contadina* (rabbit stew with white beans and polenta) and *penne cons salsa di sarde* (a sardine and fennel pasta), the menu touches all points on "the boot." On any day, there may be as many as 15 specials. The remarkably fresh seafood is especially recommended. My favorite is a savory bowl of steamed mussels in a white wine broth and a delicately seared swordfish. Frankly, whatever Chef Girogio is cooking up is bound to be good.

Monty's Bayshore Restaurant. 2550 S. Bayshore Dr., Coconut Grove. ☎ **305/858-1431.** Reservations recommended upstairs on weekends. Main courses $20–$37; sandwiches $6–$8; platters $7–$10. AE, CB, DC, MC, V. Daily 11am–2am. SEAFOOD.

This place comes in three parts: a lounge, a raw bar, and a restaurant. Among them, Monty's serves everything from steak and seafood to munchies such as nachos, potato skins, and Buffalo chicken wings. This is a fun kind of place, usually with more revelers and drinkers than diners. At the outdoor, dockside bar, there's live music nightly, as well as all day on weekends. Upstairs, an upscale dining room serves one of the city's best Caesar salads and respectable stone crab claws in season. Be sure, however, not to order the claws from May until October, since they'll serve you some imported version that simply doesn't compare. In season, however, splurge on the all-you can-eat jumbo claws for $36.95—about the same price as a plateful at Joe's Stone Crab Restaurant in South Beach.

MODERATE

Green Street Cafe. 3110 Commodore Plaza, Coconut Grove. ☎ **305/567-0662.** Reservations not accepted. Main courses $6–$16. AE, MC, V. Sun–Thurs 7am–11:30pm; Fri–Sat 7am–1am. CONTINENTAL.

Green Street is located at the "100% corner," the Coconut Grove intersection of Main Highway and Commodore Plaza that 100% of all tourists visit. The location and the loads of outdoor seating (great for people-watching) relieve the pressure on Green Street to turn out fine meals, but the food is still well above average. Continental-style breakfasts include fresh croissants and rolls, cinnamon toast, and cereal. Heartier American-style offerings include eggs and omelets, pancakes, waffles, and French toast. Soup, salad, and sandwich lunches are overstuffed chicken, turkey, and tuna-based meals. Dinners are more elaborate, with several decent pasta entrees as well as fresh fish, chicken, and burgers, including one made of lamb.

Kaleidoscope. 3112 Commodore Plaza, Coconut Grove. ☎ **305/446-5010.** Reservations recommended. Main courses $12–$15 for pasta; $14–$20 for meat and fish. AE, CB, DC, MC, V. Mon–Fri 11:30am–3pm; Mon–Sat 6–11pm; Sun 5:30–10:30pm. NOUVELLE AMERICAN.

I'd recommend Kaleidoscope, in the heart of Coconut Grove, even if it were located somewhere less exciting. The atmosphere is relaxed, with low-key, attentive service, comfortable seating, and a terrace overlooking the busy sidewalks below. Dishes are well prepared, and pastas, topped with sauces like seafood and fresh basil or pesto with grilled yellowfin tuna, are especially tasty. The linguini with salmon and fresh dill is prepared to perfection.

Although there is no special pre-theater dinner, many locals stop into this reliable and reasonable second-floor spot for an elegant meal before a show down the street at The Coconut Grove Playhouse.

The Red Lantern. 3176 Commodore Plaza (Grand Ave.), Coconut Grove. ☎ **305/529-9998.** Main courses $9–$20. AE, MC, V. Mon–Thurs 11:30am–11pm; Fri 11:30am–midnight; Sat 4pm–midnight; Sun 4–11pm. CANTONESE.

Finally, here's an interesting Chinese place that breaks the mold of the cheap, boring ones around town. Specialties include shark's fin with chicken and steamed whole snapper with black-bean sauce. There's also an assortment of vegetarian dishes and some excellent soups. My favorite is the clay-pot stew of chicken in a ginger broth. Although the atmosphere is nothing to speak of, the varied menu and interesting preparation keep locals happy and make a meal here worthwhile.

Señor Frogs. 3480 Main Hwy., Coconut Grove. ☎ **305/448-0999.** Reservations recommended on weekends. Main courses $9–$15. AE, CB, DC, DISC, MC, V. Mon–Sat 11:30am–2am; Sun 11:30am–1am. MEXICAN.

Filled with a college-student crowd, this restaurant is known for a raucous good time, its mariachi band, and especially its powerful margaritas. The food at this rocking cantina is a bit too cheesy, but tasty, if not exactly authentic. The mole enchiladas, with 14 different kinds of mild chilies mixed with chocolate, is as flavorful as any I've tasted. Almost everything is served with rice and beans in quantities so large that few diners are able to finish.

Tula. 2957 Florida Ave. (across the street from the Mayfair Hotel), Coconut Grove. ☎ **305/441-1818.** Main courses $13–$19. AE, DC, DISC, MC, V. Daily 6pm–midnight. ITALIAN.

With everything from thick-crust pizzas baked in a brick oven to perfect rosemary lamb chops, Tula is a great find in the Grove. It caters to a more sophisticated crowd than you'll find elsewhere in town. There's nothing glitzy here—just good food that's a bit pricey but worth it. The attentive waitstaff and homemade pastas and soups are as close to perfect as you'll find. Ask for wine specials; they're not advertised but often available in small quantities. For months, Tula's had a superb Italian Barollo for less than $20 that was perfect with the mushroom risotto.

INEXPENSIVE

Cafe Tu Tu Tango. 3015 Grand Ave. (on the second floor of CocoWalk), Coconut Grove. ☎ **305/529-2222.** Reservations not accepted. Main courses $4–$8. AE, MC, V. Sun–Wed 11:30am–midnight; Thurs 11:30am–1am; Fri–Sat 11:30am–2am. SPANISH/INTERNATIONAL.

This second-floor restaurant in the bustling CocoWalk is designed to look like a disheveled artist's loft. Dozens of original paintings—some only half-finished—hang on the walls and studio easels. Seating at sturdy wooden tables and chairs is either inside, on wooden floors among the clutter, or outdoors, overlooking the Grove's main drag.

Flamenco and other Latin-inspired tunes complement a menu with a decidedly Spanish flare. Hummus spread on rosemary flat bread and baked goat cheese in marinara sauce are two good starters. Entrees include roast duck with dried cranberries, toasted pine nuts, and goat cheese, plus Cajun chicken eggrolls filled with corn, cheddar cheese, and tomato salsa. Pastas, ribs, fish, and pizzas round out the eclectic offerings, and several visits have proved each consistently good. Try the sweet, potent sangria and enjoy the warm lively atmosphere from a seat with a view. Especially when the rest of the Grove has shut down, Tu Tu Tango is an oasis.

News Cafe in the Grove. 2901 Florida Ave. (behind Mayfair), Coconut Grove. ☎ **305/774-6397.** Main courses $6–$16. AE, DC, MC, V. Daily 24 hours. AMERICAN REGIONAL.

Like its predecessor in South Beach, this big modern diner offers everything from Caesar salads to hummus to burgers to omelets to ice cream sundaes. The food is predictably good and the service lively and pleasant. The best part is that it's open around the clock to serve the after-movie crowd from CocoWalk and Mayfair as well as the real late-night club-goers.

12 South Miami

This mostly residential area has some very good dining spots scattered mostly along U.S. 1. Since Hurricane Andrew, most have rebuilt and are better than ever.

MODERATE

⊕ **Anacapri.** 12669 S. Dixie Hwy. (in the South Park Center at 128th St. and U.S. 1), South Miami. ☎ **305/232-8001.** Main courses $8–$16. AE, DC, DISC, MC, V. Daily 11:30am–2:30pm; Mon–Thur 5–10:30pm; Fri–Sat 5–11:30pm; Sun 5–9pm. ITALIAN.

Neighborhood fans wait in line here happily with a glass of wine and pleasant company for somewhat heavy but flavorful Italian cuisine. Prices are reasonable and everyone is treated like a member of the family. If you're in the area, check it out. Stick with the basics, such as pastas with red sauce, which are all flavorful, although a bit heavy on the garlic and oil. An antipasto with thinly cut meats and cheeses and some good green peppers is a great start to a hearty meal.

Cafe Hammock. 500 SW 177th Ave. (in the Miccosukee Indian Gaming site on Krome Ave. and Tamiami Trail), South Miami. ☎ **305/222-4600.** Reservations accepted. Main courses $10–$22; dinner specials $5–$6. DISC, MC, V. Daily 24 hours. CONTINENTAL.

In the clanging environs of the Native American gaming village way down south, you can dine on stone crab claws and decent steak for a few bucks while overlooking hundreds of fanatical bingo players. If you can keep away from the dealers and slots and don't mind a bit of smoke, you'll be amazed at the excellent service and phenomenal specials it runs to entice gamblers to this bizarre outpost. Don't expect Native Americans in native dress; you'll find servers from New Jersey and California before you see a Miccosukee serving burgers here.

Call in advance to see if there are any worthwhile specials. Otherwise, the regular menu with intriguing-sounding offerings, such as Cajun-style cod nuggets and Bahamian conch fritters, is disappointing. Some entrees, like frog legs and grilled portobello mushrooms, are delicious, but no bargain. The alligator is also tasty, although a bit dry.

INEXPENSIVE

The Crepe Maker Cafe. 8269 SW 124th St., South Miami. ☎ **305/233-4458** or 305/233-1113. Crepes $3–$7.50. No credit cards. Mon–Sat 11am–8pm; Sun noon–6pm. FRENCH/CREPES.

Create your own delicious crêpes at this little French cafe. You can choose from ham, tuna, black olives, red peppers, capers, artichoke hearts, and pine nuts. Some of the best combinations include a Philly cheese steak with mushrooms and a classic Cordon Bleu. Delicious desert crêpes have ice creams, strawberries, peaches, walnuts, and pineapples. Enjoy your crêpe fresh off the griddle at the counter or on a bar stools. The soups are also delicious. Kids can run around in a small play area, too.

Pollo Tropical. 18700 SW 40th St., South Miami. ☎ **305/225-7858.** Main courses $3–$6. No credit cards. Sun–Thurs 11am–10pm; Fri–Sat 11am–11pm. CUBAN/FAST FOOD.

This Miami-based chain is putting up new terra-cotta–arched, fast-food places so fast you can hardly finish your meal before another one has taken root.

This is lucky for Miamians and the Southeast, where dozens of these restaurants provide hot tender chicken with a variety of healthful side dishes, such as fresh chunks of carrots, onions, zucchini, and squash on wooden skewers and a variety of salads. The chicken is marinated in a seriously secret sauce and served with well-seasoned black beans and rice. The menu, although Latin inspired, is clearly spelled out in English. Pollo Tropical is a good place to get an education in Latin *sabor* (taste).

Other locations include 1454 Alton Rd., Miami Beach (☎ **305/672-8888**), and 11806 Biscayne Blvd., North Miami (☎ **305/895-0274**). Check the phone book for others.

Shorty's. 9200 S. Dixie Hwy. (between U.S. 1 and Dadeland Blvd.), South Miami. ☎ **305/ 670-7732.** Main courses $5–$9. DISC, MC, V. Mon–Thurs 11am–10pm; Fri–Sat 11am–11pm. BARBECUE.

A Miami tradition since 1951, this hokey log cabin is still serving some of the best ribs and chicken in South Florida. People line up for the smoke-flavored, slow-cooked meat that's so tender it seems to jump off the bone into your mouth. The secret, however, is to ask for your order with sweet sauce. The regular stuff tastes bland and bottled. All the side dishes, including cole slaw, corn on the cob, and baked beans, look commercial but are necessary to complete the experience. This is B-B-Q, with a neon *B*.

A second Shorty's is located in Davie at 5989 S. University Dr. (☎ **305/ 944-0348**).

The Tea Room. 12310 SW 224th St. (at Cauley Square), South Miami. ☎ **305/258-0044.** Sandwiches and salads $6–$7; soups $3–$4. AE, DISC, MC, V. Mon–Sat 11am–4pm. ENGLISH TEA.

Do stop in for a spot of tea at this recently rebuilt tea room in historic Cauley Square off U.S. 1. The little lace-curtained room is an unusual site in this heavily industrial area better known for its warehouses than its doilies.

Sample some simple sandwiches, such as the turkey club with potato salad and a small lettuce garnish or an onion soup full of rich brown broth and stringy cheese. Daily specials, like spinach-and-mushroom quiche, and delectable desserts are a must before beginning your explorations of the old antiques and art shops in this little enclave of civility down south.

7 What to See & Do

Miami is growing rapidly, undergoing a major transformation into a world-class tourist center. To attract upscale visitors from all over the world, developers are building more and more shopping centers, high-class restaurants, and hotels. In response to the new breed of audience, the city has seen a new wave of art exhibitions, theaters, nightclubs, and better sports arenas and facilities.

The best things in Miami are still the treasures nature put there, such as the Everglades National Park and the sea and the wide sandy beaches, but don't discount the human-made attractions altogether. The city was, and still is, designed to court visitors (and their dollars) from around the world, and many of these efforts make for fantastic entertainment. Nearly destroyed in the early 1980s by developers' wrecking balls, the Art Deco district in South Beach is by far the area's most popular tourist site. It's here amid the cotton candy–colored architecture that locals and visitors skate, stroll, shop, play, dance, and dine among. Some of the city's older attractions, such as Monkey Jungle, Parrot Jungle, and the Seaquarium, are wonderful diversions as well, popular with locals and visitors alike. Older constructions built for local enjoyment, such as Villa Vizcaya or Coral Castle, are also not to be missed.

More and more visitors are coming to Miami each year—around 10 million in 1997—to get a taste of the incredibly diverse offerings scattered throughout this sprawling metropolis. No matter what your pace, you'll find yourself wishing you had more time here. But, figuring on your limited schedule, check out the suggested itineraries for a good guide on how to spend your time.

SUGGESTED ITINERARIES

If You Have 1 Day

Make your way through the Art Deco District, and tour the area's whimsical architecture along Ocean Drive. Park at Lincoln Road to walk the strip, and choose any of the excellent restaurants to have a late-afternoon snack or dinner.

If You Have 2 Days

Spend some time in Key Biscayne and include a trip to the Miami Seaquarium, especially if you have children along; kids love the killer whales and performing dolphins. Tour South Beach in the evening when the lively cafe scene and nightlife will keep you up late. On your second day, drive down to Greater Miami South to visit one or more of the attractions described in   this chapter, such as Parrot Jungle, Monkey Jungle, or Miami Metrozoo. On your way, consider a quick tour of Coral Gables and see the spectacular Biltmore Hotel. Or, if shopping is your thing, head Downtown, where you can browse galleries in the Design District and stroll in Bayside Marketplace, where, if you're feeling ambitious, you can enjoy an evening boat cruise.

If You Have 3 Days

Spend the first 2 days as described above and plan to really delve into South Beach on your third day, when you can visit the Wolfsonian, The Bass Museum, the Holocaust Memorial, and the Jewish Museum. Punctuate the afternoon with some in-line skating or biking on the boardwalk, and stops into one or more of the many cafes lining Ocean Drive. In the evening, drive down to *Calle Ocho* for dinner and a show, or head to Coconut Grove for your meal. Afterward, enjoy a Latin nightclub or a bar in CocoWalk.

If You Have 5 or More Days

You've only just begun to get a flavor of this multifaceted region. With a few extra days, take advantage of all you can do outdoors. Spend a day at the beach, collecting shells, working on your tan, or being a little more active. You can rent a charter boat to catch your own dinner, sail from the Coconut Grove Marina, jet ski, or kayak through the mangroves. You can take a tour of Villa Vizcaya, a historic tour of the city, or a funky Art Deco District walking tour. With an extra day, you can drive across the Everglades (see chapter 11, "Side Trips from Miami") or down to the Keys (see chapter 12, "The Keys"). You might even hop on a one-day cruise to Freeport or Nassau in the Bahamas (see chapter 11).

1 Miami's Beaches

There are more than 35 miles of pristine beach in Dade County. The unique characters of Miami's many beaches are as varied as the city's population. Some are shaded by towering palm trees, while others are darkened by huge condominiums. Some attract families or old-timers, others a gay singles scene, but basically, there are two distinct beach alternatives: Miami Beach and Key Biscayne.

MIAMI BEACH'S BEACHES Collins Avenue fronts more than a dozen miles of white-sand beach and blue-green waters from 1st to 192nd streets. Although most of this stretch is lined with a solid wall of hotels, beach access is plentiful, and you are free to frolic along the entire strip. There are lots of public beaches here, wide and well-maintained, complete with lifeguards, toilet facilities, concession stands, and metered parking (bring lots of quarters). Except for a thin strip close to the water, most of the sand here is hard-packed—the result of a $10-million Army Corps of Engineers Beach Rebuilding Project meant to protect buildings from the effects of eroding sand.

In general, the beaches on this barrier island become less crowded the farther north you go. A wooden boardwalk runs along the hotel side of the beach from 21st to 46th streets—about 1 1/2 miles—offering a terrific sun-and-surf experience without getting sand in your shoes. Aside from "The Best Beaches," listed below, Miami Beach's lifeguard-protected public beaches include **21st Street,** at the beginning of the boardwalk; **35th Street,** popular with an older crowd; **46th Street,** next to the

Miami Area Attractions & Beaches

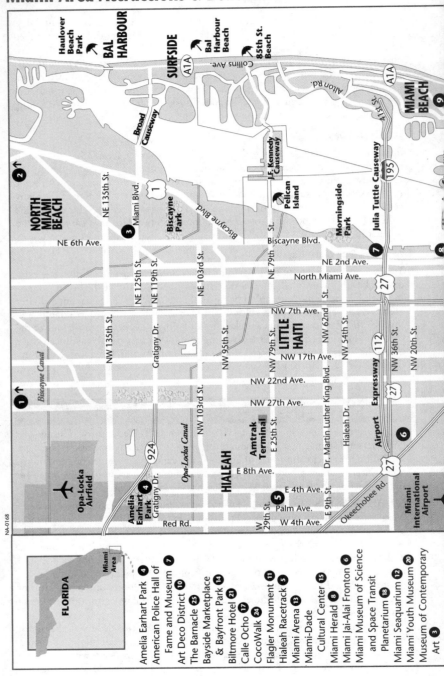

Amelia Earhart Park 4
American Police Hall of
Fame and Museum 7
Art Deco District 10
The Barnacle 25
Bayside Marketplace
& Bayfront Park 14
Biltmore Hotel 21
Calle Ocho 17
CocoWalk 24
Flagler Monument 11
Hialeah Racetrack 5
Miami Arena 13
Miami-Dade
Cultural Center 15
Miami Herald 8
Miami Jai-Alai Fronton 6
Miami Museum of Science
and Space Transit
Planetarium 18
Miami Seaquarium 12
Miami Youth Museum 20
Museum of Contemporary
Art 3

In case you want to see the world.

At American Express, we're here to make your journey a smooth one. So we have over 1,700 travel service locations in over 120 countries ready to help. What else would you expect from the world's largest travel agency?

do more

Travel

http://www.americanexpress.com/travel

In case you want to
be welcomed there.

We're here to see that you're always welcomed at establishments everywhere. That's why millions of people carry the American Express® Card—for peace of mind, confidence, and security, around the world or just around the corner.

do more

AMERICAN
EXPRESS

Cards

In case you're running low.

We're here to help with more than 118,000 Express Cash

locations around the world. In order to enroll, just call

American Express before you start your vacation.

do more

Express Cash

And just in case.

We're here with American Express® Travelers Cheques
and Cheques *for Two.*® They're the safest way to carry
money on your vacation and the surest way to get a
refund, practically anywhere, anytime.

Another way we help you...

do more

**Travelers
Cheques**

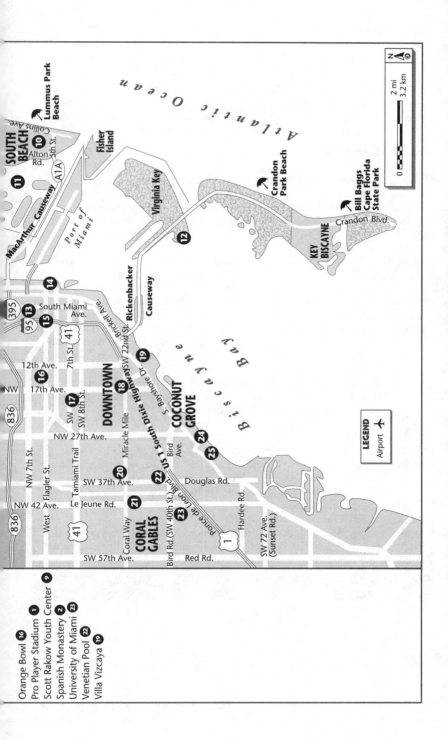

LEGEND

✈ Airport

Orange Bowl 🔞
Pro Player Stadium ➊
Scott Rakow Youth Center ➒
Spanish Monastery ➋
University of Miami ㉓
Venetian Pool ㉒
Villa Vizcaya ⑲

N

2 mi
3.2 km
0

Atlantic Ocean

Lummus Park
Beach

Fisher
Island

Virginia Key

Crandon
Park Beach

Bill Baggs
Cape Florida
State Park

Crandon Blvd.

KEY
BISCAYNE

**SOUTH
BEACH**

Collins Ave.

5th St.

Alton
Rd.

A1A

MacArthur Causeway

Port of
Miami

⑪

⑩

Rickenbacker

Causeway

⑫

Biscayne Bay

395

95

41

South Miami
Ave.

7th St.

Brickell Ave.

SW 22nd St.

⑭

⑬

⑮

12th Ave.

17th Ave.

NW

836

⑯

SW
7th St.

SW 8th St.

DOWNTOWN

Miracle Mile

⑰

⑱

⑲

S. Bayshore Dr.

**COCONUT
GROVE**

Bird
Ave.

㉔

㉓

NW 27th Ave.

NW 7th St.

West Flagler St.

Tamiami Trail

SW 37th Ave.

Le Jeune Rd.

NW 42 Ave.

41

⑳

㉑

**CORAL
GABLES**

Coral Way

SW 57th Ave.

US 1 South Dixie Highway

Bird Rd.(SW 40th St.)

㉒

Ponce de Leon Blvd.

㉓

Douglas Rd.

Hardee Rd.

SW 72 Ave.
(Sunset Rd.)

Red Rd.

1

Fontainebleau Hilton; **53rd Street,** a narrower, more sedate beach; **64th Street,** one of the quietest strips around; and **72nd Street,** a local old-timers' spot.

KEY BISCAYNE'S BEACHES   If Miami Beach is not private enough for you, try Key Biscayne. Crossing Rickenbacker Causeway ($1 toll) is almost like crossing into the Bahamas. The 5 miles of public beach here are blessed with softer sand and are less developed and more laid-back than the hotel-laden strips to the north.

THE BEST BEACHES

Here are my picks:

- **Best Party Beach:** In Key Biscayne, **Crandon Park Beach,** on Crandon Boulevard, has 3 miles of oceanfront beach, 493 acres of park, 75 grills, three parking lots, several soccer and softball fields, and a public 18-hole championship golf course. The beach is particularly wide and the water is usually so clear you can see the bottom. Admission is $2 per vehicle. It's open daily from 8am to sunset.

- **Best Beach for People-Watching:** The ultra-chic **Lummus Park Beach,** which runs along Ocean Drive from about 6th to 14th streets in South Beach, is the best place to go if you're seeking entertainment as well as a great tan. On any day of the week, you might spy models primping for a photo shoot, nearly naked sun-worshippers avoiding tan lines, and the best abs anywhere.

- **Best Swimming Beach:** The **85th Street Beach,** along Collins Avenue, is the best place to swim away from the maddening crowds. It's one of Miami's only stretches of sand with no condos or hotels looming over sunbathers. Lifeguards patrol the area throughout the day.

- **Best Windsurfing Beach: Hobie Beach,** on the right side of the causeway leading to Key Biscayne, is not really a beach, but a secluded inlet with predictable winds and a number of places where you can rent Windsurfers.

- **Best Shell-Hunting Beach:** You'll find plenty of colorful shells at **Bal Harbour Beach,** Collins Avenue at 96th Street, just a few yards north of Surfside Beach. There's also an exercise course and good shade—but no lifeguards.

- **Best All-Around Tanning Beach:** Although the state has been trying to pass ordinances to outlaw nudity, several nude beaches are thriving in the region. In Dade County, **Haulover Beach,** just north of the Bal Harbour border, attracts nudists from around the world and has created something of a boom for area businesses that cater to them.

- **Best Surfing Beach: Haulover Beach/Harbor House,** just north of Miami Beach, seems to get Miami's biggest swells. Go early to avoid the rush of young locals who wish they were in Maui.

2 The Art Deco District

Miami's best site is not a museum or an amusement park, but a piece of the city itself. Located in South Beach, the Art Deco District is a whole community made up of outrageous and fanciful 1920s and 1930s architecture. The district is roughly bounded by the Atlantic Ocean on the east, Alton Road on the west, 6th Street on the south, and Dade Boulevard (along the Collins Canal) on the north. In chapter 8, "Driving & Strolling Around Miami," you'll find a map of the neighborhood (*page 143*) as well as a detailed walking tour.

Most of the finest examples of the whimsical art deco style are concentrated along three parallel streets—Ocean Drive, Collins Avenue, and Washington Avenue—from about 6th to 23rd streets.

After years of neglect and calls for the wholesale demolition of its buildings, South Beach got a new lease on life in 1979. Under the leadership of Barbara Baer Capitman, a dedicated crusader for the art deco region and the Miami Design Preservation League, an area made up of an estimated 800 buildings was granted a listing on the National Register of Historic Places. Designers then began high lighting long-lost architectural details with soft sherbet shades of peach, periwinkle, turquoise, and purple. Developers soon moved in, and the full-scale refurbishment of the area's hotels was under way.

Today, hundreds of new hotels, restaurants, and nightclubs have been renovated or are in the process, and South Beach is on the cutting edge of Miami's cultural and nightlife scene.

EXPLORING THE AREA

If you're exploring on your own, start at the **Art Deco Welcome Center,** 1001 Ocean Dr. (☎ **305/531-3484**), which has several informative giveaways, including maps and art deco architectural information. Art deco books (including *The Art Deco Guide,* an informative compendium of all the buildings here), T-shirts, postcards, mugs, and other similarly styled items are sold here. It's open Monday to Saturday from 9am to 6pm, sometimes later.

Among the highlights to seek out is the **Essex House,** 1001 Collins Ave., at 10th Street, an excellent example of nautical moderne, complete with porthole windows and sleek "racing stripes" along its sides. Along Ocean Drive, between 6th and 8th streets look for the **Park Central** and the **Imperial, Majestic,** and **Colony hotels.** At 1020 Ocean Dr., the **Clevelander Hotel** is one of the few in the area with an original swimming pool and a deco-style sundeck area. It now hosts a popular bar scene. (See chapter 10, "Miami After Dark.")

Other particularly memorable areas for strolling include **Lincoln Road**, which is lined with galleries, cafes, and funky art and antique stores. The **Community Church,** at the corner of Lincoln Road and Drexel Avenue, is the neighborhood's first church and one of its oldest surviving buildings, dating from 1921.

Also on Lincoln Road, 1 block east of Washington Avenue, is the **Albion Hotel,** a spectacular building in streamline moderne style that dates back to 1939. It just received a $10-million–plus renovation. Just around the corner on Collins Avenue, **The Delano** is the hottest hotel in town. Although most of the original 1947 details disappeared with the overhaul in 1995, the outrageous new decor and old exterior, including a rocket-like fin on top, are worth checking out (see chapter 5, "Accommodations").

For informative walking and biking tours of the area, see "Sightseeing Cruises & Organized Tours," below.

3 Animal Parks

Kids of all ages will enjoy Miami's animal parks, which feature everything from dolphins to lions to parrots to alligators. Of course, what's a trip to Florida without having seen a gator?

✪ **Miami Metrozoo.** SW 152nd St. and SW 124th Ave. ☎ **305/251-0403.** Admission $8 adults, $4 children 3–12. Daily 9:30am–5:30pm (ticket booth closes at 4pm). From U.S. 1 south, turn right on SW 152nd St. and follow signs about 3 miles to the entrance.

This huge 290-acre complex is completely cageless—animals are kept at bay by cleverly designed moats. Especially if you're with children, it's worth it. Mufasa and Simba (of Disney fame) were modeled on a couple of Metrozoo's lions, still in residence. Plus, there are two rare white Bengal tigers, a Komodo dragon, rare koala bears, a monorail "safari," and a petting zoo. You can even ride an elephant. The zoo is about a 35-minute drive from the beaches.

✪ **Miami Seaquarium.** 4400 Rickenbacker Causeway (south side), Key Biscayne. ☎ **305/ 361-5705.** Admission $18.95 adults, $13.95 seniors over 55, $16.95 children 3–9. Daily 9:30am–6pm (ticket booth closes at 4:30pm). Take I-95 south to the Rickenbacker Causeway.

You'll want to arrive early to experience this fun and educational attraction. It takes about 4 hours to tour the 35-acre oceanarium and see all four daily shows starring the world's most impressive ocean mammals, although you can do it in about 2 hours if you're on a tight schedule. Trained dolphins, killer whales, and frolicking sea lions play with trainers and visitors. If you want, you can even volunteer for one of their big wet fishy kisses!

Monkey Jungle. 14805 SW 216th St., South Miami. ☎ **305/235-1611.** Admission $11.50 adults, $9.50 seniors and active-duty military, $6 children 4–12. Daily 9:30am–5pm (tickets sold until 4pm). Take U.S. 1 south to SW 216th St. or from Florida Turnpike, take Exit 11 and follow the signs.

See rare Brazilian golden lion tamarins. Watch the "skin-diving" Asian macaques. Yes, it's primate paradise! There are no cages to restrain the antics of the monkeys as they swing, chatter, and play their way into your heart. Screened-in trails wind through acres of "jungle," and daily shows feature the talents of the park's most progressive pupils. You've got to love primates to get over the heavy smell of the jungle; it's been here for more than 60 years.

Parrot Jungle and Gardens. 11000 SW 57th Ave., Greater Miami South. ☎ **305/666-7834.** Admission $12.95 adults, $11.95 seniors, $8.95 children 3–10. Daily 9:30am–6pm. Cafe opens at 8am. Take U.S. 1 south, turn left at SW 57th Ave. or exit Kendall Drive from the Florida Turnpike and turn right on U.S. 1.

It's loud and it's silly, but fun. Not just parrots, but hundreds of magnificent macaws, peacocks, cockatoos, and flamingos occupy this 22-acre park. Continuous shows in the Parrot Bowl Theater star roller-skating cockatoos, card-playing macaws, and more stunt-happy parrots than you ever thought possible. Alligators, tortoises, and iguanas are also on exhibit. Other attractions include a wildlife show focusing on indigenous Florida animals, an area called "Primate Experience," a children's playground, and a petting zoo.

After more than 50 years at this location, Parrot Jungle is planning to move to its own island midway between downtown Miami and the beaches; the relocation is scheduled for 1999.

4 Miami's Museum & Art Scene

Miami's museum scene has always been quirky, interesting, and inconsistent at best. Though several exhibition spaces have made forays into collecting nationally acclaimed work, limited support and political infighting have made it a difficult proposition. Recently, with the reinvention of the Wolfsonian, the reincarnation of MOCA, and the increased daring of the Miami Art Museum, the scene has improved dramatically. It's now safe to say that world-class exhibitions start here. Listed below is an excellent cross-section of the valuable treasures that have become a part of the city's cultural heritage, and as such, are as diverse as the city itself.

For gallery lovers, see "Specialized Tours," below, for scheduled gallery walks, and chapter 9, "Shopping" for a highlight of a few of the best.

South Beach Attractions

To mid Miami Beach ↗

The Bass
Museum of Art

Collins
Park

Dade Boulevard

Miami Beach
Convention Center

20th St.

19th St.

18th St.

Bay Rd.

Purdy Ave.

Dade Boulevard

West Ave.

Alton Rd.

Lenox Ave.

17th St.

James Ave.

Michigan Ave.

Lincoln
Road Mall

Lincoln Rd.

Collins Ave.

16th St.

15th St.

Española Way

Historic
Art Deco
District

14th St.

13th St.

Meridian Ave.

Miami Beach
Post Office

Flamingo
Park

12th St.

West Ave.

Alton Rd.

Lenox
Ave.

11th St.

Ocean Dr.

Beach
Patrol
Station

10th St.

Euclid Ave.

Art Deco
Welcome
Center

9th St.

Pennsylvania Ave.

Washington Ave.

Lummus
Park

8th St.

Michigan Ave.

Jefferson Ave.

7th St.

6th St.

Atlantic
Ocean

5th St.

4th St.

3rd St.

Washington Ave.

Collins Ave.

Ocean Dr.

2nd St.

1st St.

South Pointe
Park

Government Cut

SOUTH BEACH ATTRACTIONS
Bass Museum of Art ❷
Bayshore Golf Course ❶
Holocaust Memorial ❸
Sanford L. Ziff Jewish Museum
   of Florida ⓯
The Wolfsonian ⓭
BIKE & BLADE RENTALS
Fritz's Skate Shop ❽
Miami Beach Bicycle Center ⓮
Skate 2000 ⓬
GYM
Club Body Tech ⓫
ART SPACES
Colony Theater ❿
Jackie Gleason Theater of
   Performing Arts ❻
Lincoln Theatre ❼
Miami City Ballet Studio ❾
Performing Art Network
   Building ❺
INFORMATION
Miami Beach Chamber
   of Commerce ❹

0   .2 mi
0   .124 km

N

NA-0169

IN SOUTH BEACH

Bass Museum of Art. 2121 Park Ave. (just west of Collins Ave.), South Beach. ☎ **305/ 673-7530.** Admission $5 adults, $3 students with ID and senior citizens, free for children 6 and under; second and fourth Wed of the month by donation from 5–9pm. Tues–Sat 10am–5pm; Sun 1–5pm (every second and fourth Wed open 1–9pm). Closed major holidays.

An important and growing visual arts museum in Miami Beach, Bass displays European paintings, sculptures, and tapestries from the Renaissance, baroque, rococo, and modern periods as part of their small permanent collection. Temporary exhibitions alternate between traveling shows and rotations of the Bass's stock, with themes ranging from 17th-century Dutch art to contemporary architecture.

Built from coral rock in 1930, the Bass sits in the middle of six tree-topped, landscaped acres. Construction has begun here on a 12-acre expansion, due to be completed by 1999.

The Wolfsonian. 1001 Washington Ave., South Beach. ☎ **305/531-1001.** Admission $5 adults; $3.50 senior citizens, students, and children 6–12; $5 tour-group members; free on Thurs evenings. Children under 6 and members free. Tues–Sat 11am–6pm; Sun noon–5pm; Thurs 6–9pm.

Mitchell Wolfson, Jr., an eccentric collector of late 19th- and 20th-century art and other paraphernalia, was spending so much money storing his booty that he decided to buy a warehouse. It ultimately held more than 70,000 of his items, including glass, ceramics, sculptures, paintings, and photographs. He's given this incredibly diverse and controversial collection to Florida International University. The former storage facility has been retrofitted with such painstaking detail that it's the envy of curators around the world.

Be advised that The Wolfsonian has been beleaguered with money troubles recently, and may have to cut costs or sell some of the collection to raise funds for operating expenses.

✪ **Holocaust Memorial.** 1933 Meridian Ave. (at Dade Blvd.), South Beach. ☎ **305/ 538-1663.** Free admission. Daily 9am–9pm.

This heart-wrenching memorial is hard to miss and would be a shame to overlook. The powerful centerpiece is a bronze statue by Kenneth Treister that depicts millions of people crawling into an open hand to freedom. You can walk through an open hallway lined with photographs and the names of concentration camps and their victims. From the street, you'll see the outstretched arm, but do stop and tour the sculpture at ground level. What's hidden behind the beautiful stone facade is extremely moving.

IN & NEAR DOWNTOWN

The Cuban Museum of the Americas. 1300 SW 12th Ave., Little Havana. ☎ **305/ 858-8006.** $3 adults, $1 students and children. Usually open Tues–Fri noon–6pm and weekends by appointment. Closed major holidays. Hours vary drastically, so call first.

This politically charged museum created by Cuban exiles has been open with some irregularity since 1974. It displays all mediums, from ceramics to photography to sculpture to painting, by artists throughout Latin America. Exhibits change frequently. In May 1998, this museum was put up for sale. Call for details.

Florida Museum of Hispanic and Latin American Art. 4006 Aurora St. (between Bird Rd. and Ponce de Leon Blvd.), Miami. ☎ **305/444-7060.** Free admission. Tues–Fri 11am–5pm; Sat 11am–4pm. Closed Aug and major holidays.

In addition to the permanent collection of contemporary artists from Spain and Latin America, this 3,500-square-foot museum hosts monthly exhibitions of works from

A Secret Stash of Contemporary Art

Art aficionados always find their way to major art exhibitions in the cities and towns they visit, but nothing can be more exciting and more unusual than being invited to tour a private collection.

Next time you're in Miami for a weekend, consider yourself on the guest list. Your hosts are four New Yorkers, Mera and Don Rubell and their adult children, Jennifer and Jason, who together have opened two hip hotels on South Beach (The Albion and the Greenview). They have also brought with them their priceless collection of more than a thousand works of contemporary art, by the likes of Paul McCarthy, Keith Haring, Jean-Michel Basquiat, Charles Ray, and Cindy Sherman. These pieces are now on view in a former Drug Enforcement Agency warehouse in downtown Miami.

"I'm jealous," says David A. Ross, Director of New York's Whitney Museum of American Art. "There are few collections of its equal anywhere in the world."

The works, many of which are too big or too daring for your average museum, reveal the Rubells' taste for the strange, humorous and irreverent. They include McCarthy's *Cultural Gothic* (1992–1993), a motorized sculpture of a man coaxing a young boy into an act of bestiality, and Beverly Semme's *Blue Gowns* (1993), three giant gowns flowing from a neck-craning height onto the floor.

If you don't know these names, you should probably skip this stop. There's no avoiding nudity, erotica, and themes some may find offensive. The collection is open strictly by appointment only, from 11am to 4pm Fridays and Saturdays and sometimes Sundays. To schedule a visit, call the curator, Bert Rodriguez, at ☎ **305/573-6090.**

Latin America and the Caribbean Basin. Usually the exhibitions focus on a theme, such as international women or surrealism. It's not a major attraction, but for art lovers it's worth a stop. On the same block, you'll find great design stores and a few other galleries.

○ **Miami Art Museum at the Miami–Dade Cultural Center.** 101 W. Flagler St., Miami. ☎ **305/375-1700** or 305/375-3000. Admission $5 adults, $2.50 senior citizens and students with ID, free for children 11 and under, by contribution on Tues. Tues–Wed and Fri 10am–5pm; Thurs 10am–9pm; Sat–Sun noon–5pm. Closed major holidays. From I-95 south, exit at Orange Bowl–NW 8th St. and continue south to NW 2nd St.; turn left at NW 2nd St. and go 1^1/2 blocks to NW 2nd Ave.; turn right, and park at the Metro–Dade Garage. Bring the parking ticket to the lobby for validation.

The recently renamed Miami Art Museum (it was called the Center for the Fine Arts until 1996) features an eclectic mix of modern and contemporary works by such artists as Eric Fischl, Max Beckman, Jim Dine, and Stuart Davis. Rotating exhibitions span the ages and styles and often focus on Latin American or Caribbean artists. The shows are almost always superbly curated and installed, and sometimes subject to controversy from the ultra-political Cuban community.

The Miami–Dade Cultural Center, where the museum is housed, is an oasis for those seeking cultural enrichment during their trip to Miami. In addition to the acclaimed Miami Art Museum, the center houses the main branch of the Miami–Dade Public Library, which sometimes features art and cultural exhibits, and the Historical Museum of Southern Florida, which highlights the fascinating history of Florida, particular its southern region.

American Police Hall of Fame and Museum. 3801 Biscayne Blvd., Miami. ☎ **305/573-0070.** Admission $6 adults, $4 seniors over 61, $3 children 11 and under, free for police officers worldwide. 50% off coupons often available from hotel racks. Daily 10am–5:30pm. Drive north on U.S. 1 from downtown until you see the building with the real police car affixed to its side.

This strange museum appeals mostly to those fascinated by police and their gadgetry. Inside the block building is a combination of reality and fantasy that's part thoughtful tribute, part Hollywood-style drama. Just past the car featured in the motion picture *Blade Runner* is a mock prison cell, in which visitors can take pictures of themselves pretending they're doing 5 to 10. Also displayed are execution devices, including a guillotine and an electric chair. In the entry is a touching memorial to the more than 3,000 police officers who have lost their lives in the line of duty.

☺ Museum of Contemporary Art (MOCA). 770 NE 125th St., North Miami. ☎ **305/893-6211.** Admission $4 adults, $2 seniors and students with ID, free for children 12 and under. Tues–Sat 11am–5pm; Sun noon–5pm. Closed major holidays.

MOCA recently acquired a new 23,000-square-foot space in which to display its impressive collection of internationally acclaimed art with a local flavor. You can see works by Jasper Johns, Roy Lichtenstein, Larry Rivers, Duane Michaels, and Claes Oldenberg. Guided tours are offered in English, Spanish, French, Creole, Portuguese, German, and Italian.

A new screening facility allows for film presentations to complement the exhibitions. Although the $3.75-million project was built in an area otherwise avoided by tourists, MOCA is worth a drive to view important contemporary art in South Florida.

IN CORAL GABLES & COCONUT GROVE

Miami Museum of Science and Space Transit Planetarium. 3280 S. Miami Ave., Coconut Grove. ☎ **305/854-4247** for general information, 305/854-2222 for planetarium show times. Museum of Science, $6 adults, $4 seniors and children 3–12, free for children 2 and under. Planetarium, $5 adults, $2.50 children and seniors. Combination ticket, $9 adults, $5.50 children and seniors. Half-price 4:30–6pm weekdays. Museum of Science, daily 10am–6pm; call for planetarium show times. Closed major holidays. Metrorail: Vizcaya station. Or take I-95 south to Exit 1 and follow the signs.

The Museum of Science features more than 140 hands-on exhibits that explore the mysteries of the universe. Live demonstrations and collections of rare natural history specimens make a visit here fun and informative. Two or three major traveling exhibits are usually on display as well.

The adjacent Space Transit Planetarium projects astronomy and laser shows as well as interactive demonstrations of upcoming computer technology and cyberspace features. Plan to spend at least 3 or 4 hours exploring the fascinating exhibits and displays here.

Miami Youth Museum. On Level B of Paseos, 3301 Coral Way, Coral Gables. ☎ **305/446-4FUN.** Admission $4 for anyone over 1 year old. Mon–Thurs 10am–5pm; Fri 10am–9pm; Sat–Sun 11am–6pm.

This interactive "museum" is more like a theater, since it's a place where kids can explore their interests in the "grown-up world." If you're in the Gables and want to placate (and educate) the kids, check it out. You'll find a great selection of hands-on exhibits, including a mini–grocery store complete with cashier and stockboy assignments for role-playing. Maybe the kids want to pretend to be Dr. Smiles, the dentist, or publish their own newspaper from the "Hot off the Press" exhibit. Tours are offered in English and Spanish.

5 Fantastic Feats of Architecture

Not all the great buildings in Miami are in South Beach's Art Deco district. You'll also find many exciting enclaves filled with Mediterranean gems and eclectic wonders, especially in Coral Gables. Even if you aren't staying there, check out the **Biltmore Hotel** (see chapter 5, "Accommodations") and the stunning Congregational Church across the street.

Villa Vizcaya. 3251 S. Miami Ave. (just south of Rickenbacker Causeway), North Coconut Grove. ☎ **305/250-9133.** Admission $10 adults, $5 children 6–12, free for children 5 and under. Villa, daily 9:30am–5pm (ticket booth closes at 4:30pm); gardens, daily 9:30am–5:30pm. Closed Christmas. Take I-95 south to Exit 1 and follow the signs.

Sometimes referred to as the "Hearst Castle of the East," this magnificent villa is the setting for many society weddings and galas. It was built in 1916 as a winter retreat for James Deering, co-founder and former vice president of International Harvester. The industrialist was fascinated by 16th-century art and architecture, and his ornate mansion—which took 1,000 artisans 5 years to build—became a celebration of that period. Most of the original furnishings, including dishes and paintings, are still intact.

The spectacularly opulent villa wraps itself around a central courtyard. Outside, lush formal gardens, accented with statuary, balustrades, and decorative urns, front an enormous swath of Biscayne Bay, near the homes of Sylvester Stallone and Madonna.

The Barnacle State Historic Site. 3485 Main Hwy. (1 block south of Commodore Plaza), Coconut Grove. ☎ **305/448-9445.** Admission $1. Tours Fri–Sun at 10am, 11:30am, 1pm, and 2:30pm from the main house porch. Group tours Mon–Thurs with 2-week advance reservations. From downtown Miami, take U.S. 1 south to 27th Ave., make a left, and continue to South Bayshore Dr.; then make a right, follow to the intersection of Main Hwy., and turn left.

The former home of naval architect and early settler Ralph Middleton Munroe is now a museum in the heart of Coconut Grove. The house's quiet surroundings, wide porches, and period furnishings illustrate how Miami's privileged class lived in the days before skyscrapers and luxury hotels. Enthusiastic and knowledgeable state park employees offer a wealth of historical information to those interested in quiet, low-tech attractions like this one.

Coral Castle. 28655 S. Dixie Hwy., Homestead. ☎ **305/248-6344.** Admission $7.75 adults, $6.50 seniors, $5 children 7–12. Daily 9am–6pm. Closed Christmas. Take U.S. 1 south to SW 286th St.

There's plenty of competition, but Coral Castle is probably the strangest attraction in Florida. In 1923, the story goes, a crazed Latvian, suffering from unrequited love, immigrated to South Miami and spent the next 25 years of his life carving huge boulders into a prehistoric-looking, roofless "castle." It seems impossible that one rather short man could have done all this, but there are scores of affidavits on display from neighbors who swear it happened. Apparently experts have studied this phenomenon to help figure out how the Great Pyramids and Stonehenge were built.

Listen to the audio tour to learn about this bizarre spot, now on the National Register of Historic Places. The commentary lasts about 25 minutes and is available in four languages. Although Coral Castle is a bit overpriced and under-maintained, it's worth a visit when in the area.

✪ Spanish Monastery Cloisters. 16711 W. Dixie Hwy. (at NE 167th St.), North Miami Beach. ☎ **305/945-1461.** Admission $4.50 adults, $2.50 seniors, $1 children 11 and under. Mon–Sat 10am–4pm; Sun noon–4pm.

Did you know that the oldest building in the Western Hemisphere dates from 1141 and is located in Miami? The Spanish Monastery Cloisters were first erected in Segovia, Spain. Centuries later, newspaper magnate William Randolph Hearst purchased and brought them to America in pieces. The carefully numbered stones were quarantined for years until they were finally reassembled on the present site in 1954. Visitors are free to explore; you'll want to spend about an hour touring the cold, ancient structure, the beautiful grounds, and the gift shop.

Venetian Pool. 2701 DeSoto Blvd. (at Toledo St.), Coral Gables. ☎ **305/460-5356.** Admission $5 adults, $4 teens, $2 children 3–12 and under (children under 36 months not allowed in the water). June–Aug, Mon–Fri 11am–7:30pm, Sat–Sun 10am–4:30pm; Apr–May and Sept–Oct, Tues–Fri 11am–5:30pm, Sat–Sun 10am–4:30pm; Nov–Mar, Tues–Fri 10am–4:30pm, Sat–Sun 10am–4:30pm.

Miami's most beautiful and unusual swimming pool, dating from 1924, is hidden behind pastel stucco walls and is honored with a listing in the National Register of Historic Places. Underground artesian wells feed the free-form lagoon, which is shaded by three-story Spanish porticos and features both fountains and waterfalls. It can be cold in the winter months. During summer, the pool's 800,000 gallons of water are drained and refilled nightly, ensuring a cool, clean swim. Visitors are free to swim and sunbathe here, just as Esther Williams and Johnny Weissmuller did decades ago. For a modest fee, you or your children can learn to swim during special summer programs.

6 Nature Preserves, Parks & Gardens

The Miami area is a great place for outdoors-minded visitors, with beaches, parks, and gardens galore. Plus, South Florida has two national parks; see chapter 11 for coverage of the Everglades and Biscayne National Park.

BOTANICAL GARDENS & A SPICE PARK

In Miami, the **Fairchild Tropical Gardens,** 10901 Old Cutler Rd. (☎ **305/ 667-1651**), features a veritable rain forest of both rare and exotic plants on 83 acres. Palmettos, vine pergola, palm glades, and other unique species create a scenic, lush environment. It's well worth taking the free hourly tram to learn what you always wanted to know about the various flowers and trees during a 30-minute narrated tour.

Admission is $8 for adults, and free for children 12 and under accompanied by an adult. Open daily from 9:30am to 5pm. Take I-95 south to U.S. 1, turn left onto Le Jeune Road, and follow it straight to the traffic circle; from there, take Old Cutler Road 2 miles to the park.

A testament to Miami's unusual climate, the **Preston B. Bird and Mary Heinlein Fruit and Spice Park,** 24801 SW 187th Ave., Homestead (☎ **305/247-5727**), harbors rare fruit trees that cannot survive elsewhere in the country.

Definitely ask for a guide. If a volunteer is available, you'll learn some fascinating things about this 30-acre living plant museum where the most exotic varieties of fruits and spices, including ackee, mango, ugly fruits, carambola, and breadfruit, grow on strange-looking trees with unpronounceable names.

The best part? You're free to take anything that falls to the ground. You'll also find samples of interesting fruits and jellies made from the park's bounty in the gift store. Cooks who like to experiment must visit the park store, which carries exotic ingredients and cookbooks.

Admission to the spice park is $2 for adults and 50¢ for children under 12. Open daily from 10am to 5pm. Closed major holidays. Tours are $1.50 for adults

Attractions in South Miami–Dade

Coral Castle **6**
Fairchild Tropical Gardens **2**
Miami Metrozoo **3**
Monkey Jungle **4**
Parrot Jungle **1**
Preston B. Bird and Mary Heinlein
Fruit and Spice Park **5**

and $1 for children on Saturday and Sunday at 1 and 3pm. Take U.S. 1 south, turn right on SW 248th Street, and go straight for 5 miles to SW 187th Avenue.

MORE MIAMI PARKS

The **Amelia Earhart Park,** 401 E. 65th St., Hialeah (☎ **305/685-8389**), has five lakes stocked with bass and brim for fishing; playgrounds; picnic facilities; and a big red barn that houses cows, sheep, and goats for petting and ponies for riding. There's also a country store and dozens of old-time farm activities like horseshoeing, sugarcane processing, and more. Parking is free on weekdays and $3.50 per car on weekends. Open daily from 9am to sunset. To drive here, take I-95 north to the NW 103rd Street exit, go west to East 4th Avenue, and then turn right. Parking is 1 1/2 miles down the street.

At the historic **Bill Baggs Cape Florida State Recreation Area,** 1200 Crandon Blvd. (☎ **305/361-5811**), at the tip of Key Biscayne, you can explore the unfettered wilds and enjoy some of the most secluded beaches in Miami. There's also a recently reopened lighthouse. A rental shack rents bikes, hydrobikes, kayaks, and many more water toys. It's a great place to picnic, and a newly constructed restaurant serves homemade Latin food, including great fish soups and sandwiches. Just be careful that the raccoons don't get your lunch, because the furry black-eyed beasts are everywhere. Admission is $4 per car with up to eight people. Open daily from 8am to sunset.

A tour of the recently renovated lighthouse, lightkeeper's quarters, and kitchen costs $1 to $2.

Tropical Park, 7900 SW 40th St. (☎ **305/226-0796**), has it all. Enjoy a game of tennis and racquetball for a minimal fee, or swim and sun yourself on the secluded little lake. You can use the fishing pond for free, and they'll even supply you with the rods and bait. If you catch anything, however, you're on your own. Open daily from sunrise to sunset.

7 Especially for Kids

The **Scott Rakow Youth Center,** 2700 Sheridan Ave. (☎ **305/673-7767**), is a hidden treasure on Miami Beach. This two-story facility boasts an ice-skating rink, bowling alleys, a basketball court, gymnasium equipment, and full-time supervision for kids. Call for a complete schedule of organized events. The only drag is that it's not open to adults (except on Sunday). Admission is $1.50 per day for visiting children 9 to 17. Open daily from 2 to 8:30pm.

The following is a roundup of other attractions kids will especially enjoy. Details on each one can be found earlier in the chapter.

AMELIA EARHART PARK *(see page 129)*   This is the best park in Miami for kids. They'll like the petting zoos, pony rides, and private island with hidden tunnels.

MIAMI METROZOO *(see page 121)*   This completely cageless zoo offers such star attractions as a monorail "safari" and a petting zoo. Kids love the elephant rides.

MIAMI MUSEUM OF SCIENCE AND SPACE TRANSIT PLANETARIUM *(see page 126)*   At the Planetarium, kids can learn about space and science by watching entertaining films and cosmic shows. The space museum also offers child-friendly explanations for natural occurrences.

MIAMI SEAQUARIUM *(see page 122)*   Kids can get a kiss from a dolphin and watch exciting performances.

MIAMI YOUTH MUSEUM *(see page 126)*   Here children can dabble in fantasy land, playing at what they're interested in. It's one huge game of "What do you want to be when you grow up?"

8 Sightseeing Cruises & Organized Tours

Always call ahead to check prices and times. Reservations are usually suggested.

BOAT & CRUISE-SHIP TOURS

Gondola Adventures. Docked at Bayside Marina, at the Biscayne Market Place, 401 Biscayne Blvd., Miami. ☎ **305/358-6400.** Rates from $5 and up.

A real gondola in Miami? Well, it may not be the canals of Venice, but with a little imagination, the Bayside Marina will do. You can go on a simple ride around Bayside for $5, or splurge on your own private and cozy sunrise cruise to an island.

Heritage Miami II Topsail Schooner. Bayside Marketplace Marina, 401 Biscayne Blvd., Downtown. ☎ **305/442-9697.** Tickets $12 adults, $7 children 12 and under. Sept–May only. Tours leave daily at 1:30, 4, and 6:30pm, and on Fri, Sat, and Sun also at 9, 10, and 11pm.

More adventure than tour, this relaxing ride aboard Miami's only tall ship is a fun way to see the city. The 2-hour cruises pass by Villa Vizcaya, Coconut Grove, and Key Biscayne and put you in sight of Miami's spectacular skyline. Call to make sure the ship is running on schedule. On Friday, Saturday, and Sunday evenings, there are 1-hour tours to see the lights of the city.

Lady Lucille. 4441 Collins Ave. (docked across from the Fontainebleau Hotel), Miami Beach. ☎ **305/534-7000.** Tickets $15 adults, $6 children. Cruise leaves daily at 11am and 2pm.

Set your sights and sails on Miami's human-made beauty: Millionaires' Row. You can cruise along Biscayne Bay and check out Gloria Estefan's or Fitipaldi's mansion all in the comfort of an air-conditioned 150-passenger boat, complete with snacks and two full bars. The trip lasts 3 hours.

AIR TOURS

Ultralight Adventures! 3401 Rickenbacker Causeway at the marina, Key Biscayne. ☎ **305/361-3909,** or 305/478-9055 for a pager. $65 for 20 minutes, $100 for an hour. By appointment.

For the brave soul, there's an air tour over Miami and Key Biscayne on an *ultra-light*, a little open plane (of sorts) with a small motor. You won't find a better way to see all of Miami. Fun Flight lives up to its name and can even certify you to fly one of their planes and join their ranks.

SIGHTSEEING TOURS

Miami Nice Excursion, Inc., Travel and Service. 18430 Collins Ave., Miami Beach. ☎ **305/949-9180.** Admission $29–$55 adults, $25 children. Daily 7am–10pm. Call ahead for directions to various pickup areas.

Pick your destination. The Miami Nice tours will take you to the Everglades, Fort Lauderdale, the Seaquarium, Key West, Cape Canaveral, or even the Bahamas. Included in most Miami trips is a fairly comprehensive city tour narrated by knowledgeable guides. The company is one of the oldest in town.

SPECIALIZED TOURS

One good option, besides those mentioned below, is a tour led by **Dr. Paul George**. Dr. George is a history teacher at Miami-Dade Community College and a historian at the Historical Museum of Southern Florida. He also happens to be Mr. Miami. There's a set calendar of tours, but all of them are fascinating to South Florida buffs. Tours focus on neighborhoods, such as Little Havana, Brickell Avenue, or Key Biscayne, and on themes, such as cemeteries in Miami. The often long-winded discussions can be a bit much for those who just want a quick look-around, but Dr. George certainly knows his stuff. The cost is $15 to $25; reservations are required (☎ **305/375-1492**). Tours leave from the Historical Museum at 101 W. Flagler St., Downtown.

Miami Design Preservation League. The Art Deco Welcome Center, 1001 Ocean Dr., South Beach. ☎ **305/672-2014.** Walking tours $10 per person. Tours leave Sat at 10:30am and Thurs at 6:30pm. Self-guided audio tours also available 7 days a week for $5. Call ahead for updated schedules.

On Thursday evenings and Saturday mornings, the Design Preservation League sponsors walking tours that offer a fascinating inside look at the city's historic Art Deco District. Tour-goers meet for a 1 1/2-hour walk through some of America's most exuberantly "architectured" buildings. The League led the fight to designate this area a National Historic District and is proud to share the splendid results with visitors.

Art Deco Cycling Tour. 601 5th St., South Beach. ☎ **305/674-0150.** $10 per person, plus $5 for bike rental. Tours depart every other Sunday at 10am from the Miami Beach Bicycle Center.

If you'd rather bike or in-line skate than walk, catch this fun and interesting Sunday morning tour. The bicycle is the most efficient mode of transportation through the streets of South Beach, and one of the best ways to see the historic Art Deco District. Call to reserve a spot.

Biltmore Hotel Tour. 1200 Anastasia Ave., Coral Gables. ☎ **305/445-1926.** Free admission. Tours depart on Sunday at 1:30, 2:30, and 3:30pm. Call to reserve.

Take advantage of these free walking tours offered on Sunday to enjoy the hotel's beautiful grounds. The Biltmore is chock-full of history and mystery, including a few ghosts; go out there and see for yourself.

Coral Gables Art and Gallery Tour. Various locations in Coral Gables. Free. For more information, call Richard Arregui (☎ **305/447-3973**) or stop by any of the galleries in the area. First Friday of the month from 7 to 10pm.

Vans shuttle art lovers to more than 20 galleries that participate in Gables Night in the gallery section of Coral Gables. Viewers can sip wine as they gaze at American folk art; African, Native American, and Latin art; and photography. Most galleries are on Ponce de León Boulevard, between SW 40th and SW 24th streets. The vans run every 15 minutes from 7 to 10pm.

Lincoln Road Gallery Walk at the Art Center. 924 Lincoln Rd. (between Michigan and Jefferson Ave.). ☎ **305/674-8278.** Free. Tour given second Saturday of every month from 7 to 10pm.

Join a knowledgeable guide for a tour of artists' studios on the second Saturday of every month. Or feel free to wander through the more than 50 studios housed in this cooperative art complex on your own. You can also walk along the pedestrian mall to sample the works on display in other galleries. Many serve wine and appetizers. Meet at 1035 Lincoln Road at 7pm for the guided tour or start at the main gallery space at 924 Lincoln to do it on your own.

9 Water Sports

POWERBOATING

Private rental outfits include **Beach Boat Rentals,** 2400 Collins Ave., Miami Beach (☎ **305/534-4307**), where 50-horsepower, 18-foot powerboats rent for some of the best prices on the beach. Rates are $61.25 for an hour, $165.13 for 4 hours, and $225.70 for 8 hours. All rates include taxes and gas. A $250 cash or credit-card deposit is required. Cruising is permitted only in and around Biscayne Bay—ocean access is prohibited. Renters must be over 21. The rental office is at 23rd Street, on the inland waterway in Miami Beach. It's open from 9am to 6pm (weather permitting) during the high season and 9am to 8pm during the summer.

Club Nautico of Coconut Grove, 2560 S. Bayshore Dr., Coconut Grove (☎ **305/858-6258**), rents high-quality powerboats for fishing, waterskiing, diving, and cruising in the bay or ocean. All boats are Coast Guard equipped, with VHF radios and safety gear. Rates range from $199 for 4 hours and $299 for 8 hours to as much as $419 on weekends. Club Nautico is open daily from 9am to 5pm (weather permitting). Other locations include the **Crandon Park Marina,** 4000 Crandon Blvd., Key Biscayne (☎ **305/361-9217**), with the same rates and hours as the Coconut Grove location; and the **Miami Beach Marina,** Pier E, 300 Alton Rd., South Beach (☎ **305/673-2502**), where rates are $229 for 4 hours and $299 for 8 hours for a 20-foot boat; and $259 for 4 hours and $359 for 8 hours for a 24-footer. Nautico on Miami Beach is open daily from 9am to 5pm.

Key Biscayne Boat Rental, 3301 Rickenbacker Causeway, Key Biscayne, (☎ **305/361-RENT**), is next to the Rusty Pelican. If you want to cruise Key Biscayne's lovely waters, rent a 21-footer here for $175 for a half day or $250 for a full day. If you're looking for just a few hours of thrills, a 2-hour minimum for $100 is available. This place is open Monday to Friday from 9am to 5pm, and will open earlier for special fishing requests.

SAILBOATS

You can rent sailboats and catamarans through the beachfront concessions desk of several top resorts, such as the Doral Ocean Beach Resort, Sheraton Bal Harbour Beach Resort, and Dezerland Surfside Beach Hotel (see chapter 5, "Accommodations").

Sailboats of Key Biscayne Rentals and Sailing School, in the Crandon Marina (next to Sundays on the Bay), 4000 Crandon Blvd., Key Biscayne (☎ **305/361-0328** days, 305/279-7424 evenings), can also get you out on the water. A 22-foot sailboat rents for $27 an hour, or $81 for a half day. A Cat-25 or J24 is available for $35 an hour or $110 for a half day. If you've always had a dream to win the America's Cup but can't sail, Sailboats will get you started. It offers a 10-hour course over 5 days for $250 for one person or $350 for you and a buddy, $50 for each additional person.

Shake a Leg, 2600 Bayshore Dr., Coconut Grove (☎ **305/858-5550**), is a unique sailing program for disabled and able-bodied people alike. The program pairs up sailors for day and evening cruises and offers sailing lessons as well. Consider a moonlight cruise (offered monthly) or a race clinic. Shake a Leg members also welcome able-bodied volunteers for activities on and off the water. It costs $60 for nonmembers to rent a boat for 3 hours; free for volunteers. Open on Wednesday through Sunday from 9am to 5pm.

JET SKIS/WAVE RUNNERS

Don't miss a chance to tour the islands on the back of your own little watercraft. Many beachfront concessionaires rent a variety of these popular water scooters. The latest models are fast and smooth. Try **Tony's Jet Ski Rentals,** 3601 Rickenbacker Causeway, Key Biscayne (☎ **305/361-8280**), one of the city's largest rental shops, located on a private beach in the Miami Marine Stadium lagoon. Jet skis rent for about $38 for a half hour and $64 for an hour. Wave Runners rent for $45 for a half hour and $70 for an hour. Tony's is open daily from 10:30am to 6:30pm.

KAYAKS

The laid-back **Urban Trails Kayak Company** rents boats at 10800 Collins Ave. (☎ **305/947-1302**). It offers scenic routes through rivers with mangroves and islands as your destination. Most of the kayaks are sit-on-tops and most are plastic, although some fiberglass ones are available. Rates are $8 an hour, $20 for up to 4 hours, and $25 for over 4 hours. Tandems are $12 an hour, $30 for up to 4 hours, and $35 for the day. Open daily from 9am to 5pm.

The outfitters here give interested explorers a map to take with them and quick instructions on how to work the paddles and boats. If you have at least four people, you can get a guided tour for $35 per person for half a day. This is a fun way to experience some of Miami's unspoiled wildlife, and it's good exercise, too.

SCUBA DIVING

In 1981, the government began a wide-scale project designed to increase the number of habitats available to marine organisms. One of the program's major accomplishments has been the creation of nearby artificial reefs, which have attracted all kinds of tropical plants, fish, and animals. In addition, Biscayne National Park (see chapter 11, "Side Trips from Miami") offers a protected marine environment just south of Downtown.

Several dive shops around the city offer organized weekend outings, either to the reefs or to one of over a dozen old shipwrecks around Miami's shores. Check "Divers" in the Yellow Pages for rental equipment and for a full list of undersea tour operators.

Divers Paradise of Key Biscayne, 4000 Crandon Blvd. (☎ **305/361-3483**), offers two dive expeditions daily to the more than 30 wrecks and artificial reefs off the coast of Miami Beach and Key Biscayne. You can take a 3-day certification course for $399, which includes all the dives and gear. If you already have your C-card, a dive trip costs about $90 if you need equipment and only $35 if you bring your own gear. It's open Monday to Friday from 10am to 6pm and Saturday and Sunday from 8am to 6pm. Call ahead for times and locations of dives.

WINDSURFING

Many hotels rent Windsurfers to their guests, but if yours doesn't have a water-sports concession stand, head for Key Biscayne.

Sailboards Miami, Rickenbacker Causeway, Key Biscayne (☎ **305/361-SAIL**), operates out of big yellow trucks on Hobie Beach, the most popular windsurfing spot in the city. For those who've never ridden a board but want to try it, Sailboards Miami offers for $39 a 2-hour lesson that's guaranteed to turn you into a wave warrior or you get your money back. After that, you can rent a windsurf board for $20 an hour or $37 for 2 hours. If you want to make a day of it, a 10-hour card costs $130. Open daily from 10am to 5:30pm. Make your first right after the toll booth to find the outfitters.

10 More Ways to Play, Both Indoors & Out

BIKING

The cement promenade on the southern tip of the island is a great place to ride. Biking up the beach is great for surf, sun, sand, exercise, and people-watching. If you don't want to subject your bicycle to the salt and sand, try one of the many oceanfront rental places here. Most of the big beach hotels rent bicycles, as does the **Miami Beach Bicycle Center,** 601 5th St., South Beach (☎ **305/674-0150**), which charges $5 per hour or $14 per day. It's open Monday to Saturday from 10am to 7pm and Sunday from 10am to 5pm.

Bikers can also enjoy more than 130 miles of paved paths throughout Miami. The beautiful and quiet streets of Coral Gables and Coconut Grove beg for the attention of bicyclists. Old trees form canopies over wide, flat roads lined with grand homes and quaint street markers. Several bicycle trails are spread throughout these neighborhoods, including one that begins at the doorstep of **Dade Cycle,** 3216 Grand Ave., Coconut Grove (☎ **305/444-5997**); it's open Monday to Saturday from 9:30am to 5:30pm, Sunday from 10:30am to 5:30pm. MasterCard, Visa, and Discover are accepted.

In Key Biscayne, the terrain is perfect for biking, especially along the park and beach roads. If you don't mind the sound of cars whooshing by, Rickenbacker Causeway is also fantastic since it is one of the only bikeable inclines in Miami from which you get fantastic elevated views of the city and waterways. **Key Cycling,** 61 Harbor Dr., Key Biscayne (☎ **305/361-0061**), rents mountain bikes for $5 an hour or $15 a day. It's open Monday through Friday from 10am to 7pm, Saturday from 10am to 6pm, and Sunday from 11am to 4pm.

Intra Mark, 350 Ocean Dr., Key Biscayne (☎ **305/365-9762**), rents scooters for $15 an hour or $45 for a half day, and bicycles for $5 an hour or $10 for 4 hours. The eco-minded staff directs bikers to the best paths for nature-watching. You'll find this shop off the Rickenbacker Bridge across from the Rusty Pelican; it's open every day between 10am and 5pm.

Seasonal Pleasures: Pick Your Own Produce

There is a singular pleasure in getting your fingers stained red by berry juice while friends up North shovel snow. But as South Florida's farm region gets gobbled up by tract homes and shopping malls, the area's self-pick farms are disappearing, too. Some of the remaining berry fields offer ambitious pickers a chance to find their own treasures beneath the trailing vines of strawberry rows for about $2.25 a pound.

If you don't feel like waking up early to pick the juicy red jewels, at least stop by to buy a few boxes of South Florida's winter bounty. Nothing tastes like just-picked berries. They usually bloom between January and April. At other times, you may find vegetables and herbs, including cayenne, jalapeño, orange peppers, eggplant, zucchini, lettuce, cabbage, and broccoli.

On your way to any of the sites in South Dade, just look around for the bright-red "U-Pic" signs indicating a nearby strawberry or tomato farm. Also look for brightly painted trucks parked on the side of the road. They bear the fruits of someone else's labor; all you have to do is pay.

Also look for farm-fresh snack stands in South Dade.

Burr's Berry Farms, 12741 SW 216th St., in Goulds (☎ **305/235-0513**), makes outrageous fruit milk shakes and ice creams. To get to Burr's, drive south on U.S. 1 and turn right on SW 216th Street. The fruit stand is about 1 mile west of U.S. 1 on the same road as the Monkey Jungle. It's open daily from 9am to 5:30pm.

Go early to snatch up some of the fast-selling pastries, tarts, and jams at **Knaus Berry Farm,** 15980 SW 248th St., in Redland (☎ **305/247-0668**). At all hours, a line of anxious ice-cream lovers wait for fresh fruit treats from a little white window. You'll also find flowers, herbs, and other seasonal vegetables. They are most famous, though, for their fresh-from-the-oven cinnamon rolls. Buy one or buy a dozen—they freeze well. Knaus is slightly further south on U.S. 1. Turn right on 248th Street, and the stand is about $2^1/2$ miles down on the left-hand side. It's open Monday to Saturday from 8am to 5:30pm.

If you want to avoid the traffic altogether, head out to **Shark Valley** in the Everglades National Park—one of South Florida's most scenic bicycle trails and a favorite haunt of city-weary locals. See chapter 11 for more details.

Note: Children under the age of 16 are required by Florida law to wear a helmet, which can be purchased at any bike store or retail outlet selling cycling supplies.

FISHING

Bridge fishing is popular in Miami; you'll see people with poles over almost every waterway.

Some of the best surf casting in the city can be had at **Haulover Beach Park,** at Collins Avenue and 105th Street, where there's a bait-and-tackle shop right on the pier. **South Pointe Park,** at the southern tip of Miami Beach, is another popular fishing spot and features a long pier, comfortable benches, and a great view of the ships passing through Government Cut.

You can also choose to do some deep-sea fishing. One bargain outfitter, the **Kelley Fishing Fleet,** at the Haulover Marina, 10800 Collins Ave. (at 108th Street), Miami Beach (☎ **305/945-3801**), has half-day, full-day, and night fishing aboard diesel-powered "party boats." The fleet's emphasis on drifting is geared toward trolling and bottom fishing for snapper, sailfish, and mackerel, but it also schedules 2- and 3-day trips to the Bahamas. Half-day and night fishing trips are $21 for adults and $14.50 for children; full-day trips are $33 for adults and $26.50 for children; rod and reel rental is $5. Daily departures are scheduled at 9am, 1:45pm, and 8pm; reservations are recommended.

Also at the Haulover Marina is the charter boat **Helen C,** 10800 Collins Ave., Haulover (☎ **305/947-4081**). Although there's no shortage of private charter boats here, Capt. Dawn Mergelsberg is a good pick, since she puts individuals together to get a full boat. Her *Helen C* is a twin-engine 55-footer, equipped for big-game "monster" fish like marlin, tuna, dolphin, shark, and sailfish. The cost is $70 per person. Sailings are scheduled for 8am to noon and 1 to 5pm daily; call for reservations. Private charters and transportation are also available. Children are welcome.

Key Biscayne offers deep-sea fishing to those willing to get their hands dirty and pay a lot. The competition among the boats is fierce, but the prices are basically the same no matter which you choose. The going rate is about $400 to $450 for a half day and $600 to $700 for a full day of fishing. These rates are usually for a party of up to six, and the boats supply you with rods and bait as well as instruction for first-timers. Some will take you out to Key Biscayne and even out to the Upper Keys if the fish aren't biting in Miami.

You might consider the following boats, all of which sail out of the Key Biscayne marina: **Sunny Boy III** (☎ **305/361-2217**), **Queen B** (☎ **305/361-2528**), and **L & H** (☎ **305/361-9318**). Call them for reservations.

GAMBLING

Although gambling is technically illegal in Miami, there are plenty of loopholes to the rule. Gamblers can try their luck at off-shore casinos, bingo, dominoes, jai alai, card rooms, horse races, and dog races.

Especially popular is the huge outpost west of Miami, **Miccosukee Indian Gaming,** 500 SW 177th Ave., (☎ **800/741-4600** or 305/222-4600). This glitzy casino isn't Vegas, but you can play slots, all kinds of bingo, and even poker (with a $10 maximum pot).

One of many gambling "cruises to nowhere" is the **Sea Kruz.** It departs daily and most evenings from 1280 5th St., South Beach. (☎ **800/688-PLAY** or 305/ 538-8300). Tickets are $15. For an extra $5 on the lunch cruise, there's an all-you-can-eat soup-and-salad bar, and for $9 on the dinner cruise, there's an all-you-can-eat dinner with a carving station. Throw in a little dancing to a live band and the trip is complete. Ask for free chips or discount coupons, usually offered for the asking.

Casino Miami (☎ **305/577-7775**) sails every day but Mondays and most evenings from the Dupont Plaza Hotel in downtown Miami. Admission is usually the same as Sea Kruz ($15), but this boat is slightly newer and the crowd a little more subdued.

Dominoes is popular in Miami. It's played at **Flagler Dog Track,** 401 NW 38th Ct., (☎ **305/649-3000**) and at **Miami Jai Alai** (see below). Poker rooms are also available here.

GOLF

There are more than 50 private and public golf courses in the Greater Miami area. Contact the **Greater Miami Convention and Visitors Bureau** (☎ **800/283-2707** or 305/539-3063) for a complete list of courses and costs. Some of the area's best and most expensive are at the big resorts, many of which allow non-guests to play, such as the **Doral Blue Course** at the Doral Resort and Spa in West Miami; **Don Shula's**

Hotel and Golf Club, also in West Miami; and the **Biltmore** in Coral Gables. See chapter 5 for more details.

Otherwise, the following represent some of the area's best public courses. **Crandon Park Golf Course,** formerly known as The Links, 6700 Crandon Blvd., Key Biscayne (☎ **305/361-9129**), is the number-one–ranked municipal course in the state and one of the top five in the country. The park is situated on 200 bayfront acres and offers a pro shop, rentals, lessons, carts, and a lighted driving range. The course is open daily from dawn to dusk; greens fees (including cart) are $86 per person during the winter and $45 per person during the summer. Special twilight rates are available.

One of the most popular courses among real enthusiasts is the **Doral Park Golf and Country Club,** 5001 NW 104th Ave., West Miami (☎ **305/591-8800**); it's not related to the Doral Hotel or spa. Call to book in advance since this challenging 18-holer is so popular with locals. The course is open from 6:30am to 6pm during the winter and until 7pm during the summer. Cart and green fees vary, so call ☎ **305/594-0954** for information.

Known as one of the best in Miami, the **Golf Club of Miami,** 6801 Miami Gardens Dr., at NW 68th Avenue (☎ 305/829-8456), has three 18-hole courses of varying degrees of difficulty. You'll encounter lush fairways, rolling greens, and some history. The west course, designed in 1961 by Robert Trent Jones and updated in the 1990s by the PGA, was where Jack Nicklaus played his first professional tournament and Lee Trevino won his first professional championship. The course is open daily from 6:30am to sunset. Cart and greens fees are $45 to $75 per person during the winter, and $20 to $34 per person during the summer. Special twilight rates are available.

Golfers looking for some cheap practice time will appreciate **Haulover Park,** 10800 Collins Ave., Miami Beach (☎ **305/940-6719**), in a pretty bayside location. The longest hole on this par-27 course is 125 yards. It's open daily from 7:30am to 5:30pm during the winter, and to 7:30pm during the summer. Greens fees are $5 per person during the winter, and $4 per person during the summer. Hand carts cost $1.40.

HEALTH CLUBS

Although many of Miami's full-service hotels have fitness centers, you can't count on them in less upscale establishments or in the small Art Deco District hotels. Several health clubs around the city will take in non-members on a daily basis. If you're already a member at the mega–health club chain **Bally's Total Fitness,** dial ☎ **800/777-1117** to find the clubs in the area. There are no outlets on the beaches; most are in South Miami.

One of the most popular clubs, which welcomes walk-in guests, is **Club Body Tech,** 1253 Washington Ave., South Beach (☎ **305/674-8222**), where you might work out with Cindy Crawford, Madonna, or any of a number of supermodels when they're in town. This club offers star appeal and top-of-the-line equipment. Use of the facility is $14 daily, $50 weekly, with discounts for guests of most area hotels. It keeps late hours, especially in season, when it's often open until midnight.

IN-LINE SKATING

Miami's consistently flat terrain should make in-line skating easy. The heavy traffic and construction, however, make it tough to find long routes. Remember to keep a pair of sandals or sneakers with you since many area shops won't allow you inside with skates on.

Because of the popularity of blading and skateboarding, the city has passed a law prohibiting skating on the west side (the sidewalk side) of Ocean Drive in the evenings. In addition, the city has passed a law that all bladers must skate slowly and safely. You wouldn't want to mow down an elderly stroller. You can still have fun, though, and the following rental outfits can help chart an interesting course for you and supply you with all the necessary gear.

In Coral Gables, **Extreme Skate & Sport,** 7876 SW 40th St. (☎ **305/261-6699**), is one of South Florida's largest in-line skate dealers. Even if you know nothing about this trendy new sport, a knowledgeable sales staff and a large selection to choose from ensure that you can't go wrong.

In South Beach, **Fritz's Skate Shop,** 726 Lincoln Rd. Mall (☎ **305/532-1954**), rents top-quality skates, including safety pads, for $7.50 per hour, $22.50 per day, and $14 overnight. If you're an in-line skate virgin, an instructor will hold your hand for $25 an hour. The shop also stocks lots of gear and clothing.

Also in South Beach, **Skate 2000,** at 1200 Ocean Dr. (☎ **305/538-8282**) and 650 Lincoln Rd. (☎ **305/538-9491**), will help you keep up with the beach crowd by renting in-line skates and safety accessories. Rates are $8 an hour and $24 a day plus $100 deposit (credit card or cash). Skate 2000 also offers free lessons by a certified instructor on South Beach's boardwalk every Sunday at 10am. You can either rent or bring your own skates.

JOGGING

Throughout Dade County, you'll find a number of safe and well-planned jogging courses. The following are only a sampling of some of the best. For more good routes in your area or for running buddies, call the **Miami Runners Club** at ☎ **305/227-1500**.

In Key Biscayne, **Crandon Park,** at 4000 Crandon Blvd., has a 15-station fitness course as well as great secluded trails that run along the island's east side, past the old zoo and over the Causeway. In **Coconut Grove,** you can jog along the South Bayshore Drive on a clearly marked path along the bay.

In North Miami Beach, **Greynolds Park,** 17530 W. Dixie Hwy., has many trails winding past lakes and hills as well as a 15-station Vita-Course. At **Haulover Beach Park,** 10801 Collins Ave., in Miami Beach, you can run along the sandy paths with the ocean at your side through a rigorous 20-station fitness course. The **Miami Beach Boardwalk,** a wood-decked course, runs along the ocean from 21st to 46th streets. Even though you share this well-lighted path with strollers and walkers, it's a beautiful route in a safe area.

SWIMMING

There is no shortage of water here. See "Best Beaches" and also the Venetian Pool under "Fantastic Feats of Architecture," above, for descriptions of good swimming options.

TENNIS

Hundreds of tennis courts in South Florida are open to the public for a minimal fee. Most courts operate on a first-come, first-served basis, and are open from sunrise to sunset. For information and directions, call the **City of Miami Beach Recreation, Culture, and Parks Department** (☎ **305/673-7730**), or the **City of Miami Parks and Recreation Department** (☎ **305/575-5256**).

The three hard courts and seven clay courts at the **Key Biscayne Tennis Association,** 6702 Crandon Blvd. (☎ **305/361-5263**), get crowded on weekends since they're some of Miami's most beautiful. You'll play on the same courts as Lendl, Graf, Evert, McEnroe, and other greats; this the venue for one of the world's biggest annual tennis events, the Lipton Championship (see "Miami Calendar of Events," in chapter 2, "Planning a Trip to Miami"). There's a pleasant, if limited, pro shop, plus many good pros. Only four courts are lit at night, but if you reserve at least 48 hours in advance, you can usually take your pick. It costs $4 to $5 per person per hour. The courts are open daily from 8am to 9pm.

11 Spectator Sports

Check the *Miami Herald*'s sports section for a daily listing of local events and the paper's Friday "Weekend" section for comprehensive coverage and in-depth reports. For last-minute tickets, call the venue directly, since many season ticket holders sell singles and return unused tickets. Expensive tickets are available from brokers or individuals, listed in the classified sections of the local papers. Some tickets are also available through **Ticketmaster** (☎ **305/358-5885**).

BASEBALL

Especially since winning the World Series in 1997, the young **Florida Marlins** have been attracting a loyal following. For the time being, home games are at the **Pro Player Stadium,** 2267 NW 199th St., North Miami Beach (☎ **305/626-7426**). Tickets are $4 to $30. Box office hours are Monday to Friday from 8:30am to 6pm, Saturday from 8:30am to 4pm, and prior to games; tickets are also available through Ticketmaster. The team currently holds spring training in Melbourne, Florida.

BASKETBALL

The **Miami Heat,** now coached by Pat Riley, made its NBA debut in November 1988. It's one of Miami's hottest tickets. The season lasts from November to April, with most games beginning at 7:30pm at the **Miami Arena,** 721 NW 1st Ave. (☎ **305/577-HEAT**). Plans are in the works to build a new arena on the waterfront. Tickets are $14 to $44. Box office hours are Monday to Friday from 10am to 4pm (until 8pm on game nights); tickets are also available through Ticketmaster.

FOOTBALL

Miami's golden boys are the Miami Dolphins, the city's most recognizable team, followed by thousands of "dolfans." Coached by Jimmy Johnson, the team plays at least eight home games during the season, between September and December, at the **Pro Player Stadium,** 2267 NW 199th St., North Miami Beach (☎ **305/626-7426** or 305/623-6100). Tickets cost about $30 and are predictably tough to come by. The box office is open Monday to Friday from 10am to 6pm; tickets are also available through Ticketmaster (☎ **305/350-5050**).

HORSE RACING

Wrapped around an artificial lake, **Gulfstream Park,** at U.S. 1 and Hallandale Beach Boulevard, Hallandale (☎ **305/931-7223**), is both pretty and popular. Large purses and important races are commonplace at this suburban course, and the track is often crowded. Call for schedules. Admission is $3 to the grandstand, and $3 to the clubhouse. Free parking. From January 3 to March 15, post times are Wednesday to Monday at 1pm.

You might remember the pink flamingos at **Hialeah Park,** 2200 E. 4th Ave., Hialeah (☎ **305/885-8000**), from Miami Vice. This famous colony is the largest of its kind. The track, listed on the National Register of Historic Places, is one of the most beautiful in the world, featuring old-fashioned stands and acres of immaculately manicured grounds. Admission is $1 to the grandstand and $2 to the clubhouse on weekdays, and $2 and $4, respectively, on weekends. Children 17 and under enter free with an adult. Parking starts at $2. Races are held mid-March to mid-May, but the course is open year-round for sightseeing Monday to Saturday from 9am to 5pm. Call for post times.

ICE HOCKEY

The young **Florida Panthers** (☎ **954/768-1900**), have already made history. In the 1994–1995 season, they played in the Stanley Cup finals, and the fans love them. Their new stadium is located at 2555 NW 137th Way, Sunrise, in Broward County. Call for directions and ticket information.

JAI ALAI

Jai alai, sort of a Spanish-style indoor lacrosse, was introduced to Miami in 1924 and is regularly played in two Miami-area frontons. Although the sport has roots stemming from ancient Egypt, the game as it's now played was invented by Basque peasants in the Pyrenees mountains during the 17th century.

Players use woven baskets, called *cestas,* to hurl balls—*pelotas*—at speeds that sometimes exceed 170 miles per hour. Spectators, who are protected behind a wall of glass, place bets on the evening's players.

The **Miami Jai Alai Fronton,** 3500 NW 37th Ave., at NW 35th Street (☎ **305/633-6400**), is America's oldest fronton, dating from 1926. It schedules 13 games per night. Admission is $1 to the grandstand, $5 to the clubhouse. It's open year-round. There are games Monday and Wednesday to Saturday at 7pm, with matinees on Monday, Wednesday, and Saturday at noon.

Driving & Strolling Around Miami

Miami is made up of many small neighborhoods, some of which are more car-centric than others. If you're Downtown or in Coral Gables without a car, then you may as well plan to sit by the pool or in front of a television for your whole vacation. In these neighborhoods, attractions, restaurants, and shopping are spread out over many miles, and sidewalks are virtually nonexistent. Public transportation is equally elusive. To explore the greater Miami area and the beaches, you'll need a car. However, if you're staying in South Beach, you'll find a car superfluous, and even annoying. Valet rates can be as high as $18 a day, and metered spots are hard to come by.

The two driving tours below highlight Miami's architectural, cultural, and ethnic diversity. And when you're set to stroll South Beach, the walking tour will show you the way.

DRIVING TOUR 1
Miami Panorama: From the Beaches to the City and Back

Start: Joe's Stone Crab Restaurant, 227 Biscayne St. (at Washington Avenue), South Beach.
Finish: Lincoln Road at Van Dyke Cafe, 826 Lincoln Rd., (at Jefferson Avenue), South Beach.
Time: Approximately 1 hour, excluding stops and allowing for light traffic.
Best Times: Weekday evenings at sunset (when the roads tend to be less busy), or weekend mornings.
Worst Times: Weekday rush hours, from 8 to 10am and 4 to 6pm.
This driving tour follows a circular route, which will give you a good feel for the city in general. You'll drive through Miami Beach's varied neighborhoods, from the Art Deco District to condo-laden North Beach, and then onto the mainland and back again to Miami Beach's central section.

Start at:

1. **Joe's Stone Crab Restaurant** (227 Biscayne St.). This Miami Beach institution has served its inimitable stone crab claws to millions of customers since 1913. It's open 8 months a year (roughly October 15 through May 15), and it's always packed. To the south is a controversial building, South Beach's first high-rise, **Portofino**

Towers, which rises more than 46 stories. It was built by German developer Thomas Kramer in the face of public opposition in 1996.

Head east toward the beach and turn left onto Ocean Drive, where you'll be in the southern fringe of:

2. The historic **Art Deco district.** Drive north along Ocean Drive, also known as Deco Drive. On the right, you'll notice construction of several new large beachfront hotels and condos. Once past 5th Street, on the left you'll see some of the classic examples of Art Deco hotels from the 1930s and 1940s, including the **Park Central** at 640 Ocean Drive and the **Avalon** at 700 Ocean Drive. For a more detailed tour, see "A Walking Tour" below or call the **Miami Design Preservation League** (☎ **305/672-2014**), which runs a very informative walking tour on Thursday evenings and Saturday mornings.

Between 11th and 12th streets is:

3. The palatial **home of the late Gianni Versace,** where he was gunned down by a spree killer in 1997. Owned by his heirs, this Italianate mansion remains one of the only private residences on Ocean Drive.

On the next block is:

4. **The Tides** (1220 Ocean Dr.). Built in 1936, it is the largest original art deco hotel on the strip.

Continue north and notice the newer condominiums and hotels straight ahead and on the right. They are the only beachside residences on the strip (between 5th and 15th streets).

At 15th Street, you will be forced to turn left. Then make a quick right onto Collins Avenue, and look right to see:

5. **The Loews Miami Beach Hotel** (1601 Collins Ave.), with a huge circular spire. It's South Beach's only brand new hotel and the largest to be built here in more than 30 years. The Loews company invested more than $135 million to build this 800-room mega-structure, designed to handle visiting conventioneers.

Continue heading north along Collins Avenue, Miami Beach's most celebrated street, where you can get a good perspective on the diversity of the area. Look left and you'll see:

6. **Burger King,** at Lincoln Road. This is Miami's only true art deco fast-food outlet, complete with a blue-and-yellow tropical exterior, neon lights, and trademark art deco curves. On the opposite corner is a **Denny's,** with equally impressive architecture.

As you continue north, look to your right and take time to admire more:

7. **Deco hotels,** like the **National** (no. 1677), the **Delano** (no. 1685), the **Ritz** (no. 1701), the **Marseilles** (no. 1741) and the **Shelborne** (no. 1801). These hotels are some of the region's classic Deco "skyscrapers."

Continue north, past some not-yet-renovated art deco hotels, pretty foot bridges, and lots of construction. Straight ahead, you'll see a lush tropical garden behind huge Roman-style columns. This fancy greenery is just an illusion; it's really the:

8. **Fontainebleau Mural** at Collins Avenue and 44th Street. The lagoon and waterfalls pictured actually exist behind the wall in the rear of the famous Fontainebleau Hilton (4441 Collins Ave.) built by Morris Lapidus in 1954. In this hotel's grand nightclub, all the big stars of the era, such as Frank Sinatra, Sammy Davis Jr., Judy Garland, Ann Margaret, Liberace, and even Elvis Presley, performed. Plans are in the works for a major expansion that will demolish the old mural and add hundreds of rooms to the already mammoth resort.

Next door on Collins Avenue, you will pass the:

9. **Eden Roc** (4525 Collins Ave.), with a small fountain in front, another famous but smaller hotel, also garishly dressed in turquoise and white.

Driving Tour—Miami Panorama

1. Joe's Stone Crab Restaurant
2. Art Deco District Hotels
3. Home of the late Gianni Versace
4. The Tides
5. The Loews Miami Beach Hotel
6. Burger King
7. Deco Hotels
8. Fontainebleau Hotel & Mural
9. Eden Roc Hotel
10. Bal Harbour
11. Alton Road
12. Palm Island, Hibiscus Island,
    & Star Island
13. Fisher Island
14. Port of Miami
15. Miami Herald Building
16. Julia Tuttle Causeway
17. Pinetree Drive
18. The Miami Beach Convention Center
19. The Jackie Gleason Theater
20. Van Dyke's on Lincoln Rd.

BAL HARBOUR

Broad Causeway

96th St.

Harding Ave.

Collins Ave.

SURFSIDE

77th St.

71st St.

North Shore Dr.

South Shore Dr.

Normandy Dr.

Allison Island

John F. Kennedy Causeway

934

Normandy Isle

La Gorce Island

NE 79th St.

Harbor Island

North Bay Island

Treasure Island

NE 2nd Ave.

Biscayne Blvd.

N. Bay Rd.

W. 63rd St.

Creek

907

MIAMI BEACH

W. 51st St.

Biscayne Bay

11 W. 47th St.

Alton Rd.

Indian Creek

9
8 44th St.

195

16

←To Miami

Julia Tuttle Causeway

Arthur Godfrey Rd.

Sheridan Ave.

Pine Tree Dr.

Prairie Ave.

907

17 30th St.

Sunset Isles

Bay Rd.

24th St.

7

Rivo Alto Island

Belle Isle

W. 20th St. Dade Blvd.

23rd St.

City Park

18
19 6
20 5

Collins Park

Venetian Causeway

15

Lincoln Rd. Mall

Flamingo Park

Hibiscus Island

Bay Rd.

14th St.

4
3

Palm Island

Alton Rd.

11th St.

9th St.

7th St.

Ocean Dr.

Collins Ave.

Lummus Park

12 Star Island

A1A

2

41

MacArthur Causeway

1st St.

Biscayne St.

Pier Park

Atlantic Ocean

1

0.6 mi
1 km
N

14

13 Fisher Island

NA-0171

143

As you continue north, you are entering an area known as **Condo Canyon,** a huge wall of condominiums that block the ocean view and shade the roads. Continue north just past 96th Street; turn left at the sign pointing to the Business District. This is Harding Avenue. You are now in:

10. Bal Harbour, the United State's highest net worth zip code. Look right and see the huge white structure, the exclusive Bal Harbour Shops, which includes Saks Fifth Avenue, Neiman Marcus, Armani, Ungaro, Brooks Brothers, and all of Miami's fanciest boutiques.

Turn left onto Harding Avenue, which becomes Indian Creek Drive. Continue south. Just before a small elevated traffic ramp, turn right onto 63rd Street (South S.R. 907), which leads to:

11. Alton Road, where you'll see gorgeous art deco and Mediterranean Revival homes dating back to the 1920s. Continue south on Alton Road until 5th Street, and turn right. Head west over the MacArthur Causeway. Look right to see the area's most exclusive private islands:

12. Palm Island, Hibiscus Island, and Star Island. Many of Miami's elite live here, including Gloria Estefan and her husband Emilio. Leona Helmsley also owns a home here.

To the left is:

13. Fisher Island, where Oprah Winfrey, Anne Bancroft, Mel Brooks, and Luciano Pavarotti spend their vacations.

Farther along on the right is:

14. Port of Miami, the world's busiest port, where all the major cruise ships dock. Cross over the MacArthur Causeway into Miami and turn right onto Biscayne Boulevard. Look right to see the:

15. Miami Herald Building (between 13th and 16th streets), a squat yellow and brown structure housing Miami's only daily paper. This is the downtown Omni neighborhood, currently under an aggressive renewal program. A $244 million performing arts complex is to be built on the site of the old Sears tower, between 13th and 14th streets.

Continue north. At 36th Street, look for signs on the right to take you east on 195 back to Miami Beach. Admire the incredible skyline behind you and the glistening waterway all around, and look ahead for the whimsical neon-encircled palm trees welcoming you back to Miami Beach. You are crossing over the:

16. Julia Tuttle Causeway, named for Miami's founder. Once back on the beach, continue straight ahead through the commercial section of Arthur Godfrey Road (41st Street), and turn right onto:

17. Pinetree Drive, a historic street of elegant homes where the likes of John Astor and Clark Gable once lived. At 23rd Street, the road turns into Dade Boulevard. At the first traffic light (Washington Avenue), turn left. On your right, you will see:

18. The Miami Beach Convention Center (1900 Convention Center Dr.). In addition to many international exhibitions and shows, it's the site of the annual boat show in February, the world's largest. Most mornings, you will find at least one model and some photographers in the midst of a shoot along the stark white walls.

Just next door is:

19. The Jackie Gleason Theater (1700 Washington Ave.). Turn right at 17th Street and park at the municipal lot on the left. Walk south to:

20. Lincoln Road, for the area's best shopping, dining, and people watching.

☕ **WINDING DOWN**   Look for the only tall building on Lincoln Road, and choose a seat at **Van Dyke's,** 846 Lincoln Rd., South Beach (☎ **305/534-3600**).

Open until 2am, this lively and reasonably priced sidewalk cafe is always happening. (See chapter 6, "Dining").

DRIVING TOUR 2
Downtown, Coconut Grove & Coral Gables

Start and Finish: Bayside Marketplace, 401 Biscayne Blvd. (Downtown).
Time: Approximately 1¹/₂ hours, excluding stops.
Best Times: Two hours before sunset, when the city will be breathtakingly illuminated.
Worst Times: Weekday morning rush hour, from 8 to 10am.

This tour takes you through Downtown to two of Miami's oldest and best-known neighborhoods: Coconut Grove and Coral Gables.

Coconut Grove, annexed by the City of Miami in 1925, was established by northeastern artists and writers. It has a reputation as being an "in" spot for bohemians and intellectuals. The first hotel in the area was built in 1880.

Coral Gables, one of Miami's first planned developments, was created by developer George Merrick in the early 1920s. Many houses were built in a Mediterranean style along lush tree-lined streets that open onto beautifully carved plazas. The best architectural examples of the era have Spanish-style tiled roofs and are built from Miami oolite, a native limestone, commonly called "coral rock."

Start at the:

1. **Bayside Marketplace** (401 Biscayne Blvd.), and drive south along Biscayne Boulevard.
2. **Southeast Financial Center** (200 S. Biscayne Blvd.). This 55-story steel-and-glass tower was once the tallest building east of Dallas and south of Manhattan. At its bottom, Biscayne Boulevard doglegs and reveals:
3. **International Place** (100 SE First St.). Formerly owned by the ruined Centrust Bank, this spectacular wedge-shaped building, designed by the celebrated I. M. Pei & Partners, is illuminated nightly at a cost of more than $100,000 a year. For Independence Day, the night lights are red, white, and blue; for Deco Weekend, pastel colors are used.

   Stay in the left lane and cross the drawbridge over the Miami River, the mainland's most beautiful waterway and a hotbed of illegal activities. Be patient—the bridge regularly opens to let tugboats and barges through. You are now on:
4. **Brickell Avenue,** home to the largest concentration of international banks in the United States. Drive slowly. Each one of these architectural masterpieces deserves attention.

   South of SE 15th Street, Brickell Avenue becomes residential, and an equally extraordinary block of condominiums rises up along the avenue's east side, including **The Palace** (1541 Brickell Ave.), **The Imperial** (1617 Brickell Ave.), and **The Atlantis** (2025 Brickell Ave.), all designed by Arquitectonica, Miami's world-famous architectural firm. The Atlantis sports a square hole in its center, from which sprouts a lone palm tree. **Villa Regina** (1581 Brickell Ave.) would be almost plain-looking if it were not for its spectacular rainbow-colored exterior, painted by Israeli artist Yacov Agam. The **Santa Maria** (1643 Brickell Ave.), completed in 1998, is the tallest residential building south of Manhattan.

   Just past the turn-off toward Key Biscayne, you will come to a second set of traffic lights. Bear left onto South Miami Avenue, which quickly becomes South

Bayshore Drive. This two-lane road runs along Biscayne Bay, on the southern edge of Coconut Grove. At SE 32nd Road, just before the sign to the Villa Vizcaya, turn left and drive around the large cul-de-sac. On the right, you'll see:

5. **Sylvester Stallone's bayfront mansion,** with a huge coral-colored gate. Keep following the road and look right to find **Madonna's mansion.**

You may want to leave your car and stroll around **Alice C. Wainwright Park** (2845 Brickell Ave), a pocket-size park on the waterfront. Be aware that, at certain hours, you may share the space with gay cruisers. After you've driven around the cul-de-sac, return the way you came and turn left onto South Miami Avenue. Immediately look out on your left for the entrance to:

6. **Villa Vizcaya** (3251 S. Miami Ave.; ☎ **305/250-9133**), the elegant and opulent estate of International Harvester pioneer James Deering. The magnificent house and grounds are well worth wandering. The house is open daily from 9:30am to 5pm; the gardens, to 5:30pm. (See "Fantastic Feats of Architecture" in chapter 7.)

South Miami Avenue turns into South Bayshore Drive. Continue down this tree-lined street, passing Mercy Hospital, Monty's Bayshore restaurant, and the:

7. **Grand Bay Hotel** (2669 S. Bayshore Dr.) on your right and **Miami City Hall,** at the end of Pan American Drive, on your left.

At its end, South Bayshore Drive turns right, into McFarlane Road, a short street that terminates at Coconut Grove's most popular intersection. Make a sharp left onto Main Highway and cruise slowly. This is the heart of the:

8. **Grove's business district** and home to dozens of boutiques and cafes.

☕ **TAKE A BREAK** For a light snack or a long lunch, there are plenty of places to choose from. The **Green Street Café,** 3110 Commodore Plaza (☎ **305/ 567-0662**), is located on one of the Grove's busiest corners, the intersection of Main Highway and Commodore Plaza. But the cafe is a relaxed place, serving breakfast, lunch, and dinner to loungers who linger at the sidewalk tables. (See the listing in chapter 6, "Dining.")

Two blocks south of Commodore Plaza, you'll see the entrance to:

9. **The Barnacle** (3485 Main Hwy.). This former home of naval architect and early settler Ralph Middleton Munroe is now a museum open to the public (☎ **305/ 448-9445**). Tours are given Friday through Sunday every hour and a half between 10am and 2:30pm. (See "Fantastic Feats of Architecture" in chapter 7.)

On the next block, on your right, is the **Coconut Grove Playhouse** (3500 Main Hwy.). Built as a movie theater in 1926, it is one of Miami's oldest showplaces. (See "The Performing Arts" in chapter 10.)

Farther along Main Highway at the intersection of Devon Road is:

10. **The Plymouth Congregational Church.** Founded in 1897, it's one of Miami's oldest.

Main Highway ends at Douglas Road (SW 37th Avenue). Turn right, drive north about 2 miles, and make a left onto Coral Way (SW 22nd Street). This stretch between Main Highway and U.S. 1 is a bit seedy. Depending on your comfort level, you may not want to go through here at night. You are now entering Coral Gables via the village's most famous thoroughfare, dubbed the:

11. **Miracle Mile.** This stretch of shops and eateries dates from the development's earliest days and is the heart of downtown Coral Gables. To your right, on the corner of Ponce de Leon Boulevard, stands the **Colonnade Building** (133–169 Miracle Mile), a structure that once housed George Merrick's sales offices and has since been rebuilt into a top hotel, the Omni Colonnade (see chapter 5,

Driving Tour—
Downtown, Coconut Grove & Coral Gables

start here

0.6 mi
1 km

Biscayne Bay

Rickenbacker Causeway

Brickell Ave.

95

Miami River

NW 12th Ave.   SW 12th Ave.

41

DOWNTOWN

South Bay Shore Dr.

South Dixie Hwy.

Pan American Dr.

**Fair Isle
(Grove Isle)**

West Flagler St.

Tamiami Trail

41

SW 22nd St.

**Grand
Bay Hotel**

Miami City Hall

SW 27th Ave.   SW 27th   Ave.

SW 8th St.

SW 24th St.

Bird Ave.

SW

**Commodore
Plaza**

**COCONUT
GROVE**

Main Hwy.

Bayview
Rd.

Douglas Rd.

Miracle Mile

SW 37th Ave.   Douglas Rd.

Ponce de Leon   Blvd.

**finish
here**

Le Jeune Rd.

Bird Rd.

Le Jeune Rd.

Coral Way

Sevilla Ave.

Anastasia Ave.

Riviera Dr.

**CORAL
GABLES**

Anderson Rd.

South Dixie Hwy.

Granada Blvd.

Columbus Blvd.

1. Bayside Marketplace
2. Southeast Financial Center
3. International Place
4. Brickell Avenue
5. Sylvester Stallone's
   & Madonna's mansions
6. Villa Vizcaya
7. Grand Bay Hotel and Miami
   City Hall
8. Coconut Grove's business district
9. The Barnacle
10. Plymouth Congregational Church
11. Miracle Mile
12. Granada Golf Course
13. Venetian Pool
14. DeSoto Plaza & Fountain
15. Biltmore Hotel
16. Palermo, Catalonia, and
    Malaga avenues

NA-0172

147

"Accommodations"). **Coral Gables City Hall** (405 Biltmore Way), with its trademark columned rotunda, is at the end of the Miracle Mile.

Follow Coral Way to the right of City Hall and past the:

12. **Granada Golf Course,** one of two public courses in Coral Gables. After 4 blocks, turn left onto DeSoto Boulevard and look for the:

13. **Venetian Pool** (2701 DeSoto Blvd.) on your left. This is Miami's most unusual swimming pool, dating from 1924 and listed on the National Register of Historic Places. It's hidden behind pastel stucco walls and shaded by three-story Spanish porticos. It costs $4 to swim and sunbathe, but if you just want to look around for a few minutes, the cashier may let you in free. (See "Fantastic Feats of Architecture" in chapter 7.)

One block farther along DeSoto Boulevard is the:

14. **DeSoto Plaza and Fountain,** one of Coral Gables' most famous traffic circles. Designed by Denman Fink in the early 1920s, the structure consists of a column-topped fountain surrounded by a footed basin that catches water flowing from four sculpted faces.

DeSoto Boulevard picks up again on the other side of the fountain and continues for about 4 blocks to its end at Anastasia Avenue, in front of the:

15. **Biltmore Hotel** (1200 Anastasia Ave.). This grand hotel is one of Miami's oldest and prettiest properties. The enormous cost of operating the Biltmore has forced it through many hands in recent years. It once served as a veterans hospital and even a dorm for students of nearby University of Miami. Bankruptcy shut the hotel in 1990, but the Biltmore is once again open, now under the management of the Westin chain. Its 26-story tower is a replica of the Giralda Bell Tower in Seville, Spain. Go inside and marvel at the ornate marble-and-tile interior, outfitted with mahogany furniture and a medieval fireplace.

Out back, the hotel's enormous swimming pool is the largest of its kind in North America. Just beyond is the challenging and beautiful Biltmore Golf Course. The fastest way back to downtown Miami is to continue east to the end of Anastasia Avenue, and then turn right on LeJeune Road, and then left onto U.S. 1.

Take a detour on your way home to sightsee on:

16. **Palermo, Catalonia, Malaga,** and other interesting tree-lined avenues. Here you'll see many of Miami's historic homes, built in the 1920s and 1930s in Spanish and Mediterranean styles.

A WALKING TOUR
South Beach Highlights

Start: Art Deco Welcome Center, 1001 Ocean Dr. (South Beach).

Finish: Clevelander Hotel, 1020 Ocean Dr.

Time: Allow approximately 1¹/₂ hours, not including browsing in shops and galleries.

Best Times: Any day between 11am and 5pm.

Worst Times: Nights and Sundays, when galleries are closed.

The Art Deco District in South Beach is roughly bounded by the Atlantic Ocean on the east, Alton Road on the west, Sixth Street on the south, and Dade Boulevard (along the Collins Canal) to the north. This approximately one-square-mile area is listed on the National Register of Historic Places. There will certainly be plenty of people to watch while you're strolling around, and amazing architecture to admire

Walking Tour—South Beach Highlights

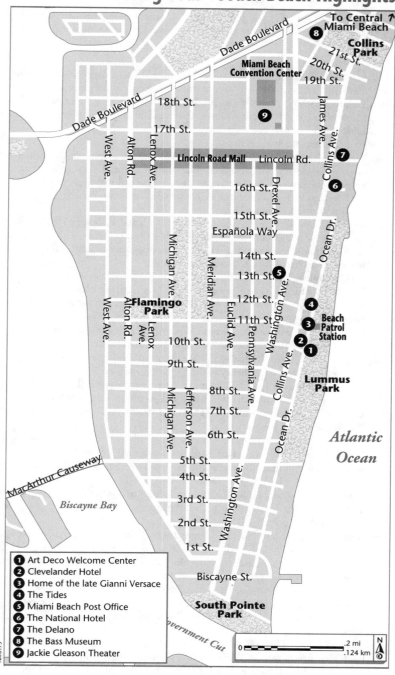

To Central Miami Beach

Collins Park

Dade Boulevard

Miami Beach Convention Center

21st St.
20th St.
19th St.

18th St.

Dade Boulevard

17th St.

West Ave.
Alton Rd.
Lenox Ave.

Lincoln Road Mall   Lincoln Rd.

James Ave.

Collins Ave.

❽
❼
❻

16th St.

Drexel Ave.

15th St.

Española Way

Michigan Ave.
Meridian Ave.

14th St.
13th St.   ❺

❾

Flamingo Park

12th St.
11th St.   ❹
❸   Beach Patrol Station

West Ave.
Alton Rd.
Lenox Ave.

10th St.
9th St.

Euclid Ave.
Pennsylvania Ave.
Washington Ave.

Ocean Dr.

❷
❶

8th St.

Jefferson Ave.
Michigan Ave.

7th St.
6th St.

Collins Ave.

Lummus Park

5th St.
4th St.

Atlantic Ocean

MacArthur Causeway

3rd St.
2nd St.

Washington Ave.

Biscayne Bay

1st St.

Biscayne St.

South Pointe Park

Government Cut

❶ Art Deco Welcome Center
❷ Clevelander Hotel
❸ Home of the late Gianni Versace
❹ The Tides
❺ Miami Beach Post Office
❻ The National Hotel
❼ The Delano
❽ The Bass Museum
❾ Jackie Gleason Theater

NA-0173

0   .2 mi
.124 km

N

as well. This tour takes you past the Deco District's highlights. If you want more details, consider taking the intriguing Art Deco walking tour (see chapter 7, "What to See & Do.")

Start at the:

1. **Art Deco Welcome Center** (1001 Ocean Dr.). This storefront office offers free maps and art deco architecture information. You can also buy art deco books, T-shirts, postcards, mugs, car sunshades, and other similarly styled items. It's open Monday to Saturday from 11am to 6pm, and usually until 9pm on Thursday, Friday, and Saturday evenings.

Just across the street is the:

2. **Clevelander Hotel** (1020 Ocean Dr.), one of the few hotels in the area with an original swimming pool and deco-style sun deck area. The huge outdoor stage, located behind the pool, hosts live rock and reggae bands almost every night, when the Clevelander becomes one of the liveliest locales on the beach.

Walk north on Ocean Drive to:

3. The late **Gianni Versace's home** (between 11th and 12th streets). The only privately owned residence on South Beach's Ocean Drive, this outrageously decadent mansion is where the Italian fashion designer was gunned down. It's now owned by his heirs and has an uncertain future.

Continue north to:

4. **The Tides** (1220 Ocean Drive), one of Ocean Drive's oldest and tallest deco buildings. Renovated in 1997 by Island Outpost, this is also perhaps the city's most elegant rehab.

Turn west and make your way to Washington Avenue, where you'll turn right. On the left side of the street, you'll see the magnificent:

5. **Miami Beach Post Office** (1300 Washington Ave.), completed in 1938 and designed by Howard L. Cheney in the Depression Moderne style as part of a Work Projects Administration (WPA) project. Step into the skylit-domed lobby, where you'll see a turret with a lantern finial and gleaming gold post boxes beneath a classic WPA mural depicting Ponce de León landing in Florida and fighting with the Native Americans.

Head east on 13th Street. Observe the similar deco features on the simple buildings along the way. Many have been repainted in brighter colors than the originals to highlight the unusual features. Turn left on Collins Avenue and look for:

6. **The National Hotel** (1687 Collins Ave.). Built in 1940, this stunning structure is now one of the beach's most beautiful hangouts.

A few doors down is:

7. **The Delano** (1685 Collins). Originally built in 1947 and renovated half a century later by Phillipe Stark and Ian Schrager, this hotel epitomizes the success of South Beach's renaissance. Note the futuristic fins on top of this 12-story super-sexy hotel.

Continue north on Collins to 21st Street. Turn left to see:

8. **The Bass Museum** (2121 Park Ave.), recently expanded and full of great art.

Another left will lead you to Dade Boulevard, and then another left to Washington Avenue, past the:

9. **Jackie Gleason Theater** and to Lincoln Road, a good place to stroll, between 16th and 17th streets west of Washington. Also charming is Española Way, a pretty street with Mediterranean Revival architecture, between 14th and 15th streets, starting at Collins Avenue.

Shopping 9

A mecca for hard-core shoppers from Latin America, the Caribbean, and the rest of Florida, Miami has everything you could ever want and some things you never dreamed of. Where else could you find a Neiman-Marcus just miles from an authentic Cuban cigar factory? A place selling exotic saltwater fish down the street from a warehouse full of opulent 15th-century French furniture? Only in Miami.

This shopping capital has strip malls, boutiques, and enclosed malls in every conceivable nook and cranny of the city, which makes for lots of competition among retailers and good bargains for those who like to hunt. In addition to the mega-malls, like Dadeland and Aventura, the city entices buyers with block after block of fancy boutiques and second-hand stores in areas like Lincoln Road and Miracle Mile. Driving along the side streets, you'll spot dozens of interesting ethnic food and clothing shops to explore. In this chapter, I've listed some of my favorite places to shop.

1 The Shopping Scene

Almost every major street in Miami is lined with an infinite variety of small stores, restaurants, motels, and fast-food joints. This is, after all, primarily a tourist town. Below I've described some of the popular retail areas, where many stores are concentrated for easy browsing.

As a general rule, **shop hours** are Monday through Saturday from 10am to 6pm and Sunday from noon to 5pm. Many stores stay open late (usually until 9pm) one night of the week (usually Thursday). Shops in trendy Coconut Grove are open until 9pm Sunday through Thursday and even later on Friday and Saturday nights. Department stores and shopping malls also keep longer hours, staying open from 10am to 9 or 10pm Monday to Saturday and noon to 6pm on Sunday.

The 6.5% state and local **sales tax** is added to the price of all non-food purchases.

Most Miami stores can wrap your purchase and **ship** it anywhere in the world via the United Parcel Service (UPS). If they can't, you can send it yourself, either through UPS (☎ 800/742-5877) or through the U.S. Mail (see "Fast Facts: Miami" in Chapter 4).

Impressions

> *Someday . . . Miami will become the great center of South American trade.*
> —Julia Tuttle, Miami's founder, 1896

SHOPPING AREAS

If you're looking for discounts on all types of goods—from watches and jewelry to luggage and leather—downtown Miami is the best district to visit. However, watch out for some unscrupulous businesses. Electronic shops have been known to sell empty boxes or switch merchandise. You also should look around Flagler Street and Miami Avenue for all kinds of cluttered bargain stores. Most signs around there are printed in both English and Spanish, for the benefit of locals and tourists alike.

COCONUT GROVE   Downtown Coconut Grove, centered on Main Highway and Grand Avenue and branching onto the adjoining streets, is one of Miami's few pedestrian-friendly zones. The Grove's wide sidewalks, lined with cafes and boutiques, provide hours of browsing pleasure. Coconut Grove is best known for its dozens of avant-garde clothing stores, funky import shops, and excellent sidewalk cafes. You can't escape Miami's ubiquitous malls, however—there's one near this cozy village center, too (see "Mayfair Shops in the Grove," under "Malls"). For more information about this area, see "City Layout" in Chapter 4.

CORAL GABLES—MIRACLE MILE   Actually only a half-mile long, this central shopping street was an integral part of George Merrick's original city plan (see "Neighborhoods in Brief" in Chapter 4). Today, the strip still enjoys popularity for its old-fashioned ladies' shops, haberdashers, bridal stores, and gift shops. Recently, newer "chain" stores, like Barnes and Noble, Old Navy, and even Starbucks, have been opening on the Mile, but you'll find that it's still lined primarily with small 1970s storefronts. It also features several good and unusual restaurants before it terminates at the Mediterranean-style City Hall rotunda (see Chapter 6, "Dining"). This strip is worth a stop on your tour of Coral Gables.

SOUTH BEACH—LINCOLN ROAD   This luxurious pedestrian mall, originally designed in 1957 by Morris Lapidus, recently underwent a multimillion-dollar renovation that included new lighting and more than 500 palm trees. Here shoppers can find an array of clothing and art and a menagerie of South Beach's finest restaurants. Future plans include the construction of a movie theater and a major grocery store. Enjoy an afternoon of gallery hopping and be sure to look into the open studios of the Miami City Ballet (see "The Performing Arts" in Chapter 10). Monthly gallery tours, periodic jazz concerts, and a weekly farmer's market are just a few of the offerings on "The Road." See "City Layout" in Chapter 4 for more information about this area.

MALLS & DEPARTMENT STORES

There are so many malls in Miami that it would be impossible to mention them all. What follows is a list of the biggest and the best shopping centers.

You can find any number of department stores, such as Saks, Macy's, Bloomingdale's, Neiman-Marcus, and Lord & Taylor, in the Miami malls listed below, but Miami's own is **Burdines,** at 22 E. Flagler St., Downtown (☎ **305/ 835-5151**), and 1675 Meridian Ave. (just off Lincoln Rd.) in South Beach (☎ **305/ 674-6311**). One of the oldest and largest department stores in Florida, Burdines specializes in high-quality, middle-class home furnishings and fashions.

Aventura Mall. 19501 Biscayne Blvd. (on the corner of 197th St. near the Dade–Broward county line), Aventura. ☎ **305/935-1110.**

Enter this large enclosed mall, and you'll find it easy to imagine you're on the outskirts of Omaha . . . or anywhere else in America, for that matter. More than 200 national chain boutiques are complemented by the megastores J. C. Penney, Lord & Taylor, Macy's, Bloomingdale's, and Sears. Parking is free.

Bal Harbour Shops. 9700 Collins Ave. (on 97th St., opposite the Sheraton Bal Harbour Hotel), Bal Harbour. ☎ **305/866-0311.**

There's not much in the way of whimsy here, just the best-quality goods from the fanciest names. Ann Taylor, Fendi, Joan & David, Krizia, Rodier, Gucci, Brooks Brothers, Waterford, Cartier, H. Stern, Tourneau—the list goes on and on. With Neiman-Marcus at one end and Saks Fifth Avenue at the other, the Bal Harbour Shops are the fanciest in Miami. The mall itself is a pleasant open-air emporium, featuring covered walkways and lush greenery. Parking starts at $1 with an endorsed ticket. Be sure to have your ticket validated. You can use an unattended machine at Saks Fifth Avenue even if you don't make a purchase. Check out the mall's Web site at www.balharbourshops.com.

Bayside Marketplace. 401 Biscayne Blvd., Downtown. ☎ **305/577-3344.**

The marketplace, filled with lively and exciting shops, has a stunning location— 16 beautiful waterfront acres in the heart of downtown Miami. Downstairs, about 100 shops and carts sell everything from plastic fruit to high-tech electronics (some of the more unique specialty shops are listed separately below). The upstairs eating arcade is stocked with dozens of fast-food choices, offering a wide variety of inexpensive international eats. Some restaurants stay open later than the stores, which close at 11pm Monday to Saturday and 8pm on Sunday. Parking is $1 per hour.

☻ Dadeland Mall. 7535 N. Kendall Dr. (intersection of U.S. 1 and SW 88th St., 15 minutes south of Downtown), Kendall. ☎ **305/665-6226.**

The granddaddy of Miami's suburban mall scene, Dadeland features more than 175 specialty shops, anchored by four large department stores—Burdines, J. C. Penney, Lord & Taylor, and Saks Fifth Avenue. Sixteen restaurants serve from the adjacent Treats Food Court. Parking is free.

The Falls Shopping Center. 8888 Howard Dr. (at the intersection of U.S. 1 and 136th Street, about 3 miles south of Dadeland Mall), Kendall. ☎ **305/255-4570.**

Tropical waterfalls are the setting for this outdoor shopping center with dozens of moderately priced, slightly upscale shops. Miami's first Bloomingdale's is here, as are Polo, Ralph Lauren, Caswell-Massey, and more than 60 other specialty shops. After a recent renovation, The Falls became the quintessential shopping experience. Macy's, Crate & Barrel, Brooks Brothers, and Pottery Barn are among the newest additions. Parking is free.

Sawgrass Mills. 12801 W. Sunrise Blvd., Sunrise (west of Fort Lauderdale). ☎ **954/ 846-2300.**

Although this mammoth mall is actually located in Broward County, it is a phenomenon worth mentioning. This behemoth holds more than 300 shops and kiosks in nearly 2.5 million square feet covering 50 acres. Wear your Nikes to trek around the shops, which include Donna Karan, Saks Fifth Avenue, Levi's, Sunglass Hut, Ann Taylor, Barneys New York, Cache, Waterford crystal, and hundreds more, all selling at 30% to 80% below retail. Since the most recent expansion, Sawgrass Mills has added another dimension to this mammoth shopping complex. The $30-million job will add 300,000 square feet of entertainment facilities, including themed restaurants and other assorted treats, such as a 24-screen movie theater.

From Miami, buses run three times daily; the trip takes just under an hour. Call for exact pick-up points along Collins Avenue and Downtown. If you are driving, take I-95 North to 595 West until Flamingo Road. Exit and turn right, driving 2 miles until Sunrise Boulevard. You can't miss this monster on the left. Parking is free, but don't forget where you parked your car.

The Streets of Mayfair. 2911 Grand Ave. (a few blocks east of Commodore Plaza), Coconut Grove. ☎ **305/448-1700.**

Recently revamped, this small and labyrinthine complex conceals a movie theater, several top-quality shops, restaurants, art galleries, and nightclubs. The emphasis is on chic, expensive elegance and intimate European-style boutiques. Valet parking is available for $1 for the first 2 hours and $1 each additional hour; $6 after 6pm.

2 Shopping A to Z

ART & ANTIQUES

Miami's art and antiques shops are scattered in small pockets around Miami. Some are in North Miami Beach, along West Dixie Highway or Miami Gardens Drive. But you'll find the bulk of the antiques district in Coral Gables, where many antique and art galleries are within walking distance of each other along Ponce de Leon Boulevard, extending from U.S. 1 to Bird Road. Listed below is a selection of galleries both in and out of these districts; of course, there are many more stores to browse in.

If you happen to be in town on the first Friday of a month, you can take a free trolley tour of the Coral Gables art district. The tour runs from 7 to 10pm; meet at Ambrosino (listed below) or any of the other participating galleries in the area. Some shops stay open later and serve refreshments to art lovers who want to turn shopping into a night out.

Ambrosino Gallery. 3095 SW 39th Ave., Coral Gables. ☎ **305/445-2211.**

This well-respected gallery shows works by contemporary Latin American artists. The knowledgeable staff is always willing to answer questions.

Dietel's Antiques. 6572 Bird Rd., Coral Gables. ☎ **305/666-0724.**

An active trade business here means lots of different styles are revolving constantly. You'll find baubles of every assortment. Stop into this little jewel as you make your way through Coral Gables' quaint antiques district.

Elite Fine Art. 3140 Ponce De Leon Blvd., Coral Gables. ☎ **305/448-3800.**

Touted as one of the finest galleries in Miami, Elite features modern and contemporary Latin American painters and sculptors.

✪ Evelyn S. Poole Ltd. 3925 N. Miami Ave., Miami. ☎ **305/573-7463.**

Known as the most fine of the fine antiques collections, the Poole assortment of European 17th-, 18th-, and 19th-century decorative furniture and accessories is housed in 5,000 square feet of space in the newly revived Decorator's Row. Here celebrity clients shop for that special "statement piece" in these vast museumlike galleries.

Gallery Antigua. 5130 Biscayne Blvd. (in the Boulevard Plaza Building). ☎ **305/759-5355.**

With Florida so close to the Caribbean, it's no surprise that an entire gallery dedicated to African-American and Caribbean artists would prosper. Gallery Antigua boasts a vast collection of prints and reproductions, as well as masks and sculptures. They do framing on the premises and will ship purchases for you.

Best Buys

Miami's best buys are fruit and fish, the region's specialties. Nowhere will you find fresher local seafood and citrus products. Here's where to shop:

CITRUS FRUIT   There was a time when it seemed as though almost every other store was shipping fruit home for tourists. Today such stores are a dying breed, although a few high-quality operations still send the freshest oranges and grapefruit. **Todd's Fruit Shippers,** P.O. Box 141951, Coral Gables, (☎ **305/448-5215**), can take your order over the phone and charge it to American Express, MasterCard, or Visa. Boxes are sold by the bushel or fractions thereof and start from about $20.

Along with fresh oranges and grapefruits, **Bins and Baskets,** 300 Alton Rd., (☎ **305/531-2467**) sells kiwi, pineapple, and a variety of tropical favorites and gourmet foods. It accepts most major credit cards and ships worldwide.

SEAFOOD   East Coast Fisheries, 330 W. Flagler St., Downtown (☎ **305/ 577-3000**), a retail market and restaurant (see the review in Chapter 6), has shipped millions of pounds of seafood worldwide from its own fishing fleet. It is equipped to wrap and send 5- or 10-pound packages of stone-crab claws, Florida lobsters, Florida Bay pompano, fresh Key West shrimp, and a variety of other local delicacies to your door via overnight mail.

Miami's most famous restaurant is **Joe's Stone Crab,** located at 227 Biscayne St., South Beach (☎ **800/780-CRAB** or 305/673-0365). Joe's makes overnight air shipments of stone crabs to anywhere in the country, but note that Joe's sells stone crabs only during the crab season, which runs from October through May.

Meza Fine Art. 275 Giralda Ave., Coral Gables. ☎ **305/461-2723.**

This gallery specializes in Latin American artists, including Carlos Betancourt, Javier Marin, and Gloria Lorenzo.

Miami Twice. 6562 SW 40th St., Coral Gables. ☎ **305/666-0127.**

Here you'll find the Old Florida furniture and decorations, such as lamps and ashtrays, that define South Florida's unique style. In addition to deco memorabilia, there are some fun old clothes, shoes, and jewelry. Since the prices can be a bit steep, bargain as you would anywhere else.

BAKERIES

Andalusia Bake Shops. 248 Andalusia Ave., Coral Gables. ☎ **305/445-8696.** Other location at 3015 Aventura Blvd., North Miami Beach (☎ 305/935-2253).

This ever-expanding chain has won fame among locals who praise it for its outstanding cakes, pastries, and breads. Also, most of the locations have a to-die-for prepared food counter serving up everything from chicken curry salad to hummus and pot pies.

Biga Corporation. 1080 Alton Rd., Miami Beach. ☎ **305/535-1008.** Another location at 305 Alcazar, Coral Gables (☎ 305/446-2111).

Six dollars for a loaf of bread! Yes, and sometimes more. You'll be happy to pay it when you sink your teeth into these inimitable old-world style loaves. Flavors range from seven grain to marble pumpernickel-rye, which is my favorite. There's a great wine and cheese selection, too.

La Boulangerie. 328 Crandon Blvd., Key Biscayne. ☎ **305/361-0281.**

Stop here for delicious sandwiches and fruit tarts (see review in Chapter 6).

La Brioche Doree. 4017 Prairie Ave., Miami Beach. ☎ **305/538-4770.**

No one makes a better croissant anywhere. Period.

BEACHWEAR

You'd expect a plethora of beachwear stores in Miami, and you'd find it. However, if you want to get away from the cookie-cutter styles available at any local mall, try these shops listed below. You're likely to find a bathing suit that makes you stand out while you're basking on the beach or out giving the waves a workout.

Alice's Day Off. 5900 SW 72nd St., South Miami. ☎ **305/284-0301.**

Alice's may have a corner on the neon trend, but it also comes out season after season with pretty and flattering floral patterns. If an itsy-bitsy bikini is not your style, Alice's has a range of more modest cuts for those not shaped like a Baywatch babe.

Aqua. 650 Lincoln Rd., South Beach. ☎ **305/674-0942.**

If the thought of cavorting on the beaches practically "au naturel" doesn't make you blush, head straight to Aqua. It has a great selection of Brazilian-cut suits all in bold colors.

Bird's Surf Shop. 250 Sunny Isles Blvd., North Miami Beach. ☎ **305/940-0929.**

If you're a hard-core surfer or just want to hang out with them, head to Bird's Surf Shop. Although Miami doesn't regularly get huge swells, if you're here during the winter and one should happen to hit, you'll be ready. The shop carries more than 150 boards. Call its surf line (☎ **305/947-7170**) before going out to find the best waves from South Beach to Cape Hatteras and even the Bahamas and Florida's West Coast.

Island Trading. 1332 Ocean Dr., South Beach. ☎ **305/673-6300.**

One more part of music mogul Chris Blackwell's empire, Island sells everything you'll need to wear in the tropical resort town, like batik sarongs, sandals, sundresses, bathing suits, cropped tops, and more. Many of the unique styles are created on the premises by a team of young and innovative designers.

Island Water Sports. 16231 Biscayne Blvd. ☎ **305/944-0104.**

You'll find everything from booties to gloves to baggies. Check in here before you rent that Waverunner or Windsurfer.

X-Isle Surf Shop. 437 Washington Ave., South Beach. ☎ **305/673-5900.** Free surf report at ☎ 305/534-7873.

Prices are slightly higher at this beach location, but the young staff is knowledgeable and tubular.

BOOKS

If you enjoy curling up with a good book in front of a blasting air conditioner—we are in Miami, after all—Miami's bookstores do the trick. There are all the usual chains, like Barnes and Noble and Borders—both with the requisite cafe inside—but there are also quite a few unique and slightly more eclectic independents.

Books & Books. 296 Aragon Ave., Coral Gables. ☎ **305/442-4408.** Another location at 933 Lincoln Rd., South Beach (☎ 305/532-3222).

Here the literati arrive in BMWs. Enjoy the antiquarian room, which specializes in art books and first-edition literature. If that's not enough intellectual stimulation for you, the shop hosts free lectures from noted authors and experts almost nightly, as well as a poetry line where you can hear a new poem every day (☎ **305/444-POEM**).

At the Lincoln Road location, you'll rub elbows with tanned and buffed South Beach bookworms sipping cappuccinos at the Russian Bear Cafe inside the store. Check your in-line skates at the door, please.

Coco Grove Antiquarian. 3318 Virginia St., Coconut Grove. ☎ **305/444-5362.**

One of very few out-of-print bookstores in Miami, Coco Grove Antiquarian specializes in books about Florida and the Caribbean, but also boasts a large selection of out-of-print cookbooks, sci-fi, and first editions.

Cuba Art and Books. 2317 Le Jeune Rd., Coral Gables. ☎ **305/567-1640.**

This shop specializes in old Cuban books about the island nation, and also sells some prints and paintings by Cuban artists. Most titles are in Spanish and focus on art and politics.

Kafka's Kafe. 1464 Washington Ave., South Beach. ☎ **305/673-9669.**

Gourmet coffee, access to e-mail and the Internet, and a wide range of foreign and domestic magazines are some of the extras you will find at this excellent used bookstore.

CHOCOLATE

If you know and love chocolate, you'll appreciate all the following stores: **Godiva Chocolatier,** at 19575 Biscayne Blvd., Miami (☎ **305/682-0537**) and 7429 N. Kendall Dr., South Miami (☎ **305/662-2429**); **Krone Chocolatier,** 9700 Collins Ave., Miami Beach, in the Bal Harbour Shops (☎ **305/868-6670**); and **Le Chocolatier,** 1840 NE 164th St., North Miami Beach (☎ **305/944-3020**).

CIGARS & CIGARETTES

Although it is illegal to bring Cuban cigars into this country, somehow *Cohibas* show up at every dinner party and nightclub in town. Not that I condone it, but if you hang around the cigar smokers in town, no doubt one will be able to tell you where you can get some of the highly prized contraband. Be careful, however, of counterfeits.

Some of the stores listed below sell excellent hand-rolled cigars made with domestic and foreign-grown tobacco. Many of the *viejos* (old men) got their training in Cuba working for the government-owned factories in the heyday of Cuban cigars.

Ba-balú. 500 Española Way, Miami Beach. ☎ **305/538-0679.** Closed Monday.

With its extensive collection of memorabilia from pre-1959 Cuba, Ba-balú offers a taste of Cuba, selling not only its hand-rolled cigars (it does about a thousand a week), but T-shirts, baseball caps, Cuban coins, bills, postcards, stamps, and coffee. Enjoy live bongo music nightly, and ask owner Herbie Sosa for a free shot of Cuban coffee.

La Gloria Cubana. 1106 SW 8th St., Little Havana. ☎ **305/858-4162.**

This tiny storefront shop employs about 45 veteran Cuban rollers who sit all day rolling the very popular torpedoes and other critically acclaimed blends. They've got back orders until next Christmas, but it's worth stopping in. They *will* sell you a box and show you around.

Miccosukee Tobacco Shop. 850 SW 177th Ave. (Krome Ave. and Tamiami Trail), Miami. ☎ **305/226-2701.**

At this remote, Native-American–owned outpost, you are spared the state taxes on cigarettes and can pick up national brands for $14 a carton, generics from $8 to $13.

Mike's Cigars. 1030 Kane Concourse (at 96th St.), Bay Harbor Island. ☎ **305/866-2277.**

Mike's recently moved to this location, but it's one of the oldest smoke shops in town. Since 1950, Mike's has been selling the best from Honduras, the Dominican Republic, and Jamaica, as well as the very hot local brand La Gloria Cubana. Most say it has the best prices, too.

South Beach News and Tobacco. 710 Washington Ave., Miami Beach. ☎ **305/673-3002.**

A walk-in humidor stocks cigars from the Dominican Republic, Honduras, and Jamaica. You'll also find a large selection of wines, coffees, and cigar paraphernalia in this pleasant little shop. Also, a hand roller comes in as he pleases to roll for the tourists.

ELECTRONICS

Electronics are a big market here. Many people travel to Miami from South America and other areas of the world to buy playthings and gadgets. You'll find many electronics stores around, but most are concentrated in downtown Miami, where the shopping can be both amazing and scary. The streets are littered with bargain electronics stores, but shop with care. Make sure any equipment you buy comes with a warranty, and try to charge your purchase instead of paying cash. I've listed a few reputable stores with several chain locations where you can safely shop.

The Sharper Image. 401 Biscayne Blvd. (in the Bayside Marketplace). ☎ **305/374-8539.** Another location in the Dadeland Mall, at 7507 N. Kendall Dr., South Miami (☎ 305/667-9970).

Electronics nuts will love this store. It tends to be high-end, both in merchandise and price, but it's free just to look and touch (yes, you're allowed), so even if you're not buying, visit the store to see what's new in the high-tech world.

Sound Advice. 12200 N. Kendall Dr., Kendall. ☎ **305/273-1225.** Other locations at 17641 Biscayne Blvd., Aventura (☎ 305/933-4434), and 1222 S. Dixie Hwy., Coral Gables (☎ 305/665-4434).

An audio-junkie's candy store, Sound Advice features the latest in high-end stereo equipment, as well as TVs, VCRs, and telephone equipment. Techno-minded, but sometimes pushy, salespeople are on hand to help.

Spy Shops International Inc. 280 NE 4th St. ☎ **305/374-4779.**

This store is perfect for James Bond wanna-bes looking to buy electronic-surveillance equipment, day and night optical devices, stun guns, mini safes, doorknob alarms, and other anti-crime gadgets.

FASHIONS
WOMEN'S

Every mall and shopping complex offers women a variety of stores to fit every style and every budget, from designer boutiques to off-price outlets, chain conglomerates to independent emporiums. Scattered throughout malls, **Banana Republic** stocks basic, well-priced clothes, while a store like **Coco Paris** (in the CocoWalk complex in Coconut Grove) carries fantasy-like outfits for evening. The stores that follow are some of the best.

A B S Clothing Collection. 226 8th St., South Beach. ☎ **305/672-8887.**

This California-based chain store fits right into South Beach. You'll find both trendy and professional stuff here, from zebra-print minis to tailored pantsuits. It's perfect for finding something to wear to stroll on Ocean Drive.

Betsey Johnson. 805 Washington Ave., South Beach. ☎ **305/673-0023.**

Here you'll find slightly wild clothes for the young and young at heart, made of stretchy materials, velvet, knits, and more.

Loehmann's. 18701 Biscayne Blvd. (Fashion Island), North Miami Beach. ☎ **305/932-4207.**

Loehmann's is the queen of discount women's clothing. If you don't mind communal dressing rooms and hordes of zealous shoppers, look here for great deals on everything from bathing suits to evening wear.

Ungaro. 9700 Collins Ave. (in the Bal Harbour Shops), Miami Beach. ☎ **305/866-1401.**

Here you'll find elegant apparel—what everyone wears to shop at Bal Harbour.

MEN'S

Brooks Brothers. 9700 Collins Ave. (in the Bal Harbour Shops), Miami Beach. ☎ **305/ 865-8686** and at 8888 Howard Dr. (in The Falls shopping complex), Kendall, ☎ 305/259-7870.

If you need a new navy blazer or some khaki trousers to roll up for an oceanfront stroll, shop here for the classics.

Giorgio's. 208 Miracle Mile, Coral Gables. ☎ **305/448-4302.**

One of the finest custom men's stores, Giorgio's features an extensive line of Italian suits and all the latest by Canelli.

Hugo Boss. 9700 Collins Ave., Miami Beach. ☎ **305/864-7753.**

Hipsters and businessmen alike love this place, where you'll find T-shirts and suits, all priced over the top.

UNISEX

More than 100 retail outlets are clustered in Miami's mile-square **Fashion District,** just north of Downtown. Miami's fashion center, which surrounds Fashion Avenue—NW Fifth Avenue—is second in size only to New York's. The district features European- and Latin-influenced designs with tropical hues and subdued pastels, and is known for swimwear, sportswear, high-fashion children's clothing, and glittery women's dresses. Most stores offer medium-quality clothing at a 25% to 70% discount, as well as on-site alterations. Most are open weekdays from 9am to 5:30pm.

Another good choice is **Old Navy,** the chain retailer owned by The Gap. Old Navy offers basic jeans, sweaters, khakis, and accessories for both men and women at extremely reasonable prices. Stores are scattered throughout Miami with central locations at 65 Miracle Mile, Coral Gables (☎ 305/529-1902), and 3885 NE 163rd St., North Miami (☎ 305/940-4640).

LINGERIE

Belinda's. 827 Washington Ave., South Beach. ☎ **305/532-0068.**

This German designer makes some of the most beautiful and intricate teddies, nightgowns, and wedding dresses. The styles are a little too Stevie Nicks for me to actually consider wearing in public, but the creations are absolutely worth admiring. The prices are appropriately up there.

Caro Cuore. 642 Collins Ave., South Beach. ☎ **305/534-6494.**

This small store stocks good-quality lingerie from its private label. Most garments are made with fancy European lace, but the store also carries a wide variety of your basic cotton.

Corset Corner. 300 Miracle Mile, Coral Gables. ☎ **305/444-6643.**

As the name suggests, this little old store on Miracle Mile sells the basic, good old-fashioned gear.

Flash Lingerie. 9700 Collins Ave. (in the Bal Harbour Shops), Bal Harbour. ☎ **305/868-7732.**

Extremely tasteful and elegant lingerie is what this shop specializes in. You'll find Cotton Club, La Perla, Lou, and other luxurious imports.

Victoria's Secret. 3015 Grand Ave., Coconut Grove. ☎ **305/443-2365.** Other locations at 401 Biscayne Blvd., Miami (☎ 305/374-8030), and Aventura Mall (☎ 305/932-0150).

You've seen the sexy catalogs—now see it up close. The many shops in town stock the basic undergarments in shimmery rayons and polys as well as a few Chinese silk robes and undies. You'll find one of the largest selections of thongs anywhere.

RESALE SHOPS

The Children's Exchange. 1415 Sunset Dr., Coral Gables. ☎ **305/666-6235.**

Selling everything from layettes to overalls, this pleasant little shop is chock-full of good Florida-style stuff for kids to wear to the beach and in the heat.

Douglas Gardens Jewish Home and Hospital Thrift Shops. 5713 NW 27th Ave., North Miami Beach. ☎ **305/638-1900.**

Lately, they have gotten smart and started to raise prices. Still, for housewares and books, you can do all right. Call to see if they are offering any specials for seniors or students.

Rags to Riches. 654 NE 125th St., North Miami. ☎ **305/891-8981.**

This is an old-time consignment shop in the thrift-store row. You might find some decent rags, and maybe even some riches. Not as upscale as it used to be, this place is still a good spot for costume jewelry and shoes.

Second Hand Rose. 18509 W. Dixie Hwy., North Miami Beach. ☎ **305/932-9888.**

You've got to dig, but sometimes you can come up with a few good finds in women's designer clothes.

SHOES

The best place for shoe shopping is at Bal Harbour Shops or in South Beach.

The Leathery. 3460 Main Hwy., Coconut Grove. ☎ **305/448-5711.**

This store sells men's and women's Timberland, Birkenstocks, Bass, Clogs, TEVAs, and more.

Little Feet and More. 7216 Red Rd., South Miami. ☎ **305/666-9655.**

You'll find Nike, Reebok, Cole Hahn, Keds, and Baby Jacks for the whole family.

FOOD MARKETS & STORES

Apple a Day Natural Food Market. 1534 Alton Rd., Miami Beach. ☎ **305/538-4569.**

This grocery store with a natural accent caters to South Beach's health-conscious crowd with your basic nuts and berries, as well as some great prepared foods and hard-to-find misos and seaweeds.

Bombay Bazaar. 2008 NE 164th St., North Miami Beach. ☎ **305/948-7258.**

This redolent little storefront is filled with bags and boxes of exotic spices, rices, and beans. Also, a small section of saris, jewelry, scarves, magazines, and videos sell well to the little Indian community that has formed around North Miami Beach. Don't bother trying to call because an incomprehensible machine picks up, and no one ever calls back.

Epicure. 1656 Alton Rd., Miami Beach. ☎ **305/672-1861.**

You've never seen tomatoes like they sell them here at Epicure. A cluster of plump, fire-engine–red beauties from Holland sells for more than $4! But they're the best. Here you'll find not only fancy produce, such as portobello mushrooms the size of a yarmulke, but also pineapples, cherries, and salad greens like you can't imagine. Epicure stocks all the usual prepared foods as well, including great chicken soup and smoked fishes. It's the beach's version of Scotty's Grocery, and you've got to love it. When you pull out your wallet, however, you'll be thinking about how much lighter it's going to be.

Gardner's Market. 7301 Red Rd., South Miami. ☎ **305/667-9953.**

Anything a gourmet or novice cook could desire can be found here. This fancy grocery store in South Miami offers the freshest and best products, from fish to cheese.

Key Biscayne Farmer's Market. 89 Harbor Dr., Key Biscayne. ☎ **305/361-1300.**

At this farmer's market, you'll find a picturesque bounty of fresh and organic fruits, vegetables, and herbs at prices that are not too insane, considering you're in Key Biscayne.

Kingston Miami Trading Company. 280 NE 2nd St., Downtown. ☎ **305/372-9547.**

Among its disorganized array of canned goods, spices, and bottles, this little grocery store has some great Jamaican specialties, including salt cod fish, scotch bonnet sauces, hard-do bread, and jerk seasoning. It also sells lots of delicious drinks, such as Irish moss, Ting, and young coconut juice.

Laurenzo's Italian Supermarket and Farmer's Market. 16385 and 16445 W. Dixie Hwy. ☎ **305/945-6381** and 305/944-5052.

These landmarks in North Miami Beach, or *NMB,* as old-timers say, are the meeting places for those in the know. Anything you want—from homemade ravioli to hand-cut imported Romano cheese to smoked salmon to fresh fish and ground pork—can be found here. The smells alone emanating from the bakery are enough to make you gain a few pounds. Be sure to see the neighboring store full of just-picked herbs, salad greens, and every type of vegetable from around the world. Incredible daily specials, such as 10 Indian River pink grapefruits for 99¢, lure thrifty shoppers from all over the city.

Scotty's Grocery. 3117 Bird Ave., Coconut Grove. ☎ **305/443-5257.**

An extensive wine selection, the freshest produce, and a knowledgeable staff make Scotty's a one-stop market. You don't have to know how to cook to be a gourmet here; you just have to know how to shop. Prices, however, are up there.

Sedano's. 13794 SW 152nd St., South Miami. ☎ **305/255-3386.**

Sedano's caters to the large Hispanic community scattered throughout Little Havana and South Miami with an assortment of ethnic fare, including fresh produce such as yuca, platanos, mamey, avocado, boniato, and guanabanas. You'll also find basic dry goods, such as coffees, beans, rice, cornmeal, and spices.

Vinham Oriental Market. 372 NE 167th St., North Miami Beach. ☎ **305/948-8860.**

Blue crabs, rice cookers, and cookbooks—this store is a one-stop shop for anything you might need for Chinese cooking. A helpful owner will instruct you.

A Taste of Old Florida

Old-fashioned smokehouses used to dot U.S. 1 and Biscayne Boulevard, but as Miami grew, they were driven out of business. As popular as they were, the old shacks couldn't generate enough money from smoked fish to compete with condominiums and shopping centers. Sadly, I've watched dozens disappear over the years.

One that remains is **Jimbo's** on Virginia Key. There's no address, since as Dan, an employee, likes to say: "We're out in the boonies."

Most days, depending on the seasons and the tides and who feels like shopping, Jimbo's sells marlin and salmon. Really, its primary business is selling bait shrimp to fishermen, but there is always some odoriferous fish splayed out for the pungent smoke. Usually, it's just been brought in from one of Jimbo's fishermen friends.

If you can find them, you'll see the old crew of Italians playing bocce, smoking, and drinking out on the bay, in a tiny sliver of backwater life tucked away from civilization. It's worth it. They're there most days if the sun is shining, and they stay until it sets.

To get to Jimbo's, drive over the Rickenbacker Causeway en route to Key Biscayne. After you've passed the second light on Crandon Boulevard, just past the MAST Academy, turn left. Drive about a mile until you see some old wooden fishing shacks (they're used as movie props). You'll find Jimbo's Shrimps across the way. To find out what they're smoking, call ☎ **305/361-7026**.

GOLF

There are hundreds of golf and pro shops throughout Miami, but these are some of the biggest and best.

Alf's Golf Shop. 524 Arthur Godfrey Rd., Miami Beach. ☎ **305/673-6568.** Another location at 15369 S. Dixie Hwy., Miami (☎ 305/378-6068).

The best pro shop on the beach, Alf's can sell you balls, clubs, gloves, and instructional videos. The knowledgeable staff has equipment for golfers of every level, and the neighboring golf course offers discounts to Alf's clients.

Edwin Watts Golf Shops. 15100 N. Biscayne Blvd., North Miami Beach. ☎ **305/944-2925.**

This full-service golf retail shop, one of the most popular in Miami, has it all, including clothing, pro-line equipment, gloves, bags, balls, videos, and books. Plus, you can ask the pros for advice on the best courses in town, as well as request coupons for discounted greens fees on various courses. There are 30 more Edwin Watts shops throughout the Southeast.

Nevada Bob's. 36th St. and NW 79th Ave. (near the airport), Miami. ☎ **305/593-2999.**

This chain store has everything at a discount: Greg Norman and Antigua clothing, pro-line equipment, and steel-shafted and Yonex clubs. There's more than 6,000 square feet of store here; you can even practice your swing at an indoor driving range with a radar gun. The staff are laid-back and very up on the latest soft and hard equipment.

HOUSEWARES

Of course, Miami has all the regulars, such as Pottery Barn, Crate & Barrel, and Williams Sonoma, but here are some of my favorites.

Dish. 939 Lincoln Rd., Miami Beach. ☎ **800/DISH-827** or 305/532-7737.

Offering an eclectic collection of dinnerware from deco era to contemporary, this funky little boutique is a must-see for the curious or the collector.

Linge de Maison Veronique. 305 Alcazar Ave., Coral Gables. ☎ **305/461-3466.**

Fussy Coral Gables housewives flock here for beautiful wares, including custom and hand-embroidered linens, layettes, bed and bath accessories, and tableware to match their china patterns.

Mr. Pottery. 18721 Biscayne Blvd., Aventura. ☎ **305/937-2638.** Other locations at 6935 Red Rd., Coral Gables (☎ 305/662-8085), and in Fashion Mall in Plantation (☎ 954/475-8796).

Good prices on a vast selection of housewares keep this store busy year-round.

Pratesi Linens Inc. 9700 Collins Ave. (in the Bal Harbour Shops), Miami Beach. ☎ **305/861-5677.**

The quality of the Italian linen here is unmatchable, but you could buy a car with what you'll pay for a full set of king-size hand-embroidered sheets.

JEWELRY

The International Jeweler's Exchange. 18861 Biscayne Blvd. (in the Fashion Island), North Miami Beach. ☎ **305/931-7032.** Closed Mondays.

At least 50 jewelers hustle their wares from individual counters at one of the city's most active jewelry centers. Haggle your brains out for excellent prices on timeless antiques from Tiffany's, Cartier, or Bulgari or on unique designs you can create yourself.

The Seybold Building. 36 NE 1st St., Downtown. ☎ **305/374-7922.**

Jewelers of every assortment gather here daily to sell their diamonds and gold. The glare is blinding as you enter this multilevel retail marketplace. You'll see handsome and up-to-date designs, but note that there aren't too many bargains to be had here.

MUSIC

Blue Note Records. 16401 NE 15th Ave., North Miami Beach. ☎ **305/940-3394.**

This place has hard-to-find progressive and underground music and a good staff of music aficionados who can tell you a thing or two. There are new, used, and discounted CDs and old vinyl, too.

Casino Records Inc. 1208 SW 8th St., Little Havana. ☎ **305/856-6888.**

The young, hip salespeople speak English and tend to be music buffs themselves. Here you'll find the largest selection of Latin music in Miami, including pop icons such as Willy Chirino, Gloria Estefan, Albita, and local boy Nil Lara. Their slogan translates to "If we don't have it, forget it." Believe me, they've got it.

CD Warehouse. 13150 Biscayne Blvd., North Miami (☎ **305/892-1048**) and at 1590 S. Dixie Hwy., Coral Gables (☎ 305/662-7100).

Buy, sell, or trade your old CDs at this eclectic music hut.

Extremes Music and News. 513 Lincoln Rd., Miami Beach ☎ **305/534-2003.**

This trendy South Beach music store stocks everything from rave and techno to rap and reggae.

Revolution Records and CDs. 1620 Alton Rd., Miami Beach. ☎ **305/673-6404.**

Here you'll find a quaint and fairly well-organized collection of CDs, from hard-to-find jazz to original recordings of Buddie Rich. They'll search for anything and let you hear whatever you like.

Specs Music. 1655 Washington Ave., South Beach. ☎ **305/534-6533.** Another location at 12451 Biscayne Blvd., North Miami Beach (☎ 305/899-0994).

Call to find out who is playing at this mega-music mall. In addition to a great collection of multicultural sounds, you'll find a lively scene most weekends.

PETS & EXOTIC ANIMALS

The tropical climate plus the constant trade with remote lands makes Miami a perfect point for exotic-animal lovers to find any furry or scaly thing imaginable.

Birdland of Miami. 6615 SW 8th St., Coral Gables. ☎ **305/261-9861.**

This store is best known for its selection of cages, but you can still find anything feathered here, including blue or yellow finches, cockatoos, and others either quiet or loquacious. If you have a special request, give them a few days, and they'll find it. The store also offers a full range of supplies, including the beautiful gilded cages it's known for, as well as fun bird toys.

Exotic Aquariums. 7399 SW 40th St., South Miami. ☎ **305/266-0978.**

Many local divers make a living collecting exotics on their dive trips. Although the practice infuriates conservationists, aquarium owners love it. Here you'll find saltwater and freshwater fish from all over the world.

Natural Selections. 14316 SW 142nd Ave., South Miami. ☎ **305/255-3357.**

Every slimy thing that made your mother screech can be had here, including geckos, lizards, snakes, and iguanas. Call for the gory details of the day.

Simbad's Bird House. 7201 SW 40th St., Miami. ☎ **305/262-6077.**

More like a small aviary than a pet store, Simbad's offers bird lovers a chance to get up close and personal with several dozen kinds of birds. The staff is knowledgeable, the birds are all friendly and touchable, and you can even watch the newborn babies being fed. The store also stocks all the necessary ingredients for a happy, healthy bird, including toys, food and custom-made cages. All birds come with a written health certificate.

World Wild. 1218 Washington Ave., South Beach. ☎ **305/535-0130.**

If you don't think they have it, they probably do. Whether you're a serious buyer or just a window shopper, come see this exotic pet store where you'll find foxes, skunks, reptiles, and even wildcats.

WINES & SPIRITS

Crown Liquors. 6751 Red Rd., Coral Gables. ☎ **305/669-0225.** Another location at 1296 NE 163rd St. (☎ 305/949-2871).

This liquor store offers one of the most diverse selections in Miami. Its ever-rotating stock comes from estate sales around the country and worldwide distributors. And since there are several stores in the chain, the owners get to buy in bulk, which results in lower prices for oenophiles. If you want one of the tastiest and most affordable champagnes ever, try its exclusive import, Billecarte Salmon.

The Estate Wines & Gourmet Foods. 92 Miracle Mile (at Douglas and Galiano), Coral Gables. ☎ **305/442-9915.**

This exceedingly friendly storefront in the middle of Coral Gables' main shopping street offers a small but well-chosen selection of vintages from around the world. It also sells a great array of gourmet cheeses, pâtés, salads, and sandwiches.

Laurenzo's. 16385 and 16445 W. Dixie Hwy., North Miami Beach ☎ **305/945-6381** and 305/944-5052.

Laurenzo's dedicates a few small aisles to its superb wine collection. A full-time expert can help you choose a bottle. Discounts are available for purchases of a case or more, but you'll get an attitude if you're a novice.

Sunny Isles Liquors. 18180 Collins Ave., North Miami Beach. ☎ **305/932-5782.**

This well-located store has on hand hundreds of brands of imported beer and hard-to-find liquor. It will also search and find decanters and minis for your collection.

10 Miami After Dark

Miami nightlife is as varied as its population. On any night, you'll find world-class opera or dance as well as grinding rock and salsa. Restaurants and bars are open late, and many clubs, especially on South Beach, stay open past dawn.

South Florida's late-night life is abuzz, too, with South Beach the center of the scene. The Art Deco District is the spawning ground for top international acts, such as Latin artist Julio Iglesias; Cuban diva Albita; controversial rappers 2 Live Crew; jazz man Nestor Torres; and rockers The Mavericks, Nil Lara, and, of course, Gloria Estefan. It's no secret that Cuban and Caribbean rhythms are extremely popular, and the sound of the conga, inextricably incorporated into Miami's club culture, makes dancing irresistible. So do some of the world's best deejays, like David Padilla, JoJo Odyssey, Junior Vazquez, and David Knapp, who mix at top clubs in the area.

One of the most striking aspects of the city is the recent growth of world-class music, dance, and theater. Miami proudly boasts a top opera company and symphony orchestra, as well as respected ballet and modern dance troupes.

The one thing Miami seems to have trouble sustaining is consistently good live music. In the past few years, Miami has watched more than a half dozen music clubs shut their doors. Some blame the lack of community support; others say it's Miami's remote geographic location, too far a drive for bands to include on their circuit; still others claim promoters in town don't work hard enough to get the word out. The truth is that there are still some excellent venues for live music, especially popular spots for jazz and Latin music. I hope these clubs will endure.

For up-to-date **entertainment listings,** check *The Miami Herald*'s "Weekend" section, which runs on Fridays, or the more comprehensive listings in *New Times,* Miami's free alternative weekly, available each Wednesday. This award-winning paper prints articles, previews, and advertisements on upcoming local events. Several **telephone hotlines**—many operated by local radio stations—give free recorded information on current events in the city. They include the Planet Radio Stuff To Do Hotline (☎ 305/770-2513), the Zeta Concert Hotline (☎ 305/770-2515), and the UM Concert Hotline (☎ 305/284-6477). Other information-oriented telephone numbers are listed under the appropriate headings below.

Tickets for many performances are handled by **TicketMaster;** call ☎ **305/ 358-5885** to charge tickets. For sold-out events, you might try **Ultimate Travel & Entertainment,** 3001 Salzedo, in Coral Gables (☎ **305/444-8499**). This well-known ticket broker is open Monday to Friday from 9am until 6pm, Saturday from 10am until 4pm.

1 Bars

There are countless bars in and around Miami with the highest concentration on trendy South Beach. Keeping track of them all would be a full-time job. Hmmm . . . and not a bad one at that. Still, the selection listed below is a mere sample. Many popular bars are in restaurants and hotels. On the beach, you'd do best to walk along Ocean Drive and especially Washington Avenue to see what's hot. In Coconut Grove, check out CocoWalk and Mayfair next door. Most of the bars listed below have no cover charge.

China Grill. 404 Washington Ave., South Beach. ☎ **305/534-2211.**

Don't bother with the food, but do stop in for an overpriced drink and some superb spectating. The dinner and bar crowd arrive decked out as if going to a disco, and from the look-over you get on the way in, you get the idea that the front-door staff would like to hang a velvet rope and do some picking at the door.

The Clevelander. 1021 Ocean Dr., South Beach. ☎ **305/531-3485.** No cover.

This old standby on one of Ocean Drive's busiest and most spacious corners is always a sure bet. You'll find a crowd gathered around the large outdoor pool area up until 5am. Cheap drinks in plastic cups complete the beachy atmosphere in this casual spring-breaky bar.

The Delano. 1685 Collins Ave., South Beach. ☎ **305/672-2000.** No cover.

I'm surprised they haven't started charging admission to this spectacular attraction. In the lobby is the Rose Bar, one of the best spots in South Beach to see beautiful people decked out in trendy splendor. Lounge on a cushy sofa or in any of the plump beds that are casually arranged throughout the lobby and backyard, and grab an expensive drink. This is a good place to start the evening before heading out to the more lively clubs in the area. Note: Don't valet park here. Not only will you pay about $15 for the privilege, you will also wait forever for the handsome valets to retrieve your car.

The Forge. 432 41st St., Miami Beach. ☎ **305/538-8533.**

Step back in time at this ultra-elegant restaurant and bar, where Wednesday night is the night to hang with dolled-up Euro-singles and New Yorkers. Call well in advance if you want to watch the parade of characters from your dinner table (see chapter 6). An elegant nightclub called Jimmy'z, a spin-off of Regine's, is adjacent. They say it's a private club, but if you dine at the restaurant or know someone, you can get in.

Howl at the Moon Saloon. 3015 Grand Ave. (on the second level of CocoWalk), Coconut Grove. ☎ **305/442-8300.** Cover $5–$10.

Drink specials are a regular fixture at night throughout the week, except Monday, when the Moon is dark. On Sunday, beers are $1.75 a pop. On Thursday night, 19- and 20-year-olds are let in, and those over 21 with a college ID can skip the cover and simply enjoy cheap buckets of beer.

Mac's Club Deuce. 222 14th St., South Beach. ☎ **305/673-9537.** No cover.

Housed in a squat, neon-covered deco building, this old dive bar is popular with bikers, barflies, and pool players who love the dark and smoky scene. It's a real local's favorite for those who like to slum it. Here you'll no doubt catch a great conversation, some old tunes on the juke box, or a good scene out the front picture window that faces a busy all-night tattoo parlor. Mac's is open daily from 8am to 5am.

Molly Malone's. 166 Sunny Isles Blvd. (just west of Collins Ave.), North Miami Beach. ☎ **305/948-3512.**

Open all day and into the next, Molly's is a divey Irish pub, popular with young and old drinkers and folk lovers alike. There's a pool table and darts, occasional Irish rock or acoustic music, and, of course, a selection of good ales and lagers.

Murphy's Law Irish Pub. 2977 McFarlane Dr., Coconut Grove. ☎ **305/446-9956.**

This wood and brass-decorated Irish pub is for those who want to escape the more antiseptic night scene at CocoWalk down the road. A big-screen TV shows sports events, but otherwise, it's just you and a pint sharing the bar with old-timers, grungers, and young professionals.

Tantra. 1445 Pennsylvania Ave. (at Española Way), South Beach. ☎ **305/672-4765.**

This super-sexy restaurant/lounge was scorching hot when it opened in late 1997 and continues to be the place for the beautiful-in-black crowd. It looks like some luxurious opium den in Marrakesh. You'll step into a small entryway covered with real grass, and then continue into the lounge, where you'll find a stone waterfall, huge Indian sculptures, smokey lanterns, and low curtained tables. This is the place to check out Miami's hippest. Plus, the food (said to have aphrodisiacal properties) is excellent, though pricey. Dinner reservations are hard to get, and a spot at the bar is even tougher, especially if you come after 11pm.

Wet Willies. 760 Ocean Dr., South Beach. ☎ **305/532-5650.**

The upstairs deck right on the main drag is one of the prime spots for watching the hectic parade of Ocean Drive. From up here, you can see the ocean as well as the spectacle of folks who walk the strip night and day. After just one Wet Willie frozen concoction, you may not be able to see much of anything. Watch out: They taste like soda pop but bite like a mad dog.

2 The Club & Music Scene

LIVE MUSIC & JAZZ

Despite the spotty success of local music, South Florida's jazz scene is very much alive with traditional and contemporary performers. Keep an eye out for guitarist Randy Bernsen, vibraphonist Tom Toyama, and flutist Nestor Torres, young performers who lead local ensembles. The University of Miami has a well-respected jazz studies program in its School of Music (☎ **305/284-6477**) and often schedules low- and no-cost recitals. Additionally, many area hotels feature live music of every assortment. Schedules are listed in the newspaper entertainment sections.

Churchill's Hideaway. 5501 NE Second Ave., Miami. ☎ **305/757-1807.** Cover usually $3, but depends on the band.

It's a dive and in a rough neighborhood, but if you want to sample Miami's local music scene, Churchill's is the place to go. You might even see a fledgling band before it makes it big. At this British pub (hence the name "Churchill's"), you can snack on rustic shepherd's pie and good English brew. And for those homesick Brits craving a good game of rugby, Churchill's is probably the only place that broadcasts English sports via satellite. Call ahead for information on upcoming bands and performance times.

The Globe. 377 Alhambra Circle (at LeJeune), Coral Gables. ☎ **305/445-3555.** No cover.

This odd little cafe is attached to a travel agency. On weekends, a red curtain transforms a corner into a stage, where you'll find decent jazz.

The Hungry Sailor. 3426 Main Hwy., Coconut Grove. ☎ **305/444-9359.** Cover Fri and Sat $5–$10. Closed Monday.

This small English-style wood-paneled pub has Watney's, Bass, and Guinness on draught and reggae regularly on tap, too. This place attracts an extremely mixed crowd. High-quality reggae and soca live music are featured Thursday through Saturday. On other nights, you might find an open mike or dance music provided by a deejay.

Rose's Bar and Lounge. 754 Washington Ave., South Beach. ☎ **305/532-0228.** Cover $3–$15 Tues–Sun, depending on show.

This hip South Beach bar features local music—live rock, jazz, or whatever else strikes your fancy or theirs—almost every night on its tiny stage. Get there early to beat the crowds and claim a spot among the sparse seating. Open every night from 5pm to 5am.

South Beach Pub. 717 Washington Ave., South Beach. ☎ **305/532-PUB1.** Cover for back room $3–$8.

This hole-in-the-wall offers your average bar up front with a small live music room in the back. Local bands as well as national touring bands pack them in at this tiny venue. Watch local papers for special Latin rock nights, where Miami's flavor is infused with some good old rock and roll.

۞ Tobacco Road. 626 S. Miami Ave. (over the Miami Ave. Bridge near Brickell Ave.), Downtown. ☎ **305/374-1198.** Cover $0–$8.

This Miami institution is a must-see. It's been around since 1912 doing more in the back room than just dancing. These days, you'll find a good bar menu along with the best live music anywhere—blues, zydeco, brass, jazz, and more. Regulars performers include The Dirty Dozen Brass band from New Orleans, who play a mean mix of zydeco and blues with an actual dozen brass players; Bill Warton and the Ingredients, who make a pot of gumbo while up on stage; Monkey Meet; Iko Iko; Chubby Carrier and his band; and many more. On Friday and Saturday nights, the music is played upstairs, and people dance like crazy, even though it's packed and there's no real dance floor. Monday, of course, is reserved for the blues. Escape the smoke and sweat in the backyard patio where air is a welcome commodity. The downright-cheap dinner specials, such as the $10 lobster dinner, are quite good and served until 2am.

Van Dyke Cafe. 846 Lincoln Rd., Miami Beach. ☎ **305/534-3600.** No cover.

Live jazz 7 nights a week until midnight—and it's free! In an elegant little upstairs lounge, the likes of Eddie Higgins, Mike Renzi, and locals such as Don Wilner, play strictly jazz for a well-dressed crowd of enthusiasts. You can have a drink or two at the pristine oak bar or enjoy some snacks from the bustling patio seats below.

DANCE CLUBS

In addition to quiet cafes and progressive poolside bars, Miami Beach pulsates with one of the liveliest night scenes in the city. Also check out "Latin Clubs" listings, later in this chapter for more places to dance.

A popular trend in Miami's club scene are "one-off" nights—events organized by a promoter and held in established venues on irregular schedules. Word of mouth, local advertising, and listings in the free weekly *New Times* are the best ways to find out about these hot events. You can also try asking a cool-looking waiter or waitress at some South Beach eatery.

And just for the record: No, Madonna, the original Material Girl, does not own a nightclub in South Beach. The club that uses her name on its oversized billboard on Washington Avenue is a strip joint, one of a handful in South Beach that cater to the area's many tourists and traveling businessmen.

Bash. 655 Washington Ave., South Beach. ☎ **305/538-2274.** BarBashClub.com. Cover $10 weeknights and $15 weekends.

This place has been around longer than most and is still pretty hot. Bash gets going late and features an eclectic mix of music, including Euro-dance, disco, and funk as well as special events, such as occasional funky fashions shows. The crowd is incredibly Euro-hip and super trendy. Open every night but Monday from 10pm to 5am.

Bermuda Bar and Grill. 3509 NE 163rd St., North Miami. ☎ **305/945-0196.** Cover $0–$10. No cover before 9pm.

This huge suburban danceteria specializes in ladies' nights (Wednesday and Thursday, there's no cover for women). Plus, it hosts cash-prize contests for women who dare to wear the skimpiest outfits. Still, everybody loves the high-energy music that packs the dance floor. Thursday is Latin night and Friday is happy hour from 5 to 8pm. Saturday is the biggest night, when all the goings-on are broadcast live on a local radio station. This place usually stays open until the sun comes up. Closed Monday and Tuesday.

Cafe Iguana. 8505 Mills Dr. (in the Kendall Town & Country Mall on the corner of 88th St. and 117th Ave.), Miami. ☎ **305/274-4948.** Cover $0–$10.

This tropical-themed bar and dance club is a bit much for low-key club-goers, but for those looking for a high-energy party, it's the place to be. Everything from male and female hot-body contests to a raging Latin night are incorporated into this nightspot.

Club St. Croix. 3015 Grand Ave., Coconut Grove (CocoWalk). ☎ **305/446-4999.** Cover $0–$15.

How many bodies can fit in one club? Club St. Croix has made it its mission to find out. If you're not blinded by the pulsating disco lights and shocking Caribbean decor, and you love loud dance music and scantily clad bodies, you'll enjoy this suburban bar scene. The Voodoo Lounge cigar bar inside the club is quiet in comparison. The club normally opens at 9pm and closes at 5am except on Thursday and Friday, when the party starts at 4pm for happy hour. Open Wednesday to Sunday.

821. 821 Lincoln Rd., South Beach. ☎ **305/531-1188.** No cover.

On most nights, 821 is more gay than straight. It's something between a neighborhood bar and a nightclub, with a deejay or live music every night. Thursday night is for women only and usually features a cabaret singer. Friday night is all boys, and they do party hard. Offering a good mix of music and people, this hotspot is a Lincoln Road staple that's open daily from 3pm until 3 or 5am.

Groove Jet. 323 23rd St. (next to the Fina gas station), South Beach. ☎ **305/532-2002.** Cover $10.

This fantastic hidden spot north of the South Beach scene has been through many incarnations. Its most recent, Groove Jet, has three distinct areas playing totally different music. Deep house, jungle, and trance tunes are usually heard in the front room with more experimental music in the back rooms. A very hip young crowd hangs in this out-of-the-way scene, which gets going late, Thursday to Sunday 11pm to 5am.

Liquid and The Lounge. 1439 Washington Ave., South Beach. ☎ **305/532-9154** for information, 305/532-8899 for table reservations. Cover $10–$15.

Liquid is reminiscent of the 1980s New York club scene, so you can expect to wait at the ropes until a disdainful bouncer chooses you. Don't dare to wear the usual casual South Beach attire; they are looking for "casual chic." Once inside, you'll find a cavernous space with up-to-the-minute dance music and two beautiful bars, VIP seating in a cozy back area, a hip-hop side room, and a downstairs lounge playing jazz and funk. Sunday night is gay. Madonna sightings are not unusual. The club opens doors at 11pm but the action starts late (around 2am).

Living Room at the Strand. 671 Washington Ave., South Beach. ☎ **305/532-2340.** Cover $5–$15.

This very Euro hotspot is the place to mix and mingle with South Beach's older, and much more sophisticated, crowd. Models and moguls alike converge here to drink and relive the art of conversation, with plenty of VIP tables to accommodate them.

Marsbar. 8505 Mills Dr. (in the Kendall Town & Country Mall on the corner of 88th St. and 117th Ave.), Miami. ☎ **305/271-6909.** Cover $5–$10.

After closing down for a while, this alternative dance club is back with a vengeance, and it's all about the '70s and '80s. The retro-only format caters to young and old alike, with youngsters and hipsters packing it in from neighboring South Miami and Kendall.

THE GAY & LESBIAN SCENE

The gay and lesbian scene is super active in South Beach. Not only are there many clubs, but there's a thriving network of gay-owned businesses. Most hotels and restaurants are gay-friendly, and many of the gay clubs are hetero-friendly as well. There are quite a few gay organizations ready to offer any information (see "Tips for Travelers with Special Needs" in chapter 2). An ultra-open lifestyle here allows for open displays of affection among gay male or female visitors.

Many of the normally "straight" clubs also have gay nights. Both Liquid and 821 host these parties. Another particularly good one is the Sunday afternoon Tea Dance at **Amnesia,** 136 Collins Ave., South Beach (☎ **305/531-5535**), where buffed boys parade around in minuscule outfits while dance music plays in the background. These parties change nights and locations from month to month, so be sure to call ahead of time.

Loading Zone. 1426 Alton Rd., Miami Beach. ☎ **305/531-5623.** No cover.

The town's only leather bar, complete with hot men, sexy videos, and, in case you forgot something, a leather shop in back.

Salvation. 1771 West Ave., Miami Beach. ☎ **305/673-6508.** Cover varies. Saturday only.

Probably the largest gay dance party in the state, with pumping dance music and some of South Beach's most recognized—and wildest—drag queens. It's a weekly party at a huge place and it goes on until the sun comes up.

Twist. 1057 Washington Ave., South Beach. ☎ **305/53-TWIST.** No cover.

One of the beach's most popular cruise bars, Twist attracts mostly male clientele but has an open-door policy. Open daily from 1pm to 5am.

Warsaw Ballroom. 1450 Collins Ave., South Beach. ☎ **305/531-4555.** Cover $10–$15.

One of Miami's oldest and most fun nightclubs, Warsaw hosts various theme nights and some of the best dance music in town. After all these years, regulars still line up down the sidewalk, waiting to get in and dance until 5am. The new owners may be slipping a bit, but it's worth checking out.

West End. 942 Lincoln Rd., South Beach. ☎ **305/538-9378.** No cover.

A mellow bar and pool hall, this Lincoln Road stand-by is a favorite hangout for women and men. Enjoy a relaxed atmosphere and a good place to meet people. Open 2pm to 5am on weekdays and noon to 5am on weekends.

LATIN CLUBS

Considering that Hispanics make up the majority of Miami's population and that there's a huge influx of Spanish-speaking visitors, it's no surprise that there are some great Latin nightclubs in the city. What's interesting is that in recent years, many new clubs have opened and are attracting a mix of curious Anglos and Europeans as well. Plus, with the meteoric rise of the international music scene based in Miami, many international stars come through the offices of MTV Latino, SONY International, and a multitude of Latin TV studios based in Miami—and they're all looking for a good club scene on weekends.

Because of the increased competition, some of Miami's older Latin clubs have gone into decline. Thankfully, however, there are still many authentic clubs that are fun to check out. If you don't already know how to dance to Latin music, consider taking a salsa class and then head out to one of the following Anglo-friendly clubs.

Alcazaba. 50 Alhambra Plaza (in the Hyatt Regency Coral Gables), Coral Gables. ☎ **305/441-1234.**

The Hyatt's Top-40 lounge plays an eclectic mix of music but exudes a decidedly Mediterranean atmosphere that mixes fantasy with reality. Cool out with some tropical drinks and authentic tapas in between songs. Happy hour—Wednesday and Friday from 5 to 7pm and Saturday from 9 to 11pm—offers half-price beer, wine, and drinks, plus a free buffet.

Cafe Nostalgia. 2212 SW 8th St. (Calle Ocho), Miami. ☎ **305/541-2631.** Cover $10 on Fri–Sat nights.

As the name implies, Cafe Nostalgia is dedicated to reminiscing about old Cuba. After watching a Celia Cruz film, you can dance to the hot sounds of Afro-Cuban jazz. With pictures of old and young Cuban stars smiling down on you and a live band celebrating Cuban heritage, Cafe Nostalgia sounds like a bit much; it's more than that. Be prepared—it's packed after midnight and dance space is mostly between the tables. Open Thursday to Sunday from 9pm to 4am. Films are shown from 10pm to midnight, followed by live music. Another branch is set to open on Miami Beach.

Where to Learn to Salsa

Are you feeling shy about hitting a Latin club because you fear your two left feet will step out? Then take a few lessons before tripping the light fantastic. Here are the names of several dance companies and dance teachers around the city who offer individual and group lessons to dancers of any origin who are willing to learn. These folks have made it their mission to teach merengue and flamenco to the gringo wannabe's and Latin left-foots.

Ballet Flamenco La Rosa (in the PAN building, 555 17th St., South Beach; ☎ 305/672-0552), wants to teach you how to flamenco, salsa, or merengue with the best of them. They are the only professional flamenco company in the area, so you'll hear those castanets going. If you're feeling shy, $50 will buy you a private lesson; otherwise, $10 an hour will allow you to learn the art of the dance with a group of other beginners.

Nobody salsas like **Luz Pinto** (☎ 305/868-9418), and she also knows how to teach the basics with patience and humor. She charges between $45 and $50 for a private lesson for up to four people and $10 per person for a group lesson. A good introduction is her multi-level group class at 7pm Sunday evenings at the PAN building. Although she teaches everything from ballroom to merengue, her specialty is Casino-style salsa, popularized in the 1950s in Cuba, Luz's homeland. A mix between disco and country square dancing, Casino-style salsa is all the rage in Latin clubs in town. If you are a very good student, you may be able to talk Luz into chaperoning a trip to a nightclub to show off your moves. She'll work out a fee based on the number of participants and their ability.

Angel Arroya has been teaching salsa to the clueless out of his home at 16464 NE 27th Ave., North Miami Beach (☎ 305/949-7799), for the past 10 years. Just $10 will buy you an hour's time in his "school." He traditionally teaches Monday and Wednesday nights, but call ahead to check for any schedule changes.

Casa Panza. 1620 SW 8th St. (Calle Ocho), Miami. ☎ **305/643-5343.** No cover.

Clap your hands or your castanets if you have them. Every Tuesday and Thursday night, Casa Panza, in the heart of Little Havana, becomes the House of Flamenco, with shows at 8 and 11pm. Patrons of the restaurant can enjoy a flamenco show or don their own dancing shoes and participate in the celebration. Enjoy a fantastic dinner before the show or have a few drinks before you do some stomping.

Mango's. 900 Ocean Dr., South Beach. ☎ **305/673-4422.** Cover $6–$15; varies by performer.

If you want to dance to a funky, loud Brazilian beat till you drop, check out Mango's on the beach. It features nightly live Brazilian and other Latin music on a little patio bar. When you need refreshment, you can choose from a wildly eclectic menu of Caribbean, Mexican, vegetarian, and Cuban specialties. Open daily from 11am to 5:30pm.

Studio 23. 247 23rd St. (adjacent to Mama Vieja Restaurant), South Beach. ☎ **305/538-1196.** Cover $5–$10.

You've heard of son? Hear it here—along with salsa, cumbia, merengue, vallenato, and house music. This neighborhood Latin disco and nightclub gets going after hours with a wild strobe-lit atmosphere. If you don't know how to do it, just wait. You'll have plenty of willing teachers on hand. Open Friday to Sunday from 8pm to 4am.

Yuca. 501 Lincoln Rd., South Beach. ☎ **305/532-9822.** Cover $25, plus two-drink minimum for the Albita performance Fri–Sat nights at 11pm.

One of the city's best restaurants (see chapter 6, "Dining") also serves up hot music in an upstairs club. If Albita is playing, don't miss her. The bill will be high and you'll be squeezed into a table no bigger than a cocktail napkin, but it's worth it for the high-energy dance music, including traditional sol, salsa, and son from the old country. No matter who is playing, you are bound to have fun at this authentic Latin hotspot. If you don't speak Spanish, sign language works here, too.

3 The Performing Arts

THEATER

In Miami, an active and varied selection of dramas and musicals are presented throughout the year. Thanks to the support of many loyal theater aficionados, especially an older crowd of New York transplants, season subscriptions are common and allow the theaters to survive, even when every show is not a hit. Some traveling Broadway shows make it to town, as well as revivals by big-name playwrights, such as Tennessee Williams, David Mamet, Neil Simon, and Israel Horowitz. The best way to find out what's playing is to check the local paper or call the theaters directly. In the summer, most theaters are dark or show a limited schedule.

The **Actors' Playhouse,** at the newly restored Miracle Theater in Coral Gables (☎ 305/444-9293), is a grand 1948 art deco movie palace with a 600-seat main theater as well as a smaller theater/rehearsal hall where a number of excellent musicals for children are put on throughout the year. In addition to these two rooms, the Playhouse recently added a 300-seat children's balcony theater. Tickets run from $16 to $50.

The **Coconut Grove Playhouse,** 3500 Main Highway in Coconut Grove (☎ 305/442-4000), was also a former movie house, built in 1927 in an ornate Spanish rococo style. Today, this respected venue is known for its original and innovative staging of both international and local dramas and musicals. The house's second, more intimate Encore Room is well suited to alternative and experimental productions. Tickets run from $15 to $35.

The **Florida Shakespeare Theatre,** on Anastasia Avenue in Coral Gables at the Biltmore Hotel (☎ 305/445-1119), stages at least one Shakespeare play, one classic, and one contemporary piece a year. This well-regarded theater usually tries to secure the rights to a national or local premiere as well. Tickets cost $22 and $26; $10 and $17 for students and seniors.

The recently renamed **Jerry Herman Ring Theatre** is on the main campus of the University of Miami in Coral Gables (☎ 305/284-3355). The University's Department of Theater Arts uses this stage for advanced-student productions of comedies, dramas, and musicals. Faculty and guest actors are regularly featured, as are contemporary works by local playwrights. Performances are usually scheduled Tuesday through Saturday during the academic year only. Tickets sell for $5 to $20.

The **New Theater,** 65 Almeria Ave., in Coral Gables (☎ 305/443-5909), prides itself on showing world-renowned works from America and Europe. As the name implies, you'll find mostly contemporary plays, with a few classics thrown in for variety. Performances are staged Thursday to Sunday year-round. Tickets are $20 on weekdays, and $25 weekends. If extra tickets are available, students pay half price.

ACTING COMPANIES

Miami's two well-known acting companies have suffered from poor financing and real-estate woes. Luckily, both have the use of the beautiful Colony Theater on Lincoln Road and the support of a loyal crew of theater aficionados. Call for schedules and locales.

The **Acme Acting Company** (☎ 305/576-7500) performs Wednesday to Saturday at 8pm, and Sunday at 7pm. They usually present off-beat contemporary plays to critical acclaim. Tickets are $15 to $25 depending on the venue; students and seniors pay $10 to $20.

The award-winning **Area Stage Company** (☎ 305/673-8002) has won respect from local and national audiences for their dramatic work in all manner of contemporary theater.

CLASSICAL MUSIC

In addition to a number of local orchestras and operas, which regularly offer high-quality music and world-renowned guest artists, each year brings a slew of special events and touring artists. One of the most important and longest-running series is produced by the **Concert Association of Florida (CAF),** 555 17th St., South Beach (☎ 305/532-3491). Known for more than a quarter of a century for its high-caliber, star-packed schedules, CAF regularly arranges the best "serious" music concerts for the city. Season after season, the schedules are punctuated by world-renowned dance companies and seasoned virtuosi like Itzhak Perlman, Andre Watts, and Kathleen Battle. Since CAF does not have its own space, performances are usually scheduled in either the Dade County Auditorium or the Jackie Gleason Theater of the Performing Arts (see below). The season lasts from October through April, and ticket prices range from $20 to $70.

Florida Philharmonic Orchestra. 169 E. Flagler St., Miami. ☎ **800/226-1812** or 305/930-1812. Tickets $15–$60. When extra tickets are available, students are allowed in for free.

South Florida's premier symphony orchestra, under the direction of James Judd, presents a full season of classical and pops programs interspersed with several children's and contemporary popular music dates. The Philharmonic performs downtown in the Gusman Center for the Performing Arts and at the Dade County Auditorium.

Miami Chamber Symphony. 5690 N. Kendall Dr., Kendall. ☎ **305/858-3500.** Tickets $12–$30.

This professional orchestra is an inexpensive alternative to the high-priced classical venues. Renowned international soloists perform regularly. The season runs October to May, and most concerts are held in the Gusman Concert Hall, on the University of Miami campus.

The New World Symphony. 541 Lincoln Rd., South Beach. ☎ **305/673-3331.** E-mail: ticketsnws.org. www.nws.org. Tickets $0–$43. Student discounts available on day of show.

This organization, led by artistic director Michael Tilson Thomas, is a stepping stone for gifted young musicians seeking professional careers. The orchestra specializes in ambitious, innovative, energetic performances and often features renowned guest soloists and conductors. The symphony's season lasts from October to May.

OPERA

✪ **Florida Grand Opera.** 1200 Coral Way, Miami. ☎ **800/741-1010** or 305/854-1643. Tickets $18–$100. Student discounts available.

Nearing its 60th birthday, this company regularly features singers from top houses in both America and Europe. All productions are sung in their original language and staged with projected English supertitles. Tickets become scarce when Placido Domingo or Luciano Pavarotti (who made his American debut here in 1965) come to town. The opera's season runs roughly from November to April, with five performances each week.

DANCE

Several local dance companies train and perform in the Greater Miami area. In addition, top traveling troupes regularly stop at the venues listed above. Keep your eyes open for special events and guest artists.

✪ **Ballet Flamenco La Rosa.** ☎ **305/672-0552** or 305/757-8475. Tickets $25 at door, $20 in advance, $18 for students and seniors.

For a taste of local Latin flavor, see this lively troupe perform impressive flamenco and other styles of dance on Miami stages.

✪ **Miami City Ballet.** Rehearsal studio on Lincoln Road Mall at Jefferson, South Beach. ☎ **305/532-4880.** Box office ☎ 305/532-7713. Tickets $17–$100.

Headquartered in a storefront in the middle of the Art Deco District's popular pedestrian mall, this Miami company has quickly emerged as a top troupe, performing both classical and contemporary works. The artistically acclaimed and innovative company, directed by Edward Villella, features a repertoire of more than 60 ballets, many by George Balanchine, and more than 20 world premieres. Stop by most afternoons to watch rehearsals through the large storefront window. Plans are in the works to move to a bigger studio by 2000. The City Ballet season runs from September to April, with performances at the Jackie Gleason Theater of the Performing Arts (see below).

MAJOR VENUES

After years of decay and a $1-million facelift, the **Colony Theater,** on Lincoln Road, South Beach (☎ **305/674-1026**), has become an architectural showpiece of the Art Deco District. This multipurpose 465-seat theater stages performances by the Miami City Ballet and the Ballet Flamenco La Rosa, as well as off-Broadway shows and other special events.

At the **Dade County Auditorium,** West Flagler Street at 29th Avenue, Miami (☎ **305/547-5414**), performers gripe about the lack of space, but for patrons, this 2,430-seat auditorium is comfortable and intimate. It's home to the city's Greater Miami Opera and also stages productions by the Concert Association of Florida, many Spanish programs, and a variety of other shows.

At the 1,700-seat **Gusman Center for the Performing Arts,** 174 E. Flagler Street in Downtown Miami (☎ **305/372-0925**), seating is tight, and so is funding, but the sound is superb. In addition to producing a regular stage for the Philharmonic Orchestra of Florida and The Miami Film Festival, the elegant Gusman Center features pop concerts, plays, film-festival screenings, and special events. The auditorium was built as the Olympia Theater in 1926, and its ornate palace interior is typical of that era, complete with fancy columns, a huge pipe organ, and twinkling "stars" on the ceiling.

Not to be confused with the Gusman Center (above), the **Gusman Concert Hall,** 1314 Miller Dr., at 14th Street in Coral Gables (☎ **305/284-6477**), is a roomy 600-seat hall that gives a stage to the Miami Chamber Symphony and a varied program of university recitals.

The elegant **Jackie Gleason Theater of the Performing Arts** (TOPA), Washington Avenue at 17th Street, South Beach (☎ **305/673-7300**), is the home of the Miami City Ballet as well as the Miami Beach Broadway Series, which recently presented *Rent, Phantom of the Opera,* and *Les Miserables.* This 2,705-seat hall also hosts other big-budget Broadway shows, classical music concerts, opera, and dance performances.

4 Movies & More

CINEMAS

In addition to the annual Miami Film Festival in February and other, smaller film events (See "Miami Calendar of Events" in chapter 2), Miami is lucky to have three wonderful art cinemas showing a range of films from *Fresa y Chocolate* to *Crumb.*

The Alliance Cinema (☎ **305/531-8504**) is tucked behind a little tropical walkway just next to Books & Books at 927 Lincoln Rd., Suite 119, in South Beach. Among other independent movies, this old hideaway shows art films, Latin American features, and lots of gay films, too. You may want to bring a pillow; the seats are old and rickety. Tickets cost $6.

Astor Art Cinema, 4120 Laguna St. (☎ **305/443-6777**), is an oasis in the midst of a desert of Cineplex Odeons and AMCs in Coral Gables. This quaint double theater hosts foreign, classic, independent, and art films and serves decent popcorn, too. Tickets are $5, $3 for seniors.

Alcazar Cinemateque, 235 Alcazar Ave., Coral Gables (☎ **305/446-7144**), is a small one-screen theater under the same ownership as the Astor, above, that shows good movies, often Spanish–language films, without the hustle and bustle of the crowded multiplexes. The Alcazar shows the more artsy of the major films as well as some obscure independents. Tickets are $6.

The Bill Cosford Cinema at the University of Miami, on the second floor of the memorial building off Campo Sano Avenue (☎ **305/284-4861**), is named after the deceased *Herald* film critic. This well-endowed little theater was recently revamped and boasts high-tech projectors, new air-conditioning, and new decor. It sponsors independent films as well as lectures by visiting filmmakers and movie stars. Andy Garcia and Antonio Banderas are a few of the big names this little theater has attracted. It also hosts the African American Film Festival and a Student Film Festival, plus collaborations with the Fort Lauderdale Festival. Admission is $5.

THE LITERARY SCENE

Books & Books, in Coral Gables at 296 Aragon Ave., and in Miami Beach at 933 Lincoln Rd., hosts readings almost every night and is known for attracting top authors, such as Colleen McCullough, Jamaica Kincaid, and Paul Levine. For details on the free readings, call ☎ **305/442-4408.**

To hear more about what's happening in Miami's literary scene, tune into the "Cover to Cover" show, broadcast at 8pm on Mondays on the public radio station, WLRN (91.3 FM).

5 Late-Night Bites

Although many dining spots in Miami stop serving at 10pm, South Beach eateries stay open very late, especially on weekends. So, if you want a quick bite after clubbing and it's 4am, don't fret. There a vast number of pizza places lining Washington Avenue in South Beach that are open past 6am. Especially good is

Pucci's, with several locations, including one at 651 Washington Ave. **La Sandwicherie,** 229 14th Street (behind the Amoco station; ☎ **305/532-8934**), serves up a great late-night sandwich until 5am. Another place of note for night owls is the **News Cafe,** 800 Ocean Dr. (☎ **305/538-6397**), a trendy and well-priced cafe with an enormous menu offering great all-day breakfasts, Middle Eastern platters, fruit bowls, or steak and potatoes. In Coconut Grove, there's another crowded News Cafe, 2901 Florida Ave. (behind Mayfair; ☎ **305/774-6397**), serving up fresh and varied food around the clock.

If your night out was at one of the Latin clubs around town, stop in at **Versailles,** 3555 SW 8th St. (☎ **444-0240**), in Little Havana. What else but a Cuban *medianoche* (midnight sandwich) will do? It might not be open all night, but its hours extend well past midnight—usually until 3 or 4am on weekends—to cater to gangs of revelers, both young and old, who like to hang out, chatter, and laugh until dawn.

Side Trips from Miami 11

As varied as Miami and its beaches are, many people like to use this centrally located spot as a jumping-off point for other destinations. Whether you'd like to tour Biscayne National Park or explore the Everglades or hop over to one of the Florida Keys, all are easily accessible from here.

1 Biscayne National Park

35 miles S of Miami

Many people who arrive at Biscayne National Park's main entrance at Convoy Point take one look around and exclaim "Are we there?" You see, the park is very large—181,500 acres to be exact—but what some visitors don't realize is that 95% of it is underwater. In 1968, President Lyndon Johnson signed a bill to conserve the barrier islands off South Florida's east coast as a national monument, a protected status one rung below a national park. After being twice enlarged, once in 1974 and again in 1980, the waters surrounding the northernmost coral reef in North America became a full-fledged national park.

There's not much for landlubbers here. The park's small mainland mangrove shoreline and 44 islands are best explored by boat. Its extensive reef system is extremely popular with divers and snorkelers. The concessionaire at Convoy Point rents canoes, runs dive trips, and offers popular glass-bottom boat tours.

Elliott Key, one of the park's 44 little mangrove-fringed islands, contains a visitors center, hiking trails, and a campground. Located about 9 miles from Convoy Point, Elliott Key is accessible only by boat. There are also campsites on Boca Chita.

JUST THE FACTS

GETTING THERE   By Car   Convoy Point, the park's mainland entrance, is 9 miles east of Homestead. To reach the park from Miami, take Florida's Turnpike to the Tallahassee Road (SW 137th Avenue) exit. Turn left, and then left again at North Canal Drive (SW 328th Street), and follow signs to the park. If you're coming from U.S. 1, whether you're heading north or south, turn east at North Canal Drive (SW 328th Street). The entrance is approximately 9 miles away.

By Boat Biscayne National Park is especially accessible to boaters. Mooring buoys abound, since it is illegal to anchor on coral. When no buoys are available, boaters must anchor on sand. Boaters should carry NOAA nautical chart no. 11451, which is available at Convoy Point. Even the most experienced yachter should be sure to carry a chart. Waters are often murky, making the abundant reefs and sandbars difficult to detect—and there are few less-interesting ways to spend a day than waiting for the tide to rise. There is a boat launch at adjacent Homestead Bayfront Park. Elliott Key has 66 slips, available free on a first-come, first-serve basis.

ACCESS POINTS The park's mainland entrance is **Convoy Point,** located 9 miles east of Homestead.

VISITORS CENTERS & INFORMATION General inquiries and specific questions should be directed to the **National Park Service,** P.O. Box 1369, Homestead, FL 33030 (☎ **305/230-7275**).

For information on park activities and tours, contact **Biscayne National Park Underwater Tours,** P.O. Box 1270, Homestead, FL 33030 (☎ **305/230-1100**).

The **Convoy Point Visitors Center,** at the park's main entrance (☎ **305/ 230-7275**), is the natural starting point for any venture into the park. In addition to providing comprehensive information on the park, rangers will show you a 10-minute slide show and a short video about Hurricane Andrew, both on request. Open Monday to Friday from 8:30am to 4pm and on Saturday and Sunday until 5pm.

ENTRANCE FEES & PERMITS Entrance is free to **Biscayne National Park.** Backcountry permits are also free, and available at the visitors center.

OPENING HOURS Biscayne National Park is always open; the visitors centers are staffed daily from about 8:30am to 5pm.

SEEING THE HIGHLIGHTS

Since Biscayne National Park is primarily underwater, the only way to truly experience it is with snorkel or scuba gear. You'll need a boat, too. Beneath the surface, the aquatic universe pulses with multicolored life. Bright parrot fish and angelfish, gently rocking sea fans, and coral labyrinths abound. Before entering the water, be sure to apply waterproof sunblock or wear a T-shirt. Once you begin to explore, it's easy to lose track of time, and the Florida sun is brutal, even during the winter months.

Afterward, take a picnic out to Elliott Key, or the recently restored Boca Chita, and feel the crisp salt air blowing off the Atlantic. Since Elliott Key is accessible only by boat, the beach is usually less crowded than those farther north.

SPORTS & OUTDOOR ACTIVITIES

CANOEING Biscayne Park offers excellent canoeing, either along the coast or across open water to nearby mangrove islands. Since tides can be strong, only experienced canoeists should attempt to paddle far from shore. If you plan to go far, first get a tide table from the visitors center (see "Just the Facts," above) and paddle with the current. Free ranger-led canoe tours are scheduled for most weekend mornings. Phone for information. You can rent a canoe at the park; rates are $8 an hour or $22 for a half-day.

FISHING Ocean fishing is excellent year-round; many people cast their lines right from the breakwater jetty at Convoy Point. A fishing license is required. Bait is not available in Biscayne, but is sold in adjacent Homestead Bayfront Park. The marina is on the right side of SW 328th Street, 6 miles before the entrance to the park. Stone crabs and Florida lobsters can be found here, but are allowed to be caught only on the ocean side and in season. There are strict limitations on size, season, number, and method of take (including spearfishing) for both fresh and saltwater fishing. The latest regulations are available at most marinas, bait and tackle shops, and at the park's visitors centers. Or you can contact the **Florida Game and Fresh Water Fish Commission,** Bryant Building, Tallahassee, FL 32301 (☎ **904/488-1960**).

HIKING   Since the majority of this park is underwater, hiking is not great, but there are some short trails worth exploring. At Convoy Point you can walk along the 370-foot boardwalk, and along the half-mile jetty that serves as a breakwater for the park's harbor. Even from here, you can usually see brown pelicans, little blue herons, snowy egrets, and a few exotic fish.

Elliott Key is accessible only by boat, but once you're there, you have two good trail options. True to its name, the Loop Trail makes a 1.5-mile circle from the bayside visitors center, through a hardwood hammock and mangroves, to an elevated oceanside boardwalk. It's likely that you'll see purple and orange land crabs scurrying around the mangrove's roots.

The Old Road is a 7-mile tropical hammock trail that runs the length of Elliott Key. Because the visitors center is located about a third of the way along the trail, you can walk (or bike) only about $2^1/_2$ miles north, or $4^1/_2$ miles south, before turning around. This trail is one of the few places left in the world to see the highly endangered Schaus' swallowtail butterfly, recognizable by its black wings with diagonal yellow bands. They're usually out from late April through July.

SNORKELING/SCUBA DIVING   The clear, warm waters of Biscayne National Park are packed with colorful tropical fish swimming in the offshore reefs. Snorkeling and scuba gear are rented and sold at Convoy Point, or bring your own.

Biscayne National Park Underwater Tours, P.O. Box 1270, Homestead, FL 33030 (☎ **305/230-1100**), operates daily snorkel trips that last about 4 hours and cost $27.95 per person. They also run two-tank dives for certified divers, and offer instruction for beginners. Prices are $34.50 per person. They are open daily from 8am until 5:30pm.

SWIMMING   You can swim at the protected beaches of Elliott Key and adjacent Homestead Bayfront Park, but neither of these beaches match other South Florida beaches for width, softness, or surf.

ORGANIZED TOURS

Biscayne National Underwater Park Tours, located at the east end of SW 328th Street, Homestead FL 33090 (☎ **305/230-1100**), offers regularly scheduled **glass-bottom boat trips.** For a fish's-eye view of Biscayne National Park's aquatic wilderness, board the 52-foot *Bocachita* for a leisurely cruise. Biscayne National Park boasts almost 200,000 acres of mangrove shoreline, living coral reefs (the only one in the continental United States) and barrier islands. Unfortunately, it's fast disappearing because of pollution and divers' carelessness, so be sure to see it while it's still here. Boats depart year-round, daily from Convoy Point every half-hour from 10am to 1pm. Tours cost $16.50 for adults and $8.50 for children 12 and under. Reservations are required.

The company also offers **guided scuba and snorkeling reef trips** led by underwater naturalists. Snorkeling tours and one-tank scuba dives depart daily at 1:30pm, and cost $27.95 and $35 per person, respectively, including equipment rental. Two-tank dive trips are offered Wednesday, Saturday, and Sunday at 8:30am. Booking is essential.

CAMPING

There are no hotels in Biscayne National Park, but camping is plentiful—for those with water transportation. Campsites are on Elliott Key and Boca Chita, and are accessible only by boat. They're equipped with showers, restrooms, and drinking fountains. With a backcountry permit, available from the ranger station, you can pitch your tent somewhere even more private. Camping is free.

2 Everglades National Park

35 miles SW of Miami

In the 1800s, before the southern Everglades were designated a national park, the only inhabited piece of this wilderness was a quiet fishing village called Flamingo. Accessible only by boat and leveled every few years by hurricanes, this mosquito-infested town never grew very popular. When the 38-mile road from Florida City was completed in 1922, many of those who did live here fled to someplace either more or less remote. Today Flamingo is a center for visitor activities and the main jumping-off point for backcountry camping and exploration. Flamingo is also home to National Park Service and concessionaire employees and their families.

Everglades National Park's northern Shark Valley entrance and the eastern approaches described in this section are the most accessible from Miami and the rest of Florida's east coast. You'll find great amenities along the way, like Indian villages, alligator farms, and boat rides. An excellent tram tour goes deep into the park along a trail that's also terrific for biking. This is also the best way to reach the park's only accommodation, the Flamingo Lodge, and its only full-service outfitters.

There are also hiking trails from Everglades City, the "western gateway" to Everglades National Park. This entrance is home to a number of good boat tours of the area and provides access to a maze of boat-accessible islands and swamps.

JUST THE FACTS

GETTING THERE & ACCESS POINTS   Everglades National Park has four entrances. The following three are the most popular and most convenient to visitors from Florida's east coast, including Miami. No matter which part of Miami you are starting in, the drive should take no longer than an hour. Unless, of course, you're traveling during rush hour (between 8 and 9:30am or from 4 until 6pm), when the roads, especially S.R. 836, will be backed up, and your driving time perhaps doubled.

The **main entrance,** in Homestead on the park's east side, is located 10 miles southwest of Florida City. From Miami, take S.R. 836 west to the Florida Turnpike south until it ends in Florida City. Signs will point you southwest onto the road that leads into the park, S.R. 9336. The main entrance's park ranger station is open 24 hours.

The **Shark Valley entrance,** on the park's north side, is on the Tamiami Trail (U.S. 41), about 35 miles west of downtown Miami. From Miami, take S.R. 836 west to the Florida Turnpike south; exit on Tamiami Trail (U.S. 41), and go west for approximately 30 miles. The park will be on your left side. Shark Valley is known for its 15-mile trail loop that's used for an excellent interpretive tram tour, bicycling, and walking. This entrance is open daily from 8:30am to 5:30pm, with some seasonal variation. Call ahead.

Chekika, popular with day visitors, picnickers, and campers, is halfway between the two entrances above in the northeast section of the park. Chekika can be reached from Miami as though you were going to Shark Valley (see above). After exiting on Tamiami Trail (Highway 41), head west 5 miles to Krome Avenue (177th Avenue);

Impressions

There are no other Everglades in the world. They are, they have always been, one of the unique regions of the earth, remote, never wholly known. Nothing anywhere else is like them: their vast glittering openness, wider than the enormous visible round of the horizon, the racing free saltiness and sweetness of their massive winds, under the dazzling blue heights of space.

—Marjory Stoneman Douglas, *The Everglades: River of Grass,* 1947

turn left, and then proceed to SW 168th Street (Richmond Avenue) and head west (left) until you reach a stop sign. Turn right; the entrance will be on the left side. There are picnic facilities and a 20-site campground. You can enter Chekika from 8:30am until sundown.

If you're coming from Florida's west coast, use the fourth entrance in **Everglades City.**

VISITOR CENTERS & INFORMATION   General inquiries and specific questions should be directed to **Everglades National Park Headquarters,** 40001 S.R. 9336, Homestead, FL 33034 (☎ **305/242-7700**). Ask for a copy of *Parks and Preserves,* a free newspaper that's filled with up-to-date information on goings-on in the Everglades. Headquarters are staffed by helpful phone operators daily from 8:30am until 4:30pm.

Note that all hours listed are for the high season, generally November through May. During the slow summer months, many offices and outfitters keep shorter hours.

The **Flamingo Lodge, Marina, and Outpost Resort,** in Flamingo (☎ **800/ 600-3813** or 941/695-3101; fax 941/695-3921), is the one-stop clearinghouse—and the only option—for in-park accommodations, equipment rentals, and tours.

Especially since its recent expansion, the **Ernest F. Coe Visitor Center,** at the park's main entrance in Homestead, is the best place to stop to gather information for your trip. In addition to free brochures outlining trails, wildlife, and activities, and information on tours and boat rentals, you will also find state-of-the-art educational displays, films, and interactive exhibits. A gift shop sells postcards, film, insect repellent, unusual gift items, and the best selection of books about the Everglades. It is open from 8am until 5pm daily.

The **Royal Palm Visitor Center,** a small nature museum located 3 miles past the park's main entrance, is a smaller information center at the head of the popular Anhinga and Gumbo–Limbo trails. It's open daily from 8am until 4pm.

The **Shark Valley Information Center** at the park's northern entrance and the **Flamingo Visitor Center** are also staffed by knowledgeable rangers who provide brochures and personal insight into the goings-on in the park. They are open from 8:30am until 5pm.

ENTRANCE FEES, PERMITS & REGULATIONS   Permits and passes can be purchased at the main park entrance, the Chekika entrance, or the Shark Valley entrance stations only.

Even if you are just visiting Everglades National Park for an afternoon, you need to buy a 7-day permit, which costs $10 per vehicle. Pedestrians and cyclists are charged $5 each and $4 at Shark Valley.

An Everglades Park Pass, valid for a year's worth of unlimited entrances, is available for $20. U.S. citizens may purchase a 12-month Golden Eagle Passport for $50, which is valid for entrance into any U.S. national park. U.S. citizens aged 62 and

Everglades National Park

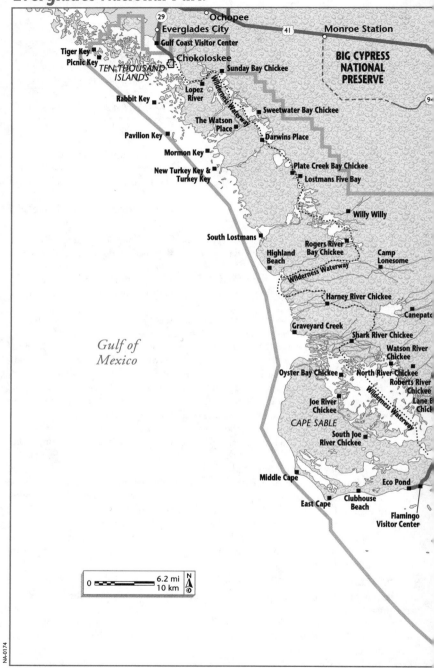

Ochopee

29

Everglades City

Gulf Coast Visitor Center

41

Monroe Station

Tiger Key

Picnic Key

Chokoloskee

BIG CYPRESS
NATIONAL
PRESERVE

TEN THOUSAND
ISLANDS

Sunday Bay Chickee

94

Lopez
River

Rabbit Key

The Watson
Place

Sweetwater Bay Chickee

Pavilion Key

Darwins Place

Mormon Key

New Turkey Key &
Turkey Key

Plate Creek Bay Chickee

Lostmans Five Bay

Willy Willy

South Lostmans

Rogers River
Bay Chickee

Camp
Lonesome

Highland
Beach

Wilderness Waterway

Harney River Chickee

Canepatc

Graveyard Creek

Shark River Chickee

Gulf of
Mexico

Watson River
Chickee

Oyster Bay Chickee

North River Chickee

Roberts River
Chickee

Joe River
Chickee

Wilderness Waterway

Lane B
Chick

CAPE SABLE

South Joe
River Chickee

Middle Cape

Eco Pond

Clubhouse
Beach

East Cape

Flamingo
Visitor Center

0   6.2 mi
     10 km

N

NA-0174

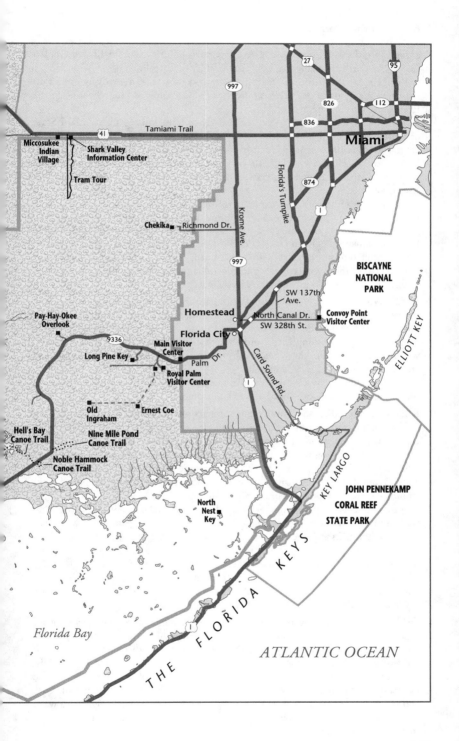

Miccosukee
Indian
Village

Shark Valley
Information Center

Tram Tour

Tamiami Trail

Miami

27

95

997

826

112

836

874

I

Florida's Turnpike

Chekika

Richmond Dr.

Krome Ave.

997

**BISCAYNE
NATIONAL
PARK**

SW 137th
Ave.

Pay-Hay-Okee
Overlook

Homestead

North Canal Dr.
SW 328th St.

Convoy Point
Visitor Center

ELLIOTT KEY

Florida City

9336

Main Visitor
Center

Long Pine Key

Royal Palm
Visitor Center

Palm   Dr.

Card Sound Rd.

I

Old
Ingraham

Ernest Coe

Hell's Bay
Canoe Trail

Nine Mile Pond
Canoe Trail

Noble Hammock
Canoe Trail

North
Nest
Key

KEY LARGO

**JOHN PENNEKAMP

CORAL REEF

STATE PARK**

Florida Bay

THE FLORIDA KEYS

I

ATLANTIC OCEAN

older pay only $10 for a Golden Age Passport—that's valid for life. A Golden Access Passport is available free to U.S. citizens with disabilities.

Permits are required for campers wanting to stay overnight either in the backcountry or in primitive campsites. See "Camping & Houseboating in the Everglades," in "Where to Stay," below.

Those who want to fish without a charter captain must get a standard State of Florida saltwater fishing license. It's available in the park at Flamingo Lodge or any tackle shop or sporting goods store nearby. Nonresidents pay $17 for a 7-day license and $7 for 3 days. Florida residents can get a fishing license good for the whole year for $14. Snook and crawfish licenses must be purchased separately at a cost of $2.

Charter captains carry vessel licenses that cover all paying passengers. Ask to be sure. Freshwater fishing licenses are available at various bait and tackle shops outside the park at the same rates. A good one close by is **Don's Bait & Tackle** at 30710 S. Federal Hwy. in Homestead right on U.S. 1. (☎ **305/247-6616**). Most of the area's freshwater fishing, limited to murky canals and human-made lakes near housing developments, is hardly worth the trouble when so much good saltwater fishing is available.

Firearms are not allowed anywhere in the park.

SEASONS   There are two distinct seasons in the Everglades: high season and mosquito season. High season is also dry season, lasting approximately from late November to May. This is the best time to visit, as low water levels attract the largest variety of wading birds and their predators. As the dry season wanes, wildlife follows the receding water, and by the end of May, the only living things you are sure to spot will cause you to itch.

Many establishments and operators in the area either close or curtail offerings in the summer, so always call ahead to check schedules.

RANGER PROGRAMS   More than 50 ranger programs, free with admission, are offered each month during high season and give visitors an opportunity to gain an expert's perspective. Some programs take place regularly, such as **Glade Glimpses,** a walking tour during which rangers point out flora and fauna and discuss issues affecting the Everglade's survival. These tours are scheduled at 10:15am, noon, and 3:30pm daily. The **Anhinga Ambles,** a similar program that takes place on the Anhinga Trail, starts at 10:30am, 1:30pm, and 4pm.

A more interesting program, the **Slough Slog,** is offered occasionally. Participants wade into the park and through the muck, stopping at an alligator hole, which is a particularly interesting and vital ecological community unto itself. Lace-up shoes and long pants (preferably ones you don't care about) are required. On Saturday and Sunday rangers can choose programs they want to offer in some time slots.

Park rangers tend to be helpful, well informed, good-humored, and happy to answer questions. Since times, programs, and locations vary from month to month, check a schedule, available at any of the visitor centers (see above).

SAFETY   There are dangers inherent in this vast wilderness area. Always let someone know your itinerary before you set out on an extended hike. It's mandatory that you file an itinerary when camping overnight in the backcountry. When on the water, watch for weather changes; severe thunderstorms and high winds often develop very rapidly. Swimming is not recommended because of the presence of alligators, sharks, and barracudas. Watch out for the region's four indigenous poisonous snakes: diamondback and pygmy rattlesnakes, coral snakes (identifiable by their colorful rings), and water moccasins (which swim on the surface of the water). Bring insect repellent to ward off mosquitoes and biting flies.

First aid is available from park rangers. The nearest hospital is in Homestead, 10 miles from the park's main entrance.

SEEING THE HIGHLIGHTS

There are many ways to experience the Everglades. Shark Valley offers a fine introduction to the park, but visitors shouldn't expect to spend more than a few hours there. Bicycling or taking a guided tram tour can be a satisfying experience, but neither fully captures the park's wonders. Likewise, boaters who choose to explore via the Everglades City entrance to the park are likely to see a lot of mangroves and not much else. To get the most out of your trip to the Everglades, make sure that you venture into the park through the main entrance, pick up a trail map, and dedicate at least a day to exploring from there.

Stop first along the **Anhinga and Gumbo–Limbo trails,** which start right next to each another, 3 miles from the park's main entrance. These trails provide a thorough introduction to Everglades flora and fauna and are highly recommended to first-time visitors. There's more water and wildlife here than in most parts of the Everglades, especially during dry season. Alligators, turtles, river otters, herons, egrets, and other animals abound. Arrive early to spot the widest selection of exotic birds, since many travel deeper into the park during daylight hours. You might spot the anhinga, a large black fishing bird so used to humans that it often builds its nest in plain view. Take your time—at least an hour is recommended. If you treat the trails and modern boardwalk as pathways to get through quickly, rather than destinations to experience and savor slowly, you'll miss out on their still beauty and hidden treasures.

Those who love to mountain bike, and who prefer solitude, might check out the infrequently traveled **Old Ingraham Highway.** This dirt road delves deeper into the Glades and isn't used by most visitors. Since it's sometimes closed, check at the visitor center when you arrive.

Don't miss climbing the observation tower at the end of the quarter-mile–long **Pa-hay-okee Trail.** The seemingly endless vistas of undulating grass give the impression of a semiaquatic Serengeti. Flocks of tropical and semitropical birds traverse the landscape, alligators and fish stir the surface of the water, and small grottoes of trees thrust up from the sea of grass. From here, you can fully appreciate the vastness of the hidden world you've entered.

If you want to get closer to nature, a few hours in a **canoe** along any of the trails allows paddlers the chance to sense the park's fluid motion and to become a part of the ecosphere. Visitors who choose this option end up feeling more like explorers than merely observers. (See "Sports & Outdoor Activities," below).

No matter which option you choose (and there are many), I strongly recommend staying for the **7pm program,** available during high season at the Long Pine Key Amphitheater. This talk by one of the park's rangers, along with the accompanying slide show, gives a detailed overview of the park's history, natural resources, wildlife, and threats to its survival.

SPORTS & OUTDOOR ACTIVITIES

BIKING   The relatively flat 38-mile paved **Main Park Road** is excellent for bicycling, as are many park trails, including Long Pine Key. Cyclers should expect to spend 2 to 3 hours along the main path.

If the park isn't flooded from excess rain (which it often is, especially in spring), **Shark Valley** in Everglades National Park is South Florida's most scenic bicycle trail. Many locals haul their bikes out to the Glades for a relaxing day of wilderness-trail riding. You'll share the flat paved road only with other bikers and a menagerie of wildlife. Don't be surprised to see a gator lounging in the sun or a deer munching on some grass. Otters, turtles, alligators, and snakes are other common companions in the Shark Valley area.

You can rent bikes at the **Flamingo Lodge, Marina, and Outpost Resort** (see "Where to Stay," below) for $17 per 24 hours, $14 per full day, $8.50 per half day (any 4-hour period), and $3 per hour. Bicycles are also available from Shark Valley Tram Tours, at the park's Shark Valley entrance (☎ **305/221-8455**), for $3.25 per hour; rentals can be picked up any time after 8:30am and must be returned by 4pm.

BIRDING   More than 350 species of birds make their homes in the Everglades. Tropical birds from the Caribbean and temperate species from North America can be found here, along with exotics that have blown in from more distant regions. Eco and Mrazek ponds, near Flamingo, are two of the best places for bird watching, especially in early morning or late afternoon in the dry winter months. Pick up a free birding checklist from a visitor center (see "Just the Facts," above), and ask a park ranger what's been spotted in recent days.

BOATING   Motorboating around the Everglades seems like a great way to see plants and animals in remote habitats. However, environmentalists are taking stock of the damage motorboats (especially airboats) inflict on the delicate ecosystem (see "Airboat Tours" below). If you choose to motor, remember that most of the areas near land are "no wake" zones, and for the protection of nesting birds, landing is prohibited on most of the little mangrove islands. There's a long list of restrictions and restricted areas, so get a copy of the park's boating rules from National Park Headquarters before setting out (see "Just the Facts," above).

The Everglades's only marina—accommodating about 50 boats with electric and water hookups—is the **Flamingo Lodge, Marina, and Outpost Resort,** located in Flamingo. The well-marked channel to Flamingo is accessible to boats with a maximum 4-foot draft and is open year-round. Reservations can be made through the marina store (☎ **941/695-3101, ext. 304**). Skiffs with low-power 15-horsepower motors are available for rent for $90 per day, $65 per half day (any 5-hour period), and $22 per hour. A $50 deposit is required.

CANOEING   The most intimate view of the Everglades comes from the humble perspective of a simple low boat. A canoe will give you a closer look into the park's shallow estuaries, where water birds, sea turtles, and endangered manatees make their homes.

Everglades National Park's longest "trails" are designed for boat and canoe travel, and many are marked as clearly as walking trails. The **Noble Hammock Trail,** a 2-mile loop, takes 1 to 2 hours, and is recommended for beginning canoers. The **Hell's Bay Trail,** a 3- to 6-mile course for hardier paddlers, takes 2 to 6 hours, depending on how far you choose to go. Park rangers can recommend other trails that best suit your abilities, time limitations, and interests.

Canoes can be rented at the **Flamingo Lodge, Marina, and Outpost Resort** (see "Where to Stay," below) for $40 for 24 hours, $32 per full day, $22 per half day (any 4-hour period), and $8 per hour. You can also rent family canoes for $50, $40, $30, and $12, respectively. A deposit is required. Skiffs, kayaks, and tandem kayaks are also available. The concessionaire will shuttle your party to the trailhead of your choice and pick you up afterward. Rental facilities are open daily from 6am to 8pm.

FISHING   About one-third of Everglades National Park is open water. Freshwater fishing is popular in brackish **Nine-Mile Pond** (25 miles from the main

Robert Is Here Selling Fruit

One of the best parts about the drive to the Everglades is a stop at one of Florida's best-known fruit stands, called **Robert Is Here**—and he usually is. Homestead native Robert Moehling has been selling home-grown treats at this ever-expanding roadside stand and adjacent farm for nearly 40 years. He's graduated from hawking cucumbers from a cardboard box to selling local and gourmet products from around the world. You'll find the freshest and biggest pineapples, bananas, papayas, mangos, and melons anywhere, as well as his famous shakes in unusual flavors like key lime, coconut, orange, and cantaloupe. In addition to what's usually found at greenmarkets, Robert also stocks exotic offerings like carambola, mamey, lychees, sugar apples, and sea grapes. The bottled jellies, hot sauces, and salad dressings make great souvenirs or gifts for foodie friends from home. To get there from Miami, take the Florida Turnpike or U.S. 1 to SW 344th Street or Palm Drive. Turn right. You'll see the stand about a mile down on the left at the corner of SW 192nd Avenue. You can't miss it if you're headed to the Everglades National Park. To find out what's in season, call ☎ **305/246-1592**.

entrance) and other spots along the Main Park Road, but because of the high mercury levels found in the Everglades, freshwater anglers are warned not to eat their catch. Before casting, check in at a visitor center, as many of the park's lakes are preserved for observation only. Fishing licenses are required. See "Just the Facts," above.

Saltwater anglers will find that snapper and sea trout are plentiful. Charter boats and guides are available at **Flamingo Lodge, Marina, and Outpost Resort** (see "Where to Stay," below). Phone for information and reservations.

ORGANIZED TOURS

AIRBOAT TOURS   Shallow-draft, fan-powered airboats were invented in the Everglades by frog hunters tired of polling through the rushes. But although it is the most efficient way to get around, airboating is not permitted in the park. These shallow-bottom runabouts tend to inflict severe damage on the animals and plants. However, just outside the boundaries of the park are many outfitters offering airboat rides. If you choose to ride on one, you might consider bringing earplugs; these high-speed boats are loud. Airboat rides are offered at the **Miccosukee Indian Village,** just west of the Shark Valley entrance on U.S. 41, the Tamiami Trail (☎ **305/223-8380**). Native American guides will take you through the reserve's rushes at high speed and stop along the way to point out alligators, native plants, and exotic birds. The cost is just $7. The **Everglades Alligator Farm,** 4 miles south of Palm Drive (S.R. 9336) (☎ **305/247-2628**), also offers half-hour guided airboat tours from 9am until 6pm daily. Their price, which includes admission to the park, is $12 for adults, $6 for children.

MOTORBOAT TOURS   Both Florida Bay and backcountry tours are offered at the **Flamingo Lodge, Marina, and Outpost Resort** (see "Where to Stay," below). Florida Bay tours cruise nearby estuaries and sandbars, while six-passenger backcountry boats visit smaller sloughs. Both are available in 1 1/2- and 2-hour versions that cost an average of $16 for adults, $8 for children, under 6 free. There are also charter-fishing and sightseeing boats that can be booked through the main reservation number (☎ **941/695-3101**). Tours depart throughout the day, and reservations are recommended.

TRAM TOURS   At the park's Shark Valley entrance, open-air tram buses take visitors on 2-hour naturalist-led tours that delve 7½ miles into the wilderness. Passengers can disembark at the trail's midsection and climb a 65-foot observation tower that offers great views of the Glades. The tour itself also offers wonderful views that include plenty of wildlife and endless acres of sawgrass. Tours run November to April only, daily from 9am to 4pm, and are sometimes stalled by flooding or particularly heavy mosquito infestation. Reservations are recommended from December to March. The cost is $8 for adults, $4 for children 12 and under, and $7 for seniors. For further information, contact **Shark Valley Tram Tours** at ☎ 305/221-8455.

SHOPPING

You won't find big malls or lots of boutiques in this area, but there is an outlet center, the **Keys Factory Shops** (☎ 305/248-4727), at 250 E. Palm Dr. (where the Fla. Turnpike meets U.S. 1), in Florida City. Here you'll find more than 60 stores, including Nike Factory Store, Bass Co. Store, Levi's, OshKosh, and Izod. Travelers can pick up a free discount coupon booklet from the Customer Service Center called the Come Back Pack. The outlet is open daily until 9pm, except Sunday when it closes at 6pm.

A necessary stop is one of Florida's best-known fruit stands, **Robert Is Here** (☎ 305/246-1592). Robert has been selling homegrown treats for nearly 40 years at the corner of SW 344th Street (Palm Drive) and SW 192nd Avenue (see box above). You'll find the freshest and biggest pineapples, bananas, papayas, mangos, and melons anywhere as well as his famous shakes in unusual flavors such as key lime, co-conut, orange, and cantaloupe. Exotic fruits, bottled jellies, hot sauces, and salad dressings are also available. This is a great place to pick up culinary souvenirs and sample otherwise unavailable goodies. Open daily 8am until 7pm.

Along Tamiami Trail, there are several roadside shops hawking Indian handicrafts, including one at the **Miccosukee Indian Village** (☎ 305/223-8380), just west of the Shark Valley entrance. At nearly every one, you'll find the same stock of feathered dream-catchers, stuffed alligator heads and claws, turquoise jewelry, and other trinkets. Do note the unique and colorful handmade cloth Miccosukee dolls.

WHERE TO STAY

IN EVERGLADES NATIONAL PARK

Flamingo Lodge, Marina, and Outpost Resort. 1 Flamingo Lodge Hwy., Flamingo, FL 33034. ☎ 800/600-3813 or 941/695-3101. Fax 941/695-3921. 127 units. A/C TEL. High season, $75–$89 double; $99–$125 cottage; $110–$130 suite. Summer/fall, from $65 double; from $79 cottage; from $85 suite. Rates for cottages and the suite are for up to four people. AE, DC, DISC, MC, V.

The Flamingo Lodge is the only lodging actually located within the boundaries of Everglades National Park. This sprawling, woodsy complex offers rooms over-looking the Florida Bay in either a two-story simple motel or the lodge. Situated right in the center of the action, it can sometimes feel like summer camp.

VCRs and videos are available for guests in the regular rooms or in the suite, but not in more primitively outfitted cottages. Still, the cottages are an especially good choice if you plan to stay more than a night or two. They have small kitchens with dishes and flatware, but no television, and are also larger, more private, and almost romantic.

Facilities include a very good restaurant (see "Where to Dine," below) and bar, freshwater swimming pool, gift shop, and coin-op laundry (available from 8am to 10pm). Binoculars, bikes, canoes, and kayaks can be rented at the front desk, open daily from 6am to 11pm, and fishing poles and ice chests are available at the marina. The hotel is open year-round. Reservations are accepted daily from 8am to 5pm. Guests are treated to free coffee in the lobby. And, of course, the vast resources of the Everglades are just outside the door.

CAMPING & HOUSEBOATING IN THE EVERGLADES

Campgrounds are available in Flamingo and Long Pine Key, where there are more than 300 campsites designed for tents and RVs. They have level parking pads, tables, and charcoal grills. There are no electrical hookups, and showers are cold water. Private ground fires are not permitted, but supervised campfire programs are conducted during winter months. Reservations may be made in advance through the national park reservation service at ☎ **800/365-CAMP.** Campsites cost $14 per night and have a 14-day consecutive stay limit, 30 days a year maximum.

Camping is also available in the backcountry year-round on a first-come, first-served basis. It's accessible only by boat, foot, or bicycle. Campers must register in person at a ranger station in either Flamingo or Everglades City or by telephone no more than 24 hours before the start of their trip. Campers can use only designated campsites, which are plentiful and well marked on visitor maps.

Many backcountry sites are *chickees*—covered wooden platforms on stilts. They're accessible only by canoe. Ground sites are located along interior bays and rivers. Beach camping is also popular. In summer especially, mosquito repellent is necessary.

Houseboat rentals are one of the park's best-kept secrets. Available through the Flamingo Lodge, motorized houseboats make it possible to explore some of the park's more remote regions without having to worry about being back by nightfall. You can choose from two different types of houseboats. The first, a 40-foot pontoon boat, sleeps six to eight people in a single large room separated by a central head (bathroom) and shower. There's also a small galley (kitchen) that contains a stove, an oven, and a charcoal grill. Prices aren't cheap unless you have a good-sized group. The boat rents for between $340 and $475 for 2 nights (there's a 2-night minimum in high season). One-night rental in the buggy summer season costs $275.

The newer, sleeker Gibson fiberglass boats sleep six and have a head and shower, air-conditioning, electric stove, and full rooftop sundeck. They rent for $575 for 2 nights (with a 2-night minimum). With either boat, the 7th night is free when renting for a full week.

Boating experience is helpful, but not mandatory, as the boats cruise up to only 6 miles per hour and are surprisingly easy to use. Reservations should be made far in advance; call **Flamingo Lodge, Marina, and Outpost Resort** (☎ **800/600-3813** or 941/695-3101).

NEARBY IN HOMESTEAD & FLORIDA CITY

Homestead and Florida City, two adjacent towns almost blown off the map by Hurricane Andrew, have come back better than before. Located along U.S. 1 about 35 miles south of Miami and 10 miles from the park's main entrance, these somewhat rural towns offer several budget chain hotels, including a **Days Inn** (☎ **305/245-1260**) in Homestead and a **Hampton Inn** (☎ **800/426-7866** or 305/247-8833) right off the Turnpike in Florida City. The best option is the **Best Western Gateway to the Keys,** 1 Strano Blvd. (U.S. 1), Florida City, FL 33034 (☎ **800/528-1234** or 305/246-5100), with rates in high season starting at about $85. This two-story, pink-and-white hotel was opened in late 1994 and offers contemporary style and comfort. The suites and some larger rooms offer convenient extras, such as a microwave, a coffeemaker, an extra sink, and a small fridge. There's also a swimming pool, Jacuzzi, and self-service laundromat.

WHERE TO DINE
IN FLAMINGO

If you aren't cooking up your own catch or eating a picnic under the shade of the hammocks, the only restaurant in the park is a very civilized alternative, **Flamingo Restaurant** (☎ 941/695-3101), in the Flamingo Lodge (See "Where to Stay," above). Besides the spectacular view of Florida Bay and numerous Keys from the large, airy dining room, you'll also find fresh fish, including my very favorite, mahi-mahi. All fish is prepared grilled, blackened, or deep-fried; dinner entrees come with salad or conch chowder, steamed vegetables, and black beans and rice or baked potato. More adventurous offerings include a fantastic Caribbean steak marinated in jerk seasonings and citrus chicken marinated in fruit juices. The large menu has something for everyone, including basic and very tasty sandwiches, pastas, burgers, and salads. You may need reservations for dinner, especially in season. Prices are surprisingly moderate, with full meals starting at about $11 and going no higher than $20.

NEARBY, IN HOMESTEAD & FLORIDA CITY

You won't find fancy nouvelle cuisine in this suburbanized farm country, but there are plenty of fast-food chains along U.S. 1 and a few old favorites worth checking out.

Housed in a squat, one-story, windowless stone building that looks something like a medieval fort, the **Capri Restaurant,** 935 N. Krome Ave., Florida City (☎ **305/ 247-1542**), has been serving hearty Italian-American fare since 1958. Great pastas and salads complement a full menu of meat and fish dishes. Portions are big. It serves lunch and dinner every day (except Sunday) until 11pm.

Another landmark is **Potlikker's,** 591 Washington Ave. (at the corner of NE 6th Street), in Homestead (☎ **305/248-0835**), featuring fried fish and shrimp baskets, along with barbecued chicken and ribs, roast pork, grilled fish, and lots of local veggies. It's good, unadulterated Southern feed at popular prices. Main courses range from $6 to $13. The kitchen is open every day from 7am until 9pm.

The **Miccosukee Restaurant** (☎ **305/223-8380**), just west of the Shark Valley entrance on the Tamiami Trail (U.S. 41), was destroyed in Hurricane Andrew, but reopened in 1995. Back and better, they serve authentic pumpkin bread, fry bread, fish, and not-so-authentic Native American interpretations of tacos and fried chicken. This interesting spot is worth a stop for lunch or dinner, served daily from 8am until 3pm. Meals cost from $5 to $14.

3 Cruises and Other Caribbean Getaways

CRUISES

Some of the most popular destinations from Miami are the Bahamian islands where gambling is a big draw, or any of the dozens of nearby Caribbean islands. Travel to Cuba is strictly prohibited from Miami (or anywhere in the United States), although many people choose to go there from Mexico, Jamaica, or the Bahamas.

The Port of Miami is the world's busiest cruise ship port, with a passenger load of close to three million annually. The popularity of these cruises shows no sign of tapering off, and the trend in ships is toward bigger, more luxurious liners. Usually all-inclusive, cruises offer value and simplicity compared to other vacation options. Most of the Caribbean-bound cruise ships sail weekly out of the Port of Miami. They are relatively inexpensive, can be booked without advance notice, and make for an excellent excursion.

All the shorter cruises are well equipped for gambling. Their casinos open as soon as the ship clears U.S. waters—typically 45 minutes after leaving port. Usually, four full-size meals are served daily, with portions so huge they're impossible to finish. Games, movies, and other on-board activities ensure you're always busy. Passengers can board up to 2 hours before departure for meals, games, and cocktails.

There are dozens of cruises to choose from—from a 1-day excursion to a trip around the world. You can get a full list of options from the **Metro-Dade Seaport Department,** 1015 North America Way, Miami, FL 33132 (☎ **305/371-7678**). It's open Monday through Friday from 8am to 5pm.

The cruise lines and ships listed below offer 2- and 3-day excursions to the Caribbean, Key West, and other longer itineraries that change often. If you want more information, contact the individual line or, for Bahamas cruises, call the **Bahamas Tourist Office,** 19495 Biscayne Blvd., Suite 809, Aventura, FL 33180 (☎ **305/932-0051**). All passengers must travel with a passport or proof of citizenship for re-entry into the United States.

For details on Caribbean cruises, pick up a copy of *Frommer's Caribbean Cruises and Ports of Call.*

Carnival Cruise Lines (☎ **800/327-9501** or 305/599-2200; www.carnival.com) has 3- and 4-day cruises to Key West and the Caribbean as well as 7-day excursions that include stops in Mexico and Latin America. At press time, Carnival had four ships based at the Port of Miami, including *Destiny,* the world's largest. Cruises usually depart from Miami every Friday, Saturday, Sunday, and Monday. Prices range from $400 to $3,000, not including port charges, which can be as high as $100 per person.

Cunard (☎ **800/528-6273** or 305/463-3000; www.cunardline.com), which moved here in late 1997, is the most luxurious of Miami's lines, launching some of the most elegant ships ever to take to the seas. Its Miami ships include the *Queen Elizabeth 2,* the *Royal Viking Sun,* and the *Vistafjord.* Itineraries are usually at least 10 days long. Prices start at $1,300.

Norwegian Cruise Line (☎ **800/327-7030** or 305/436-0866; www.ncl.com) has four ships based in Miami during the winter months and usually one in the summer. Ships go to Key West, the Bahamas, and the Western Caribbean. Its shortest cruises are 3 days; the longest is 15 days, from Miami to France. Rates range from $349 for an inside cabin on the shortest cruises to $4,500 for the very best cabin on the transcontinental journey.

Royal Caribbean Cruise Line (☎ **800/327-6700** or 305/539-6000; www.rccl.com), one of the premier lines in Miami, has about half a dozen ships coming out of Miami at any given time. It mostly does Caribbean cruises and some Bahamas destinations. The *Legend of the Seas* and the *Splendor of the Seas* offer 3-and 4-night Bahamas trips starting at $400. Longer trips can range from $1,600 per person to $7,500 for an 11-night cruise through the Caribbean.

FLIGHTS & WEEKEND PACKAGES

For those who want a quick getaway to the Caribbean without the experience of cruising, many airlines and hotels team up to offer extremely affordable weekend packages.

For example, one of the Bahamas' most elegant and family-friendly resorts, **The Atlantis** on Paradise Island, hosts guests who like watersports or like to play the slots, poker, or anything else in its active casinos. The Sun Club bought and totally revamped this 30-year-old club in 1994. Reasonably priced 3-day packages start at about $390, depending on departure date. It's generally cheaper to fly midweek.

Flights on **Paradise Airlines** (☎ 800/786-7202) depart at least twice daily from Miami International. You can also choose to stay in the company's other luxurious resorts, The Paradise Beach Resort or the Ocean Club. Book package deals through **Paradise Island Vacations** (☎ 800/722-7466).

Other groups that arrange competitively priced packages include **American Flyaway Vacations,** operated by American Airlines (☎ 800/321-2121); **Bahamas Air** (☎ 800/222-4262 or 593-1910); **Pan Am Air Bridge** (☎ 305/371-8628); and the slightly rundown **Princess Casino** in Freeport (☎ 305/359-9898). Call for rates, since they vary dramatically throughout the year and also depend on what type of accommodations you choose.

The Keys 12

The islands of the Keys are scattered across the sea like the loose beads of an exotic coral necklace. Each of the more than 400 islands that make up this 150-mile chain has a distinctive character. While some are crammed with strip malls and tourist traps, most are filled with unusual species of tropical plants, birds, and reptiles. All are surrounded by calm blue waters and graced by year-round warmth.

Despite the intriguing landscape, the stark rocky coast hardly looks inviting from the bow of a ship. When Spanish explorers Juan Ponce de León and Antonio de Herrera sailed amid these craggy, dangerous rocks in 1513, they and their men dubbed the string of islands "Los Martires" (The Martyrs) because they thought the rocks looked like men suffering in the surf. It wasn't until the early 1800s that the larger islands were settled by pirates, who amassed great wealth by salvaging cargo from ships ruined nearby. Actually, these shipwrecks were often caused by the "salvagers," who occasionally removed vital markers in the sea.

Wars, fires, hurricanes, mosquitoes, and the Depression took their toll on these resilient islands in the early part of this century, causing wild swings between fortune and poverty. In 1938, the spectacular Overseas Highway (U.S. 1) was finally completed atop the ruins of Henry Flagler's railroad, opening the region to tourists who had never been able to drive to this seabound destination.

These days, the highway connects more than 30 of the populated islands in the Keys. The hundreds of small, undeveloped islands that surround these "mainline" keys are known locally as the "backcountry" and are home to dozens of exotic animals and plants. To get to them, you must take to the water—a vital part of any trip to the Keys. Whether you fish, snorkel, dive, or just cruise, include some time on a boat in your itinerary; otherwise, you really haven't seen the Keys.

The sea and the teeming life beneath it are the main attractions here. Warm, shallow waters nurture living coral that supports a complex delicate ecosystem of plants and animals—sponges, anemones, jellyfish, crabs, rays, sharks, turtles, snails, lobsters, and thousands of types of fish. This vibrant underwater habitat thrives on one of only two living tropical reefs in the entire North American continent (the other is off the coast of Belize). As a result, anglers, divers, snorkelers, and water-sports enthusiasts of all descriptions come to explore. The heavy traffic has taken its toll on this fragile eco-scape, but efforts are underway to protect it.

Although the atmosphere throughout the Keys is that of a low-key beach town, don't expect to find many impressive beaches here. With the exception of a few private beachfront resorts and some small, sandy beaches in Bahia Honda State Park and in Key West (see "Beaches" under "The Great Outdoors," below), there are no wide natural beaches to speak of once you head south of Miami. To appease beach-hungry visitors, some hoteliers ship in Caribbean sand to create tiny stretches of sand near the sea.

The Keys are divided into three sections, both geographically and in this chapter. The **Upper and Middle Keys** are closest to the Florida mainland, so they are popular with weekend warriors who come by boat or car to fish, drink, or relax in towns like Key Largo, Islamorada, and Marathon. Further on are the **Lower Keys,** a small unspoiled swath of islands teeming with wildlife. Here in the protected regions of the Lower Keys is where you're most likely to catch sight of the area's many endangered animals. With patience, you may spot the rare eagle, egret, or Key deer. Also, keep an eye out for alligators, turtles, rabbits, and a huge variety of birds.

The last section is **Key West,** literally at the end of the road. Made famous by the Nobel Prize–winning rogue Ernest Hemingway, this tiny island is the most popular destination in the Florida Keys, overrun with cruise-ship passengers and day-trippers, as well as franchises and T-shirt shops. Still, you'll find in this "Conch Republic" a tightly knit community of permanent residents who cling fiercely to their live-and-let-live attitude—an atmosphere that has made Key West famously popular with gay travelers.

1 Exploring the Keys by Car

After you have gotten off the Florida Turnpike and landed on U.S. 1, which is also known as the Overseas Highway (see "Getting There" under "Essentials," below), you'll have no trouble negotiating these narrow islands.

The Overseas Highway is the only main road connecting the Keys. Although some find the long, straight drive from Miami to Key West tedious, it can be enjoyable if you linger and explore the diverse towns and islands along the way. If you have the time, I recommend allowing at least 3 days to work your way down to Key West.

Most of U.S. 1 is a narrow, two-lane highway, with some wider passing zones along the way. The speed limit is usually 55 m.p.h. (35–45 m.p.h. on Big Pine Key and in some commercial areas). Despite the protestations of island residents, there has been talk of expanding the highway, but by publication date, plans had not been finalized. Even on the narrow road, you can usually get from downtown Miami to Islamorada within an hour. If you're determined to drive straight through to Key West, allow at least $3^{1}/_{2}$ hours. No matter what, avoid driving anywhere in the Keys on Friday afternoons or Sunday evenings, when the roads are jammed with weekenders from the mainland.

To **find an address** in the Keys, don't bother looking for building numbers; most addresses (except in Key West and parts of Marathon) are delineated by mile markers (MM), small green signs on the bay side of the road that announce the distance from Key West. The markers start at number 127, just south of the Florida mainland. The zero marker is in Key West, at the corner of Whitehead and Fleming streets. Addresses in this chapter are accompanied by a mile marker (MM) designation when appropriate.

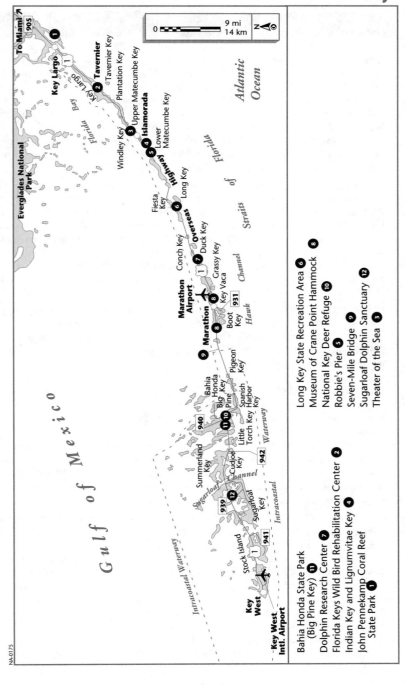

The Florida Keys

To Miami 905
Key Largo 1
1
Key Largo
Florida Bay
2 Tavernier
Tavernier Key
Plantation Key
3 Upper Matecumbe Key
Windley Key
4 Islamorada
5 Lower Matecumbe Key
Overseas Highway
Fiesta Key
6 Long Key
Conch Key
7 Duck Key
1
Grassy Key
8 Key Vaca
931
Marathon Airport
8 Boot Key
9 Marathon
Hawk Channel
Pigeon Key
Bahia Honda
Big Pine Key
Spanish Harbor Key
11 10
940
Little Torch Key
942 Waterway
Cudjoe Key
Summerland Key
Cudjoe Channel
939 12
Sugarloaf Channel
Sugarloaf Key
Stock Island
941
1
Key West Intl. Airport
Key West
Intracoastal Waterway
Intracoastal Waterway

Everglades National Park

Gulf of Mexico

Straits of Florida

Atlantic Ocean

0   9 mi
     14 km
N

NA-0175

Bahia Honda State Park (Big Pine Key) 11
Dolphin Research Center 7
Florida Keys Wild Bird Rehabilitation Center 2
Indian Key and Lignumvitae Key 4
John Pennekamp Coral Reef State Park 1

Long Key State Recreation Area 6
Museum of Crane Point Hammock 8
National Key Deer Refuge 10
Robbie's Pier 5
Seven-Mile Bridge 9
Sugarloaf Dolphin Sanctuary 12
Theater of the Sea 3

197

2 The Great Outdoors

BEACHES   Most people don't realize that the Keys really have very few beaches to speak of. The centerpiece of the Lower Keys and its greatest asset is **Bahia Honda State Park,** U.S. 1 at MM 37.5, Big Pine Key (☎ **305/872-2353**). This wonderful park has one of the most beautiful coastlines in South Florida and one of the only natural beaches in the Keys, though it's never wider than 5 feet, even at low tide. In addition to a few man-made beaches at resorts along the way, and a tiny patch of beach called **Anne's beach** at MM 73.5, you'll also find a few beaches in Key West, including **Smathers Beach** off South Roosevelt Boulevard, west of the airport; **Higgs Beach** along Atlantic Boulevard, between White Street and Reynolds Road; and **Fort Zachary Beach,** off the western end of Southard Boulevard.

BICYCLING   The almost flat 126 miles of U.S. 1 that run down the Florida Keys are tailor-made for cyclists, if it weren't for the cars. There are bike paths paralleling the road from MMs 106 to 86, but the rest of the route is on narrow shoulders, making cycling the Keys for serious cyclists only. Larger islands, like Marathon, Big Pine, and Key West, offer good family cycling on dedicated paths and smaller side streets. In Marathon, try Sombrero Beach Road, from the Overseas Highway to the public beach (at MM 50). On Big Pine, cruise along Key Deer Boulevard (at MM 30)—those with fat tires can ride into the National Key Deer Refuge. And on Key West, just about any street will do.

BIRD WATCHING   A stopping point for migratory birds on the "Eastern Flyway," the Keys are populated with a large proportion of West Indian bird species, especially during spring and fall. The small vegetated islands of the Keys are the only nesting sites in the United States for the great white heron and white-crowned pigeons. They're also one of a very few breeding places for the reddish egret, the roseate spoonbill, the mangrove cuckoo, and the black-whiskered vireo. The **Dry Tortugas,** a chain of seven coral islands 70 miles west of Key West, contain some of the best birding spots in the world. Accessible only by boat or plane, the islands are a mecca for the most serious birders. See "The Dry Tortugas," below, for more in-depth information.

Many factors are threatening the health of the bird populations on the Keys; paramount among them is loss of habitat. Forty percent of the shallow water mangrove pools on the Upper Keys were lost to human development between 1955 and 1985, and transitional wetlands, shallow water mangrove sites, freshwater ponds, and hardwood hammocks continue to be filled and developed.

DIVING & SNORKELING   According to 22,000 votes cast by readers of *Scuba Diving* magazine, the Florida Keys are the best place to dive in America, topping even California and Hawaii. The Keys are surrounded by one of the world's largest barrier-reef systems in relatively shallow water, which attracts a plethora of sealife. **John Pennekamp Coral Reef State Park** (at MM 102.3) is an especially popular place to dive and snorkel (see " The Upper & Middle Keys: Key Largo to Marathon," below), offering regular excursions to its protected reefs. If you aren't a certified diver, you can take a quick course that will allow you to go out with an instructor, or you might want to try *snuba-diving,* a relatively new version of diving offered in Key Largo, where the swimmers go down attached to a communal air breathing unit without cumbersome tanks. Dive shops abound and are listed geographically below.

FISHING   South Florida and the Florida Keys just might have more boats, rods, and reels than any place else on earth. Almost two dozen local fish species—including amberjack, barracuda, snapper, king mackerel, sailfish, tarpon, swordfish,

The Ten Keymandments

The Keys have always attracted independent spirits, from Ernest Hemingway and Tennessee Williams to Jimmy Buffett, Mel Fisher, and Zane Grey. Writers, artists, and free-thinkers have long drifted down here to escape from society's rigid demands.

Standards do seem to be different here. In 1982, for example, when drug-enforcement agents blocked off the main highway leading into Key West, residents did what they do best—they threw a party. The festivities marked the "independence" of the newly formed "Conch Republic." The distinctive flag with its conch insignia now flies throughout the island.

Although you'll generally find a very laid-back and tolerant code of behavior in the Keys, some rules do exist. Be sure to respect the Ten Keymandments while you're here, or suffer the consequences.

- Don't anchor on a reef. (Reefs are Alive. Alive. A-L-I-V-E.)
- Don't feed the animals. (They'll want to follow you home, and you can't keep them.)
- Don't trash our place. (Or we'll send Bubba to trash yours.)
- Don't touch the coral. (After all, you don't even know them.)
- Don't speed. (Especially on Big Pine Key, where deer reside and tar-and-feathering is still practiced.)
- Don't catch more fish than you can eat. (Better yet, let them go. Some of them support schools.)
- Don't collect conch. (This species is protected. By Bubba.)
- Don't disturb the bird nests. (They find it very annoying.)
- Don't damage the seagrass. (And don't even think about making a skirt out of it.)
- Don't drink and drive on land or sea. (There's absolutely nothing funny about it.)

and white marlin—attain a weight of 50 pounds or more, the respectable minimum for seasoned trophy hunters. There are three different kinds of fishing in the Keys: deep-sea fishing for big-game fish like marlin, sailfish, and tuna; reef fishing for "eating fish," such as snapper and grouper; and backcountry fishing for bonefish, tarpon, and other "stalking" fish.

Unless you're fishing from land, a pier, or a sanctioned bridge, a saltwater-fishing permit is mandatory. Permits cost $7 for 3 days and $17 for 7 days and can be purchased from almost any bait or boat shop.

If your catch will not be eaten or mounted, release your fish to preserve the area's severely depleted fish population. Always pay close attention to your baited hooks; they will tempt hungry birds. Over 80% of bird injuries are caused by fishing hooks and monofilament. If you accidentally hook a bird, never allow it to fly off without first removing any attached fish line. Never discard fishing line in the water.

HIKING   You can hike throughout the Keys, on both marked trails and meandering coastlines. The best places to trek through nature are the Bahia Honda State Park (at MM 29.5), National Key Deer Refuge (at MM 30), Crane Point Hammock (at MM 50.5), Long Key State Recreation Area (at MM 68), and John Pennekamp Coral Reef State Park (at MM 102.3). See "Outdoor Sights & Activities" and "Two Exceptional State Parks," below, for complete information.

KAYAKING & CANOEING   The Overseas Highway (U.S. 1) touches on only a few dozen of the many hundreds of islands that make up the Florida Keys. I can think of no better way to explore the uninhabited shallow backcountry than by kayak or canoe. You can go places big boats just can't get to because of their large draft. Sometimes the lumbering ancient manatees will cuddle up to the boats, thinking they are another friendly species. For a more enjoyable time, ask for a sit-inside–type boat—you'll stay drier. Also, a fiberglass (as opposed to plastic) boat with a rudder is generally more stable and easier to maneuver. Many area hotels rent kayaks and canoes to guests, as do a multitude of outfitters, listed geographically below.

3 The Upper & Middle Keys: Key Largo to Marathon

48 to 105 miles SW of Miami

The Upper Keys are a popular, year-round refuge for South Floridians who take advantage of the islands' proximity to the mainland. This is the fishing and diving capital of America, and the swarms of outfitters and billboards never let you forget it.

Key Largo, once called "Rock Harbor" but renamed to capitalize on the success of the 1948 Humphrey Bogart film, is the largest Key and is more developed than its neighbors to the south. Dozens of chain hotels, restaurants, and tourist information centers service the many water enthusiasts who come to explore the nation's first underwater park, John Pennekamp Coral Reef State Park, and its adjacent marine sanctuary. **Islamorada,** the unofficial capital of the Upper Keys, offers the area's best atmosphere, food, fishing, entertainment, and lodging. In these "purple isles," nature-lovers can enjoy nature trails, historic explorations, and big-purse fishing tournaments. **Marathon,** smack in the middle of the chain of islands, is one of the most populated Keys. It is part fishing village, part tourist center, and part nature preserve. This island's highly developed infrastructure includes resort hotels, a commercial airport, and a highway that expands to four lanes. Thankfully, high-rises have yet to arrive.

ESSENTIALS

GETTING THERE   If you're coming from the Miami airport, take Le Jeune Road (NW 42nd Avenue) to Route 836 west. Follow signs to the Florida Turnpike (about 7 miles). The turnpike extension connects with U.S. 1 in Florida City. Continue south on U.S. 1.

If you're coming from Florida's west coast, take Alligator Alley to the Miami exit and then turn south onto the turnpike extension. Have plenty of quarters for the tolls.

American Eagle (☎ 800/433-7300) has daily nonstop flights from Miami to Marathon, which is near the midpoint of the chain of Keys and at the very southern end of the area referred to here as the Upper and Middle Keys. Fares range depending on the season, from $88 to $336 round-trip.

Greyhound (☎ 800/231-2222) has buses leaving Miami for Key Largo every day. At press time, prices were $13 one-way. Seats fill up in season, so come early. It's first come, first serve.

VISITOR INFORMATION   Avoid the many "Tourist Information Centers" that dot the main highway. Most are private companies hired to lure visitors to specific lodgings or outfitters. You are better off sticking with the official, not-for-profit centers that are extremely well located and staffed. In particular, the **Key Largo Chamber of Commerce** (U.S. 1 at MM 106, Key Largo, FL 33037; ☎ **800/822-1088** or 305/451-1414; Fax 305/451-4726; www.floridakeys.org) runs an excellent facility, with free direct-dial phones and plenty of brochures. Now headquartered in a handsome clapboard house, the chamber operates as an information clearinghouse for all of the Keys. It's open daily from 9am to 6pm.

The **Islamorada Chamber of Commerce,** in the Little Red Caboose (U.S. 1 at MM 82.5, P.O. Box 915, Islamorada, FL 33036; ☎ **800/322-5397** or 305/664-4503; Fax 305/664-4289; E-mail: islacc@ix.netcom.com), also offers maps and literature on the Upper Keys.

You can't miss the big blue visitors center at MM 53.5. It is the **Greater Marathon Chamber of Commerce** (12222 Overseas Hwy., Marathon, FL 33050; ☎ **800/842-9580** or 305/743-5417; Fax 305/289-0183; www.flakeys.com).

OUTDOOR SIGHTS & ACTIVITIES

One of the area's only beaches, **Anne's beach** (at MM 73.5) is really more of a picnic spot than a full-fledged beach. Still, die-hard suntanners congregate on this tiny strip of coarse sand. Others venture off the walkways into the mangroves or enjoy the wide wooden boardwalk that connects a dozen or so chicki huts, which are open-sided huts with wooden roofs. This mini-park was dedicated to Anne Eaton, a local naturalist. Parking is free, and there are clean, safe bathrooms at the park's northern end.

Indian Key and Lignumvitae Key. Off Indian Key Fill, Overseas Hwy., MM 79. ☎ **305/664-4815.**

If you are interested in seeing the Keys in their natural state, before modern development, you must venture off the highway and take to the water. Two backcountry islands that offer a glimpse of the "real" Keys are Indian Key and Lignumvitae Key. Visitors come to relax and enjoy the islands' colorful birds and lush *hammocks* (elevated pieces of land above a marsh).

Named for the *lignum vitae* ("wood of life") trees found there, **Lignumvitae Key** supports a virgin tropical forest, the kind that once thrived on most of the Upper Keys. Over the years, human settlers have imported "exotic" plants and animals to the Keys, irrevocably changing the botanical makeup of many backcountry islands and threatening much of the indigenous wildlife. Over the past 25 years, the Department of Natural Resources has successfully removed most of the exotic vegetation, leaving this 280-acre site much as it existed in the 18th century. The island also holds a historic house built in 1919 that has survived numerous storms and major hurricanes

Indian Key, a much smaller island on the Atlantic side of Islamorada, was occupied by Native Americans for thousands of years before European settlers arrived. The 10-acre historic site was also the original seat of Dade County before the Civil War. You can see the ruins of the previous settlement and tour the lush grounds on well-marked trails.

If you want to see both islands, plan to spend half a day. To get there, you can rent your own boat at **Robbie's Rent-A-Boat** (U.S. 1 at MM 77.5 on the bay side). Rates range from $60 for a 14-foot boat for half a day to $155 for an 18-foot boat for a full day. It's then a $1 admission fee to each island, which includes an informative hour-long guided tour by park rangers. This is a good option if you are a confident boater.

However, I also recommend taking Robbie's **ferry service** for $15, which includes the $1 park admission. Trips to both islands cost $25 per person. (If you are planning to visit only one island, make it Lignumvitae.) Not only is the ferry more economical, but it's easier to enjoy the natural beauty of the islands when you aren't negotiating the shallow reefs along the way. The runabouts, which carry up to six people, depart from Robbie's Pier Thursday to Monday at 9am and 1pm for Indian Key, and at 10am and 2pm for Lignumvitae Key. In the busy season, you may need to book as early as 2 days before departure. Call ☎ **305/664-4815** for information from the park service or ☎ **305/664-9814** for Robbie's.

✪ **Museum of Crane Point Hammock.** 5550 Overseas Hwy. (MM 50), Marathon. ☎ **305/ 743-9100.** Admission $7.50 for adults; $6 for seniors over 64; $4 for students and free for children under 6. Mon–Sat 9am–5pm; Sun noon–5pm.

Crane Point Hammock is a little-known but very worthwhile stop, especially for those interested in the rich botanical and archaeological history of the Keys. This privately owned 64-acre nature area is considered one of the most important historical sites in the Keys. Although Crane Point Hammock is surrounded by shopping centers and condominiums, it contains what is probably the last virgin thatch palm hammock in North America. It also has an archaeological dig site with pre-Columbian and prehistoric Bahamian artifacts.

Now headquarters for the Florida Keys Land and Sea Trust, the hammock's small nature museum has simple, informative displays of the Keys' wildlife, including a walk-through replica of a coral-reef cave and life-size dioramas with tropical birds and Key deer. A popular single-room children's museum lets kids play with a miniature railway station, walk though a Native American thatched hut, and touch a variety of sea creatures in a small saltwater touch tank.

Outside, visitors are encouraged to wander through the museum's quarter-mile nature trail amid species of exotic plants that grow nowhere else in the country.

✪ **Seven-Mile Bridge and Pigeon Key.** Between MM 40 and 47 on U.S. 1. ☎ **305/ 289-0025.**

A stop at the Seven-Mile Bridge is a rewarding and relaxing break from the drive south. Built alongside the ruins of oil magnate Henry Flagler's incredible Overseas Railroad, the "new" bridge (between MM 40 and 47) is still considered an architectural feat. The wide arched span, completed in 1982 at a cost of more than $45 million, is impressive, its apex being the highest point in the Keys. The new bridge and especially its now-defunct neighbor provide an excellent vantage point from which to view the stunning waters of the Keys. Take a few minutes or spend a few hours to appreciate this free attraction. The old "ghost bridge" is the perfect place to watch the sunset, especially if you have had enough of the bars.

In the daytime, you may want to jog, walk, or bike along the scenic 4-mile stretch of bridge, or join local fishermen, who use shrimp as bait to catch barracuda, yellowtail, and dolphin on what is known as "the longest fishing pier in the world." To get there from the southbound lane of the Overseas Highway, slow down just before the bridge and turn right, off the road, into the unpaved parking lot at the foot of the bridge.

Recently opened to the public, **Pigeon Key,** at the curve of the old bridge, is an intriguing historical site that has been under renovation since late 1995. It was once the camp for a railroad crew who built in the early part of the century. From here, your vista includes both bridges, many old wooden cottages, and a truly tranquil stretch of lush foliage and sea.

The Key is open every day except Monday from 9am to 5pm. Admission is $2 and free for children under 8. Shuttle service is provided for visitors who don't want to walk or bike the 2-mile trail to the 5-mile island. Cars cannot drive on the old bridge. Parking is available at the Knight's Key end of the bridge, at MM 48, or at the Visitor's Center at the old train car across the highway.

VISITING WITH THE ANIMALS

☉ **Dolphin Research Center.** U.S. 1 at MM 59 (on the bay side), Marathon. ☎ **305/ 289-1121.** Swim with the Dolphins, $90 per person. Call on the first day of the month to book for the following month. Educational walking tours five times every day: 10am, 11am, 12:30pm, 2pm, and 3:30pm. Admission $9.50 adults; $7.50 seniors; $6 children 4–12; free for children 3 and under. (Prices are scheduled to increase.) MC, V. Daily 9:30am–4pm. Look for the 30-foot statue of a dolphin.

Don't miss this experience. If you've always wanted to touch, swim, or play with dolphins, this is the place to do it. Of the three such centers in the continental United States (all located in the Keys), the Dolphin Research Center is the most organized and informative. The group's main goal is to educate the public and to protect these unusually smart beasts.

Although some people argue that training dolphins is cruel and selfish, the knowledgeable trainers at the Dolphin Research Center will tell you that the dolphins need stimulation and enjoy human contact. They certainly seem to. They nuzzle and seem to smile and kiss the lucky few who get to swim with them in the daily program. The "family" of 15 dolphins swims in a 90,000-square-foot natural saltwater pool carved out of the shoreline.

The procedure for making reservations is quite unbending. If you can't book your choice of dates, don't despair. You can still take a walking tour or a half-day class in how to do hand signals and feed the dolphins from docks. Kids must be at least 12 years old.

Florida Keys Wild Bird Rehabilitation Center. U.S. 1 at MM 94, Tavernier. ☎ **305/ 852-4486.** Donations suggested. Daily 8:30am–6pm. Heading south on U.S. 1, look right for the wooden bird sculptures to point the way.

Wander through lush canopies of mangroves on narrow wooden walkways to see some of the Keys's most famous residents—the large variety of native birds, including broad-wing hawks, great blue and white herons, roseate spoonbills, white ibis, cattle egrets, and a number of pelicans. This not-for-profit center operates as a hospital for the many birds who have been injured. If you have the stomach for it, ask to see naturalist Laura Quinn at work removing a fish hook from a bird's throat or untangling fishing line from a broken wing. Or come at feeding time, usually about 2pm, when you can watch the dedicated staff feed the hundreds of hungry beaks. Keep alert. The big-billed pelicans often poke their heads down from the low structures just to check out who is visiting.

☉ **Robbie's Pier.** U.S. 1 at MM 77.5, Islamorada. ☎ **305/664-9814.** Admission $1. Bucket of fish $2. Daily 8am–5pm. Look for the Hungry Tarpon restaurant sign on the right after the Indian Key channel.

One of the best and definitely one of the cheapest attractions in the Upper Keys is the famed Robbie's Pier. Here, the fierce steely tarpons, a prized catch for backcountry anglers, have been gathering for the past 20 years. You may recognize these prehistoric-looking giants that grow up to 200 pounds; many are displayed as trophies and mounted on local restaurant walls. To see them live, head to Robbie's Pier, where tens and sometimes hundreds of these behemoths circle the shallow waters waiting for you to feed them. New kayak tours promise an even closer glimpse.

Theater of the Sea. U.S. 1 at MM 84.5, Islamorada. ☎ **305/664-2431.** Fax 305/664-8162. Admission $15.25 adults; $8.75 children 3–12. Swim with the Dolphins and Trainer for a Day programs by reservation; $85 and $75 per person, respectively. Daily 9:30am–4pm.

Established in 1946, the Theater of the Sea is one of the world's oldest marine zoos. Although the facilities could use some sprucing up, the dolphin and sea lion shows are entertaining and informative, especially for children who can also see sharks, sea turtles, and tropical fish. The price is a bit steep for the rather limited resources here. Still, if you want to swim with the dolphins and you haven't booked well in advance, this is the place you may be able to get in with just a few hours—or days—notice as opposed to the more rigid Dolphin Research Center in Marathon (see above). After an hour's orientation session where you'll learn everything you've ever wanted to know about these incredible swimming mammals—from their food preferences to their mating habits—you can climb into one of the three lagoons to frolic with and touch the playful beasts. Though the water is murky and individual time with the animals is short, for those who have dreamed of swimming beside these clever creatures, this is a great experience. Cat lovers will be thrilled to learn that the facility also serves as a haven for dozens of stray cats who have free run of the entire grounds and gift shop. Those who are allergic or sensitive to cat fur and smells should skip this stop.

TWO EXCEPTIONAL STATE PARKS

One of the best places to discover the diverse ecosystem of the Upper Keys is in its most famous park, ✪ **John Pennekamp Coral Reef State Park,** located on U.S. 1 at MM 102.5, in Key Largo (☎ **305/451-1202**). Named for a former *Miami Herald* editor and conservationist, the 188-square-mile park is the nation's first undersea preserve. It's a sanctuary for part of the only living coral reef in the continental United States. The original plans for Everglades National Park included this part of the reef within its boundaries, but opposition from local homeowners made its inclusion politically impossible.

Because the water is extremely shallow, the 40 species of corals and more than 650 species of fish here are particularly accessible to divers, snorkelers, and glass-bottomed–boat passengers. You can't see the reef from the shore. To experience this park, visitors must get in the water. Your first stop should be the visitor center, which is full of educational fish tanks and a mammoth 30,000-gallon saltwater aquarium that re-creates a reef ecosystem. At the adjacent dive shop, you can rent snorkeling and diving equipment and join one of the boat trips that depart for the reef throughout the day. Visitors can also rent motorboats, sailboats, Windsurfers, and canoes. The 2-hour glass-bottomed–boat tour is the best way to see the coral reefs if you refuse to get wet.

Canoeing around the park's narrow mangrove channels and tidal creeks is also popular. You can go on your own in a rented canoe, or in winter, sign up for a tour led by a local naturalist. Hikers have two short trails to choose from: a boardwalk through the mangroves and a dirt trail through a tropical hardwood hammock. Ranger-led walks are usually scheduled daily from the end of November to April. Phone for schedule information and reservations.

Park admission is $2.50 per vehicle for one occupant; for two or more, it is $4 per vehicle, plus 50¢ per passenger; $1.50 per pedestrian or bicyclist. Call ☎ **305/451-1621** for information. On your way into the park, ask the ranger for a map. Glass-bottomed–boat tours cost $13 for adults and $8.50 for children 11 and under. Snorkeling tours are $23.95 for adults and $18.95 for children 17 and under, including equipment. Sailing and snorkeling tours are $28.95 for adults, $23.95 for children 17 and under, including equipment but not tax. Canoes rent for $8 per hour or $28 for 4 hours. Reef boats (powerboats) rent for $25 to $45 per hour; call ☎ **305/451-6325.** Open daily from 8am to 5pm; phone for tour and dive times. Also, see below for more options on diving, fishing, and snorkeling these reefs.

Long Key State Recreation Area, U.S. 1 at MM 68, Long Key (☎ **305/664-4815**) is one of the best places in the Middle Keys for hiking, camping, and canoeing. This 965-acre is situated atop the remains of an ancient coral reef. At the entrance gate, ask for a free flyer describing the local trails and wildlife.

You can hike along two nature trails. The Golden Orb Trail is a 1-mile loop around a lagoon that attracts a large variety of birds. Rich in West Indian vegetation, this trail leads to an observation tower that offers good views of the mangroves. Layton Trail, the only part of the park that doesn't require an admission fee, is a quarter-mile shaded loop that goes through tropical hammocks before opening onto Florida Bay. The trail is well marked with interpretive signs; you can easily walk it in about 20 minutes.

The park's excellent 1¹/2-mile canoe trail is also short and sweet, allowing visitors to loop around the mangroves in about an hour—it couldn't be easier. You can rent canoes at the trailhead for about $4 per hour. Long Key is also a great spot to stop for a picnic if you get hungry on your way to Key West.

Railroad builder Henry Flagler created the Long Key Fishing Club here in 1906, and the waters surrounding the park are still popular with game fishers. In summer, sea turtles lumber onto the protected coast to lay their eggs.

Admission is $3.25 per car plus 50¢ per person (except for the Layton Trail, which is free). Open daily from 8am to sunset.

WATER SPORTS A–Z

There are literally hundreds of outfitters in the Keys who will set up all kinds of water activities, from cave dives to parasailing. If those recommended below are booked up or unreachable, ask the local chamber of commerce for a list of qualified members.

BOATING   In addition to the rental shops in the state parks, you will find dozens of outfitters along U.S. 1 offering a range of runabouts and skiffs for boaters of any experience level. **Captain Pip's,** U.S. 1 at MM 47.5, Marathon (☎ **800/ 707-1692** or 305/743-4403), rents 18.5- to 24-foot motorboats with 90 to 225 horsepower engines for $110 to $170 per day.

Robbie's Rent-a-Boat, U.S. 1 at MM 77.5, Islamorada (☎ **305/664-9814**), rents 14- to 27-foot motorboats with engines ranging from 15 to 200 horsepower. Boats cost $60 to $205 for a half day and $80 to $295 for a whole day.

CANOEING/KAYAKING   I can think of no better way to explore the uninhabited, shallow backcountry than by kayak or canoe. You can reach places big boats just can't get to because of their large draft. Sometimes manatees will cuddle up to the boats, thinking them another friendly species.

For a more enjoyable time, ask for a sit-inside boat—you'll stay drier. Also, a fiberglass (as opposed to plastic) boat with a rudder is generally more stable and easier to maneuver. Many area hotels rent kayaks and canoes to guests, as do the outfitters listed here. **Florida Bay Outfitters,** U.S. 1 at MM 104, Key Largo (☎ **305/ 451-3018**), rents canoes and sea kayaks for use in and around John Pennekamp Coral Reef State Park for $20 to $30 for a half day and $35 to $50 for a whole day. Canoes cost $25 for a half day and $35 for a whole day. At **Coral Reef Park Co.,** on U.S. 1 at MM 102.5, Key Largo (☎ **305/451-1621**), you can rent canoes and kayaks for $8 per hour, $28 for a half day; most canoes are sit-on-tops.

DIVING & SNORKELING   The **Florida Keys Dive Center,** on U.S. 1 at MM 90.5, Tavernier (☎ **305/852-4599;** fax 305/852-1293), takes snorkelers and divers to the reefs of John Pennekamp Coral Reef State Park and environs every day. PADI training courses are also available for the uninitiated. Tours leave at 8am and 12:30pm and cost $25 per person to snorkel (including mask, snorkels, and fins) and $40 per person to dive (plus an extra $30 if you need to rent all the gear).

At **Hall's Dive Center & Career Institute,** U.S. 1 at MM 48.5, Marathon (☎ **305/743-5929;** fax 305/743-8168), snorkelers and divers can choose to dive at Looe Key, Sombrero Reef, Delta Shoal, Content Key, and Coffins Patch. Tours are scheduled daily at 9am and 1pm. If you mention this guide, you will get a special discounted rate of $30 per person to snorkel (including equipment) and $40 per person to dive. Choose from a wide and impressive array of equipment. Rental is extra.

With **Snuba Tours of Key Largo** (☎ 305/451-6391), you can dive down to 20 feet attached to a comfortable breathing apparatus that really gives you the feeling of scuba diving without having to be certified. You can tour shallow coral reefs teeming with hundreds of colorful fish and plant life, from sea turtles to moray eels. Reservations are required; call to find out where and when to meet—usually in the late afternoon from the Westin or the Cheeca Lodge. A 2- to 3-hour underwater tour costs $70, including all equipment. If you have never dived before, you may require a 1-hour lesson in the pool, which costs an additional $40. The best part is you can bring the kids—as long as they are at least 8 years old.

FISHING Robbie's **Partyboats & Charters,** on U.S. 1 at MM 84.5, Islamorada (☎ **305/664-8070** or 305/664-4196), located at the south end of the Holiday Isle Docks (see the Holiday Isle Resort in "Where to Stay," below), offers day and night deep-sea and reef fishing trips aboard a 65-foot party boat. Big-game–fishing charters are also available, and "splits" are arranged for solo fishers. Party-boat fishing costs $25 for a half day, $40 for a full day, and $30 at night. Charters run $400 for a half day, $600 for a full day; splits begin at $65 per person. Phone for information and reservations.

Bud n' Mary's Fishing Marina, on U.S. 1 at MM 79.8, Islamorada (☎ **800/ 742-7945** or 305/664-2461; fax 305/664-5592), one of the largest marinas between Miami and Key West, is packed with sailors offering guided backcountry fishing charters. This is the place to go if you want to stalk tarpon, bonefish, and snapper. If the seas are not too rough, deep-sea and coral fishing trips can be arranged. Charters cost $400 to $500 for a half day, $600 to $800 for a full day, and splits begin at $125 per person.

The Bounty Hunter, 15th Street, Marathon (☎ **305/743-2446**), offers full- and half-day outings. For years, Captain Brock Hook's huge sign has boasted no fish, no pay. You're guaranteed to catch something. Choose your prey from shark, barracuda, sailfish, or whatever else is running. Prices are $350 for a half day, $375 for three-quarters of a day, and $450 for a full day. Rates are for groups of no more than six people.

SHOPPING

On your way to the Keys, you'll find an outlet center, the **Keys Factory Shops** (☎ 305/248-4727), at 250 E. Palm Dr. (where the Fla. Turnpike meets U.S. Hwy. 1), in Florida City. The center holds more than 60 stores, including Nike Factory Store, Bass Co. Store, Levi's, Osh Kosh, and Izod. Travelers can pick up a free discount coupon booklet called the Come Back Pack from the Customer Service Center. The outlet is open daily until 9pm, except Sunday when it closes at 6pm.

The Upper and Middle Keys have no shortage of tacky tourist shops selling shells and T-shirts and other hokey souvenirs, but for real Keys-style shopping, check out the weekend **flea markets**. One of the best is held every Saturday and Sunday bayside at MM 103.5 (☎ 305/451-0677). Dozens of vendors open their stalls from 9am until 4 or 5pm selling every imaginable sort of antiques, T-shirts, plants, shoes, books, toys and games, as well as a hearty dose of good old-fashioned junk.

A mecca for fishing and sports enthusiasts is **The World Wide Sportsman** (☎ **305/664-4615**), which opened in late 1997 at MM 81.5. It's not only the largest fishing store in the Keys, but also a meeting place for anglers from all over the world. Every possible gizmo and gadget, plus hundreds of T-shirts, hats, books, and cute gift items are displayed in its more than 25,000 square feet. The sales people are knowledgeable and eager to help. Travel specialists can even arrange for charter trips and backcountry tours. The store is open daily from 7am until 8:30pm. The staff is also happy to relay weather and travel data to interested callers. Ask for the tackle department, which is where the weather station operates.

WHERE TO STAY

U.S. 1 is lined with chain hotels in all price ranges. In the Upper Keys, the best moderately priced options are the **Holiday Inn Key Largo Resort & Marina,** U.S. 1 at MM 99.7 (☎ **800/THE KEYS** or 305/451-2121), and right next door, at MM 100, the **Ramada Limited Resort & Casino** (☎ **800/THE KEYS** or 305/451-3939). Both hotels share three pools and a casino boat; however, the Ramada is cozier and offers slightly cheaper rates. Also, the **Best Western Suites at Key Largo,** 201 Ocean Dr., MM 100 (☎ **800/462-6079** or 305/451-5081), is just 3 miles from John Pennekamp Coral Reef State Park. Another good option in the Upper Keys is **Islamorada Days Inn,** U.S. 1 at MM 82.5 (☎ **800/DAYS-INN** or 305/664-3681). In the Middle Keys, the **Howard Johnson** at 13351 Overseas Hwy, MM 54 in Marathon (☎ **800/321-3496** or 305/743-8550), also offers reasonably priced oceanside rooms.

Since the real beauty of the Keys lies mostly beyond the highways, there is no better way to see this area than by boat. Why not stay in a floating hotel? Especially if traveling with a group, houseboats can be economical. To rent a houseboat, call Ruth and Michael Sullivan at **Smilin' Island Houseboat Rentals** (MM 99.5), Key Largo, FL (☎ **305/451-1930**). Rates are from $750 to $1,350 for 3 nights. Boats accommodate up to six people.

For land options, consider these recommendations, grouped first by price, and then geographically from north to south. I've used the following guide for per-night prices: very expensive, more than $250; expensive, $180 to $250; moderate, $90 to $180; and inexpensive, less than $90.

Very Expensive

Cheeca Lodge. U.S. 1 at MM 82 (P.O. Box 527), Islamorada, FL 33036. ☎ **800/327-2888** or 305/664-4651. Fax 305/664-2893. 267 units. A/C MINIBAR TV TEL. Winter $240–$610 double, $315 suite; off-season $160–$425 double, $275 suite. AE, CB, DC, DISC, MC, V.

One of the better places to stay in the Upper Keys, Cheeca has been hosting celebrities, royalty, and politicians since its opening in 1949. This lodge offers all the amenities of a world-class resort in a very laid-back setting. You may not feel compelled to leave the sprawling grounds, but it's good to know the hotel is conveniently situated near the best restaurants and nightlife. Located on 27 acres of beachfront property, this rambling resort is known for its excellent sports facilities, including diving and snorkeling programs and one of the only golf courses in the Upper Keys.

Although rooms are not particularly plush, all are spacious and have small balconies. The nicer ones overlook the ocean and have large marble bathrooms. Almost all rooms have entrances accessible from open-air hallways, and guests can park their cars in private spots near their rooms. The staff is always available, but thankfully not overly visible.

Dining/Diversions: The Atlantic's Edge restaurant is one of the best in the Upper Keys (see "Where to Dine," below). A pool bar and comfortable lounge offer more casual options throughout the day and evening.

Amenities: Concierge, room service, dry-cleaning and laundry services, in-room massage, newspaper delivery, baby-sitting, express checkout, valet parking, free coffee and refreshments in lobby. Kitchenettes, VCRs and video rentals, three outdoor heated pools, kids' pool, five hot tubs, beach, access to nearby health club, Jacuzzi, bicycle rental, 9-hole, par-3 golf course, children's nature programs, conference rooms, car-rental desk, sundeck, six lighted tennis courts, water-sports equipment rental, tour desk, nature trail, boutiques.

✪ **Hawk's Cay Resort.** U.S. 1 at MM 61, Duck Key, FL 33050. ☎ **800/432-2242** or 305/743-7000. Fax 305/743-5215. 176 units. A/C TV TEL. Winter $220–$350 double, $400–$850 suite; off-season $160–$250 double, $300–$750 suite. AE, DC, DISC, MC, V.

Located on its own 60-acre island just outside of Marathon in the Middle Keys, Hawk's Cay is a sprawling and impressive resort encompassing a marina as well as a saltwater lagoon that's home to a half-dozen dolphins. It's especially popular with families, who appreciate the many activities and reasonably priced diversions. It's also more casual than other resorts, like Cheeca Lodge, which offers many of the same amenities. The manicured grounds are dotted with handsome two- and three-story flamingo-colored buildings. The guest rooms within are all quite similar—views account for the differences in price. All are large and have walk-in closets, small refrigerators, a sliding glass door opening onto a private balcony, and Caribbean-style bamboo furnishings padded with colorful fabrics. If you want to splurge, the top-floor suites have separate seating areas with pull-out sofas and large wraparound terraces with spectacular views.

Dining/Diversions: Three good restaurants and a lounge have a wide range of food, from Italian to seafood. A well-stocked ship's store has snacks and basic groceries. A lively lounge features live music every evening and most weekend afternoons.

Amenities: Concierge, room service, overnight laundry, in-room massage, express checkout, transportation to airport and golf course, free refreshments in lobby. Outdoor heated pool, a new adults-only private pool, beach, small fitness room, Jacuzzi, nearby golf course, sundeck, eight tennis courts (two lighted), water-sports equipment, bicycle rental, game room, children's center or programs, self-service laundry, marina store and gift shop, conference rooms, car-rental desk.

Westin Beach Resort. U.S. 1 at MM 97, Key Largo, FL 33037. ☎ **800/728-2738,** 800/325-3535, or 305/852-5553. Fax 305/852-8669. 210 units. A/C MINIBAR TV TEL. Winter $239–$289 double, from $389 Jacuzzi suite; off-season $210–$260 double, from $389 Jacuzzi suite. AE, DC, DISC, MC, V.

Under new ownership since 1996, this resort has benefited from an extensive $3-million renovation. In addition to an overall rehab, the resort distinguishes itself by its secluded yet convenient location. It is set back on 12 private acres of gumbo-limbo and hardwood trees, making it invisible from the busy highway. Despite its hideaway location, the sprawling pink-and-blue four-story complex is surprisingly large. A three-story atrium lobby is flanked by two wings that face 1,200 feet of the Florida Bay. The large guest rooms have tasteful tropical decor and private balconies. The suites are twice the size of standard rooms and have better-quality wicker furnishings and double-size balconies. Ten suites feature private spa tubs and particularly luxurious bathrooms with adjustable showerheads, bidets, and lots of room for toiletries.

Dining/Diversions: The hotel restaurant offers terrific views of the bay and surf-and-turf dinners nightly. A casual cafe serves breakfast, lunch, and dinner both inside and outdoors. A poolside snack bar serves sandwiches, salads, and refreshments. The top-floor lounge has a dance floor and a pool table.

Amenities: Concierge, 24-hour room service, newspaper delivery, dry-cleaning and laundry service, in-room massage, twice-daily maid service, baby-sitting, secretarial services, express checkout, free morning coffee in lobby, valet parking. Two outdoor heated swimming pools, beach, small but modern fitness room with Universal equipment, Jacuzzi, nature trails, two lighted tennis courts, water-sports equipment rental, children's programs, conference rooms, hair salon.

EXPENSIVE

Jules' Undersea Lodge. 51 Shoreland Dr. (P.O. Box 3330), Key Largo, FL 33037. ☎ **305/ 451-2353.** Fax 305/451-4789. 1 unit. A/C TV TEL. $195–$295 per person. Rates include breakfast and dinner as well as all equipment and unlimited scuba diving in the lagoon. AE, DISC, MC, V. From U.S. 1 south, at MM 103.2, turn left onto Transylvania Avenue, across from the Central Plaza shopping mall.

Originally built as a research lab in the 1970s, this small underwater compartment now operates as a single-room hotel. As expensive as it is unusual, Jules' is most popular with diving honeymooners. The lodge rests on pillars on the ocean floor. To get inside, guests swim under the structure and pop up into the unit through a 4×6-foot "moon pool" that gurgles soothingly all night long. The 30-foot–deep underwater suite consists of a bedroom and galley and sleeps up to six. There is a television and VCR. Also, room service will bring breakfast, lunch, and daily newspapers in waterproof containers at no extra charge. Needless to say, this novelty is not for everyone.

Marriott Key Largo Bay Beach Resort. 103800 Overseas Hwy. (MM 103.8), Key Largo FL 33037. ☎ **800/932-9332** or 305/453-0000. Fax 305/453-0093. E-mail: baybeach@reefnet.com. 150 units. A/C MINIBAR TV TEL. Winter $209–$269, suites $500; off-season $139–$179, $250 suites. AE, DC, DISC, MC, V.

When this mammoth chain resort was built in 1993, many thought the sleepy little island town would be forever spoiled. On the contrary, this pristine, two-story Marriott created some major competition for the area's older resorts and the run-down 1950s motels, resulting in an overall upgrade of the neighboring accommodations. While it is hardly quaint, the amenities-laden complex built on 17 acres has everything an active or resting traveler could want, including a decent-sized beach. All guests are welcome to sail for free on a gambling cruise ship that anchors in international waters from 2pm until 2am daily. Rooms are decorated in a pleasant (if generic) tropical style and include extras such as coffeepots, hair dryers, and safes. Most rooms (all but 22) also offer balconies overlooking the stunning Florida bay. For real pampering, consider the enormous suites, which can easily sleep a family of five. All have large wraparound terraces and large sitting areas. With its rates being slightly cheaper than the nearby Westin and Cheeca Lodge, you'll find it a good value. It's one of the hotels most convenient to Miami (about an hour drive). Reserve early; winter weekends usually book up months in advance.

Dining/Diversions: A casual bayside grill offers casually elegant dining, and an outdoor tiki bar has snacks and cocktails throughout the afternoon and evening.

Amenities: Concierge, room service, dry-cleaning and laundry services, in-room massage, newspaper delivery, baby-sitting, express checkout. Large outdoor pool, Jacuzzi, three small beach areas, VCRs on request, gym, bicycle rental, conference rooms, sundeck, access to nearby tennis and racquetball courts, water-sports equipment rental, business center, tour desk, children's programs, game room, nature trail, boutiques.

✪ The Moorings. 123 Beach Road near MM 81.5 on the ocean side, Islamorada, FL 33036. ☎ **305/664-4708.** Fax 305/664-4242. 17 cottages. A/C TV TEL. In season, $165–$200 smaller one-bedrooms, $350 large one-bedrooms. Oceanfront, two- and three-bedroom cottages $2,450–$6,300 weekly. Discounts off-season. Two-night minimum for smaller cottages; 1-week minimum for larger cottages. MC, V.

Staying at the Moorings is more like staying at your second home than at a hotel. You'll never see another soul on this 18-acre resort if you choose not to. There isn't even maid service unless you request it. The romantic whitewashed houses are spacious and modestly decorated with funky island prints, bamboo, and tropical motifs. All have full kitchens and most have washers and dryers. Some have CD players and VCRs; ask when you book. The real reason to come to this cool resort is to relax on the more than 1,000-foot beach (one of the only real beaches around) and to soak up some old-fashioned Keys simplicity. There is a simple hard tennis court, a few kayaks and Windsurfers, but absolutely no motorized water vehicles. There is no room service or restaurant (although Morada Bay across the street is excellent). This is a place for people who like each other a lot. If you want to be pampered, pamper each other. Picture yourself in a wide rope hammock under a palm tree watching the sun set with a glass of wine and a good book by your side. Leave the kids at home unless they are extremely well-behaved and not easily bored.

Amenities: Laundry and dryers, full kitchens, some VCRs, large sandy beach, sundeck, large pool, boats, jogging trails.

MODERATE/INEXPENSIVE

Banana Bay Resort & Marina. U.S. 1 at MM 49.5, Marathon, FL 33050. ☎ **800/BANANA-1** or 305/743-3500. Fax 305/743-2670. 60 units. A/C TV TEL. Winter $95–$175 double; off-season $75–$125 double. Rates include breakfast. Children 4 and under stay free in parents' room. Weekend and 3- and 7-night packages available. AE, DC, DISC, MC, V.

It doesn't look like much from the sign-cluttered Overseas Highway, but when you enter the lush grounds of Banana Bay, you will realize you're in one of the most bucolic and best-run properties in the Upper Keys. Built in the early 1950s as a fishing camp, the resort is a maze of pink-and-white two-story buildings hidden among banyans and palms. Guest rooms are very similar, but those with better views are more expensive. The rooms are moderately sized, and many have private balconies where you can enjoy complimentary coffee and newspapers every morning.

The restaurant serves breakfast, lunch, and dinner by the pool or in a kitschy old dining room. A waterfront tiki bar offers great sunset views. Head down to the marina to sign up for charter fishing, sailing, and diving. Kids will enjoy the small game room and free use of bicycles.

✪ Conch Key Cottages. Near U.S. 1 at MM 62.3 (RR 1, Box 424), Marathon, FL 33050. ☎ **800/330-1577** or 305/289-1377. Fax 305/743-8207. 12 units. A/C TV. Winter $100 efficiency, $126 one-bedroom apt, $147 one-bedroom cottage, $194–$249 two-bedroom cottage; off-season $72 efficiency, $115 one-bedroom apt, $132 one-bedroom cottage, $147–$215 two-bedroom cottage. DISC, MC, V.

Occupying its own private micro-island just off U.S. 1, Conch Key Cottages is a unique and comfortable hideaway run by live-in owners Ron Wilson and Wayne Byrnes, who are constantly fixing and adding to their unique property. This is a place to get away from it all; the cottages aren't close to much, except maybe one or two interesting eateries. The cabins, which were built at different times over the past 40 years, overlook their own stretch of natural, but very small, private beach and have screened-in porches and cozy bedrooms and baths. Each has a hammock and barbecue grill. Request one of the new two-bedroom cottages, completed in 1997—especially if you are traveling with the family. They are the most spacious and well designed, practically tailor-made for couples or families. On the other side of the pool are a handful of efficiency apartments that are similarly outfitted, but enjoy no beach frontage. All have fully equipped kitchens. There's also a small heated freshwater pool.

Faro Blanco Marine Resort. 1996 Overseas Hwy., U.S. 1 at MM 48.5, Marathon, FL 33050. ☎ **800/759-3276** or 305/743-9018. 123 units, 31 houseboats with 4 units each. A/C TV TEL. Winter $65–$150 cottage, $99–$200 houseboat, $185 lighthouse, $240 condo; off-season $55–$125 cottage, $79–$150 houseboat, $150 lighthouse, $210 condo. AE, DISC, MC, V.

Spanning both sides of the Overseas Highway and all on waterfront property, this huge, two-shore marina and hotel complex offers something for every taste. Freestanding, camp-style cottages with a small bedroom are the resort's least expensive accommodations, but are in dire need of rehabilitation. Old appliances and a musty odor also make them the least desirable units on the property. There are some larger apartments with modern furniture and cleaner bathrooms and kitchens.

The houseboats are the best choice and value. Permanently tethered in a tranquil marina, these white rectangular boats look like floating mobile homes and are uniformly clean, fresh, and recommendable. They have colonial American–style furnishings, fully equipped kitchenettes, front and back porches, and water, water everywhere. The boats are so tightly moored, you hardly move at all, even in the roughest weather.

Finally, there are two unusual rental units located in a lighthouse on the pier. Circular staircases, unusually shaped rooms and showers, and nautical decor make it quite a unique place to stay, but some guests might find it claustrophobic. Guests in any of the accommodations can enjoy the Olympic-size pool, any of the four casual restaurants, a fully equipped dive shop, barbecue and picnic areas, and a playground.

Holiday Isle Resort. U.S. 1 at MM 84, Islamorada, FL 33036. ☎ **800/327-7070** or 305/664-2321. Fax 305/664-2703. 199 units. Winter $85–$425; off-season $65–$350. AE, CB, DISC, MC, V.

A huge resort complex encompassing five restaurants, lounges, and shops, and four distinct (if not distinctive) hotels, the Holiday Isle is one of the biggest resorts in the Keys. It attracts a spring-break kind of crowd year-round. Its Tiki Bar claims to have invented the rum runner drink (151-proof rum, blackberry brandy, banana liqueur, grenadine, and lime juice), and there's no reason to doubt it. Hordes of partiers are attracted to the resort's nonstop merrymaking, live music, and beachfront bars. As a result, some of the accommodations can be noisy.

Rooms can be bare-bones budget to oceanfront luxury, as the broad range of prices reflect. Even the nicest rooms could use a good cleaning. El Captain and Harbor Lights, two of the least expensive hotels on the property, are both austere and basic. Like the other hotels here, rooms could use a thorough rehab. Howard Johnson's, another Holiday Isle property, is a little farther from the action and a tad more civilized. If you plan to be there for a few days, choose an efficiency or suite; both have kitchenettes. Guests can choose between two outdoor heated pools and a kids' pool. They also offer water-sports equipment rental, gift boutiques, and a shopping arcade.

✪ **Kona Kai Resort & Gallery.** 97802 Overseas Hwy. (U.S. 1 at MM 97.8), Key Largo, FL 33037. ☎ **800/365-7829** or 305/852-7200. Fax 305/852-4629. E-mail: KonaKai@aol.com. 11 units. Winter $141–$165 rms; $175–$400 suites; off-season $94–$145 rms, $117–$205 suites. Three- to 4-night minimum stay usually required. AE, DISC, MC, V.

No one seems to get quite as thrilled over the Florida Key's low-key beauty as a transplanted city boy. The garrulous proprietor of Kona Kai, Joe Harris, is the quintessential New Yorker and an enthusiastic tour guide. He and his partner, Ronnie

Farina, former executives with NBC television, bend over backward to accommodate guests' every need. It's all about personal service. It's also about 2 acres of tropical fruits, such as carambola, passion fruits, bananas, key limes, guava, Florida pistachios, and more. A small tennis court, pool, Jacuzzi, Ping-Pong table, volleyball, and all kinds of water sports are available for those who want a physical workout. For the adventurous, Joe and Ronnie will organize excursions to the Everglades, the backcountry, or wherever. No phones in the rooms and a 4-day minimum stay required in the winter make relaxing imperative. The rooms, all very private and simply furnished, are spaced out and protected by low walls of tropical trees. An impressive art gallery doubles as the property's office and lobby. Photos by renowned local artist Clyde Butcher will inspire even the most tenderfooted to explore the natural wonders of the Keys.

Lime Tree Bay Resort Motel. U.S. 1 at MM 68.5 in Layton, Long Key, FL 33001. ☎ **800/ 723-4519** or 305/664-4740. Fax 305/664-0750. 30 units. A/C TV TEL. $75–$110 motel rooms or efficiencies; $115–$150 cottages; $105–$125 deluxe motel rooms; $150–$180 one bedroom suite; $155–$230 two-bedroom suites. AE, DC, DISC, MC, V.

The Lime Tree Bay Resort is the only hotel in the tiny town of Layton (pop. 183). Midway between Islamorada and Marathon, the hotel is only steps from Long Key State Recreation Area. Motel rooms and efficiencies have tiny bathrooms with standing showers, but are clean and well maintained. The best deal is the two-bedroom bay-view apartment. The large living area with new fixtures and furnishings leads out to a large private deck where you can enjoy a view of the gulf from your hammock. A full kitchen and two full baths make it a comfortable space for six people.

This affordable little hideaway has all the amenities you could want, including shuffleboard, tennis, a small pool, water sports, and a little cafe with a small but decent menu. It's situated on a very pretty piece of waterfront graced with hundreds of mature palm trees and lots of other tropical foliage.

INEXPENSIVE

Bay Harbor Lodge. U.S. 1 at MM 97.7 (off the southbound lane of U.S. 1), Key Largo, FL 33037. ☎ **305/852-5695.** 16 units. A/C TV TEL. $58–$78 double; $78–$98 efficiency; $85–$125 cottage. MC, V.

A small, simple retreat that's big on charm, the Bay Harbor Lodge is an extraordinarily welcoming place. The lodge is far from fancy, and the wide range of accommodations are not all created equal. The motel rooms are small and ordinary in decor, but even the least expensive is recommendable. The efficiencies are larger motel rooms with fully equipped kitchenettes. The oceanfront cottages are larger still, have full kitchens, and represent one of the best values in the Keys. The vinyl-covered furnishings and old-fashioned wallpapers won't win any design awards, but elegance isn't what the "real" Keys are about. The 1$^{1}/_2$ lush acres of grounds are planted with banana trees and have an outdoor heated pool and several small barbecue grills. Guests are free to use the rowboats, paddleboats, canoes, kayaks, and snorkeling equipment. Bring your own beach towels.

CAMPING

John Pennekamp Coral Reef State Park. U.S. 1 at MM 102.5 (P.O. Box 487), Key Largo, FL 33037. ☎ **305/451-1202.** 47 campsites. Phone or in-person camping reservations only. $24–$26 per site. MC, V.

One of Florida's best parks (see above), Pennekamp offers 47 well-separated campsites, half available by advance reservation, the rest distributed on a first-come, first-served basis. The car-camping sites are small but well equipped with bathrooms

The Truth About Keys Cuisine

There are few world-class chefs in the Florida Keys, but that's not to say the food isn't great. Restaurants here serve very fresh fish and a few local specialties—most notably conch fritters and chowder, Key lime pie, and stone crab claws and lobster when they're in season.

Although a commercial net-fishing ban has diminished the stock of once abundant fish in these parts, even the humblest of restaurants can be counted on to take full advantage of the gastronomic treasures of their own backyard. The Keys have everything a cook could want: the Atlantic and the Gulf of Mexico for impeccably fresh seafood; a tropical climate for year-round farmstand produce, including great tomatoes, beans, berries, and citrus fruit; and a freshwater swamp for rustic delicacies such as alligator, frog's legs, and hearts of palm.

Conch fritters and chowder are mainstays on most tourist-oriented menus. Because the queen conch was listed as an endangered species by the U.S. government in 1985, however, the conch in your dish was most likely shipped fresh-frozen from the Bahamas or the Caribbean.

Key lime pie consists of the juice of tiny yellow key limes (a fruit unique to South Florida), along with condensed milk, all in a graham cracker crust. Experts debate whether the true Key lime pie should have a whipped cream or a meringue topping, but all agree that the filling should be yellow—never green.

Florida lobster is an entirely different species from the more common Maine variety, and has a sweeter meat. You'll see only the tails on the menu because the Florida lobster has no claws. **Stone crabs** are my all-time favorite. They've been written about and talked about by kings, presidents, and poets. Although you'll find them on nearly every menu in season, consider buying a few pounds of jumbos at the fish store to take to the beach in a cooler. Don't forget to ask them to crack them for you and to get a cup of creamy mustard sauce. You'll be glad to know that after their claws are harvested, the crabs grow new claws, thus ensuring a long-lasting supply of these unique delicacies.

If you are around at the right time of year—generally, October to March for stone crabs and August to March for lobster—then every meal is sure to be fantastic. When they're fresh, it's tough to make these crustaceans anything but delicious.

and showers. A little lagoon nearby attracts many large wading birds. Reservations are held until 5pm, and the park must be notified of late arrival by phone on the check-in date. Pennekamp opens at 8am and closes around sundown. No pets.

Long Key State Recreation Area. U.S. 1 at MM 67.5 (P.O. Box 776), Long Key, FL 33001. ☎ **305/664-4815**. 60 campsites. $24–$26 per site for one to four people. MC, V.

The Upper Keys's other main state park is more secluded than its northern neighbor and more popular. All sites are located oceanside and surrounded by narrow rows of trees and nearby toilet and bath facilities. Reserve well in advance, especially in winter.

WHERE TO DINE

Although not known as a culinary hot spot, the Upper and Middle Keys do offer some excellent restaurants, many of which specialize in seafood. Often visitors (especially those who fish) take advantage of accommodations that have kitchen facilities and cook their own meals. Also, most restaurants will clean and cook your catch for a nominal charge.

VERY EXPENSIVE

✪ **Atlantic's Edge.** In the Cheeca Lodge, U.S. 1 at MM 82, Islamorada. ☎ **305/664-4651.** Reservations recommended. Main courses $20–$36. AE, CB, DC, DISC, MC, V. Daily 5:30–10pm. SEAFOOD/REGIONAL.

Ask for a table by the oceanfront window to feel really privileged at this, the most elegant restaurant in the Keys. Although the service and food are first-class, don't get dressed up—a sport coat will be fine, but isn't necessary. You can choose from an innovative, varied menu, which offers several choices of fresh fish, steak, chicken, and pastas. The crab cakes, made with stone crab when in season, are the very best in the Keys; served on a warm salad of baby greens with a mild sauce of red peppers, they're the stuff cravings are made of. Other excellent dishes include a Thai-spiced fresh baby snapper and the vegetarian angel-hair pasta with mushrooms, asparagus, and peppers in a rich broth. Service can sometimes be less than efficient, but is always courteous and professional.

EXPENSIVE

Barracuda Grill. U.S. 1 at MM 49.5 (bay side), Marathon. ☎ **305/743-3314.** Reservations not accepted. Main courses $11–$25. AE, DISC, MC, V. Mon–Sat 6–10pm. BISTRO/SEAFOOD.

Owned by Lance Hill and his wife, Jan (who used to be a sous chef at Little Palm Island), this casual spot serves excellent seafood and traditional bistro fare. It's too bad it's open only for dinner. Some of the favorite dishes are old-fashioned meat loaf, classic beef Stroganoff, rack of lamb, and seafood stew. The pork tenderloin roasted with red onions and figs is one of the menu's best selections. In addition, this small barracuda-themed restaurant features a well-priced American wine list with a vast sampling of California vintages.

✪ **Marker 88.** U.S. 1 at MM 88 (bay side), Islamorada. ☎ **305/852-9315.** Reservations not usually required. Main courses $14–$29. AE, DC, DISC, MC, V. Tues–Sun 5–11pm. SEAFOOD/REGIONAL.

An institution in the Upper Keys, Marker 88 has been pleasing locals, visitors, and critics since it opened in the early 1970s. Chef-owner Andre Mueller has created a "gourmet" restaurant in a tropical-fish house setting. The wide range of standard fare is tinged with his take on nouvelle cuisine. Taking full advantage of his island location, Andre offers dozens of seafood selections, including Keys lobster, Bahamas conch, Everglades frogs' legs, Florida Bay stone crabs, Gulf Coast shrimp, and an impressive variety of fish from around the country. After you've figured out what kind of seafood to have, you can choose from a dozen styles of preparation. The Keys's standard is *meuniere,* which is a subtle, tasty sauce of lemon and parsley. I love the more dramatic *rangoon,* with currant jelly, cinnamon, and fresh tropical fruits, including bananas and mangos. Although everything looks tempting, don't over-order—portions are huge. The waitresses, who are pleasant enough, require a bit of patience, but the food is worth it.

✪ **Morada Bay.** U.S. 1 at MM 81.6, Islamorada. ☎ **305/664-0604.** Reservations recommended for large groups. Main courses $16–$22; sandwiches $7–$8. AE, MC, V. Mon–Thurs 11:30am–10pm; Fri–Sun 11am–11pm. CARIBBEAN/AMERICAN.

This lovely bayside bistro offers a great setting for its super-fresh, innovative seafood, as well as some more basic offerings, such as chicken fajitas, hamburgers, and salads. Salads like the Sunshine Salad are large and generously lavished with slices of avocado, mango, and tomato. When in season, delicious raw oysters are imported from

Long Island. Fish dishes are always fresh. I like mine jerked with a peppery coating and nearly black finish. If you can't decide, share a few items from the tapas menu: jumbo shrimp cocktails, fried calamari, conch fritters, smoked fish dip, or a charcuterie of sausages and hams on country bread.

MODERATE

Lazy Days Oceanfront Bar and Seafood Grill. U.S. 1 at MM 79.9, Islamorada. ☎ **305/ 664-5256.** Main courses $11–$20. AE, DISC, MC, V. Tues–Sun 11:30am–10pm. SEAFOOD/ AMERICAN.

Opened in 1992, the Lazy Days quickly became one of the most popular restaurants around, mostly because of the large portions and lively atmosphere. Meals are pricier than the casual dining room would suggest, but the food is good enough and the menu varied. Steamed clams with garlic and bell peppers make a tempting appetizer. The menu focuses on—what else?—seafood, but you can also find Italian dishes. Most main courses come with baked potato, vegetables, a tossed salad, and French bread, making appetizers redundant.

☉ Lorelei Restaurant and Cabana Bar. U.S. 1 at MM 82, Islamorada. ☎ **305/664-4656.** Reservations not usually required. Main courses $9–$22. Daily 7am–10pm. Outside bar serves lunch menu 11am–9pm. Bar closes at midnight. SEAFOOD/BAR FOOD.

Don't resist the siren call of the enormous, sparkling, roadside mermaid—you won't be dashed into the rocks. This big old fish house and bar is a great place for a snack, a meal, or a beer. Inside, a good-value menu focuses mainly on seafood. When in season, lobsters are the way to go. For $20, you can get a good-sized tail—at least a 1-pounder—prepared any way you like. Other fare includes the standard clam chowder, fried shrimp, and doughy conch fritters. Salads and soups are hearty and satisfying. For those tired of fish, the menu also offers a few beef selections. The outside bar has live music every evening, and you can order snacks and light meals from a limited menu that is satisfying and well priced. Enjoy the live entertainment every night.

INEXPENSIVE

☉ Henry's Bakery and Gourmet Pizza Shop. U.S. 1 at MM 82.5 (adjacent to Days Inn), Islamorada. ☎ **305/664-4030.** Pastas $7–$9.50; pizzas $8–$18; sandwiches and salads $4.50– $8. Mon–Sat 6am–10pm (sometimes later on weekends). No credit cards. BAKERY/PIZZERIA.

It would be easy to drive right past this tiny storefront bakery, which serves the best pizzas and sandwiches in town. My favorite is freshly sliced turkey on homemade warm French bread, with a splash of superbly tangy vinaigrette. Most days Henry bakes fresh multi-grain, semolina, and Italian bread, too. Stop by early for delicious pastries and croissants. If you want pizza, consider the decadent Sublime Pie with lobster tail, roasted bell peppers, and sun-dried tomatoes. The crust has the perfect texture—just a bit chewy, but not too doughy. The shop has only one table inside, so order to go, or call for delivery in the evenings after 5pm.

☉ Islamorada Fish Company. U.S. 1 at MM 81.5 (up the street from Cheeca Lodge), Islamorada. ☎ **800/258-2559** or 305/664-9271. Main courses $8–$20. DISC, MC, V. Mon– Sat 8am–9pm; Sun 9am–9pm. Also, just up the block, **Islamorada Fish Company Restaurant & Bakery,** MM 81.6. ☎ **305/664-8363.** DISC, MC, V. Thurs–Tues 6am–9pm; Wed 6am–2pm. SEAFOOD.

The original Islamorada Fish Company has been selling seafood out of its roadside shack since 1948. It's still the best place to pick up a cooler of stone crab claws in season (October through early April). Enjoy spectacular views from picnic tables on the store's bayside dock while munching on their famous (and fattening) Islamorada fish sandwich, served with melted American cheese, fried onions, and cole slaw. A few hundred yards up the road is the newer establishment, which looks like an average diner, but has a selection of fantastic seafood and pastas. It's also the place to eat breakfast. Locals gather for politics and gossip as well as delicious grits, oatmeal, omelets, and homemade pastries (the fresh donuts are great dunked in coffee).

Key Largo's Crack'd Conch. U.S. 1 at MM 105.5 (ocean side). ☎ **305/451-0732.** Main courses $9–$13; sandwiches $5–$7. AE, MC, V. Thurs–Tues noon–10pm. SEAFOOD.

This colorful little shack looks appealing from the road and isn't a bad place to stop, especially if you like beer. Over a hundred imported and domestic lagers, porters, stouts, and ales are available. Food choices, on the other hand, are not as varied or as predictable. The Crack'd Conch will deliver decent baskets of fried clams, shrimp, chicken, and, of course, conch. Soups are okay, but certainly not made from scratch. The zesty conch salad and the messy po' boy sandwiches are the best options. Prices are higher than they ought to be, considering the quality and atmosphere, but it won't break you.

THE UPPER & MIDDLE KEYS AFTER DARK

Nightlife in the Upper Keys tends to start before the sun goes down, often at noon, since most people—visitors and locals alike—are on vacation. Also, many anglers and sports-minded folk go to bed early.

Opened in the early 1990s by some young locals tired of tourist traps, **Hog Heaven,** at MM 85.3 just off the main road on the ocean side in Islamorada (☎ **305/664-9669**), is a welcome respite from the neon-colored cocktail circuit. This whitewashed biker bar offers a waterside view and diversions that include big-screen TVs and video games. The food isn't bad, either. The atmosphere is cliquish since most patrons are regulars, so start up a game of pool or skeet to break the ice.

No trip is complete without a stop at the Tiki Bar at the **Holiday Isle Resort,** U.S. 1 at MM 84, Islamorada (☎ **800/327-7070** or 305/664-2321). Hundreds of revelers visit this oceanside spot for drinks and dancing any time of day, but the live rock music starts at 8:30pm.

In the afternoon and early evening (when everyone is either sunburned, drunk, or just happy to be alive and dancing to live reggae), head for **Kokomo's,** just next door to the thatched-roof Tiki Bar. Kokomo's often closes at 7:30pm on weekends, so get there early. For information, call the Holiday Isle Resort.

Locals and tourists mingle at the outdoor cabana bar at Lorelei's (see "Where to Dine," above). Most evenings after 5pm, you'll find local bands playing on a thatched roof stage—mainly rock and roll, Caribbean, and sometimes blues.

Woody's Saloon and Restaurant, on U.S. 1 at MM 82, Islamorada (☎ **305/664-4335**), is a lively, wacky, raunchy place serving up mediocre pizzas and live bands almost every night. The house band, Big Dick and the Extenders, showcases a 300-pound Native American who does a lewd, rude, and crude routine of jokes and songs starting at 9pm, Tuesday through Sunday. He is a legend. By the way, don't think you're lucky if you are offered the front table: It's the target seat for Big Dick's haranguing. Avoid the lame karaoke performance on Sunday and Monday evenings. There's a small cover charge most nights. Drink specials, contests, and the legendary Big Dick keep this place packed until 4am almost every night.

For a more subdued atmosphere, try the handsome wood bar at **Zane Grey's** (on the second floor of World Wide Sportsman at MM 81.5). Outside, enjoy a view of the calm waters of the bay, or inside, soak up the history of some real old anglers. Original manuscripts and photographs are displayed in mahogany cases. You feel like a real swell in this stained-glass, clubby atmosphere. It is open from 11am to 11pm, and later on weekends. Call to find out who is playing on weekends (☎ **305/ 664-4244**), when there is live entertainment and no cover charge.

4 The Lower Keys: Big Pine Key to Coppitt Key

110–140 miles SW of Miami

Big Pine, Sugarloaf, Summerland, and the other Lower Keys are less developed and more tranquil than the Upper Keys. If you're looking for haute cuisine and a happening nightlife, look elsewhere. If you're looking to commune with nature or adventure in solitude, you've come to the right place. Unlike their neighbors to the north and south, the Lower Keys are devoid of rowdy spring-break crowds, boast few T-shirt and trinket shops, and have almost no late-night bars. What they do offer are the very best opportunities to enjoy the vast natural resources—on land and water— that make the area so rich. Stay overnight in the Lower Keys, rent a boat, and explore the reefs—it might be the most memorable part of your trip.

ESSENTIALS

GETTING THERE   See "Essentials" for the Upper and Middle Keys. Continue south on U.S. 1. The Lower Keys start at the end of the Seven-Mile Bridge.

VISITOR INFORMATION   The **Lower Keys Chamber of Commerce,** ocean side of U.S. 1 at MM 31 (P.O. Box 430511), Big Pine Key, FL 33043 (☎ **800/ 872-3722** or 305/872-2411; fax 305/872-0752; E-mail: lkchamber@aol.com), is open Monday through Friday from 9am to 5pm and Saturday from 9am to 3pm. The pleasant staff will help with anything a traveler may need. Call, write, or stop in for a comprehensive, detailed information packet.

WHAT TO SEE & DO

The centerpiece of the Lower Keys and its greatest asset is **Bahia Honda State Park,** U.S. 1 at MM 37.5, Big Pine Key (☎ **305/872-2353**), which has one of the most beautiful coastlines in South Florida and one of the only natural beaches in the Keys. Bahia Honda is a great place for hiking, bird watching, swimming, snorkeling, and fishing. The 524-acre park encompasses a wide variety of ecosystems, including coastal mangroves, beach dunes, and tropical hammocks. There are miles of trails packed with unusual plants and animals and a small white beach. Although the beach is never wider than 5 feet even at low tide, this is one of the Keys' best beach areas. Shaded seaside picnic areas are fitted with tables and grills.

True to its name (Spanish for "deep bay"), the park has relatively deep waters close to shore that are perfect for snorkeling and diving. Head to the stunning reefs at Looe Key where the coral and fish are more vibrant than anywhere in the United States. Snorkeling trips depart daily from March through September and cost $22 for adults, $18 for youths 6 to 14, and free for children 5 and under. Call ☎ **305/872-3210** for a schedule.

Admission to the park is $4 per vehicle (and 50¢ per person), $1.50 per pedestrian or bicyclist, free for children 5 and under. Open daily from 8am to sunset.

The most famous residents of the Lower Keys are the tiny Key deer. Of the estimated 300 existing in the world, two thirds live on Big Pine Key's **National Key Deer Refuge.** To get your bearings, stop by the rangers' office at the Winn-Dixie Shopping Plaza near MM 30.5 off U.S. 1. They'll give you an informative brochure and map of the area. It is open Monday through Friday from 8am to 5pm.

If the office is closed, head out to the Blue Hole, a former rock quarry now filled with the fresh water that's vital to the deer's survival. To get there, turn right at Big Pine Key's only traffic light onto Key Deer Boulevard (take the left fork immediately after the turn), and continue 1½ miles to the observation site parking lot, on your left. The half-mile Watson Hammock Trail, about a third of a mile past the Blue Hole, is the refuge's only marked footpath. Try coming out here in the early morning or late evening to catch a glimpse of these gentle, dog-sized deer. Refuge lands are open daily from half an hour before sunrise to half an hour after sunset. Whatever you do, do not feed the deer—it will threaten their survival. Call the park office (☎ **305/872-2239**) to find out about the infrequent free tours of the refuge, scheduled at different times throughout the year.

The only human-made attraction in the Lower Keys is the **Sugarloaf Bat Tower,** off U.S. 1 at MM 17 (next to Sugarloaf Airport on the bay side). In a vain effort to battle the ubiquitous troublesome mosquitoes in the Lower Keys, developer Clyde Perkey built this odd structure to lure bug-eating bats. Despite his alluring design and a pungent bat aphrodisiac, his guests never showed. Since 1929, this wooden, flat-topped, 45-foot-high pyramid has stood empty and deserted, except for the occasional tourist who stops to wonder what it is. There is no sign or marker to commemorate this odd remnant of ingenuity. It's worth a 5-minute detour to see it. To get there, turn right at the Sugarloaf Airport sign, and then right again onto the dirt road that begins just before the airport gate; the tower is about 100 yards ahead.

OUTDOOR ACTIVITIES A-Z

BICYCLING   If you have your own bike, or your lodging offers rental (many do), the Lower Keys is a great place to get off busy U.S. 1 to explore the beautiful back roads. On Big Pine Key, cruise along Key Deer Boulevard (at MM 30). Those with fat tires can ride into the National Key Deer Refuge.

BIRD WATCHING   Bring your birding books. A stopping point for migratory birds on the Eastern Flyway, the Lower Keys are populated with many West Indian bird species, especially during spring and fall. The small vegetated islands of the Keys are the only nesting sites in the United States for the great white heron and the white-crowned pigeon. They're also some of the very few breeding places for the reddish egret, the roseate spoonbill, the mangrove cuckoo, and the black-whiskered vireo. Look for them on Bahia Honda and the many uninhabited islands nearby.

BOATING   Dozens of shops rent powerboats for fishing and reef exploring. Most also rent tackle, sell bait, and have charter captains available. **Bud Boats,** at the Old Wooden Bride Fishing Camp and Marina, MM 30 in Big Pine Key (☎ **305/ 872-9165**), has a wide selection of well-maintained boats. Depending on the size, rentals cost between $70 and $250 for a day, between $50 and $130 for a half day. Another good option is **Jaybird's Powerboats,** U.S. 1 at MM 33, Big Pine Key (☎ **305/872-8500**). They rent for full days only. Prices start at $127 for a 19-footer.

CANOEING & KAYAKING   The Overseas Highway (U.S. 1) touches on only a few dozen of the many hundreds of islands that make up the Keys. To really see the Lower Keys, rent a kayak or canoe—perfect for these shallow and exciting waters. **Reflections Kayak Nature Tours,** operating out of Parmer's Place Resort Motel, on U.S. 1 at MM 28.5, Little Torch Key (☎ **305/872-2896**), offers fully outfitted backcountry wildlife tours, either on your own or with an expert. A former U.S. Forest Service guide, Mike Wedeking, keeps up an engaging discussion describing the area's fish, sponges, coral, osprey, hawks, eagles, alligators, raccoons, and deer. The 3-hour tours cost $45 per person and include spring water, fresh fruit, granola bars, and use of binoculars. Bring a towel and sea sandals or sneakers.

FISHING   A day spent fishing, either in the shallow backcountry or in the deep sea, is a great way to ensure yourself a fresh fish dinner, or you can release your catch and just appreciate the challenge. **Larry Threlkeld's Strike Zone Charters,** U.S. 1 at MM 29.5, Big Pine Key (☎ 305/872-9863), is one of the area's best chartered boats in either the deep sea or the backcountry. Prices start at $250 to $400 for a half day. Especially if you have enough anglers to share the price, it isn't too steep. They may be able to match you with other interested visitors. Call a day or two in advance to see. Reef fishing trips are also offered by **Scandia-Tomi,** U.S. 1 at MM 25, Summerland Key (☎ 305/745-8633; fax 305/872-0520). They have a six-passenger maximum.

HIKING   You can hike throughout the flat marshy Keys, on both marked trails and meandering coastlines. The best places to trek through nature are **Bahia Honda State Park** at MM 29.5 and **National Key Deer Refuge** at MM 30 (for more information on both, see "What to See & Do," above). Bahia Honda Park has a free brochure describing an excellent self-guided tour along the Silver Palm Nature Trail. You'll traverse hammocks, mangroves, and sand dunes and cross a lagoon. You can do the walk (which is less than a mile) in under half an hour and can explore a great cross-section of the natural habitat in the Lower Keys.

SNORKELING/DIVING   Snorkelers and divers should not miss the Keys' most dramatic reefs at the Looe Key National Marine Sanctuary. Here you'll see more than 150 varieties of hard and soft coral, some centuries old, as well as every type of tropical fish, including the gold and blue parrot fish, moray eels, barracudas, French angels, and tarpon. **Looe Key Dive Center,** U.S. 1 at MM 27.5, Ramrod Key (☎ 305/872-2215), offers a mind-blowing 2¹/₂-hour tour aboard a 45-foot catamaran with two shallow 1-hour dives for snorkelers and scuba divers. Snorkelers pay $30, and divers with their own equipment pay $65. Good-quality rentals are available. (See "What to See & Do," above, for other diving options.)

SHOPPING

Certainly not known for great shopping, the Lower Keys do happen to be home to many good visual artists, particularly those who specialize in depicting their natural surroundings. **The Artists in Paradise Gallery,** on Big Pine Key in the Winn-Dixie Shopping Plaza, near MM 30.5, 1 block north of U.S. 1 at the traffic light (☎ 305/872-1828), displays an ever-changing selection of watercolors, oils, photos, and sculptures. This cooperative gallery displays the work of more than a dozen artists who share the task of watching the store. Usually hours are daily from 10am to 6pm. Even more impressive is the ✪ **Gallery at Kona Kai** (see "Where to Stay," below), which shows dramatic black-and-white photos, oils, watercolors, and more.

WHERE TO STAY

There are a number of cheap fish shacks along the highway for those who want bare-bones accommodations. So far, there are no national hotel chains in the Lower Keys. For information on lodging in cabins or trailers at local campgrounds, see "Camping," below.

VERY EXPENSIVE

✪ **Little Palm Island.** Launch is at the ocean side of U.S. 1 at MM 28.5, Little Torch Key, FL 33042. ☎ 800/343-8567 or 305/872-2524. Fax 305/872-4843. 28 bungalows, 2 houseboat suites. A/C MINIBAR. Winter $495–$625 suite; off-season $400–$425 suite. No children under 16. AE, CB, DC, DISC, MC, V.

Under new ownership since 1997, Little Palm Island received a much-needed renovation, which included new roofs, a new dining room, and a thorough update of the guest rooms. This exclusive resort—host to presidents and royalty—is not just a place to stay while in the Lower Keys; it is a resort destination all its own. Built on a private 5-acre island, it's accessible only by boat. Guests stay in thatched-roof villas amid lush foliage and flowering tropical plants. Many villas have ocean views and private sundecks with rope hammocks. Inside, the romantic suites have all the comforts and conveniences of a luxurious contemporary beach cottage, but without telephones, TVs, or alarm clocks. Note that on the breezeless south side of the island, you may get invaded by mosquitoes, even in the winter. Bring spray and lightweight long-sleeved clothing. Known for its innovative and pricey food, Little Palm also hosts guests just for dinner or lunch. If you are staying on the island, opt for the full American plan, which includes three meals a day for about $100 per person. If you pay à la carte, you could spend that much just on dinner. At these prices, Little Palm appeals to those who aren't keeping track. Note that children are not welcome.

Dining/Diversions: The Little Palm Restaurant offers fine dining either indoors or alfresco at inflated prices. A pool bar offers refreshments and light snacks all day.

Amenities: Concierge, room service, dry cleaning, laundry, newspaper delivery, twice-daily maid service, in-room massage, courtesy van from Key West or Marathon airport. Outdoor pool with small waterfall, wide beach, in-room Jacuzzi tubs, sauna, sundeck, water-sports equipment, jogging trail, boutique.

MODERATE

Barnacle Bed & Breakfast. 1557 Long Beach Dr. (P.O. Box 780), Big Pine Key, FL 33043. ☎ **800/465-9100** or 305/872-3298. Fax 305/872-3863. 4 units. A/C TV TEL. Winter $95–$125 double; off-season $85–$125 double. No children under 16. Rates include breakfast. DISC, MC, V. From U.S. 1 south, turn left at the Spanish Harbor Bridge (MM 33) onto Long Beach Rd. Look left for the stone wall and signs to the house on the left.

Joan Cornell, the Barnacle's owner, was once an innkeeper in Vermont; she knows what amenities travelers are looking for and goes out of her way to accommodate. Her Big Pine Key home has only four bedrooms, each with its own character. Two are upstairs in the main house—their doors open into the home's living room, which contains a small Jacuzzi-style tub. For privacy, the remaining two rooms are best; each has its own entrance and is out of earshot of the common areas. The Cottage Room, a free-standing, peak-topped bedroom, is best, outfitted with a kitchenette and pretty furnishings. The accommodations are standard, not luxurious. All rooms have small refrigerators and private baths. The property has its own private sandy beach where you can float all day on the inn's rafts, rubber boat, or kayak. Beach towels, chairs, bicycles, and coolers are available at no charge. Children are not welcome.

Deer Run Bed and Breakfast. Long Beach Dr. (P.O. Box 431), Big Pine Key, FL 33043. ☎ **305/872-2015.** Fax 305/872-2842. E-mail: deerrunbb@aol.com. 3 units. Winter, from $110 double; off-season, from $95 double. No children under 16. Rates include full American breakfast. No credit cards. From U.S. 1 south, turn left at the Big Pine Fishing Lodge (MM 33); continue for about 2 miles.

Located directly on the beach, Sue Abbott's small, homey, smoke-free B&B is a real find. One upstairs and two downstairs guest rooms are comfortably furnished with queen-size beds, good closets, and touch-sensitive lamps. Rattan and 1970s-style chairs and couches furnish the living room, along with 13 birds and three cats. Breakfast, which is served on a pretty, fenced-in porch, is cooked to order by Sue herself. The wooded area around the property is full of deer, which are often spotted on the beach as well. Ask to use one of the bikes to explore nearby nature trails. The owner prefers adults and mature children only.

INEXPENSIVE

✪ **Parmer's Place Cottages.** Barry Ave. (P.O. Box 430665), near MM 28.5, Little Torch Key, FL 33043. ☎ **305/872-2157.** Fax 305/872-2014. 41 units. In winter and during festivals, from $77 double, from $93.50 efficiency; off-season, $55–$65 double, from $75 efficiency. AE, DISC, MC, V. Turn right onto Barry Ave. Resort is a half mile down on the right.

Parmer's, a fixture here for more than 20 years, is well known for its charming hospitality and helpful staff. This downscale resort offers modest but comfortable cottages. Every unit is different. Some face the water, some are a few steps away from the water, some have small kitchenettes, and others are just a bedroom. Room 26, a one-bedroom efficiency, is especially nice, with a small sitting area that faces the water. Room 6, a small efficiency, has a little kitchenette and an especially large bathroom. The rooms all have linoleum floors, dated 1970s-style painted rattan furnishings, fake flowers, and thrift-store art. They're very clean. Many can be combined to accommodate large families. Facilities include a horseshoes court, boat ramp, and a heated swimming pool.

CAMPING

Bahia Honda State Park (☎ **305/872-2353**) offers some of the best camping in the Keys. It is as loaded with facilities and activities as it is with campers. However, don't be discouraged by its popularity—this park encompasses more than 500 acres of land. There are 80 campsites and six spacious and comfortable cabin units. If you're lucky enough to get one, the park's cabins represent a very good value. Each holds up to eight guests and comes complete with linens, kitchenettes, and utensils. Ask for a cabin overlooking the bay, which offers the best views and most privacy. You'll enjoy the wraparound terrace, barbecue pit, and rocking chairs.

Camping here costs about $25 per site for one to four people without electricity and $26 with electricity. Depending on the season, cabin prices change: From December 15 to September 14, it's about $125 per cabin for one to four people; from September 15 to December 14, it's $97.28 per cabin. Additional people (over four) cost $6. MasterCard and Visa are accepted.

Another excellent value can be found at the **KOA Sugarloaf Key Resort,** near MM 20. This oceanside facility has 200 fully equipped sites that rent for about $53 a night (no-hook-up sites cost about $36). Or pitch a tent on the 5 acres of lush waterfront property. The resort also rents out travel trailers. The 22-foot Dutchmen sleeps six and is equipped with eating and cooking utensils. It costs about $100 a day. More luxurious trailers go for $160 a day. All major credit cards are accepted. For details, contact P.O. Box 420469, Summerland Key, FL 33042 (☎ **800/562-7731** or 305/745-3549; fax 305/745-9889; E-mail: sugarloaf@koa.net).

WHERE TO DINE

There aren't many fine dining options in the Lower Keys, but the following are worth a stop for those passing through.

MODERATE

✪ **Mangrove Mama's Restaurant.** U.S. 1 at MM 20, Sugarloaf Key. ☎ **305/745-3030.** Main courses $13–$19; lunch $2–$9; brunch $5–$7. MC, V. Daily 11:30am–10pm (11am in season). SEAFOOD/CARIBBEAN.

As dedicated locals who come daily for happy hour will tell you, Mangrove Mama's is a true Lower Keys institution and a dive in the best sense of the word. The restaurant is a shack that used to have a gas pump as well as a grill. Now, guests share the property with some miniature horses (out back) and stray cats. A handful of simple tables, inside and out, are shaded by banana trees and palm fronds. Fish is, not surprisingly, the menu's mainstay, although soups, salads, sandwiches, and omelets are also good. Grilled teriyaki chicken and club sandwiches are tasty alternatives to fish, as are meatless chef's salads and spicy barbecued baby-back ribs.

✪ **Monte's.** U.S 1 at MM 25, Summerland Key. ☎ **305/745-3731.** Main courses $10–$14; lunch $3–$8. No credit cards. Mon–Sat 9:30am–10pm; Sun 10am–9pm. SEAFOOD.

Monte's has survived for more than 20 years because the food is very good and incredibly fresh. Certainly nobody goes to this restaurant/fish market for its atmosphere: Plastic place settings rest on plastic-covered picnic-style tables in a screen-enclosed dining patio. The day's catch may include shark, tuna, lobster, stone crabs, or shrimp.

INEXPENSIVE

✪ **Coco's Kitchen.** 283 Key Deer Blvd. (in the Winn-Dixie Shopping Center), Big Pine Key. ☎ **305/872-4495.** Main courses $5–$12; lunch $2–$5; breakfast $1–$4.50. No credit cards. Mon–Sat 7am–7:30pm. Turn right at the traffic light near MM 30.5. Stay in the left lane. CUBAN/NICARAGUAN.

This tiny storefront has been dishing out black beans and rice and shredded beef to Cuban food fans for more than 10 years. The owners, who are actually from Nicaragua, cook not only superior Cuban food but also some local specialties, Italian food, and Caribbean food. The best bet is the daily special, which may be roasted pork or fresh grouper, served with rice and beans or salad and crispy fries. Top off the huge, cheap meal with a rich caramel-soaked flan.

No Name Pub. ¹/₄ mile south of No Name Bridge on N. Watson Blvd., Big Pine Key. ☎ **305/872-9115.** Pizzas $8–$18; subs $5. MC, V. 11am–11pm. Turn right at Big Pine's only traffic light (near MM30.5) onto Key Deer Blvd. Turn right on Watson Blvd. At stop sign, turn left. Look for a small wooden sign on the left marking the spot. PUB FOOD/PIZZA.

This funky old bar out in the boonies serves snacks and sandwiches until 11pm on most nights and drinks until midnight. Pizzas are tasty—thick-crusted and super-cheesy. Try one topped with local shrimps, or consider a bowl of chili with all the fixings—hearty and cheap. Also decent is the smoked fish dip. Everything is served on paper plates. Locals hang out at the rustic bar, one of the Florida Keys's oldest, drinking beer and listening to a jukebox heavy with 1980s selections. The decor—if you can call it that—is basic. Walls and ceilings are plastered with thousands of autographed dollar bills. Ask the waitress for a stapler to affix yours. At sunset, look outside and you may see one of the famed Key deer.

THE LOWER KEYS AFTER DARK

Although the mellow islands of the lower Keys aren't exactly known for wild nightlife, there are some friendly bars and restaurants where locals and tourists gather to hang out and drink.

One of the most scenic is **Sandbar** (☎ **305/872-9989**), a wide-open breezy wooden house built on slender stilts and overlooking a wide channel on Barry Avenue (near MM 28.5). It attracts an odd mix of bikers and blue-hairs daily from 11am until 11pm. Pool tables are the main attraction, but there's also live music some nights. The drinks are reasonably priced and the food isn't too bad, either. For another fun bar scene, see **No Name Pub,** listed above in "Where to Dine."

5 Key West

The locals, or "conchs" (pronounced "conks"), and the developers here have been at odds for years. This once low-key island has been thoroughly commercialized—there's a Hard Rock Cafe smack in the middle of Duval Street and thousands of cruise ship passengers descending on Mallory Square each day. It's definitely not the seedy town Hemingway and his cronies once called their own.

Laid-back Key West still exists, but it's now found in different places: the backyard of a popular guesthouse, for example, or an art gallery, or a secret garden, or the hip hangouts of Bahama Village. And, of course, there's always the sea.

The heart of town offers a more wild time. Here you'll find good restaurants, fun bars, live music, rickshaw rides, and lots of shopping. Don't bother with a watch or tie. This is the home of the perennial vacation.

ESSENTIALS

GETTING THERE   For directions by car, see "Essentials" for the Upper and Middle Keys, above. Continue south on U.S. 1. When entering Key West, stay in the far-right lane onto North Roosevelt Boulevard, which becomes Truman Avenue in Old Town. Continue for a few blocks, and you will find yourself on Duval Street, in the heart of the city. If you stay to the left, you'll also reach the city center after passing the airport and historic houseboat row, where a motley collection of boats make up one of Key West's most interesting neighborhoods.

Several regional airlines fly nonstop from Miami to Key West; fares are about $120 to $300 round-trip. **American Eagle** (☎ **800/443-7300**) and **US Airways Express** (☎ **800/428-4322**) land at **Key West International Airport,** South Roosevelt Boulevard (☎ **305/296-5439**), on the southeastern corner of the island.

Greyhound (☎ **800/231-2222**) has buses leaving Miami for Key West every day. At press time, prices were $32 one-way and $60 round-trip. Seats fill up in season, so come early. It's first come, first served.

GETTING AROUND   With limited parking, narrow streets, and congested traffic, driving in Key West can be a nightmare. Consider ditching the car for a bicycle. The island is small and as flat as a board, which makes it easy to negotiate, especially away from the crowded downtown. Many tourists also choose to cruise by moped, an option that can make navigating the streets risky, especially since there are no helmet laws in Key West. Spend the extra money and rent a helmet; there are hundreds of serious accidents each year.

Rates for simple one-speed cruisers start at about $6 per day (from $30 per week). Tacky, pink mopeds start at about $25 per day and $100 per week. The best shops include **The Bike Shop,** 1110 Truman Ave. (☎ **305/294-1073**); the **Moped Hospital,** 601 Truman Ave. (☎ **305/296-3344**); and **Tropical Bicycles & Scooter Rentals,** 1300 Duval St. (☎ **305/294-8136**).

PARKING   Note that parking in Key West's Old Town is particularly limited. There is a well-placed **municipal parking lot** at Simonton and Angela streets just behind the firehouse and police station. You may want to stash your car there while you enjoy the very walkable downtown section of Key West.

VISITOR INFORMATION   The **Florida Keys and Key West Visitors Bureau,** P.O. Box 1147, Key West, FL 33041 (☎ **800/FLA-KEYS**), offers a free vacation kit packed with visitor information. **The Key West Chamber of Commerce,** 402 Wall St., Key West, FL 33040 (☎ **800/527-8539** or 305/294-2587), also offers both

Attractions

Aquarium  18
Audubon House & Tropical Gardens 23
Cemetery 9
Chamber of Commerce 21
East Martello Museum and Gallery 2
Ernest Hemingway Home and Museum 25
Fort Zachary Beach 29
Higgs Beach 6
Lighthouse Museum 26
Mallory Square 19
Mel Fisher Maritime Heritage Museum 22
Smathers Beach 3

Accommodations

Big Ruby's 24
The Brass Key 4
Blue Lagoon Resort 1
Chelsea House 12
The Grand 5
Island City House Hotel 7
Key West Hilton Resort & Marina 20
Key West International Hostel 13
La Pensione 10
Marquesa Hotel 11
Marriott's Beach Resort 15
Oasis 8
Ocean Key House 17
Pier House Resort & Caribbean Spa 16
Rainbow House 14
South Beach Oceanfront Motel 28
Southernmost Point Guest House 27

general and specialized information. The lobby is open daily from 8:30am to 6pm; phones are answered from 8am to 8pm. **The Key West Visitors Center** also provides information on accommodations, goings-on, and restaurants; the number is ☎ **800/LAST-KEY**. It's open weekdays from 8am to 5:30pm and weekends from 8:30am to 5pm. Gay travelers will want to call the **Key West Business Guild** (☎ **305/294-4603**), which represents more than 50 guesthouses and B&Bs in town, as well as many other gay-owned businesses. Ask for its 52-page color brochure. Or try **Good Times Travel** (☎ **305/294-0980**), which will set up lodging and package tours on the island.

ORIENTATION   A mere 2- by 4-mile island, Key West is simple to navigate, even though there is no real order to the arrangement of streets and avenues. As you enter town on U.S. 1 (also called Roosevelt Boulevard), you will see most of the moderately priced chain hotels and fast-food restaurants. The better restaurants, shops, and outfitters are crammed onto Duval Street, the main thoroughfare of Key West's Old Town. On surrounding streets are the many inns and lodges in picturesque

Victorian/Bahamian homes. On the southern side of the island is the coral beach area and some of the larger resort hotels.

The area called Caribbean Village has only recently become open to tourists. With several cool restaurants and guesthouses opened over the years, this hippie-ish neighborhood, complete with street-roaming chickens and cats, is the most urban and rough you'll find in the keys. You might see a few seedy drug dealings on street corners, but it's nothing to be overly concerned with. Resident business owners tend to keep a vigilant eye on the neighborhood. It looks worse than it is.

SEEING THE SIGHTS

✪ Audubon House & Tropical Gardens. 205 Whitehead St. (between Greene and Caroline sts.). ☎ **305/294-2116.** Admission $7.50 adults; $3.50 children 6–12. Daily 9:30–5pm (last admission at 4:45pm). Discounts for students and AAA and AARP members.

This well-preserved home dating from the early 19th century stands as a prime example of early Key West architecture. Named after the renowned painter and bird expert, John James Audubon, who was said to have visited the house in 1832, the graceful two-story home is a peaceful retreat from the bustle of nearby Duval Street and Mallory Square. Included in the price of admission is a self-guided audio-tape tour that lasts just under half an hour. With voices of several characters from the house's past, the tour never gets boring—although it is at times a bit hokey. See rare Audubon prints, gorgeous antiques, historical photos, and lush tropical gardens and, while you're at it, learn a little about the island's colorful history. Even if you don't want to spend the time and money to explore the grounds and home, check out the impressive gift shop, which sells a variety of fine mementos at reasonable prices.

Ernest Hemingway Home and Museum. 907 Whitehead St. (between Truman Ave. and Olivia St.). ☎ **305/294-1575** or 305/294-1136. Admission $6.50 adults; $4 children. Daily 9am–5pm.

One-time Key West resident Ernest Hemingway has become somewhat of a tourist icon down here; the novelist's gruff image is emblazoned on T-shirts and mugs and is used to sell everything from beer to suntan lotion. Hemingway's particularly handsome stone Spanish Colonial house, built in 1851, was one of the first on the island to be fitted with indoor plumbing and a built-in fireplace. The author lived here from 1928 until 1940, along with about 50 six-toed cats, whose descendants still roam the premises. It was during those years that the Nobel Prize winner wrote some of his most famous works, including *For Whom the Bell Tolls, A Farewell to Arms,* and "The Snows of Kilimanjaro." Fans may want to take the optional half-hour tour. It's interesting and included in the price of admission.

Key West Cemetery. Entrance at Margaret and Angela sts. Free admission. Daily dawn to dusk. Tours can be arranged by calling **305/294-WALK.**

This funky picturesque cemetery is the epitome of the quirky Key West image, as irreverent as it is humorous. Many tombs are stacked several high, condominium style—the rocky soil made digging 6 feet under nearly impossible for early settlers. Pets are often buried beside their owners. Many of the memorials are emblazoned with nicknames, a common Key West informality literally taken to the grave. Look for headstones labeled "The Tailor," "Bean," "Shorty," and "Bunny." Other headstones also reflect residents' lighthearted attitudes toward life and death. "I Told You I Was Sick" is one of the more famous epitaphs, as is the tongue-in-cheek widow's inscription "At Least I Know Where He's Sleeping Tonight."

East Martello Museum and Gallery. 3501 S. Roosevelt Blvd. ☎ **305/296-3913.** Admission $6 adults; $2 children 8–12; free for children 7 and under. Daily 9:30am–5pm (last admission is at 4pm).

Adjacent to the airport, the East Martello Museum is located in a Civil-War–era brick fort that itself is worth a visit. The museum contains a bizarre variety of exhibits that collectively do a thorough job interpreting the city's intriguing past. Historical artifacts include model ships, a deep-sea diver's wooden air pump, a crude raft from a Cuban "boat lift," a supposedly haunted doll, a Key West–style children's playhouse from 1918, and a horse-drawn hearse. Exhibits illustrate the Keys's history of salvaging, sponging, and cigar making. And if all that's not enough, the museum also exhibits modern works by local artists. After seeing the galleries, climb a steep spiral staircase to the top of a lookout tower for good views over the island and ocean.

☼ **Key West Aquarium.** 1 Whitehead St. (at Mallory Square). ☎ **305/296-2051.** Admission $8 adults; $4 children 4–12; free for children under 4. Tickets are good for 2 consecutive days. Look for discount coupons from local hotels, at Duval Street kiosks, and from trolley and train tours. Daily 10am–6pm.

The oldest attraction on the island, the Key West Aquarium is a modest but fascinating exhibit. A long hallway of eye-level displays showcase dozens of variety of fish and crustaceans. See delicate sea horses swaying in the backlit tanks. Kids can touch sea cucumbers and sea anemones in a shallow touch tank in the entryway. If you can, catch one of the free guided tours offered daily at 11am, 1pm, 3pm, and 4pm, when you can witness the dramatic feeding frenzy of the sharks, tarpon, barracudas, stingrays, and turtles. Tickets are good for 2 consecutive days, a bonus for kids with short attention spans.

Key West Lighthouse Museum. 938 Whitehead St. ☎ **305/294-0012.** Admission $6 adults; $2 children 7–12; free for children 6 and under. Daily 9:30am–5pm (last admission at 4:30pm).

When the Key West Lighthouse was opened in 1848, many locals mourned. Its bright warning to ships signaled the end of a profitable era for wreckers, pirate salvagers who looted reef-stricken ships. The story of this, and other Keys lighthouses, is illustrated in a small museum that was formerly the keeper's quarters. When radar and sonar made the lighthouse obsolete, it was opened to visitors as a tourist attraction. It's worth mustering the energy to climb the 88 claustrophobic steps to the top, where you'll be rewarded with magnificent panoramic views of Key West and the ocean.

☼ **Mel Fisher Maritime Heritage Museum.** 200 Greene St. ☎ **305/294-2633.** Admission $6.50 adults; $2 children 6–12; free for children 5 and under. Open daily 9:30am–5pm.

This museum honors local hero Mel Fisher, who, along with a crew of other salvagers, found a multimillion-dollar treasure trove in 1985 aboard the wreck of the Spanish galleon *Nuestra Señora de Atocha.* The admission price is somewhat steep, but if you're into diving, pirates, and the mystery of sunken treasures, check out this small informative museum, full of doubloons, pieces of eight, emeralds, and solid-gold bars. A dated but informative film provides a good background of Fisher's incredible story. The museum also features a new exhibit about the USS *Maine* titled "Battleship."

ORGANIZED TOURS

BY TROLLEY-BUS   Yes, it's more than a bit hokey to sit in these red cars, but it's worth the embarrassment. The city's whole story is packed into a neat, 90-minute package on the **Conch Tour Train,** which covers the island and all its rich, raunchy history. The "train's" engine is a propane-powered jeep disguised as a locomotive. Tours depart from both Mallory Square and the Welcome Center, near where

Hanging Out in Key West

The primary activity in Key West is relaxing. Most visitors, whether they have come from Dusseldorf or Fort Lauderdale, look forward to a trip here to escape the hectic pace of "real" life. The island does not disappoint.

Many folks never venture farther than their lodging's poolside. In fact, many accommodations host evening happy hours to encourage guests to stay put. But with hundreds of outdoor cafes and bars in and around the city center, there are many wonderful spots to hang out in Key West. Duval Street is the hub.

A tradition in Key West, the **Mallory Square Sunset Celebration** can be relaxing or overwhelming, depending on your vantage point. Every evening, locals and visitors gather at the docks behind Mallory Square (at the westernmost end of Duval Street) to celebrate the day gone by. Secure a spot on the docks to experience the carnival of portrait artists, acrobats, food vendors, and animal acts. Better yet, get a seat at the Hilton's **Sunset Deck** (☎ **305/294-4000**), a luxurious bar on top of its restaurant at the intersection of Front and Greene streets. From the civilized calm of a casual bar, you can look down on the mayhem with a drink in hand.

If you want to get away from crowds altogether, head to the beaches at the southern end of the island. At **Indigenous Park,** at Atlantic Avenue and White Street, you can catch an assortment of locals playing bocce on many weekday evenings. They aren't your stereotypical set of old Italian cronies, either. "Organized" teams compete for a championship title between late August and December and from January through May. Stop by after 6pm to watch a few sets. At other times, bring a picnic or a good book and enjoy the quiet ocean views.

Perhaps the most perfect retreat for any weary traveler is **Nancy's Secret Garden,** a peaceful tropical shade garden nestled in Key West's busy downtown. Nancy Forrester opened her haven to the public in 1994 in an effort to raise money to keep up the maintenance on this 1-acre miracle. She calls the beautifully maintained site, which includes a small gallery and gift shop, a work of "installation art." There are no explanatory signs or recorded descriptions. This is a place for people who aren't looking to be educated, entertained, or enlightened. With the help of dedicated volunteers, she keeps the place open from 10am until 5pm every day. For a fee of $6, picnickers, nature lovers, or tourist-weary travelers can escape to the serene spot. To get there, walk down Duval Street, away from Mallory Square. Turn left on Fleming, and after one long block, turn right onto Simonton Street (just behind the Marquesa Hotel). On your left is a tiny alley named Free School Lane. The garden is just beyond the swinging wooden gates. There may or may not be a sign—Nancy can't decide.

U.S. 1 becomes North Roosevelt Boulevard, on the other side of the island. For more information, contact the Conch Train at 1 Key Lime Sq., Key West (☎ **305/294-5161;** fax 305/292-8993). The cost is $15 for adults, $7 for children 4 to 12, and free for children 3 and under. Daily departures are every half hour from 9am to 4:30pm.

The other option to get a good perspective on this history-packed island is the **Old Town Trolley.** Drivers maintain a running commentary as the open-air tram loops around the island's streets past all the major sights. The main advantage of this 90-minute tour is that riders can get off at any of 14 stops, explore a museum or visit a restaurant, and then reboard later at will. Trolleys depart from Mallory Square and other points around the island. For details, contact them at 1910 N. Roosevelt Blvd. (☎ **305/296-6688**). Tours are $16 for adults, $7 for children 4 to 12, and free for children 3 and under. Departures are daily every half hour (though not always on the hour or half hour) from 9am to 4pm.

BY AIR   Proclaimed by the mayor as "the official air force of the Conch Republic," **Island Airplane Tours,** at Key West Airport, 3469 S. Roosevelt Blvd. (☎ **305/294-8687** for reservations), offers windy rides in its open-cockpit 1940 Waco biplanes over the reefs and around the islands. Thrill seekers—and they only—will also enjoy a spin in the company's S2-B aerobatics airplane that does loops, rolls, and sideways figure-eights. Company owner Fred Cabanas was "decorated" in 1991, after he spotted a Cuban airman defecting to the United States in a Russian-built MiG fighter. Sightseeing flights cost $50 to $200, depending on the duration.

BY BOAT   The **Pride of Key West/Fireball,** at 2 Duval St. (☎ **305/296-6293;** fax 305/294-8704), is a 58-foot glass-bottomed catamaran that goes on both day and evening coral-reef tours and sunset cruises. Reef trips cost $20 per person; sunset cruises are $25 per person and include snacks, sodas, and a glass of champagne.

The **Wolf,** at Schooner Wharf, Key West Seaport (☎ **305/296-9653;** fax 305/294-8388), is a 44-passenger topsail schooner, equipped with a cannon, that sets sail daily for daytime and sunset cruises around the Keys. Key West Seaport is located at the end of Greene Street. Day tours cost $25 per person; sunset sails cost $30 per person and include champagne, wine, beer, soda, and live music.

OTHER TOURS   For a lively look at Key West, try a 2-hour tour of the island's five **most famous pubs.** It starts daily at 2:30pm, lasts 1 1/2 hours, costs $21, and includes four drinks. Another fun tour, for those interested in the paranormal, is the nightly **ghost tour.** Cost is $18 for adults and $10 for children. Guests report sightings periodically. Both tours are offered by Key West Tour Association. New in 1998 is a **cemetery tour** at 10:30am (☎ **305/294 WALK**).

SPORTS & OUTDOOR ACTIVITIES

BICYCLING & MOPEDING   A popular mode of transportation for locals and visitors, bikes and mopeds are available at many rental outlets in the city (see "Getting Around," above). Escape the hectic downtown scene and explore the island's scenic side streets. Head away from Duval Street to South Roosevelt Boulevard and the beachside enclaves along the way.

BEACHES   At the end of the chain of Keys are finally a few beaches, although they do not compare to the state's wide natural wonders up the coast. Here are your beach-going options: **Smathers Beach,** off South Roosevelt Boulevard west of the airport; **Higgs Beach,** along Atlantic Boulevard between White Street and Reynolds Road; and **Fort Zachary Beach,** located off the western end of Southard Boulevard.

Although there is an entrance fee ($3.75 per car, plus more for each passenger), I recommend Fort Zachary, since it also includes a great historical fort, a Civil War museum, and a large picnic area with tables, barbecue grills, bathrooms, and showers.

DIVING   One of the area's largest scuba schools, **Dive Key West Inc.,** 3128 N. Roosevelt Blvd. (☎ **800/426-0707** or 305/296-3823; fax 305/296-0609; E-mail: divekeywest@flakeysol.com; divekeywest.com), offers instruction on all levels. Its dive boats take participants to scuba and snorkel sites on nearby reefs.

Wreck dives and night dives are two of the special offerings of **Lost Reef Adventures,** 261 Margaret St. (☎ **800/952-2749** or 305/296-9737). Regularly scheduled runs and private charters can be arranged. Phone for departure information.

FISHING   As any angler will tell you, there's no fishing like Keys fishing. Key West has it all: bonefish, tarpon, dolphin, tuna, grouper, cobia, and more. Sharks, too. When it comes to fishing, this is it.

Step aboard a small exposed skiff for an incredibly diverse day of fishing. In the morning, you can head offshore for sailfish or dolphin, and then by afternoon, get closer to land for a shot at tarpon, permit, grouper, or snapper. Here in Key West, you can probably pick up more cobia—one of the best fighting and eating fishes around—than anywhere else in the world. For a real fight, ask your skipper to go for the tarpon—the greatest fighting fish there is, famous for its dramatic "tail walk" on the water after it's hooked. Shark fishing is also popular.

You'll find plenty of competition among the charter fishing boats in and around Mallory Square. However, you should know that the bookers from the kiosks in town generally take 20% of a captain's fee in addition to an extra monthly fee. So you can usually save yourself money by booking directly with a captain or going straight to one of the docks. You can negotiate a good deal at **Charter Boat Row,** 1801 N. Roosevelt Ave. (across from the Shell station), home to more than 30 charter fishing and party boats. Just show up to arrange your outing, or call **Garrison Bite Marina** (☎ 305/292-8167) for details.

The advantage of the smaller, more expensive charter boats is that you can call the shots. They'll take you where you want to go, to fish for what you want to catch. These "light tackles" are also easier to maneuver, which means you can go to backcountry spots for tarpon and bonefish, as well as out to the open ocean for tuna and dolphin. You'll really be able to feel the fish, and you'll get some good fights. Larger boats, for up to six or seven people, are cheaper and best for kingfish, billfish, and sailfish. Consider Jim Brienza's 27-foot *Sea Breeze,* docked at 25 Arbutus Dr. (☎ 305/294-6027), if you want a light tackle experience. For a larger boat, try Capt. Henry Otto's 44-foot *Sunday,* docked at the Hyatt in Key West (☎ 305/294-7052).

The huge commercial party boats are more for sightseeing than serious angling, though you can get lucky and get a few bites at one of the fishing holes. One especially good deal is the *Gulfstream II* (☎ 305/296-8494), an all-day charter that goes out daily from 9:30am until 4pm. You'll pay $30, plus $3 for a rod and reel. This 65-foot party boat usually has at least 30 other anglers. Bring your own cooler or buy snacks on the boat. Beer and wine is allowed.

For serious anglers, nothing compares to the light tackle boats that leave from **Oceanside Marina** (☎ 305/294-4676) in Stock Island, at 5950 Peninsula Avenue, a mile and a half off U.S. 1. It's a 20-minute drive from Old Town on the Atlantic side. There are more than 30 light tackle guides, which range from flatbed, backcountry skiffs to a 28-foot open boats. There are also a few larger charters and a head or party boat that goes to the Dry Tortugas. Call the dockmaster for details.

For the light tackle experience of your life, call **Captain Bruce Cronin** at ☎ 305/294-4929 or **Captain Kenny Harris** at ☎ 305/294-8843, two of the more famous (and pricey) captains still working these docks. You'll pay from $450 to $500 for a full day, usually about 8am until 4pm, and from $200 to $350 for a half day.

GOLF   One of the area's only courses is **Key West Golf Club** (☎ 305/294-5232), an 18-hole course located just north of the island of Key West at MM 4.5 (turn onto College Road to the course entrance). Designed by Rees Jones, the course has plenty of mangroves and water hazards on its 6,526 yards. It's open to the public and has a new pro shop. Call ahead for tee-time reservations.

SHOPPING

Like any tourist destination, Key West has an abundance of tacky tourist shops. It also happens to have a wide variety of fantastic antiques stores, designer boutiques, art galleries, and bookstores.

On Duval Street, T-shirt shops outnumber almost any other business. If you must get a wearable memento, be careful of unscrupulous salespeople. Despite efforts to curtail the practice, many shops have been known to rip off unwitting shoppers. A few too many Rum Runners sometimes result in some very expensive souvenirs. It pays to check the prices and the exchange rate before signing any sales slips. You are entitled to a written estimate of any T-shirt work before you pay for it.

At Mallory Square is the **Clinton Street Market,** an over–air-conditioned mall of kiosks and stalls designed for the many cruise ship passengers who never venture beyond this super-commercial zone. Amid the dreck are some delicious coffee and candy shops and some high-priced hats and shoes. There's also a free and clean rest room.

Once the main industry of Key West, cigar making is enjoying renewed success at the handful of factories that survived the slow years. Stroll through **"Cigar Alley,"** between Front and Greene streets, where you will find *viejitos*—little old men—rolling fat stogies just as they used to do in their homeland across the Florida Straits. Stop at the **Key West Cigar Factory,** at 308 Front St. (☎ **305/294-3470**), for an excellent selection of imported and locally rolled smokes, including the famous El Hemingway. Remember, buying or selling Cuban-made cigars is illegal. Shops advertising "Cuban Cigars" are usually referring to domestic cigars made from tobacco grown from seeds that were brought from Cuba decades ago.

If you are looking for local or Caribbean art, you will find nearly a dozen galleries and shops clustered on Duval Street between Catherine and Fleming streets. You'll also find some excellent shops scattered on the side streets. One worth seeking out is the ✪ **Haitian Art Co.,** 600 Frances St. (☎ **305/296-8932**), where you can browse through room upon room of original paintings from well-known and obscure Haitian artists in a range of prices from a few dollars to a few thousand. Also, check out **Cuba, Cuba!** at 814 Duval St. (☎ **305/295-9442**). Here you will find paintings, sculpture, and photos by Cuban artists.

A favorite stop in the Keys is the deliciously fragrant **Key West Aloe** at 524 Front St. (between Simonton and Duval streets; ☎ **305/294-5592**). Since 1971, this shop has been selling a simple line of bath products, including lotions, shampoos, and soothing balms for those who have spent too much time in the hot tropical sun. Sweet aromas waft from the several outlets in town. At the main shop (open until 8pm), you can find great gift baskets, tropical perfumes, and candies and cookies, too. In addition to frangipani, vanilla, and hibiscus scents, sample Key West for Men, a unique and alluringly musky best-seller. You can also call for a catalogue.

Literature and music buffs will appreciate the many bookshops and record stores on the island. **Key West Island Bookstore** (☎ **305/294-2904**) at 513 Fleming St. carries new, used, and rare books and specializes in fiction by residents of the Keys, including Hemingway, Tennessee Williams, Shel Silverstein, Ann Beattie, Richard Wilbur, and John Hersey. **Flaming Maggie's** (☎ **305/294-3931**) at 800 Cartoline St. carries a wide selection of gay books. Both shops are open daily.

For anything else, from bed linens to candlesticks to clothing, go to downtown's oldest and most renowned department store, **Fast Buck Freddie's,** at 500 Duval St. (☎ **305/294-2007**). It's open daily from 10am to 6pm in season, 11am to 7pm in the summer, and until 10pm most Saturdays and some evenings in season. For the same merchandise at more reduced prices, try ✪ **Half Buck Freddie's,** 726 Caroline St. (☎ **305/294-6799**). Here you can shop for out-of-season bargains and "rejects" from the main store. Half Buck is open on Thursday, Friday, Saturday, and Sunday only, from 11am to 5pm.

WHERE TO STAY

You'll find a wide variety of places to stay in Key West, from resorts with all the amenities to seaside motels, quaint bed-and-breakfasts, and clothing-optional guesthouses. Unless you're in town during Key West's most popular holidays—Fantasy Fest (around Halloween), Hemingway Days (in July), and Christmas and New Year's—or for a big fishing tournament (many are held from October to December)—you can almost always find a place to stay at the last minute. However, you may want to book early, especially in the winter, when prime properties fill up and many require 2- or 3-night minimums. Prices at these times are also extremely high. Finding a room for under $100 a night is nearly impossible.

If you don't find a room that works for you or you want something different, try **Reservation Hotline of Key West,** one of the most pleasant reservation services in town. Rita Logan will help you sort out the many small lodgings that couldn't all be reviewed here and can also recommend private homes or condos. Call ☎ **800/ 546-5397** or 305/745-9977 between 9am and 6pm, Monday through Saturday. During high season, this service is open on Sundays, too. **The Key West Innkeepers Association,** P.O. Box 6172, Key West, FL 33041 (☎ **800/492-1911** or 305/ 292-3600), can also help find lodging in any price range from its dozens of members and affiliates.

Most major hotel chains have at least one location in Key West; many are clustered on North Roosevelt Boulevard (U.S. 1). Moderately priced options include **Howard Johnson,** 3031 N. Roosevelt Blvd. (☎ **800/942-0913** or 305/296-6595); the **Ramada Inn,** 3420 N. Roosevelt Blvd. (☎ **800/330-5541** or 305/294-5541); the **Econo Lodge,** 3820 N. Roosevelt Blvd. (☎ **800/553-2666** or 305/294-5511); the **Holiday Inn Beachside,** 3841 N. Roosevelt Blvd. (☎ **800/292-7706** or 305/ 294-2571); and the **Quality Inn,** 3850 N. Roosevelt Blvd. (☎ **800/228-5151** or 305/294-6681). The Howard Johnson and the Holiday Inn are the only hotels with gulf-view rooms; the other hotels listed are just across the street. Duval Street is less than 5 minutes away by car or taxi.

If you want a national chain closer to Key West's historic section, you might try **Holiday Inn La Concha Hotel** at 430 Duval St. (☎ **800/745-2191**). It is centrally located, but rates are high for the mediocre rooms (from $160 in season). Like much of Key West, service here can be brusque. Avoid the Best Western Hibiscus Hotel located at 1313 Simonton St. The property is in bad shape, management is rude, and prices are high.

Gay travelers will want to call the Key West Business Guild (☎ **305/294-4603**), which represents more than 50 guesthouses and B&Bs in town, as well as many other gay-owned businesses. Be advised that most gay guesthouses have a clothing-optional policy. One of the most elegant and popular ones is **Big Ruby's** (☎ **800/477-7829** or 305/296-2323) at 409 Applerouth Lane (a little alley just off Duval Street). A low cluster of buildings surround a lushly landscaped courtyard where a hearty breakfast is served each morning and wine is poured at dusk. The mostly male guests hang out by a good-sized pool tanning in the buff. Also popular is **Oasis** at 823 Fleming Street (☎ **305/296-2131**). It's super-clean and friendly. Guests can enjoy a central location and a 14-seat hot tub.

Another luxurious property is **The Brass Key** at 412 Frances St. (☎ **305/ 296-4719**), which is more romantic and traditionally decorated and welcomes many lesbian travelers as well. *Out and About* gave it a five-star rating. For women only, the **Rainbow House** (☎ **305/292-1450**) is a large, gorgeous guesthouse with lots of amenities, including two pools and two hot tubs.

VERY EXPENSIVE

✪ Key West Hilton Resort and Marina. 245 Front St. (at the end of Duval St.), Key West, FL 33040. ☎ **800/221-2424** or 305/294-4000. Fax 305/294-4086. 211 units. A/C MINIBAR TV TEL. Winter $259–$475 double, $325–$750 suite; off-season $169–$375 double, $250–$750 suite. Sunset Key Cottages. Winter $870–$1395; off-season $670–$925. AE, DC, DISC, MC, V.

Completed in the fall of 1996, this Hilton is a truly luxurious addition to downtown's hotel scene. This rambling two-building hotel is at the very end of Duval Street in the middle of all of Old Town's action. The sparkling new rooms are large and well appointed, with tropical decor and all the modern conveniences. Choose a suite in the main building if you want a large Jacuzzi in your living room. Otherwise, the marina building has great views. This giant will no doubt be very popular with corporate and convention visitors.

Amenities: Concierge, room service, laundry and dry-cleaning services, newspaper delivery, in-room massage, nightly turndown, twice-daily maid service, express checkout, valet parking, complimentary in-room coffee, secretarial services. Outdoor heated pool, offshore secluded beach, health club, Jacuzzi, sundeck, water-sports equipment, full-service marina, bicycle rental, game room, business center, self-service laundry, conference rooms, gift shops and boutiques.

Marriott's Reach Resort. 1435 Simonton St., Key West, FL 33040. ☎ **800/874-4118** or 305/296-5000. Fax 305/296-2830. 149 units. A/C MINIBAR TV TEL. Winter $309–$419 double; off-season $170–$310 double. AE, CB, DC, DISC, MC, V. Valet parking $9 per day.

The Reach is one of the few hotels on the island with its own strip of sandy beach. The drawback here is the location; the hotel is a 15-minute walk away from the center of the Duval Street action. Supported by stilts that leave the entire ground floor for car parking, the hotel offers four floors of rooms designed around atriums. The guest rooms are large and feature tile floors, sturdy wicker furnishings, and tropical colors. Each contains a small service bar with a sink, fridge, and tea/coffeemaker, and has a vanity area separate from the bathroom. The rooms are so nice you can easily forgive the small closets and diminutive dressers. All have sliding glass doors that open onto balconies, and some have ocean views.

Ample palm-planted grounds surround a small pool area. There's also a private pier for fishing and suntanning. The protected waters are tame and shallow.

Amenities: Concierge, room service, dry cleaning, newspaper delivery, in-room massage, baby-sitting, express checkout. Outdoor heated swimming pool, beach, health spa, Jacuzzi, sauna, bicycle rental, business center, tour desk, conference rooms, sailboats, Windsurfers, beauty salon.

✪ Pier House Resort and Caribbean Spa. 1 Duval St. (near Mallory Docks), Key West, FL 33040. ☎ **800/327-8340** or 305/296-4600. Fax 305/296-9085. 154 units. A/C MINIBAR TV TEL. Winter $275–$450 double, $450–$795 suite; off-season $195–$350 double, $325–$645 suite. Children under 16 stay free in parents' room. AE, CB, DC, DISC, MC, V.

Pier House is one of the area's best resort choices, offering luxurious rooms, top-notch service, and even a full-service spa. Its excellent location—at the foot of Duval Street and just steps from Mallory Docks—is the envy of every hotel on the island. Set back from the busy street, on a short strip of beach, this hotel is a welcome oasis of calm.

The accommodations here vary tremendously, from relatively simple business-style rooms to romantic guest quarters complete with integrated stereo systems and whirlpool tubs. Their best waterfront suites and rooms have recently been renovated. Although every accommodation has either a balcony or a patio, not all overlook the water. My favorites, in the two-story spa building, don't have any view at all. But what they lack in scenery, they make up for in opulence; each well-appointed spa room has a sitting area and a huge Jacuzzi bathroom.

Dining/Diversions: The restaurant serves very respectable meals in a dark dining room or on an umbrella-covered patio overlooking the docks. Old Havana Docks is a good waterfront bar, especially at sunset.

Amenities: Concierge, room service, laundry services, newspaper delivery, in-room massage, express checkout. Heated swimming pool, beach, health club, spa treatments, two Jacuzzis, sauna, sundeck, water-sports equipment rentals, bicycle rental, tour desk, conference rooms, beauty salon.

EXPENSIVE

Island City House Hotel. 411 William St., Key West, FL 33040. ☎ **800/634-8230** or 305/294-5702. Fax 305/294-1289. 24 units. A/C TV TEL. Winter $165 studio, $195–$225 one-bedroom suite, $255–$285 two-bedroom suite; off-season $95 studio, $125–$155 one-bedroom suite, $165–$190 two-bedroom suite. Rates include breakfast. AE, CB, DC, DISC, MC, V.

A little resort unto itself, the Island City House consists of three separate unique buildings that share a common jungle-like patio and pool. The first building, unimaginatively called the Island City House building, is a historic three-story wooden structure with wraparound verandas that allow guests to walk around the entire edifice on any floor. The warmly dressed old-fashioned interiors here include wood floors and many antique furnishings. Many rooms have full-size kitchens, queen-size beds, and sumptuous floral window treatments. The tile bathrooms could use more counter space, and the room lighting isn't always perfect, but eccentricities are part of this hotel's charm.

The unpainted wooden Cigar House has particularly large bedrooms similar in ambience to those in the Island City House. Most rooms are furnished with wicker chairs and king-size beds and have big bathrooms (although lacking in counter space). As with the Island City House, rooms facing the property's interior courtyard are best. The Arch House is the least appealing of the three buildings, but still very recommendable. Built of Dade County pine, the Arch House's cozy bedrooms are furnished in wicker and rattan and come with small kitchens and baths.

Amenities: Newspaper delivery, free coffee in lobby, dry cleaning, laundry service, in-room massage, baby-sitting. Kitchenettes, VCR rental and complimentary videos, outdoor heated pool, Jacuzzi, bicycle rental, sundeck, self-service laundromat.

✪ **Marquesa Hotel.** 600 Fleming St. (at Simonton St.), Key West, FL 33040. ☎ **800/869-4631** or 305/292-1919. Fax 305/294-2121. 40 units. A/C MINIBAR TV TEL. Winter $215–325; off-season $135–$235. No children under 12 allowed. AE, DC, MC, V.

One of my very favorite properties, the Marquesa offers all the charm of a small historic hotel with the amenities of a large resort. It encompasses four different buildings, two adjacent swimming pools, and a three-stage waterfall that cascades into a lily pond. Two of the hotel's houses are luxuriously restored Victorian homes with rooms outfitted with extra-plush antiques and oversize contemporary furniture. The rooms in the two other, newly constructed buildings are even richer; many have four-poster wrought-iron beds with bright floral spreads. The green marble baths are lush and spacious. The decor is simple, elegant, and spotless. These are the only hotel rooms I have ever seen that I would like my home to resemble.

Amenities: Concierge, valet, newspaper delivery, twice-daily maid service, valet parking. Two outdoor swimming pools (one is heated), access to nearby health club.

Ocean Key House. Zero Duval St., Key West, FL 33040. ☎ **800/328-9815** or 305/296-7701. Fax 305/292-7685. www.oceankeyhouse.com. 96 units. A/C MINIBAR TV TEL. Winter, from $160 double, $340–$525 one-bedroom suite, $420–$700 two-bedroom suite; off-season, $135 double, $225–$495 one-bedroom suite, $320–$600 two-bedroom suite. Children 17 and under stay free in parents' room. AE, CB, DC, DISC, MC, V.

You can't get much more central than this modern hotel, located across from the Pier House at the foot of Duval Street. Still, for the same price as the best rooms, you may do better at one of the more intimate accommodations, such as the Marquesa or the Pier House. Most of the guest rooms here are suites, ample-sized accommodations fitted with built-in couches. Many rooms have sliding glass doors that open onto small balconies, some of which enjoy unobstructed water views. All suites have Jacuzzi tubs in either the master bedroom or living room. The standard guest rooms are much less desirable. They are small and dark and have no views.

Dining/Diversions: A casual dockside grill serves lunch and dinner. Breakfast is served at an indoor/outdoor cafe.

Amenities: Concierge, room service, dry-cleaning and laundry services. VCRs and video rentals, outdoor heated pool, access to nearby health club, Jacuzzi in every suite, conference rooms, sundeck, water-sports concession, tour desk.

MODERATE

Chelsea House. 707 Truman Ave., Key West, FL 33040. ☎ **800/845-8859** or 305/296-2211. Fax 305/296-4822. 20 units. A/C TV TEL. Winter $120–$180 double, $360 apt; off-season $75–$125 double, $250 apt. Rates include breakfast. Pets $10 extra. AE, CB, DC, DISC, MC, V.

Despite its decidedly English name, the Chelsea House is "all American," a term that in Key West isn't code for "conservative." Chelsea House caters to a mixed gay/straight clientele and displays its liberal philosophy most prominently on the clothing-optional sundeck. One of only a few guesthouses in Key West that offers TVs, VCRs, private baths, and kitchenettes in each guest room, Chelsea House has a large number of repeat visitors. The apartments come with full kitchens and separate living areas, as well as palm-shaded balconies in back. The baths and closets could be bigger, but both are adequate and serviceable.

When weather permits, which is almost always, breakfast is served outside by the pool. There is private parking. Note that children 14 and under are not accepted.

☉ La Pensione. 809 Truman Ave. (between Windsor and Margaret sts.), Key West, FL 33040. ☎ **800/893-1193** or 305/292-9923. Fax 305/296-6509. 9 units. A/C TEL. Winter, from $158 double with Frommer's discount; summer, from $98 double with Frommer's discount. Rates include breakfast and represent a 10% discount for readers who mention this guide. AE, DC, DISC, JCB, MC, V.

This classic bed-and-breakfast in the 1891 home of a former cigar executive distinguishes itself from other similar inns by its extreme attention to details. The friendly knowledgeable staff treat the stunning home and the guests with extraordinary care. The comfortable rooms all have air-conditioning, ceiling fans, king-size beds, and private bathrooms. Many have French doors opening onto spacious verandas. Although the rooms have no phones or televisions, the distractions of Duval Street— only steps away—should keep you adequately occupied during your visit. Breakfast, which includes made-to-order Belgian waffles, fresh fruit, and a variety of breads or muffins, can be taken on the wraparound porch or at the communal dining table. No children are allowed.

South Beach Oceanfront Motel. 508 South St. (at the Atlantic Ocean), Key West, FL 33040. ☎ **800/354-4455** or 305/296-5611. Fax 305/294-8272. 50 units. A/C TV TEL. Winter $105–$199 double; off-season $69–$140 double. AE, MC, V.

This standard two-story motel is located directly on the ocean, within walking distance of Duval Street. Because the structure is perpendicular to the water, most of the rooms overlook a pretty Olympic-size swimming pool rather than a wide swath of beach. The best—and by far most expensive—are the lucky pair of beachfront rooms on the end (numbers 115 and 215).

All rooms share similar aging decor and include standard furnishings. The smallish bathrooms could use a makeover, and include showers but no tubs. There's a private pier, an on-site water-sports concession, and a laundry room available for guest use. When making reservations, ask for a room that's as close to the beach (and as far from the road) as possible. If you'll be there a while, ask for one of the rooms with a kitchenette; there is no restaurant on the premises.

Southernmost Point Guest House. 1327 Duval St., Key West, FL 33040. ☎ **305/294-0715.** Fax 305/296-0641. 6 units. A/C TV TEL. Winter $95–$175 double, $150 suite; off-season $55–$125 double, $95 suite. Rates include breakfast. AE, MC, V.

One of the only inns that actually welcomes children and pets, this romantic and historic guesthouse is a real find. The antiseptically clean rooms are not as fancy as the house's ornate 1885 exterior. Each room has basic beds and couches and a hodge-podge of furnishings, including futon couches, high-back wicker chairs, and plenty of mismatched throw rugs. Each room is different. Room 5 is best; situated upstairs, it has a private porch, an ocean view, and windows that let in lots of light. Every room has a refrigerator and a full decanter of sherry. Mona Santiago, the hotel's kind, laid-back owner, provides chairs and towels that can be brought to the beach, which is just a block away. Plus, guests can help themselves to wine as they soak in the new 14-seat hot tub. Kids will enjoy the swings in the backyard and the pet rabbits.

INEXPENSIVE

Blue Lagoon Resort. 3101 N. Roosevelt Blvd., Key West, FL 33040-4118. ☎ **305/296-1043.** Fax 305/296-6499. 72 units. A/C TV TEL. Winter $80–$240; off-season $50–$110. MC, V.

More than half of the rooms at this funky oceanside resort rent for less than $100 year-round—an all too unusual occurrence in Key West, especially for full-service resorts. The rooms, furnished in heavy cedar wood, are basic and a bit run-down but still decent—along the lines of a Howard Johnson or other budget accommodation. Second-floor rooms are generally quieter. The pricier waterfront rooms aren't really worth the extra money (although some include a jet ski ride). Guests tend to be young college-aged kids out for a wild time. Although pretty far from Old Town, the resort is convenient by scooter and car, and it is literally surrounded by Wave Runners, boats, parasailing, and diving fun.

✪ **The Grand.** 1116 Grinnell St. (between Virginia and Catherine sts.), Key West, FL 33040. ☎ **888/947-2630** or 305/294-0590. E-mail: thegrand@conch.net. 10 units. A/C TV TEL. Winter $68–$98 rms; $118 suites. AE, DISC, MC, V.

Don't expect cabbies or locals to know about this gem. Opened in 1997, this guesthouse wasn't even in the phone book its first or second year. Lucky for you! It's got everything you could want, including a very moderate price tag. All rooms have private baths, air-conditioning, telephones, and private entrances. The floors are painted in bright colors, and beds are dressed in light tropical prints. It's run by another one of those happy-to-be-alive Northeastern transplants, Elizabeth Rose, who goes out of her way to provide any and all services for her appreciative guests. Room number 2 on the back side of the house is the best deal; it's small, but it has a porch and the most privacy. Suites are a real steal, too. The large two-room units come with a complete kitchen. The house is in a modest residential section of Old Town, only about 7 blocks from Duval Street. With the exception of the youth hostel/motel, other accommodations in this price range tend to be in Caribbean Village, a more seedy part of Key West. This is without a doubt the best bargain in town.

Key West International Hostel. 718 South St., Key West, FL 33040. ☎ **800/51-HOSTEL** or 305/296-5719. Fax 305/296-0672. 100 units. A/C TV. Winter $17 for IYHF members, $20 for non-members dorm beds; $75–$105 motel rms. Off-season, from $15 for IYHF members, from $18 for non-members dorm beds; $50–$85 motel rms. DISC, MC, V.

This well-run hostel is a 3-minute walk to the beach and to Old Town. It's not the Ritz, but it's affordable. Very busy with European backpackers, this is a great place to meet people. The dorm rooms are dark and sparse, but clean enough. The higher-priced motel rooms are a good deal, especially those equipped with full kitchens. Facilities include a pool table under a tiki-hut roof and bicycle rentals for $6 per day. There is also cheap food available for breakfast, lunch, and dinner. As in all community living arrangements, you'll want to watch your valuables; there are mini safes in each room.

WHERE TO DINE

Key West offers a vast, tempting array of food. You'll find many ethnicities represented, from Thai to Cuban, plus the usual drive-through franchises (mostly up on Roosevelt Boulevard). There is even a Hard Rock Cafe on Duval Street. Wander Old Town and browse menus after you have exhausted the list below. If you don't feel like venturing out, call **We Deliver** (☎ **305/293-0078**), a service that for a small fee (between $3 and $6) will bring you anything you want from any of the area's restaurants or stores. We Deliver operates between 3 and 11pm. **Fausto's Food Palace,** open since 1926, will deliver groceries, beer, wine, or snacks to stock your fridge (☎ **305/294-5221** or 305/296-5663). Fausto's has a $25 minimum.

VERY EXPENSIVE

Cafe des Artistes. 1007 Simonton St. (near Truman Ave.). ☎ **305/294-7100**. Reservations recommended. Main courses $23–$39. AE, MC, V. Daily 6–11pm. FRENCH.

Open over a dozen years, the Cafe des Artistes's impressive longevity is the result of its winning combination of food and atmosphere. Traditional French meals benefit from a subtle tropical twist. The food is served with sincerity by uniformed waiters well versed in the virtues of fine food. Start with the duck-liver pâté made with fresh truffles and old cognac, or Maryland crabmeat served with an artichoke heart and herbed tomato confit. Nouvelle and traditional French entrees include lobster flambé with mango and basil and wine-basted lamb chops rubbed with rosemary and ginger.

Louie's Backyard. 700 Waddell Ave. ☎ **305/294-1061**. Reservations highly recommended. Main courses $25–$30; lunch $8–$15. AE, CB, DC, MC, V. Daily 11:30am–3pm and 6–10:30pm. CARIBBEAN CONTEMPORARY.

Louie's, once known as Key West's most elegant restaurant, has lost its luster. Its location, nestled amid blooming bougainvillea on a lush slice of the gulf, remains one of the most romantic on earth. Unfortunately, the gorgeous real estate doesn't improve the uneven food, sluggish service, and snooty attitude. Part of the problem is that the kitchen doors seem to be constantly swinging. Depending on who is cooking, you may or may not have an interesting or tasty meal. Try the weekend brunches, which tend to be more reliable than dinners, or, to be assured of a good time, you may just want to sit at the dockside bar and enjoy a cocktail at sunset.

EXPENSIVE

Antonia's. 615 Duval St. ☎ **305/294-6565.** Reservations suggested. Main courses $17–$24; pastas $12–$15. AE, DC, MC, V. Daily 6–11pm. NORTHERN ITALIAN.

The food is great but the atmosphere a bit fussy for Key West. If you don't have a reservation in season, don't bother. The management is less than accommodating. Still, if you are organized and don't mind paying high prices for dishes that elsewhere go for much less, try this old stand-by. From the perfectly seasoned homemade focaccia to an exemplary crème brûlée, this elegant little standout is amazingly consistent. The menu includes a small selection of classics, such as zuppa di pesce, rack of lamb in a rosemary sauce, and veal marsala, and never disappoints. However, the way to go is with the nightly specials. If offered, try the flaky, tender mutton snapper served with a light anchovy cream sauce (or your choice). The presentation is simple but elegant; the sauce, perfectly subtle. You can't go wrong with either fresh pastas or beef dishes.

✪ **Bagatelle.** 115 Duval St. ☎ **305/296-6609.** Reservations recommended. Main courses $16–$24; lunch $5–$12. AE, DC, DISC, MC, V. Daily 11:30am–3pm and 5:30–10pm. SEAFOOD/ TROPICAL.

Reserve a seat at the elegant second-floor veranda overlooking Duval Street's mayhem. From the calm above, enjoy any of the selections from this large menu. You may want to start your meal with the excellent herb-and-garlic stuffed whole artichoke or the sashimi-like seared tuna rolled in black peppercorns. Also recommended is a lightly creamy garlic-herb pasta topped with gulf shrimp, Florida lobster, and mushrooms. The best chicken and beef dishes are given a tropical treatment: grilled with papaya, ginger, and soy.

✪ **Mangoes.** 700 Duval St. (at Angela St.), Key West. ☎ **305/292-4606.** Reservations recommended for parties of six or more. Main courses $12–$24; pizzas $10–$12; lunch $7–$14. AE, CB, DC, DISC, MC, V. Daily 11am–midnight; pizza until 1am. Upstairs bar (Limbo) 7pm–4am. AMERICAN/REGIONAL.

This restaurant's large brick patio, directly on Duval, is so seductive to passersby that it's packed almost every night of the week. The food and service are some of the best in the Keys. Appetizers include conch chowder laced with sherry, lobster dumplings with tangy Key lime sauce, and grilled shrimp cocktail with spicy mango chutney. Spicy sausage with black beans and rice, crispy curried chicken, and local snapper with passion fruit sauce are typical among the entrees, but Mangoes's outstanding individual-size designer pizzas are the best menu items by far. They're baked in a Neapolitan-style oven fired by buttonwood. Mangoes enjoys a good buzz among locals.

MODERATE

✪ **Blue Heaven.** 729 Thomas St. (at the corner of Petronia St., in Bahama Village), Key West. ☎ **305/296-8666.** Main courses $9–$23; lunch $5.25–$12; breakfast $3–$8.50. DISC, MC, V. Mon–Sat 8am–3:30 pm and 6–10:30pm; Sun 8am–1pm and 6–10:30pm. SEAFOOD/AMERICAN/NATURAL.

This little hippie-run gallery and restaurant has become the place to be in Key West—and with good reason. Be prepared to wait in line. The food here is some of the best in town, especially for breakfast. You can enjoy homemade granolas, huge tropical fruit pancakes, and seafood Benedict. Dinners are just as good and run the gamut from just-caught fish dishes to Jamaican-style jerk chicken, curried soups, and vegetarian stews. But if you're a neat freak, don't bother. Some people are put off by the dirt floors and roaming cats and birds. The building used to be a bordello, where Hemingway was said to hang out watching cockfights. A newly opened bakery/coffeehouse has proved a big hit.

Mangia, Mangia. 900 Southard St. (at Margaret St.), Key West. ☎ **305/294-2469.** Reservations not accepted. Main courses $9–$14.50. AE, MC, V. Daily 5:30–10pm. ITALIAN/AMERICAN.

Mangia, Mangia is one of Key West's best values. Locals appreciate that they can get inexpensive good food here in a town of so many tourist traps. Off the beaten track, in a little corner storefront, this great Chicago-style pasta place serves some of the best Italian food in the Keys. The family-run restaurant offers superb homemade pastas of every description, including one of the tastiest marinaras around. The simple grilled chicken breast brushed with olive oil and sprinkled with pepper is another good choice. You wouldn't know it from the glossy glass front room, but there's a fantastic little outdoor patio dotted with twinkling pepper lights and lots of plants. You can relax out back with a glass of one of their excellent wines or homemade beer while you wait for your table.

○ **Pepe's.** 806 Caroline St. (between Margaret and Williams sts.), Key West. ☎ **305/294-7192.** Main courses $11–$20; lunch $5–$9; breakfast $2–$9. DISC, MC, V. Daily 6:30am–10:30pm. AMERICAN.

This old dive has been serving good, basic food for nearly a century. Steaks and Apalachicola Bay oysters are the big draw for regulars who appreciate the rustic bar-room setting and historic photos on the walls. Look for original scenes of Key West in 1909, when Pepe's first opened. If the weather is nice, choose a seat on the patio under a stunning mahogany tree. Burgers, fish sandwiches, and standard chili satisfy hearty eaters. Buttery sautéed mushrooms and rich mashed potatoes are the best comfort food in Key West. Stop by early for breakfast when you can get old-fashioned chipped beef on toast and all the usual egg dishes. In the evening, there are reasonably priced cocktails on the deck.

Turtle Kraals Wildlife Grill. 213 Margaret St. (corner of Caroline St.), Key West. ☎ **305/294-2640.** Main courses $12–$20. DISC, MC, V. Mon–Thurs 11am–1am; Fri–Sat 11am–2am. SOUTHWESTERN/SEAFOOD.

You'll join lots of locals in this out-of-the-way converted warehouse that serves innovative seafood at great prices. Try the twin lobster tails stuffed with mango and crabmeat or any of the big quesadillas or fajitas. Kids will like the wildlife exhibits and the very cheesy menu. Blues bands play most nights; there's never a cover.

INEXPENSIVE

The Deli. 926 Simonton St. (corner of Truman St.), Key West. ☎ **305/294-1464.** Full meals $5–$13; sandwiches $2–$7. DISC, MC, V. Daily 7:30am–9:30pm. DINER/AMERICAN.

In operation since 1950, this family-owned, corner eatery has kept up with the times. It's really more of a diner than a deli and has a vast menu with all kinds of hearty options, from meatloaf to yellowtail snapper. Avoid the lobster sandwich, which is fried and a bit greasy. Other seafood options are good. A daily selection of more than a dozen vegetables includes the usual diner choices of beets, corn, and coleslaw with some distinctly Caribbean additions, such as rice and beans and fried plantains. Most dinners include a choice of two vegetables and homemade biscuits or corn bread.

Breakfasts are made to order and attract a loyal following of locals. The Deli also offers ice cream sundaes and gourmet coffees.

✪ **El Siboney Restaurant.** 900 Catherine St. (at Margaret St.), Key West. ☎ **305/296-4184.** Main courses $5–$13. No credit cards. Mon–Sat 11am–9pm. CUBAN.

For good, cheap Cuban food, stop at this corner dive that looks more like a gas station than a diner. Be prepared however, to wait like the locals for succulent roast pork, Cuban sandwiches, grilled chicken, and *ropa vieja,* all served with heaps of rice and beans. This tiny storefront is a worthwhile, very affordable choice in a town with lots of glossy tourist traps.

PT's Late Night. 920 Caroline St. (at the corner of Margaret St.), Key West. ☎ **305/ 296-4245.** Main courses $5–$14; lunch $5–$12. DISC, MC, V. Daily 11am–4am. AMERICAN.

This place is worth knowing about not only because it's one of the only places in town serving food past 10pm, but it also happens to serve good food at extremely reasonable prices. The sports-bar atmosphere might make you wonder, but I've never been disappointed, although service can be a bit slow and brusque. Let's say it's 1am, you're starving, and you've just parked your bike outside: You'll be ecstatic when your heaping plate of nachos arrives. Fajitas are served sizzling hot with a huge platter of fixings, including beans, rice, lettuce, jalapeños, and tomatoes. Super-fresh salads are so big they can be a meal in themselves. There are also nightly specials, such as corned beef and cabbage on Monday and roast turkey with all the trimmings on Thursday. This place is worth knowing about at any time of day.

KEY WEST AFTER DARK

Duval Street is the Bourbon Street of Florida. Amid the T-shirt shops and clothing boutiques, you'll find bar after bar serving stiff drinks to revelers who bounce from one to another. Bands and crowds vary from night to night and season to season. Your best bet is to start at Truman Avenue and head up Duval to check them out for yourself. Cover charges are mostly unheard of, so stop into a dozen and see which you like.

Captain Tony's. 428 Greene St. ☎ **305/294-1838.**

Just around the corner from Duval's beaten path, this smoky old wooden bar is about as authentic as you'll find. It comes complete with old-time regulars who remember the island before cruise ships docked here; they say Hemingway drank, caroused, and even wrote here. The owner, Captain Tony Tarracino, a former controversial Key West mayor, has recently capitalized on the success of this once-quaint tavern by franchising the place.

Durty Harry's. 208 Duval St. ☎ **305/296-4890.**

This large entertainment complexes features live rock bands almost every night. You can wander to one of the many outdoor bars or head up to Upstairs at Rick's, an indoor/outdoor dance club that gets going late. For the more racy singles or couples, there is the Red Garter, a pocket-size strip club popular with bachelor and divorce parties. The hawker outside reminds couples that "The family that strips together sticks together."

Jimmy Buffett's Margaritaville Cafe. 500 Duval St. ☎ **305/292-1435.**

This cafe, named after another Key West legend, is a worthwhile stop. Although Mr. Buffett moved to glitzy Palm Beach years ago, his name is still attracting large crowds. This kitschy restaurant/bar/gift shop features live bands every night—from rock to blues to reggae and everything in between. The touristy cafe is furnished with plenty of Buffett memorabilia, including gold records, photos, and drawings. The margaritas are high-priced but tasty. The cheeseburgers aren't worth singing about.

Limbo. 700 Duval St. (corner of Angela St.). ☎ **305/292-4606.**

This secret little hideaway, above the well-known restaurant Mangoes (see "Where to Dine," above), is a great bar. Music ranges from house/techno to calypso, rock, jazz, blues, and classical guitar; they boast, "We've had it all." Cozy individual booths allow patrons to talk while catching a great view of the crowd that sometimes dances in the small space near the outside deck.

Sloppy Joe's. 201 Duval St. ☎ **305/294-5717.**

You'll have to stop in here just to say you did. Scholars and drunks debate whether this is the same Sloppy Joe's that Hemingway wrote about, but there's no argument that this classic bar's turn-of-the-century wooden ceiling and cracked tile floors are Key West originals. The popular and raucous bar is crowded with tourists almost 24 hours a day, and almost always has live music.

THE GAY SCENE

In Key West, the best music and dancing can be found at the predominantly gay clubs. While many of the area's other hot spots are geared toward tourists who like to imbibe, the gay clubs are for those who want to rave—mostly locals (or at least, recent transplants). None of the spots described here discriminate—anyone open-minded and fun is welcome. Cover varies, but is rarely more than $10.

The gay nightlife was once dominated by The Copa. However, an arsonist put an end to the former legend in 1995. Back and better than ever in its place at 623 Duval St. is a bigger, more modern club called ✪ **Epoch** (☎ 305/296-8521). The music is still an eclectic mix, with everything from techno to house to disco. With a bigger dance floor, a huge outside deck overlooking Duval Street, and a new state-of-the-art sound system, this a better choice than ever for people of any orientation who appreciate a good dance club.

Another popular late-night spot is **One Saloon,** 524 Duval St. (☎ 305/296-8118), featuring great drag and lots more disco. A mostly male clientele frequents this hot spot from 9pm until 4am. Escape to the outdoor garden bar if it gets too steamy inside.

Sunday nights are fun at two local spots. **Tea by the Sea,** on the pier at the Atlantic Shores Motel, 510 South St. (☎ 305/296-2491), attracts a faithful following of regulars and visitors alike. Show up after 7:30pm. Better known around town as La-Te-Da, **La Terraza,** at 1125 Duval St. (☎ 305/296-6706), is a great spot to gather poolside for the best martini in town—but don't bother with the food.

6 The Dry Tortugas

70 miles W of Key West

As long as you have come this far, you might as well take a trip to the Dry Tortugas, especially if you're into bird watching, which is the primary draw of these seven small islands. Few people realize that Florida's Keys don't end at Key West.

Ponce de León, who discovered this far-flung cluster of coral keys in 1513, named them "Las Tortugas" because of the many sea turtles, which still flock to the area during the nesting season in the warm summer months. Oceanic charts later carried the preface "dry" to warn mariners that fresh water was unavailable here. Modern intervention has made drinking water available, but little else.

These underdeveloped islands make a great day trip for travelers interested in seeing the truly natural anomalies of the Florida Keys—especially the birds. The Dry Tortugas are nesting grounds and roosting sites for thousands of tropical and subtropical oceanic birds. Visitors will also find a historical fort, good fishing, and terrific snorkeling around shallow reefs.

GETTING THERE

BY BOAT   The Yankee Fleet, based in Key West (☎ **800/634-0939** or 305/294-7009), offers day trips from Key West for sightseeing, snorkeling, or both. Cruises leave daily at 7:30am from the Land's End Marina, at Margaret Street. Breakfast is served onboard. The journey takes 3 hours. Once on the island, called Garden Key, you can join a guided tour or explore it on your own. Boats return to Key West by 7pm. Tours cost $85 per person, including breakfast; $50 for children 16 and under; $75 for seniors, students, and military personnel. Snorkeling equipment rental is free. Phone for reservations.

BY PLANE   The best option for air service from Key West to the Dry Tortugas is **Seaplanes of Key West,** based at Key West Airport (☎ **800/950-2FLY** or 305/294-0709). Flights depart at 8am, 10am, noon, and 2pm. The 40-minute trip, almost twice as fast as the competitors, at about 500 feet offers a great introduction to these little-known islets. Fares, which include snorkeling equipment and a cooler for use on the island, start at $159 for adults for a half-day excursion and $275 for a full-day. Rates for kids under 12 are discounted by about 30%. Call for detailed rate schedules and flight plans.

EXPLORING THE DRY TORTUGAS

Fort Jefferson, a huge six-sided 19th-century fortress, is built almost at the water's edge of Garden Key, giving the appearance that it floats in the middle of the sea. The monumental structure is surrounded by formidable 8-foot-thick walls that rise up from the sand to nearly 50 feet. Impressive archways, stonework, and parapets make this 150-year-old monument a grand sight. With the invention of the rifled cannon, the fort's masonry construction became obsolete, and the building was never completed. For 10 years, from 1863 to 1873, Fort Jefferson served as a prison, a kind of "Alcatraz East." Among its prisoners were four of the "Lincoln Conspirators," including Samuel A. Mudd, the doctor who set the broken leg of fugitive assassin John Wilkes Booth. In 1935, Fort Jefferson became a National Monument administered by the National Park Service. For more information about Fort Jefferson and the Dry Tortugas, call ☎ **305/242-7700.**

OUTDOOR ACTIVITIES

BIRD WATCHING   Bring your binoculars and your bird books. Bird watching is the reason to visit this little cluster of tropical islands. The islands, uniquely situated in the middle of the migration flyway between North and South America, serve as an important rest stop for the more than 200 winged varieties that pass through here annually. The season peaks from mid-March to mid-May, when thousands of birds—including thrushes, orioles, boobies, swallows, noddy, and snooty terns—show up. In season, migrant birds in a continuous procession fly over or rest at the islands. About 10,000 terns nest here each spring, and many other species from the West Indies can be found year-round.

DIVING & SNORKELING   The warm, clear, shallow waters of the Dry Tortugas combine to produce optimum conditions for snorkeling and scuba diving. Four endangered species of sea turtles—the green, leatherback, Atlantic ridley, and hawksbill—can be found here, along with a myriad of marine species. The region just outside the seawall of Garden Key's Fort Jefferson is excellent for underwater touring; an abundant variety of fish, corals, and more live in just 3 or 4 feet of water.

FISHING   Fishing for snapper, tarpon, grouper, and other fish is popular. The mandatory saltwater fishing permit costs $7 for 3 days and $17 for 7 days. No bait or boating services are available in the Tortugas, but there are day docks on Garden Key as well as a cleaning table. The water is roughest in winter, but the fishing is excellent year-round. Outfitters from Key West can arrange day charters (see "Sports & Outdoor Activities," above).

For real ocean adventure, contact **Florida Fish Finder,** 8262 NW 58th St., Miami, FL 33166 (☎ **305/513-9955;** fax 305/513-9955), which specializes in 2- and 3-day fishing trips to the Dry Tortugas. This rugged 115-foot fishing boat leaves from Stock Island, MM 5 (about 5 miles north of Key West). Two-day trips leave Friday night, return Sunday afternoon, and cost $200 per person. The price includes sleeping accommodations in bunk beds, bait, and tackle, but not food. For an extra fee, you can purchase breakfast, lunch, and dinner, or bring your own cooler of food and snacks. Three-day trips leave the last Friday morning of every month, return the following Sunday afternoon, and cost $240 per person. Phone for reservations. Bring a towel, your camera, a cooler, and a bathing suit.

CAMPING

The rustic beauty of tiny Garden Key is a camper's dream. Don't worry about sharing your site with noisy RVs or motor homes; they can't get here. This is the most isolated spot in Florida. The abundance of birds doesn't make it quiet, but camping here—literally a stone's throw from the water—is as picturesque as it gets. Campers are allowed to pitch tents only on Garden Key. Picnic tables, cooking grills, and toilets are provided, but there are no showers. All supplies must be packed in and out. Sites are free and are available on a first-come, first-served basis. No stoves are permitted. For more information, call the **National Park Service** (☎ **305/242-7700**).

Appendix

AIRLINES

Air Canada
☎800/776-3000
www.aircanada.ca

Alaska Airlines
☎800/426-0333
www.alaskaair.com

America West Airlines
☎800/235-9292
www.americawest.com

American Airlines
☎800/433-7300
www.americanair.com

British Airlines
☎800/247-9297
☎0345/222-111 in Britian
www.british-airways.com

Canadian Airlines International
☎800/426-7000
www.cdnair.ca

Continental Airlines
☎800/525-0280
www.flycontinental.com

Delta Air Lines
☎800/221-1212
www.delta-air.com

Hawaiian Airlines
☎800/367-5320
www.hawaiianair.com

Kiwi International Air Lines
☎800/538-5494
www.jetkiwi.com

Midway Airlines
☎800/446-4392

Northwest Airlines
☎800/225-2525
www.nwa.com

Southwest Airlines
☎800/435-9792
www.iflyswa.com

Tower Air
☎800/34-TOWER (800/348-6937) outside New York
☎718/553-8500 in New York
www.towerair.com

Trans World Airlines (TWA)
☎800/221-2000
www.twa.com

United Airlines
☎800/241-6522
www.ual.com

USAirways
☎800/428-4322
www.usair.com

Virgin Atlantic Airways
☎800/862-8621 in Continental U.S.
☎0293/747-747 in Britain
www.fly.virgin.com

CAR RENTAL AGENCIES

Advantage
☎800/777-5500
www.arac.com

Alamo
☎800/327-9633
www.goalamo.com

Auto Europe
☎800/223-5555
www.autoeurope.com

Avis
☎800/331-1212 in the Continental U.S.
☎800/TRY-AVIS in Canada
www.avis.com

Budget
☎800/527-0700
www.budgetrentacar.com

Dollar
☎800/800-4000
www.dollarcar.com

Enterprise
☎800/325-8007
www.pickenterprise.com

Hertz
☎800/654-3131
www.hertz.com

Kemwel Holiday Auto
☎800/678-0678
www.kemwel.com

National
☎800/CAR-RENT
www.nationalcar.com

Payless
☎800/PAYLESS
www.paylesscar.com

Rent-A-Wreck
☎800/535-1391
rent-a-wreck.com

Thrifty
☎800/367-2277
www.thrifty.com

Value
☎800/327-2501
www.go-value.com

MAJOR HOTEL & MOTEL CHAINS

Best Western International
☎800/528-1234
www.bestwestern.com

Clarion Hotels
☎800/CLARION
www.hotelchoice.com/cgi-bin/res/webres?clarion.html

Comfort Inns
☎800/228-5150
www.hotelchoice.com/cgi-bin/res/webres?comfort.html

Courtyard by Marriott
☎800/321-2211
www.courtyard.com

Days Inn
☎800/325-2525
www.daysinn.com

Doubletree Hotels
☎800/222-TREE
www.doubletreehotels.com

Econo Lodges
☎800/55-ECONO
www.hotelchoice.com/cgi-bin/res/webres?econo.html

Fairfield Inn by Marriott
☎800/228-2800
www.fairfieldinn.com

Hampton Inn
☎800/HAMPTON
www.hampton-inn.com

Hilton Hotels
☎800/HILTONS
www.hilton.com

Holiday Inn
☎800/HOLIDAY
www.holiday-inn.com

Howard Johnson
☎800/654-2000
www.hojo.com/hojo.html

Hyatt Hotels & Resorts
☎800/228-9000
www.hyatt.com

ITT Sheraton
☎800/325-3535
www.sheraton.com

La Quinta Motor Inns
☎800/531-5900
www.laquinta.com

Marriott Hotels
800/228-9290
www.marriott.com

Motel 6
☎800/4-MOTEL6 (800/466-8536)

Quality Inns
☎800/228-5151
www.hotelchoice.com/cgi-bin/res/webres?quality.html

Radisson Hotels International
☎800/333-3333
www.radisson.com

Ramada Inns
☎800/2-RAMADA
www.ramada.com

Red Carpet Inns
☎800/251-1962

Red Lion Hotels & Inns
☎800/547-8010
www.travelweb.com

Red Roof Inns
☎800/843-7663
www.redroof.com

Residence Inn by Marriott
☎800/331-3131
www.residenceinn.com

Rodeway Inns
☎800/228-2000
www.hotelchoice.com/cgi-bin/res/webres?rodeway.html

Super 8 Motels
☎800/800-8000
www.super8motels.com

Travelodge
☎800/255-3050

Vagabond Inns
☎800/522-1555
www.vagabondinns.com

Wyndham Hotels and Resorts
☎800/822-4200 in Continental U.S. and Canada
www.wyndham.com

Index

See also Accommodations & Restaurants indexes, below.
Page numbers in italics refer to maps.

GENERAL INDEX

RESTAURANTS

FROMMER'S® COMPLETE TRAVEL GUIDES
(Comprehensive guides with selections in all price ranges—from deluxe to budget)

Alaska
Amsterdam
Arizona
Atlanta
Australia
Austria
Bahamas
Barcelona, Madrid & Seville
Belgium, Holland & Luxembourg
Bermuda
Boston
Budapest & the Best of Hungary
California
Canada
Cancún, Cozumel & the Yucatán
Cape Cod, Nantucket & Martha's Vineyard
Caribbean
Caribbean Cruises & Ports of Call
Caribbean Ports of Call
Carolinas & Georgia
Chicago
China
Colorado
Costa Rica
Denver, Boulder & Colorado Springs
England
Europe
Florida

France
Germany
Greece
Hawaii
Hong Kong
Honolulu, Waikiki & Oahu
Ireland
Israel
Italy
Jamaica & Barbados
Japan
Las Vegas
London
Los Angeles
Maryland & Delaware
Maui
Mexico
Miami & the Keys
Montana & Wyoming
Montréal & Québec City
Munich & the Bavarian Alps
Nashville & Memphis
Nepal
New England
New Mexico
New Orleans
New York City
Nova Scotia, New Brunswick & Prince Edward Island
Oregon
Paris
Philadelphia & the Amish Country

Portugal
Prague & the Best of the Czech Republic
Provence & the Riviera
Puerto Rico
Rome
San Antonio & Austin
San Diego
San Francisco
Santa Fe, Taos & Albuquerque
Scandinavia
Scotland
Seattle & Portland
Singapore & Malaysia
South Pacific
Spain
Switzerland
Thailand
Tokyo
Toronto
Tuscany & Umbria
USA
Utah
Vancouver & Victoria
Vermont, New Hampshire & Maine
Vienna & the Danube Valley
Virgin Islands
Virginia
Walt Disney World & Orlando
Washington, D.C.
Washington State

FROMMER'S® DOLLAR-A-DAY GUIDES
(The ultimate guides to comfortable low-cost travel)

Australia from $50 a Day
California from $60 a Day
Caribbean from $60 a Day
England from $60 a Day
Europe from $50 a Day
Florida from $60 a Day
Greece from $50 a Day
Hawaii from $60 a Day
Ireland from $50 a Day

Israel from $45 a Day
Italy from $50 a Day
London from $70 a Day
New York from $75 a Day
New Zealand from $50 a Day
Paris from $70 a Day
San Francisco from $60 a Day
Washington, D.C., from $60 a Day

FROMMER'S® MEMORABLE WALKS

Chicago
London

New York
Paris

San Francisco

FROMMER'S® PORTABLE GUIDES

Acapulco, Ixtapa/
  Zihuatenejo
Bahamas
California Wine
  Country
Charleston & Savannah
Chicago

Dublin
Las Vegas
London
Maine Coast
New Orleans
New York City
Paris

Puerto Vallarta, Manzanillo
  & Guadalajara
San Francisco
Sydney
Tampa Bay & St. Petersburg
Venice
Washington, D.C.

FROMMER'S® NATIONAL PARK GUIDES

Grand Canyon
National Parks of the American West
Yellowstone & Grand Teton

Yosemite & Sequoia/
  Kings Canyon
Zion & Bryce Canyon

THE COMPLETE IDIOT'S TRAVEL GUIDES

(The ultimate user-friendly trip planners)

Cruise Vacations
Planning Your Trip to Europe
Hawaii

Las Vegas
Mexico's Beach Resorts
New Orleans

New York City
San Francisco
Walt Disney World

SPECIAL-INTEREST TITLES

The Civil War Trust's Official Guide to
  the Civil War Discovery Trail
Frommer's Caribbean Hideaways
Israel Past & Present
New York City with Kids
New York Times Weekends
Outside Magazine's Adventure Guide
  to New England
Outside Magazine's Adventure Guide
  to Northern California

Outside Magazine's Adventure Guide
  to the Pacific Northwest
Outside Magazine's Guide to Family Vacations
Places Rated Almanac
Retirement Places Rated
Washington, D.C., with Kids
Wonderful Weekends from Boston
Wonderful Weekends from New York City
Wonderful Weekends from San Francisco
Wonderful Weekends from Los Angeles

THE UNOFFICIAL GUIDES®

(Get the unbiased truth from these candid, value-conscious guides)

Atlanta
Branson, Missouri
Chicago
Cruises
Disneyland

Florida with Kids
The Great Smoky
  & Blue Ridge
  Mountains
Las Vegas

Miami & the Keys
Mini-Mickey
New Orleans
New York City
San Francisco

Skiing in the West
Walt Disney World
Walt Disney World
  Companion
Washington, D.C.

FROMMER'S® IRREVERENT GUIDES

(Wickedly honest guides for sophisticated travelers)

Amsterdam
Boston
Chicago

London
Manhattan

New Orleans
Paris

San Francisco
Walt Disney World
Washington, D.C.

FROMMER'S® DRIVING TOURS

America
Britain
California

Florida
France
Germany

Ireland
Italy
New England

Scotland
Spain
Western Europe

WHEREVER YOU TRAVEL, *H*ELP IS NEVER FAR AWAY.

From planning your trip to

providing travel assistance along

the way, American Express®

Travel Service Offices are

always there to help.

American Express Travel Service Offices are found in central locations throughout Miami and the Keys.

Travel